W9-CGM-154

POMPEII

edited by
FILIPPO COARELLI

photography by
ALFREDO and PIO FOGLIA

POMPEII

texts by
FILIPPO COARELLI
EMIDIO DE ALBENTIIS
MARIA PAOLA GUIDOBALDI
FABRIZIO PESANDO
ANTONIO VARONE

translation by
PATRICIA A. COCKRAM

BARNES & NOBLE
NEW YORK

© 2006 by MAGNUS EDIZIONI SpA, Udine, Italy
English-language translation © Riverside Book Company, Inc.,
New York

This 2006 edition published by Barnes & Noble Publishing, Inc.
by arrangement with Riverside Book Company, Inc., New York.

All rights reserved. No part of this publication may be reproduced,
stored in a retrieval system, or transmitted, in any form or by
any means, electronic, mechanical, photocopying, recording, or
otherwise, without prior written permission from the publisher.

Preceding pages:

Fresco with theatrical mask from Pompeii, now in the National
Archeological Museum of Naples.

Fresco with sea horses, *in situ,* the Villa of the Mysteries, Pompeii.

Fresco with an imaginary bird, from the House of the Golden
Bracelet, Pompeii.

editorial co-ordination:
Elisabetta Feruglio

graphic design and layout:
Gilberto Brun

editor:
Jessica Basso

The color drawing with the reconstruction of the Forum is by
Monica Falcone.
The drawings of the plans of the houses and public buildings are
by Alessandro Trapassi.

photolithos:
RBG, Maniago, Pn.

editor, English-language edition
Brian Eskenazi

2006 Barnes & Noble Publishing

ISBN-13: 978-0-7607-8475-4
ISBN-10: 0-7607-8475-2

Printed and bound in Singapore

1   3   5   7   9   10   8   6   4   2

Table of Contents

History of the City, Excavations, and Studies

Pompeii is unquestionably the best-known archeological site in the world, as its daily crowds of visitors attest. Its universal fame began practically at the very moment of its discovery, two and a half centuries ago. In the beginning, as one might expect in an elitist society such as Europe's before the French Revolution, interest in Pompeii was limited almost exclusively to research by eighteenth- and nineteenth-century artists and intellectuals making the traditional "Grand Tour," who left behind an astonishing number of travel accounts, descriptions, sketches, and paintings. Literary and artistic culture became deeply impregnated with images of Pompeii: the founder of classical archeology, Johann J. Winckelmann, would find his primary source of inspiration there, and we see similar effects on such great literary figures as Goethe, and famous musicians like Mozart, among those most responsible for the classical fashion that swept Europe.

After the Neo-Classicists, even the Romantics found an important source of inspiration in Pompeii, one that reached all the way to the popular level. "Historical" novels such as E.G. Bulwer-Lytton's *The Last Days of Pompeii*, published in 1834, had a powerful effect on the collective imagination, not only in Europe but overseas as well. This influence became even more widespread in the twentieth century, when a new technology—the movies—appropriated Bulwer-Lytton's novel and released numerous versions of it.

This ever-expanding interest in Pompeii can be seen on two levels, the "high" and the "low." The former involves the scientific approach required by such a unique and important discovery as Pompeii; in fact, a specialization called "pompeiianism" developed, which can be seen as an extension of the antiquarian studies of the eighteenth and nineteenth centuries, and which was practiced by "pompeiianists." Its only object of study was Pompeii itself—or at most the other cities also destroyed by Vesuvius—even though this approach attributed a far more central importance to the city than it really had in antiquity,

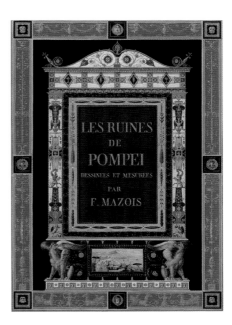

Les ruines de Pompéi, edited by F. Mazois and published between 1824 and 1838, is still a primary work for the study of Pompeii and its civilization.

Map of the Bay of Naples from 1794, in which we can see, besides the islands of Procida, Ischia and Capri, the exact location of Vesuvius.

Facing page:
Pair of feminine theatrical masks, House of the Golden Bracelet.

Refined architectural elements are found in the richest dwellings in Pompeii, such as this fountain in the House of the Scientists, decorated with a delicate mosaic of small polychrome tiles.

an importance that was merely the direct result of the catastrophe that destroyed it. What is generally defined as "Pompeiian" ("Pompeiian houses," "Pompeiian painting," etc.) was not exclusive to Pompeii at all; it was characteristic of numerous other urban agglomerations in ancient Italy, and this one Vesuvian city was not different from them in any particular way. In fact, these studies were dealing with a center of only average importance, surpassed in the Campania region alone by Capua, Pozzuoli, and Naples, and probably also by Nola and Nucera. Consequently, the excessive emphasis placed on Pompeii seriously distorted ancient reality, making it difficult to evaluate the city in the larger context of Roman Italy and, therefore, to comprehend its real role and importance. What more recent studies tend to introduce is just this reconsideration of Pompeii and a revision of these contexts. In any case, from now on, we must give up trying to understand Pompeii only through Pompeii.

On the "low" level, an ever expanding public interest in archeology has tended to become reduced to the theme of the "daily" on the one hand, and of the esoteric on the other, especially because of Egyptian and Oriental archeology. How many television shows have we seen on the "mysteries" of the pyramids, of the Etruscans, or of the Knights Templar? Part of Pompeii's fascination derives from the discovery that in essence its citizens were human beings like us. We experience a somewhat childish amazement at recognizing ourselves in the people of antiquity, who "ate like us," "slept like us," and "made love like us."

We must also emphasize, however, that the past interests us primarily because it is *not* like the present, because it allows us to reconstruct the distance, the difference—and therefore an historical perspective—not only in terms of the past, but also of the future. If things are different today, it is a sign that tomorrow too may be different—and perhaps even better! The world is not the same everywhere, nor is man ever the same as in the past. We hope that this book may contribute to re-establishing this elementary truth.

The Rediscovery of Pompeii

In 95 A.D., sixteen years after the terrible eruption that had destroyed Pompeii and Herculaneum, the memory of the disaster was still very much alive. The fascination it evoked was captured by the poet Statius, who was then living in Naples, in view of Vesuvius. "When the crops have grown back and these deserts have again become green," he wrote (*Silvae*, 4.4.79-86), "how can our descendants possibly imagine that cities and people are buried under their feet, and that their ancestors' fields disappeared under a sea of fire?"

The memory of the vanished city was carried on without interruption, thanks to the writers, historians and poets who had narrated its end. As late as 1502, inspired by this same tradition, the Neapolitan poet Jacopo Sannazaro, a follower of Virgil, imagined in his *Arcadia* the rediscovery of Pompeii in the place then referred to as *la Civita* which, as successive discoveries would show, actually corresponded to the site of the city. Even though

one of the greatest experts of the time, the German Lucas Holstenius, had already confirmed this conjecture by 1637, the location of Pompeii and Herculaneum remained controversial for a very long time: Stabia was mistakenly thought to have been on the site of the Civita, while Herculaneum was located, also erroneously, at Torre del Greco, ignoring the proliferation of discoveries during the period that should have made the answer clear. In

1592, for example, the architect Domenico Fontana, tracing the canal for an aqueduct that would carry the waters of the Sarno River to Torre Annunziata, crossed the hill, cutting into the walls of many buildings, and uncovered many inscriptions, one of which explicitly cited the Pompeiian Physical Venus. In 1689, in the course of excavations for a well on the steep slope of Vesuvius, in the Pompeii area, several inscriptions surfaced, one of which expressly mentioned Pompeii, but a local authority claimed that it referred not to the city but to the villa of a certain Pompeius. In 1693, other excavations at the Civita revealed the presence of well-preserved ancient remains. Then, in 1709, the Theater of Herculaneum was discovered. It was not clear what it was, however, until 1738, when systematic excavations were resumed at the request of the Bourbon King Charles III. The discovery of an inscription that mentioned the *theatrum Herculanensem* eliminated all doubt.

It took a few more years to settle the location of Pompeii. Rocco Gioacchino di Alcubierre, a Spanish-born engineer, who was responsible for the excavations at Herculaneum, decided to undertake systematic excavations to resolve the question of the ancient city buried in the vicinity of the Civita. Paradoxically, he was convinced, contrary to the opinions of other specialists like Martorelli and Mazzocchi, that the city was Stabia. On March 23, 1748, he began excavations with twelve workmen, not far from the Temple of Fortuna Augusta. Later, he turned his attention to a patch of terrain where a large indentation seemed to indicate the presence of a building used for performances, and the first findings confirmed this. An excited Alcubierre quickly baptized the building the "Stabian Theater." In reality, it was Pompeii's Amphitheater. It was not until August 16, 1763, when T. Suedius Clemens discovered one of a group of columns used as field-markers, which specifically named the city, that the question could be resolved: the Civita was Pompeii itself.

Exploration continued with great zeal under Charles III's successor, Ferdinand I. In 1765 excavation of the theater began, followed immediately by that of the entire Triangular Forum. The discovery of the Temple of Isis, perfectly preserved, had already taken place in 1764, contributing greatly to the fashion for "Egyptology," closely linked to Masonic lodges, that spread through Europe in those years, one of the most famous manifestations of which was the opera *The Magic Flute* by Mozart, who had visited the building.

The excavations increased notably in the years between 1770 and 1815 under Ferdinand

This reproduction of the House with the Colored Capitals is from the noted work *Le case e i monumenti di Pompei*, published by the Niccolini brothers beginning in 1854.

A beautiful image of the Temple of Isis, in a reproduction from *Le case e i monumenti di Pompei* by the Niccolini brothers.

I, then during the French occupation, and again with the Restoration. The Basilica, the first building in the Forum, was discovered, followed by the rest of the public square with all of its adjacent buildings. After 1823 a large number of private houses were uncovered, among them the House of the Faun. In the last years of the Bourbon rule, activity slowed noticeably, but would be taken up again on a grand scale, using new methods, with the foundation of the Kingdom of Italy in 1861. After 1860 the director of excavations was Giuseppe Fiorelli, the real originator of new scientific excavation methods in the Vesuvian cities. A new map was compiled, dividing the city into regions, with precise numbering for each block and individual entrance. This indispensable basis for a rigorous inventory of the buildings is still used today. Frescoes were no longer removed and carried to the Archeological Museum of Naples, but remained in place, and this made it necessary to devise new methods of excavation and restoration, as well as to rebuild the roofs of the buildings. After this point too, a new procedure was established, using plaster casts, to recover the bodies of the Pompeiians who had died in the course of the eruptions, as well as all the other perishable remains, like trees, wooden objects, etc., that had left their shapes in the solidified ashes. Fiorelli's successors, Ruggero, De Petra, Pais, and Sogliano, continued the systematic excavation of the living quarters, in particular the western ones. Between 1910 and 1924 impressive excavations were completed under Vittorio Spinazzola in the southern and

A plaster cast produced with the method devised by Giuseppe Fiorelli, the true founder of modern scientific excavation techniques for the Vesuvius cities.

eastern quarters, especially around Via dell'Abbondanza.

The more recent history of Pompeii's excavation is mainly associated with the enduring work of Amedeo Maiuri, superintendent of Pompeii from 1924 to 1961. We owe many discoveries to him—the Large Gymnasium next to the Amphitheater, the House of Menander, the Villa of the Mysteries—as well as an endless number of publications, the introduction of new excavation methods, and new methods of restoration. The stratigraphic tests Maiuri instituted in the subsoil of the city—under the walls, the buildings of the Forum, the Temple of Apollo, and the Triangular Forum—made it possible to reconstruct the city's earliest history. Particularly revealing was the removal of masses of excavation materials which had completely submerged the external facade of the city, especially on the west and south sides; these materials were then used to improve the swampy areas of the Sarno and to build the autostrada from Naples to Pompeii.

Today the activities of the superintendent's office and of the numerous scientific missions, both Italian and foreign, who work at Pompeii are concentrated on the exploration and study of already-excavated sites, from which they hope to document the various historical stages. For now, no new work-sites are being opened in unexplored zones. In fact, the primary and most pressing need is to document the results of the old excavations, information which is for the most part still unpublished; this knowledge is essential for under-

taking and concluding the work of restoration and appraisal that, after decades of neglect or scant attention, is now urgent and indispensable for the very survival of Pompeii.

The History of Pompeii

In the beginning, according to Strabo, "the Oscans occupied both Naples and its neighbor Pompeii" (*Geography V,* 4, 3). Later they would be besieged by "the Etruscans and the Pelasgians, and after them, the Samnites." These traces of ethnic history coincide fairly well with what we know about the rest of the Campania region (Capua, for example) and with the archeological testimony that has come out of the ground of Pompeii itself. The Oscans can be considered the oldest indigenous population, who founded the nucleus of the habitations around the Forum. As for the Pelasgians, they were almost surely Greeks. The Greeks had already colonized the north of Campania in the eighth century B.C., and their presence in Pompeii seems to be confirmed by the Doric Temple and by the second ring of walls, which show technical characteristics that are purely Greek.

One legend attributed the founding of the city to Hercules, and explained its name as related to the *pompé,* processions with which the hero would have celebrated his victory over Geryon. This is clearly a false etymology, but it is based on a Greek word and does, therefore, appear to refer to a myth of the city's origins that may have been introduced by the Greeks, who would surely have been visitors to the port of Pompeii from very early times.

In the second half of the fifth century B.C., Pompeii, like almost all of the Campania region, was occupied by people from the interior of the peninsula and became, from then on, a Samnite city. The first reliable historical reports on the city refer to her port, situated at the mouth of the Sarno, which must have flowed very close to its southern walls. We know, again from Strabo, that the port was used as a commercial emporium by Nola, Nucera, and Acerra, cities from the central-southern interior of Campania, probably dating from very ancient times. It was probably from here that they exported the agricultural produce of the fertile plains and salt from the Herculean marshes north of Pompeii. This function as a port-of-call is mentioned in the oldest remaining historical reference to Pompeii, which tells us that in 310 B.C., during the second Samnitic war, a Roman military fleet landed there to sack the territory of Nucera (Livy IX, 38, 2-3).

Facing page:
Feminine statue in bronze, inspired by a Greek model of the fifth century B.C., from the Villa of the Pisoni at Herculaneum and now in the National Archeological Museum of Naples.

Immediately afterwards, following the defeat of the Samnites in that war, Pompeii entered Rome's orbit as an ally, along with the league to which she belonged, the dominant center of which was Nucera. Thus, prematurely, began the long process of Romanization, which would be concluded definitively more than two centuries later. In the course of the Social War, which pitted the Italics against Rome (91-89 B.C.), Pompeii was occupied by Sulla. Along with the other Italics, the city no doubt acquired forthwith the rights of Roman citizens, transforming itself into a municipality. Finally,

in 80 B.C., after the end of the civil war between Marius and Sulla, a military colony was founded there. From that moment forward, Pompeii could consider herself a fully Roman city, and her successive affairs—as in the rest of Italy, by then completely pacified from within by a world empire—were now characteristic of provincial cities, happily anonymous, like all people without a history.

Only three episodes would interrupt this peaceful life. The Catilene Conspiracy apparently saw the active participation of the native Pompeiians, who were eager to recover rights they had been deprived of in favor of Sulla's colonies. Later, under Nero, in 59 A.D., the city's Amphitheater was the site of an intensely bloody event, amply documented by Tacitus (*Annals* XIV, 17): during a gladiator spectacle, a scuffle broke out between the Pompeiians and the Nucerians, between whom, according to long-standing Italic tradition, there was apparently profound hostility. There were many dead and wounded, and

In the port of Pompeii, as in others in the Vesuvius area, there was regular commerce in semi-precious stones and jewelry of quite distant origin, like this sapphire and this carnelian, both from the first century A.D., decorated with mythological motifs and found in Pompeii in the House of the Gemmario, or gem-dealer. Below, a carving in vitreous paste with Alexander the Great depicted as Achilles (first century A.D.), found in Pompeii and now in the National Archeological Museum of Naples.

Following pages:
An evocative view of one of the honorary arches of the Forum, presumably dedicated to Nero; on the right, the ruins of the macellum, whose columns attest to the richness of the ancient architecture.

Facing page:
Intersection of Via dell'Abbondanza and Via Stabiana. The large stones set in the middle of the crossing enabled pedestrians to avoid the dirt and mud that often covered the streets.

after a quick investigation, the emperor forbade gladiator spectacles in Pompeii for ten years.

The punishment was not to last long, however, because only three years later, in 62 A.D., a terrible catastrophe crushed the city: southern Campania was hit by an extremely violent earthquake, impressively documented by ancient authors. On February 5th of that year, Pompeii, which must have been near the epicenter, was razed to the ground, and the nearby cities of Nucera and Herculaneum also suffered very serious damage. Traces of the quake are evident even today, despite the hurried reconstruction of the buildings which, in at least one case, was explicitly recorded: on the outer perimeter of the Temple of Isis, an inscription declares that "Numerius Popidius Celsinus, son of Numerius, rebuilt from its foundations the Temple of Isis, destroyed in the earthquake."

Between August 24th and 25th in 79 A.D., after a series of very violent tremors from the earthquake, Vesuvius began to erupt. We have an actual journalistic chronicle of the event, thanks to two letters that Pliny the Younger wrote in response to a specific request from Tacitus, who wanted to use the information in his *Historiae*. This work by Tacitus has not come down to us, but we do have the letters of Pliny (*Ad Familiares* VI:16 and 20). Just a boy at the time of the eruptions, he was across the bay at Miseno with his mother and his uncle, Pliny the Elder, who was the commander of the military fleet stationed in that Campania city.

A much later account by Dionysius Cassius lingers on the wonders that supposedly preceded and accompanied the eruptions, products of the popular imagination, which is always fertile in such cases:

Many huge men appeared, surpassing human stature—like the descriptions of the Giants—first on the mountain, then in the surrounding countryside and in the cities; they roamed the earth and appeared in the sky, day and night. After this there came a terrible drought and such violent earthquakes that they made all the plains tremble and the seas shake.

Fresco portraying the historic clash between the Nucerians and the Pompeiians, which took place in the city's Amphitheater during a gladiator spectacle, now in the National Archeological Museum of Naples.

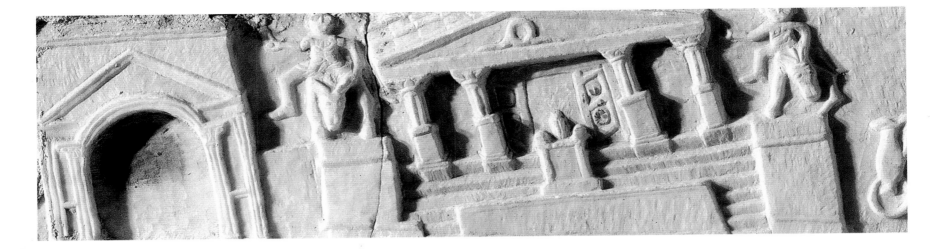

Marble relief with a scene of the earthquake of 62 A.D. Pompeii, from the atrium of the House of L. Cecilius Iucundus, 62-79 A.D., Archeological Superintendency of Pompeii.

Facing page:
Detail of a fresco from the House of the Golden Bracelet.

Image by Gavin Hamilton, a Scottish painter and antiquarian as well as a collector and authority on ancient marbles.

One could hear roaring underground and howling on the surface, and the sea rumbled, and the sky echoed the noise. Then an extraordinary din could be heard, as if the mountains were crashing down, and soon enormous masses rolled down, until they reached the farthest limits of the countryside, then came fire and such thick fog that it darkened the atmosphere and obscured the sun as in an eclipse. Night replaced the day, darkness the light, and many thought that the Giants were rebelling again (many images of them then appeared in the mist, and the blare of a trumpet was heard); others thought that the whole universe had been enveloped in chaos and fire. And consequently many fled from the houses into the streets, others from the streets into the houses, some from the sea to the land, others from the land to the sea, since, in their confused state, they felt that any place they had not yet reached must be safer than the one in which they found themselves. Finally, an enormous quantity of ash erupted, which filled all the earth, the sea and the air, destroying men, fields and crops in various ways, killing all the fish and the birds, and in addition burning two entire cities, Herculaneum and Pompeii, while the inhabitants of the latter were at the theater (*Historia Romana, LXVI, 21*).

Filippo Coarelli

LEGEND

Unless otherwise indicated, all images are on site
or from Pompeii.

MANN = National Archeological Museum of Naples

SAP = Archeological Superintendence of Pompeii

Public Life

Urban development

Pompeii's unique circumstances and her history and discovery are an ideal terrain for studying and understanding an ancient city in its entirety. In fact, not only does the excavated surface make up a considerable part of the whole urban area, estimated at about three-fifths, but more important, the entire complex presents the completely homogeneous conditions of the community at the time of the eruption in 79 A.D. Unlike practically all other cases of extensive exploration in urban areas, in this instance the excavation was not stumbled upon in a tangle of superimposed structures, a condition that generally makes the isolation of well-preserved homogeneous phases impossible. This was true even in cities like Ostia, which had already been abandoned by the end of antiquity, and it is inevitably the case with still-living cities like Rome.

In Pompeii's case, the removal of a uniform layer of ashes and lapilli, or lava pebbles, made it possible to expose extensive homogeneous sectors without much difficulty other

Via di Mercurio, which ends at the tower of the same name. This important main street was a continuation of Via del Foro, which led to the Civic Forum, the center of the city's economic, political, and social life.

A historic photograph of Amedeo Maiuri during the discovery of the fresco of Venus in the garden of the House of Venus in the Shell. Tiny grains of pumice from the eruption of Vesuvius are visible at the bottom.

Map of Pompeii
In 1858, Giuseppe Fiorelli worked out a "cadastral" system dividing the city into nine *regiones*, which he numbered counter-clockwise.

than that posed by the need to reinforce the most fragile structures. This also made it possible to examine in a comprehensive way the individual public and private buildings, as well as the reciprocal relations among them, and therefore the urban context as a whole and its contemporary connections.

Despite the presence of such favorable conditions, however, the study of Pompeii's city plan, her structures and her history is a field of research that has been undertaken only relatively recently, and the results are largely incomplete and controversial even today. This is undoubtedly because of the unusual nature of Pompeii studies, a tradition that has been influenced almost exclusively by antiquarian interests that were typical of the earliest inquiries in the eighteenth and nineteenth centuries. This tradition leaves out a great number of the wider historic and geographic contexts and has long been an almost insuperable obstacle to the introduction of more modern modes of inquiry and thus to excavations that could clarify the comprehensive nature of the urban setting and its origins—and therefore its history. To fill in this serious gap it is necessary first to create an extensive, coordinated program of in-depth excavations, which is only now just beginning.

The "modern" phase of Pompeii studies began during the period between the two world wars and is linked to the name of Amedeo Maiuri. This phase is now in full development, but it is still very far from having gone far enough, even at the level of simple documentation. This explains a certain insecurity and confusion in current studies, and the continued impossibility of reaching a comprehensive understanding of the urban history of Pompeii that goes beyond the level of a simple working hypothesis.

Consequently, the summary we propose here, based on the data currently at our disposal and taking into account an ongoing and often very lively debate, can only be presented as a very personal proposal, one which will surely require adjustments and modifications along the way, as research furnishes new data and new answers.

To understand the completely mistaken ideas about the city's urban development still held in the second half of the nineteenth century, one need only consider the system created by Giuseppe Fiorelli that divided the city into nine regions, which nonetheless had the merit of furnishing for the first time an indispensable distributive layout of the neighborhoods, and which is still the system in use. This was not merely an abstract, avowedly modern repartition for exclusively empirical ends, but a real attempt to reconstruct the actual early divisions, as Fiorelli himself explicitly affirms: "Because the area was enclosed by a ring of walls and divided into nine segments with two cornerstones and two east-west roads . . . in trying to assign numerical order to these nine segments . . . I believed that the one situated to the right of the earliest cornerstone must be considered the first and the one following it to the east the second, given that the towers numbered by the Samnites, which are attached to the city walls here and there, proceeded in the same order, and almost the same order is evident in other regions under Roman control under Augustus" (*Description of Pompeii*, Naples, 1975, 23 *passim*).

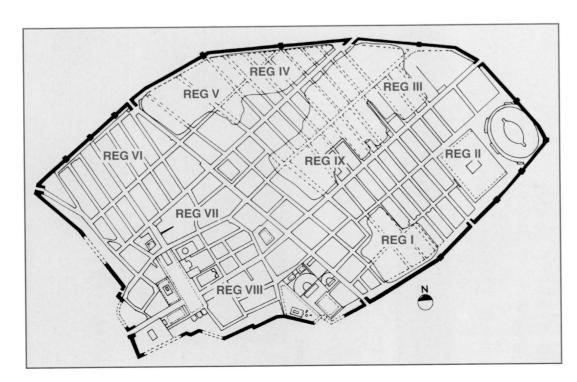

REG IV
REG V
REG III
REG VI
REG IX
REG II
REG VII
REG I
REG VIII
N

We will see later that such a scheme could not possibly represent the actual ancient one, which we can now reconstruct in a radically different way, based on inscriptions and archeological data.

Beginning with the monumental work of Amin von Gerkan (1940), we learned that the

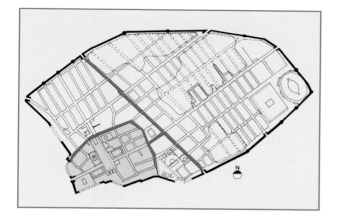

primitive settlement of the city, the so-called "Altstadt," involved the area immediately surrounding the Forum, where we can clearly recognize, amid the more regular web of the surrounding regions, a nucleus with a roughly ovoid layout, characterized by small square or rhomboidal city blocks, whose borders—possi-

bly marked by a primitive *agger*, or rampart, which was later demolished and no traces of which remain—can be recognized as the *Via dei Soprastanti,* the *Via degli Augustali,* the *Vicolo del Lupanare,* and the *Via dei Teatri.* Certain criticism, for the most part unfounded, notwithstanding, we now have a clear idea that the temple's first configuration, probably in the form of a sacred area without an actual temple building, must date from the second half of the seventh century B.C. This has been confirmed by archeological discoveries in the area of the city's main sanctuary, the Temple of Apollo.

This first inhabited nucleus was superimposed, or so it seems, on an earlier site, characterized by two axial streets: *Via Consolare* and *Via Stabiana.* The origins of this nucleus would seem to be explained by synecology, since it corresponds in time with the abandonment of many Iron-Age villages, lost in the Sarno River valley, in the second half of the seventh century B.C.

Via Consolare has an irregular, sinuous path, typical of a "natural" street, and is preserved mainly within the regular web of Region VI, whose completion can be dated, as we shall see, around the middle of the sixth century B.C., a date that apparently constitutes an end *ante quem* for the street itself. This stretch seems to lose its identity as it connects to the "Altstadt" and must therefore date from

Following pages:
The intersection of Via Consolare and Vicolo di Narciso, with a rectangular stone fountain. In the background at the left is the Herculaneum Gate, beyond which is Pompeii's largest necropolis.

The dark area on the map indicates the "Altstadt," the original nucleus from which the city of Pompeii later developed.

Panoramic view of the "old" city of Pompeii next to the "modern" city which now has over thirty-thousand inhabitants.

With Via di Vesuvio, Via Stabiana divides the city from north to south, connecting the northern and southern gates, *Porta Stabiana* and *Porta Vesuvio*. Its slope has suggested that it may have followed the path of an earlier large canal for the removal of rainwater.

an even earlier, hence pre-urban, era. The southeast continuation of this axis comes to rest at the Triangular Forum, and its alignment seems to correspond, probably not accidentally, with that of the Doric Temple. This temple, clearly outside the oldest settlement of the "Altstadt," has been correctly identified as a market sanctuary, closely attached to the port at the mouth of the Sarno, which would have been just south of the city walls.

This axial street is identified with the Samnitic "viu Sarinu," the salt road or *Via del sale* mentioned in an Oscan inscription, onto which opened the "veru Sarinu," the *Salis Port*, identified as what is today called the *Porto Ercolano*. Thus we can see a connection, certainly dating at least from the protohistoric age, between the port of the Sarno and the Herculean Salt Marshes mentioned by Columella (X, 135).

Via Stabiana, which is also outside the early inhabited center and seems to have been another very ancient thoroughfare, runs along a natural canal, cut deeply into the lava bank on which the city rose. It seems obvious to view it as connecting the urban centers at the Campania region's interior and the port at the mouth of the Sarno, with Pompeii, as we know from Strabo, serving as their market during the historic era.

The oldest Pompeii settlement, the "Altstadt," thus seems to have been connected to two important protohistoric roads, giving the new center a dominant position completely analogous to what we can also reconstruct for other cities along the Tyrrhenian seacoast, and in particular for Rome itself. There the relationships between primitive roadways (e.g. the Via Salaria, "salt road"), sites for the supply of salt such as the marshes at the mouth of the Tiber, the river-markets, and the connected sanctuaries like the Great Herculean Altar in the Bovine Forum all present structural characteristics articulated

Porta Ercolano, the Herculeaneum Gate, seen from Via dei Sepolcri, in a reproduction by W. Gell.

according to a nearly identical model, though of considerably older formation.

A large expansion of the urban area is indicated by the construction of a fortification wall, constructed of *pappamonte*, an unusual stone created by the sedimentation of volcanic material. We will return to this structure below, but for now we are interested only in recording that this was a very large enclosure, corresponding more or less to the layout of the later proto-Samnitic one, with the possible exception of the east side, of which no trace has been found to date. Recent excavations, including those by De Caro, have shown that this was a work of considerable antiquity, from around 580 to 560 B.C. This date is revolutionary for the city's urban history and obliges us to rethink all preceding theories, putting in doubt both the "revisionist" and minimalist hypotheses about the extent of the archaic city. Nevertheless, there is a fairly widespread scholarly tendency that continues to put forward, based on isolated data of questionable significance, a very late date for the occupation of this space, sometimes pushing the date even to the first century B.C., and explaining the existence of this archaic enclosure through an analogy with Samnitic centers in the interior, where indeed we do find large walled enclosures, but which we can recognize as simple places of refuge, and which cannot be interpreted as urban centers of great dimensions.

In general, such a solution is unacceptable for an area urbanized as early as the Campania region, in a period when Pompeii had already entered into the Etruscan and Greek sphere of influence. Such a proposal fails to take into account, among other things, the existence of

The Herculaneum Gate was built of mixed *opus vittatus*, a technique that consisted of a mortar and stone nucleus with a facing of small blocks of tufa or travertine alternating with bricks.

33

This honorary arch, said to be "of Caligula," is found at the beginning of Via di Mercurio; it was completely faced with marble and topped with an equestrian statue.

The beautiful fountain in the House of the Grand Fountain is located in Region VI. This area was the object of extensive urban studies carried out by Amedeo Maiuri during the 1940s.

analogous and better-known situations, like that of Capua. Besides, the available dates for Pompeii itself, however meager they may still be, are more than sufficient to suggest a radically different solution, in particular for what appears to be the oldest extension of the primitive "Altstadt," that is Region VI, which occupies the area immediately to the north of the Forum and includes both the Forum and the walls.

This neighborhood has a regular and planned layout, made up of rectangular city blocks, developed in a north-south direction, and it seems to be oriented towards the sanctuary of Apollo. Its principal axis is identified as Via di Mercurio, which is wider than the others and occupies a central position relative to them, opening onto the Forum and extending to the south of it, turning into Via delle Scuole.

Maiuri's excavations demonstrated the obviously very old date of this thoroughfare—and consequently of the region's whole road system connected to it—by revealing the presence of a gate, later eliminated, at the point where the road meets the oldest walls made of pappamonte, and the later ones—still from the fifth century B.C.—built with rectangular vertical stone panels. We can confirm the dating of this gate because it was eliminated in a later period, at the time of the completion of the first Samnitic enclosure, around 300 B.C. This permits us not only to fix the date of the gate itself, and of the Region VI road plan, at an earlier date than this, but also to link them both to an older phase of the walls, the one in pappamonte, which we know goes back to the second quarter of the sixth century B.C. Consequently, this would also seem to be the date when the street grid of Region VI was completed.

That this grid was immediately occupied by living quarters, at least in its central sector, was demonstrated in the 1940s by several investigations made by Maiuri on the interiors of two houses that face each other on Via di Mercurio: the House with the Fountain, on the west side, and House VI 10, 6 on the east. The remains of structures in pappamonte appeared on the underlying levels, oriented in the same way as the later buildings. Even if we do not have access to definite stratigraphic data, the techniques and materials used, together with the presence of archaic ceramics and of Etruscan graphics, seem to demonstrate that we are dealing with archaic habitations. This conclusion is confirmed in a definitive way by the level at which these walls emerge, which seems much lower than the general level of the neighborhood, completed around the beginning of the third century B.C., compared to the walls of the first Samnitic phase. One notes, furthermore, a distinct difference between the levels of the constructions located on the two sides of Via di Mercurio, which attests to the presence in the archaic age of a steep incline from west to east, levelled in the following phase. Other investigations under the House of Pansa (VI 6, 1) have revealed the presence of analogous structures in pappamonte, thus showing that the urbanization of the neighborhood was not limited to the immediate environs of Via di Mercurio, but extended widely, at least towards the west. The presence of decidedly ancient structures in other sectors of Region VI, for example the House of the Centaur (VI 9, 3-57), leads to similar conclusions.

Intersection of Via di Mercurio, Via del Foro, Via delle Terme, and Via della Fortuna.

The cortina wall between Tower II and the *Porta di Nocera*, the Nucera Gate.

had attracted the scholars' attention. Their explorations made it possible to show that this was an archaic element *in situ*, but did not lead to the discovery of other pertinent structures. This isolated column originally rose in an open area devoid of any construction, on an archaic level that can be dated, based on the materials discovered, between 620 and 520 B.C. A considerable number of carbonized tree branches suggested the presence of a beech forest and made it possible to exclude, consequently, the urbanization of the area before the third century B.C. The first houses completed in this zone could not therefore have an earlier date than the beginning of the second century B.C.

These dates, certainly interesting in terms of the local situation, were arbitrarily generalized for the entire neighborhood and led to the conclusion that its urbanization could not have predated the years between the end of the third and the beginning of the second centuries B.C., when the area was filled in with a large quantity of earth and made level.

If this conclusion had been tenable, the entire urban history of Pompeii would have been revolutionized, and the earliest phases would now turn out to have been much later than was generally thought. Nevertheless, even if one did not consider previously examined data like the archaic phases of the walls and the houses in pappamonte in Region VI, which decisively argue against such a reconstruction,

A completely different reconstruction seems to emerge, however, from the excavations undertaken by the State University of Milan in the block of the House of the Etruscan Column (VI 5), where the presence of an isolated tuscanic column, which gives the house its name,

one must point out that the elements that emerged from the House of the Etruscan Column can be interpreted in a radically different manner than that proposed by the excavators.

In the first place, the archaic column cannot be a "votive column," as they proposed. The presence of miniature chalices among the materials excavated must obviously be connected to the existence of an archaic sanctuary, which we can reconstruct as an open area, a *temenos*, with an altar and a divine image located on a column, according to a model widely seen in both Greece and Italy, and of which the votive sanctuary of the Assembly, the so-called *Lapis niger,* provides one of the most famous examples.

Such an interpretation can clearly be confirmed by the presence of the numerous beech trees, which were considered by the excavators to be proof of the absence of construction and therefore of a non-urbanized situation. It reality, the beech is a tree that does not grow naturally in southern Europe at altitudes below 2,000 feet; a beech forest at sea level is an absolute impossibility. Consequently, this can only have been an artificial planting, connected with a *lucus*, a sacred grove, the natural complement of a sanctuary, the presence of which has already been proven at this location. It should be noted that the beech is a plant sacred to Jupiter; in fact, on Rome's Esquiline hill there was a *lucus Fagutalis,* a sacred grove for *Iuppiter Fagutalis,* "Jupiter of the Beech." We can deduce from this that the area corresponding to the House of the Etruscan Column was occupied, in the archaic age and until the end of the third century B.C., by a sanctuary probably sacred to Jupiter, which was later eliminated, and perhaps transferred to the Forum, as we shall see below.

Consequently, the absence of construction in the zone until the end of the third century B.C. tells us nothing about the initial date of the urbanization of Region VI, much less of the rest of the city. This is an example of something correctly observed, but badly interpreted, and above all arbitrarily extended to the entire neighborhood, and even to the entire city.

We are thus able to confirm what had seemed the most reasonable reconstruction based on the available data: the neighborhood that corresponds to Region VI is in effect an early expansion of the primitive "Altstadt" and can still be dated to the sixth century B.C. It is connected to, and thus undoubtedly contemporary with, the most ancient city walls, those in pappamonte, as is demonstrated by the close link between Via di Mercurio, the supporting axis of the quarter, and the gate that originally opened in the wall, aligned with this

road. This allows us to fix the first half of the sixth century B.C. (and even more precisely, about 580-560 B.C.) as the completion date for this extremely important expansion of the urban area, which assumed the characteristics of a true city from then on.

The notable extension of the archaic walls in pappamonte poses, however, a problem concerning the overall dimensions the city had assumed till then. Was it limited to the "Altstadt" and Region VI, or did it also encompass sectors of the zone to the east, which was included inside the walls?

Several elements seem to point towards the second solution, even if for now it is impossible to define the borders and the look of this possible archaic quarter. In the first place, we have ascertained the notable antiquity of the area pertaining to the Triangular Forum, attested to by the Doric Temple, which goes back to the middle of the sixth century B.C. As we have already seen above, this sanctuary, probably having to do with trade, seems to constitute the end of two very ancient roads, coming respectively from the salt marshes—Via Consolare—and the interior of the Campania—Via Stabiana. The archaic ceramic shards found in the eastern sector of the city, besides being rare, confirm the probable presence of very old habitations, now attested also by the discovery of wall structures from the sixth-century B.C. under the Amaranthus House (I 9, 11-12) in Region I.

The presence of a completely distinctive system of square city blocks in two parallel lines, to the east of Via Stabiana and facing it,

In the House of the Etruscan Column, excavations carried out by the University of Milan showed that this tuscanic column originally stood in an open area devoid of construction.

The stone fountain located on Via dell'Abbondanza, probably a representation of Concordia.

incompatible with the general layout of the eastern sector of the city and therefore autonomous—and certainly of later date than that sector—could indicate the surviving traces of an archaic quarter, contemporaneous with Region VI but different from it, a quarter originally located outside the walls and connected to the port, similar to Rome's Aventine Hill.

The last recognizable urban system in the city's sphere is the one, mentioned above, that we see in the eastern sector of Pompeii. This is a clearly homogeneous system situated, unlike that of Region VI, on an east-west axis, the main arteries of which are Via dell'Abbondanza on the south and the thoroughfare made up of Via delle Terme, Via della Fortuna, and Via di Nola on the north, axes that each come to an end at one of the eastern gates of the city, the Sarno and Nola Gates, respectively. The recent nature of this settlement is recognizable above all along the lines where it meets the more ancient settlements to the west of Via Stabiana. This is particularly evident in the route of Via

dell'Abbondanza, whose westernmost section angles clearly towards the north to merge with Via Marina, the principal east-west axis of the "Altstadt." Farther north, on the other hand, we find no such analogous phenomenon. The east-west roads of Region VI proceed parallel to the Via delle Terme-Via della Fortuna axis. It is doubtful in any case that this was the original situation of the quarter, since such an alignment is not perpendicular to its north-south axis, which was also its main one. A similar divergence, which creates rhomboidal city blocks, would be difficult to reconcile in a newly-established quarter, created in a virgin area. It seems possible therefore that the east-west roads assumed their current path only at a later period, at the time of the definitive urbanization of the city's eastern sector. One sign that could confirm this hypothesis emerged recently from an excavation completed in House VII 4, 62, behind the Temple of Fortuna Augusta, immediately to the south of Via di Mercurio: here an older

An evocative long view of Via dell'Abbondanza showing the endless row of what were once shops and dwellings. In the foreground is the so-called Fountain of Abundance.

The Sarno, in an unpolluted stretch. The Romans disembarked at the river's mouth to sack the Nucera territory during the second Samnitic war.

building was discovered from the end of the fourth century B.C., probably meant for public banquets. It is oriented on an axis perpendicular to Via di Mercurio, and differently from the adjacent Via della Fortuna, which as a consequence appears to have assumed its current path only afterwards. Now we can date the settlement of the eastern "new city" to the end of the fourth and the beginning of the third century B.C.

Evidence of this comes from the proven relationship between this sector and the walls of the first Samnitic period, whose chronology must be attributed, based on recent excavations, to the same period. The principal axes of the new urban system are in fact strictly connected to the gates on the east side of the city: Via dell'Abbondanza, as we have seen, runs towards the Sarno Gate; and the parallel road to the north, Via delle Terme-Via della Fortuna-Via di Nola, runs to the Nola Gate. Now these two gates—probably like the walls of the eastern side, as well—seem to appear for the first time in relation to the first Samnitic phase. But the excavations undertaken at various times around the Nola Gate have not revealed any traces of the two earlier phases, neither the one in pappamonte nor the one in limestone with orthostatic stone panels, which did, however, appear in the other sectors of the fortification. This seems to indicate that the oldest walls in the eastern zone followed a different, probably more internal, path.

The very close connection between the walls and gates of the first Samnitic phase and the urbanization of the "new city" shows that we are dealing with parts of a single project of overall restructuring of the city, which we can attribute to the years around 300 B.C.

This is not a meaningless date: it corresponds in fact to a historical moment of crucial importance for the whole southern Campania region, as well as for Pompeii itself. In 310 B.C., during the second Samnitic War, the city was overrun in an attack by the Romans who, having landed at the mouth of the Sarno, pushed forward to sack the territory of Nucera. A few years later, in 307 B.C., this territory fell into the hands of Rome and was immediately incorporated as an ally into the sphere of the Roman-Italic confederation. Pompeii, as a member of the Nucera confederation, suffered the same fate, and was a Roman *urbs foederata* from then on until the Social War.

It would be hard not to connect these events with the city's radical urban restructuring, especially given that other indications point in the same direction.

The orientation of the Forum, a fundamental part of the "Altstadt," appears clearly determined by Vesuvius, whose summit, one can easily see, is aligned along the axis made up by the Forum and Via di Mercurio. A sacred implication for this choice appears probable, even more so since Vesuvius, identified with Jupiter, was venerated in Campania on the same level as a god, as attested by the presence of a *Iuppiter Vesuvius* at Capua. In light of these considerations, the position of the Temple of Jupiter to the north of the Forum,

Travellers must have been a common sight on the many Roman roads that connected the entire territory.

A reconstruction in perspective of the Forum of Pompeii.

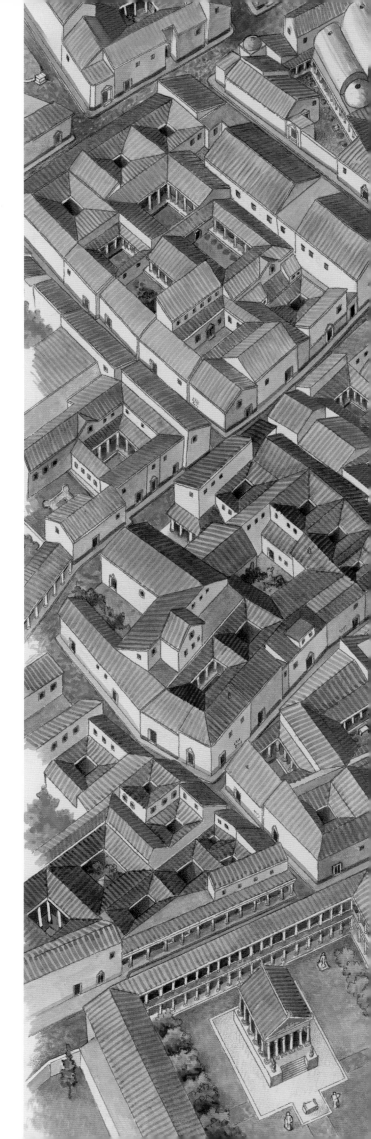

The map shows the orientation of Pompeii and Nucera towards Mount Torrenone.

Public Buildings in the Forum

First of all I will describe the proper arrangement of public buildings in the forum, the place in which magistrates administer both public and private affairs. The Greeks make their forums square, adorned by dense colonnades with epistyles of marble or other stone above which are walkways framed with timber. This practice cannot be followed in the cities of Italy, due to our ancient custom of presenting gladiator spectacles in the forum. Therefore the spaces between the columns of the loggia must be wider, for the convenience of the spectators, and the bankers' stalls are then placed all around under the porticoes and above the terraces. . . . The size of the forum is based on the number of inhabitants, so that its area is neither too small nor too large for the population. The width is set at two thirds of the length, so that the forum is oblong in shape and suitable for the spectacles. . . . The basilicas should be adjacent to the forum and connect with it on the warmest side, so that the merchants may receive the public during winter without any fear of the cold. . . . The public treasury, the prison, and the place of assembly must adjoin the forum, and their size must be proportional to it. And most of all, the assembly hall must be a building worthy of the city and its inhabitants.

Vitruvius, *On Architecture,* V, 1

like that of the probable *lucus Iovis* in Region VI as well, hardly appears accidental.

The residential axis was then rotated about one hundred degrees. As has been noted, the object of this new orientation was probably Mount Torrenone, as happened also at Nucera, whose urban plan was likely contemporary with that of the "new city" of Pompeii—a particularly significant fact, since Nucera was the leading city of the confederation. This choice was probably determined by the presence on the mountain of the league's federal sanctuary, to which we can perhaps attribute the theater from the second century B.C. discovered several decades ago at Foce di Sarno.

All this takes us back to a resettlement or reorganization of the Nucerian league at the time it joined the Roman-Italic confederation. We have already noted that the urban layouts of Pompeii and of Nucera are completely analogous to those of contemporary Latin colonies such as that of Paestum. We are therefore looking at a phenomenon of early Romanization.

The city's topographic design, in the final urban form that it assumed around 300 B.C., can be reconstructed, not only beginning with the street grid and the partitions established for its urban space, but also based on epigraphic documents.

In this regard, we must also consider a fundamental linguistic fact, for the most part ignored: the city's very name. The etymology of Pompeii probably comes from the name of the number five in Oscan, *pumpe*: that is, the "city divided into five," a pentapolis. The name seems to be the original one and is in any case already established by the end of the

Preceding pages:
The Civic Forum was the center of public, political, and commercial life in Pompeii. It consisted of a long porticoed plaza, closed on three sides, with various buildings facing it.

The localities of four of Pompeii's five urban tribes (the name of the fifth, located in Regions I and II, is unknown).

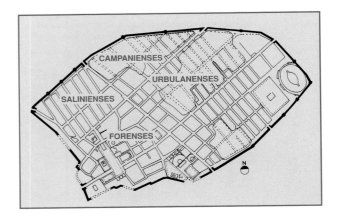

fourth century B.C. It seems to confirm the "synecologic" origins of the city, created by the fusion of a group of earlier villages, probably five. The organization into so many topographic sectors must have been retained even through the successive restructuring analyzed above. It is, in fact, easily distinguishable within the final layout, the one we can date about 300 B.C., and epigraphic documents seem to confirm it.

The urban area is clearly divided by Via Stabiana into two sectors of somewhat different dimensions. To the west of the road two easily recognizable autonomous areas are related to the earliest evolution of the city, and are therefore important historically. We refer obviously to the "Altstadt," the primitive settlement around the Forum, and its succeeding northern expansion, Region VI.

To the east of Via Stabiana, the remaining area was subdivided at the time of the new city's final urban restructuring into three

Pompéi. Vue prise au dessus de L'Odéon et du Théatre tragique: this beautiful image by A. Guesdon shows Pompeii seen from above with all its most important buildings.

sectors, bounded by two main east-west roads, Via di Nola on the north, and Via dell'Abbondanza on the south, whose route was determined by the division of Via Stabiana into three identical segments.

The correspondence between these subdivisions of five sectors, visible on the ground and an actual ancient demarcation, probably as a result of political-administrative needs, can be verified from several epigraphic documents, in particular election notices, whose specifics correspond directly with the neighborhoods of the

city as already reconstructed. In these documents, four entities are mentioned: *Forenses, Salinienses, Canpanienses*, and *Urbulanenses*. The Forenses are recorded in documents located in Via dell'Abbondanza, at the eastern edge of Region VIII: this can refer only to the inhabitants of this region, the interior of which in fact contains the Forum. The Forenses are therefore to be considered residents of the quarter identified with the "Altstadt."

The inscriptions that mention the Salinienses —three in all—are located on Via Consolare and in Region VII: it is consequently evident that they are connected to the northern quarter that makes up the oldest expansion of the ancient city. They therefore concern the inhabitants of that quarter, which must include Region VI and probably also Region VII. There is no doubt that the name must be connected to Via Saliniensis, later Via Consolare, and with the Saliniensis Gate, later Herculaneum Gate, both belonging to Region VI.

The three documents concerning the Campanienses were all discovered along the north side of Via di Nola. There is therefore no doubt that the neighborhood concerned can be identified as that situated to the north of that road, between it and the walls, and therefore as regions IV and V. The name derives surely from that of a Campana Gate which, after recent explorations demonstrated the nonexistence of a Capua Gate corresponding to Tower IX, must be recognized as the one we now call the Vesuvius Gate.

The Urbulanenses, finally, are mentioned in four inscriptions, all located on the north side of Via dell'Abbondanza. We must then identify the quarter in question with that lying between it and Via di Nola, which includes Regions III and IX. The name undoubtedly derives from the original name of Nola Gate, *Porta Urbulana,* or *veru Urublanu*, from an Oscan inscription, which we will examine below. There remains a fifth area, comprising Regions I and II, whose name we do not know.

We are thus able to definitively exclude an alternative interpretation given to this list of names, which would have designated them as villages of the Pompeii territory, the existence of which, furthermore, does not appear in any document. These are, in reality, names derived from those of the city's principal gates, which were located inside the various regions. They were, as we have seen, the Porta Saliniensis (Herculaneum Gate), the Porta Campana (Vesuvius Gate), and the Porta Urbulana (Nola Gate). The Forenses could also have derived their name not only from the Forum, but from the Porta Forensis, which is probably none other than the *Porta Marina,* which headed toward the sea.

As to the function of these regions, we should consider primarily the political-administrative one: these must in fact have been voting districts, as confirmed by their mention in electoral notices. In other words, these were districts for curias or clans, which were always

epigraph is surely the same as that which ran between Via dell'Abbondanza and Via di Nola, which actually made up the median axis of the eastern sectors of the city.

It is probable that only the main roads had names, while the others might have been indicated by progressive numbers beginning from the previous streets. This seems to be the case, for example, with the road that divides blocks I and II in Region I, where we see the graffito "Via III." It is, in fact, the third road to the south of Via dell'Abbondanza.

Walls and War

At the time of the city's maximum expansion, the walls of Pompeii were 10,560 feet long. It is possible to distinguish in them numerous phases and reconstructions, which we know better today thanks to a series of tests made between the 1920s and the 1950s by Maiuri and to more

Aerial view of the Civic Forum in which all the buildings are clearly identifiable: clockwise from the left we can see the Basilica, the Temple of Apollo, the *Forum Olitor,* the Temple of Jupiter, the macellum, the Sanctuary of the Public Lares, the Temple of Vespasian, the Building of Eumachia, and the *Comitium,* or Assembly.

uneven in number in order to assure a majority when an assembly was called. We will return to this below.

We know very little about the names of the ancient Pompeii roads. Other than Via Saliniensis, *viu Sarinu* in Oscan, we know only of a *Via Pompeiana,* which probably refers to a road running outside the city, as must also be the case for Via Stabiana, Via Decuviaris, and Via Iovia mentioned in the same Oscan inscription. The *viu Mefiu,* "Median Road," recorded in another Oscan

recent explorations conducted by Stefano De Caro and the State University of Milan.

Not counting minor interventions, we can recognize five principal stages:

1) A wall completed in the friable local rock called pappamonte and in soft lava, which was encountered in the northwest section of the enclosure, between the Herculaneum Gate and the Vesuvius Gate, and in the southeastern section near the Nucera Gate. Maiuri did not consider this an autonomous phase, but

merely the foundation of the later fortifications, which were created in a double bombard of vertical limestone slabs with a filling, or *emplecton*, in between. De Caro's 1982 exploration in a section near the fairly well-preserved Nucera Gate showed that this not only had a different and independent existence, but also one of considerable antiquity. It can be seen to date as far back as the second quarter of the sixth century B.C. This obliges us to reconstruct Pompeii's oldest history in a way that is radically different from the most traditional notions, since around 570 B.C. Pompeii appears to have been provided with a wall that enclosed a very large area, one only slightly smaller than that of the later Samnitic city. The dearth of traces of this oldest phase—and of the following one—along the eastern side of the city, where the Nola

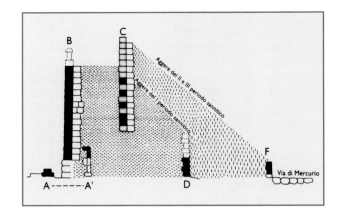

and Sarno gates seem to have appeared for the first time only at the time of the first Samnitic phase of the enclosure, and therefore around 300 B.C., leads us to believe that in

Drawing by Amedeo Maiuri of a cross-section of the urban wall, showing the different phases of its construction.

Painting of a naval battle from the House of the Vettii.

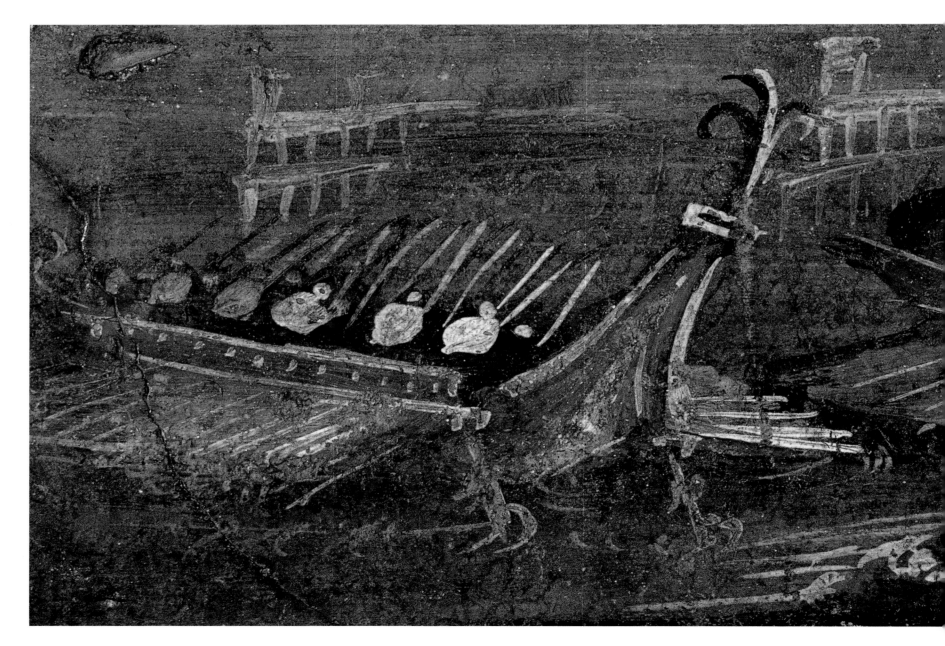

this sector the walls ran somewhat more toward the interior. Only future discoveries will clear up this point, which for now must remain open.

This oldest phase, associated with the city's first northward expansion, Region VI, probably corresponds to the period of Etruscan occupation, recorded by Strabo, much like what happened in other centers of the Campania region, most notably Capua.

2) Between the end of the sixth century B.C. and the beginning of the fifth, the wall in pappamonte was destroyed and almost immediately rebuilt in a more complex form. This structure in a double cortina of limestone slabs, with a filling in between, was a typical feature of other Greek cities in Campania, such as Naples, in the middle of the fifth century B.C. The prevalence of Hellenic elements in the city, following the Etruscan phase, also recorded once by Strabo, is confirmed in Pompeii by the existence of the Triangular Forum's Doric Temple, which is a little older, dating from the middle of the sixth century B.C.

3) A decisive qualitative leap took place with the construction of a third ring of walls, the first walls of the Samnitic era, completed in square limestone blocks from the Sarno, actually a sort of travertine, around 300 B.C., and therefore contemporary with Pompeii's entrance into the Italic confederation dominated by Rome. As has previously been seen, this phase was closely connected to a new urban plan, mainly discernible in the city's eastern sector, and Pompeii then took on the

The system of fortifications in Pompeii was very sophisticated and effective; at the time of maximum expansion, the city's walls measured over 10,560 feet in length.

The Nola Gate is at the end of Via di Nola. The helmeted divinity illustrated in relief on the keystone of the arch is extremely unusual.

dimensions and organizational characteristics that continued until the end of its history.

The new walls show a complex structure, specially reinforced on the north side, which was the most vulnerable, since it lacked the natural defense of an incline. Here the two-tiered wall was replaced by an *agger*, a rampart, banked against a facade of square limestone blocks and shored up on the inside by a shorter wall as a buttress. This situation was very similar to that of the agger walls of Rome.

The gates evolved a complex structure too, easily recognized in the best-preserved examples such as the Stabia Gate and the Nola Gate, which were transformed into veritable castles, flanked on the front by two towers inside the perimeter. These preparations, undoubtedly furnished with powerful projectile weapons and adapted to advances in assault techniques, still did not come close to the technical level of contemporary Greek fortifications.

4) Although the precise chronology of the second Samnitic phase is uncertain, the traditional dating at the end of the third century B.C., at the time of the war with Hannibal, seems likely. This phase consisted primarily of partial reconstruction and expansion of the previous structure. The path of the enclosure remained substantially unchanged, but several sections, probably damaged, were rebuilt with square blocks of Nucera tufa. The northern

Cross-section of a tower on the walls. There were twelve towers in Pompeii, distributed mainly on the northern and eastern sides of the city.

Here is what remains of Tower X, near the Vesuvius Gate. The towers were numbered counter-clockwise beginning on the south side and ending at the Herculaneum Gate.

section was given particular attention because it was the most exposed and therefore required exceptional reinforcement. The ramparts were considerably amplified, with the addition of a new internal counterscarp wall and especially of a second, taller wall, just inside the facade, which thus created a sentry walkway. The gates of the north side were restored and reinforced as well, while to a large extent those on the south side, like the Stabia Gate,

which were less vulnerable to attack because they were protected by a steep incline, retained their primitive aspect.

5) The following phase of the wall can be dated with confidence to the late-Samnitic period, and therefore the last decades of the second century B.C. In this case as well there was mainly a partial rebuilding of the earlier fortification, with very few modifications to its

Facing page:
Detail of a carving in sardonyx showing Nike crowning Ares. The god, known to the Romans as Mars, is seated and wears a crested helmet, as Nike, holding a long palm branch in her right hand, offers him the crown (MANN).

Fresco from the House of Sallust depicting the love affair of Mars and Venus (MANN).

path. In several sections, possibly those damaged during the war with Hannibal, restorations were executed in concrete with a facing of *opus incertum,* a technique that had spread starting in the beginning of the second century B.C. The most important innovation was the addition of towers, twelve in number, concentrated in particular along the north and east sides, those most exposed. These structures, situated so as to span the inner and outer walls, were made up of three floors, with narrow embrasures on the lower floors and larger windows on the third, undoubtedly intended for the most powerful projectile weapons, the catapults. A back door opened on the side of each tower, probably replacing one that originally opened at the same position in the wall. Particular care had been taken with the decoration, in first style, plastered with large expanses in relief, a technique that shows the importance of prestige in these structures, in addition to their military functions.

The twelve towers were numbered counter-clockwise starting on the south side and ending at the Herculaneum Gate, as we know from Oscan epigraphic texts, the so-called *"eituns"* inscriptions, which we will examine below, and from the preserved fragments of large numbers that were carved into the plaster covering the upper part of these structures, discovered during recent excavations near the Nola Gate. These numbers, probably present also on the interior walls, allowed the defenders to orient themselves more easily in the course of an eventual siege. The gates also underwent restorations and were enriched in their turn with ornamental elements such as the helmeted head of a divinity in relief that is still present on the inside of the Nola Gate.

Soldiers

We must consider the general availability of men in comparison to the size of the city, its topographic features, the posting of guards and patrols, and any other tasks for which the city may require men. This is part of what must be done for the proper assignment of duties. . . . First of all it is necessary to select persons who are the most sensible and have the greatest experience of war, who can assist the authorities during the battle. Then it remains only to choose men who will not be fatigued and to organize them into companies, so that they will be ready and able to go on sorties and reinforce any units that may be in trouble, or any other such tasks . . . as to the others, those who are strongest and youngest should be sent to the guard posts and on the walls, while the rest are divided into groups, according to the duration of the night and the number of sentries. . . . If there is a sudden alarm in a city without proper defenses, the most rapid response consists of assigning to each tribe, by means of a lottery, one section of the walls, to which they will immediately send their men. The length of wall to be defended will be determined by the number of men in each tribe. . . . In the same way, if a fortress should be garrisoned by allies, each of them should be assigned a section of wall to defend. Even during times of peace, it is necessary to organize the citizens. First, each street should have as its captain a man who stands out for his ability and intelligence, someone around whom the people will gather if at night there is some unforeseen event. . . . It is moreover necessary for each captain to choose the meeting place in advance, so that he may position the men on the ramparts.

Aeneas Tacticus,
*On the Defense of
Fortified Positions,* I, 1

6) Pompeii's walls, in their final configuration, must have undergone Sulla's siege during the Social War in 89 B.C. Traces of bombardment by Roman war machines can be seen on the northern section of the outer wall, between the Vesuvius and Herculaneum Gates, where the main attack would have been concentrated. Afterwards, there were extensive restorations, witnessed both epigraphically and archeologically, at the Marine Gate and especially at the Herculaneum Gate, which was entirely rebuilt in brick and composite stone at the beginning of the Sulla Colony, right after 80 B.C.

pened at Herculaneum as well. This intrusion of the private into the public sphere—definitely illegal even if tolerated—must have taken place even in the shelter of the exterior side of the enclosure, since, a few years before the eruption that destroyed the city, an emissary from the Emperor Vespasian, the tribune Titus Suedius Clemens, had to liberate the exterior area from the unlawful buildings that had invaded it, probably after the earthquake of 62 A.D. This event is confirmed by the inscribed boundary stones placed a short distance from the walls (CIL X 1018): "By

Above left: Catapult balls probably used during the siege carried out by the Sulla army in April of 89 B.C. during the Social War. *Above right:* Small stones used in a Roman era slingshot.

The walls of Pompeii from the publication by W. Gell and J. Gandy, *Pompeiana: The Result of Excavations Since 1819.*

From then on the walls to a great extent lost their defensive function, even though they certainly preserved the tax boundaries of the city. The west and south sides—that is, the most panoramic ones, facing the sea and the mouth of the Sarno—were taken over by buildings, mostly luxurious urban villas, that largely effaced their structure, and this hap-

order of the Emperor Caesar Vespasian Augustus, the tribune Titus Suedius Clemens, having made an investigation and checked the measurements, has restored to the city of Pompeii the public areas occupied by private citizens."

A group of inscriptions in Oscan (six in all, but originally surely much more numerous), painted in large red letters at various points in the city, are known as "*eituns*" inscriptions, from a word that recurs frequently in them. They are, as has been understood for a long time, precious evidence of Sulla's siege of 89 B.C. and of the organization of the troops who defended the city on that occasion. They furnish, furthermore, valuable information about the topography of Pompeii in the late Samnitic period.

With few variants, these texts repeat the same formula: for example, "for the next crossing the (detached) soldiers (must go) between tower 12 and the Salt Gate, where Maraius Atrius son of Vibius is commander" (Vetter 23). Other topographic indications read: "between tower 10 and 11;" "between the houses of Mamercus Castricius and of Maraius Spurius son of Lucius;" "between the public building and the (temple) of Minerva;" "[past?] Via Mediana, as far as the tower to the left of *Porta Urublana* (Nola Gate) and [left] at *Porta Urublana* to the Mefira tower."

The places where these inscriptions are located, along with their content, make it possible to reconstruct their function. With one exception, they were almost all found along the two main axes of the city, Via delle Terme-Via della Fortuna-Via di Nola and Via dell'Abbondanza, on the side facing the walls, immediately before the intersections of the transverse roads leading to the indicated sections of the walls. It is evident that these were street directions intended for the troops defending Pompeii during Sulla's siege, most of whom were unquestionably not from Pompeii and had only a slight familiarity with the city's topography. The indications of the section of wall to which each soldier was assigned, together with the commander responsible for him, made it possible to avoid the confusion that could occur in the case of an enemy attack on the walls. This is how we know, among other things, the precise number of towers and the direction in which the numbering ran, since the last of them, the twelfth, was located immediately to the east of the Herculaneum Gate, the "Salt Gate," while the next one to the east was the eleventh. Besides the ancient name of the Herculaneum Gate these inscriptions recorded that of the Nola Gate, *veru Urublanu*, or Porta Urublana, from which, as we have seen, the name of the Urbulanenses section derived. Also mentioned are the Doric Temple (the "Temple of Minerva") and a nearby building called the *tribud tùvtikad*, which can be translated as *public house* or *public villa*, and the "median tower," evidently the seventh. Indicated as well are "Via Mediana," an intermediate street, for the most part not excavated, between Via di Nola and Via dell'Abbondanza, and two private houses situated on the western side of the city, where the absence of towers and gates did not provide any other way of indicating the corresponding wall sections.

Government and the Forum

We can largely reconstruct political and judicial life in Pompeii, at least in the last two centuries of the city's history, by analyzing the Forum's functional structures and the city's numerous inscriptions, in conjunction with what we already know about other cities in ancient Italy.

The supreme magistrate, the *meddix tuticus*, was assisted by *aediles*, ministers of public buildings, and *quaestors*, who were primarily finance ministers. All of these positions were annual, as was common in antiquity. The popular assembly, which may have been called the *komparakio*, elected these magistrates by a method that is unknown to us. A senate made up of local notables, possibly called the *kombennio*, was concerned with important political and administrative functions.

The best-known activities of these magistrates were those concerned with building, as

Following pages:
Broad panoramic view of the Civic Forum with the Temple of Jupiter in the middle and the grand staircase topped by the columns of the facade. Visible on the right are the *macellum* and the Sanctuary of the Public Lares.

Fresco found in the House of Julia Felix and depicting a scene of daily life in the Forum which, judging from the picture, was always very crowded (MANN).

Statue of Marcus Holconius Rufus, one of the most eminent citizens of Pompeii. Beside being military tribune, he was *sacerdos Caesaris Augusti*, five times *duovir iure dicundo*, twice *duovir quinquennalis*, and had even attained the title of *patronus coloniae*, the highest municipal honor (MANN).

witnessed by a number of inscriptions in the Oscan language. The *aediles* had responsibility mainly for general works, and the *quaestors* for public and sacred buildings. It was always made clear that their work estimates were subject to the local senate's approval. The *meddices*, on the other hand, were exempt from these obligations and appear to have intervened only rarely in building activities. There are only three known examples of their building activities, but they are extremely significant. They concern, respectively: the walls and gates, attested by an inscription on the Nola Gate; a *passtata*, or portico, of unspecified location but possibly that of the Triangular Forum; and finally the well and *monopteros* situated in front of the Temple of Hercules. It would appear, consequently, that their authority was mainly in the military and religious sphere.

As in most of the Italian peninsula, Pompeii undoubtedly acquired the rights of Roman citizenship after the Social War, around 89 B.C. The existence of a Roman municipality predating the Sulla colony has been disputed, but it seems to be confirmed by the existence of a kind of magistracy, a four-man committee, the *quattorviri*, mentioned in stone inscriptions and also in ancient electoral programs published in Oscan. Such committees were exclusive to municipalities and could not possibly belong to a colony, whose highest magistrate consisted of a *duoviri iure dicundo*, a two-man legal team. The dearth of evidence is evidently due to the municipality's brief duration. In fact, at the end of the civil war between Marius and Sulla, probably around 80 B.C., Pompeii was punished with the installation of one of Sulla's colonies of military veterans, because, like most of the Samnites, it had undoubtedly supported the losing Marius faction. From then on and until the city's end, it would consist of a colony governed by *duoviri iure dicundo*, the highest legal authority in the city, and by *duoviri aediles*. The former, as their title attests, were responsible for jurisdiction, administration in general and the presidency of the local senate, which was an assembly of local council members, the *decurioni*. Like the Roman aediles, the decurions were responsible for the maintenance of roads, public buildings, and temples, and for the supervision of markets and the organization of games. Every five years the duoviri iure dicundo assumed the title of *quinquennales*, and as Roman censors had to conduct the census and revise the list of decurions, who, as in other cities, had to number one hundred. Along with the magistrates, this local senate held most of the administrative and financial power, and was also responsible for maintaining relations with Rome, in naming patrons, the high-ranking persons charged with representing the colony there.

The transition to a colony was traumatic and caused profound social and political change in the civic fabric. The creation of a military colony essentially meant the settlement of an entire legion, that is between forty-five hundred and five thousand veterans, who with their families must have amounted to a combined figure of at least fifteen to twenty thousand persons. Every family group was assigned an allotment of land, for the most part acquired through forced expropriation from the local population, especially from Sulla's adversaries, who were killed or exiled. The officers of the legion, commoners who were centurions or tribunes, to whom the largest allotments were given, automatically became decurions, members of the ruling class, and the colony's magistrates were chosen from among them. All of this must inevitably have profoundly transformed the social body, even if those Pompeiians who had not been banished, mainly those who had supported Sulla, remained a considerable part—but still a definite minority—of the population.

It is impossible to ignore the inevitable consequences of this situation, including the economic, social, and political tensions that resulted, especially in the colony's first years, at least until the Caesarian legislature arrived to remedy the damage caused by Sulla's dictatorship and restored, among other things, political rights even to the children of the

A beautiful sundial. About thirty of them were found in private gardens and public places in Pompeii, made of various materials, from marble to tufa.

exiles. An important indication of these tensions comes to us in a speech by Cicero, the one that he gave in Sulla's defense in 62 B.C.

The previous year, Cicero, who was consul at the time, had foiled the Catiline Conspiracy, which had managed to recruit those who had been marginalized by Sulla's oligarchic restructuring along with other malcontents. In an about-face that lent credibility to already persuasive suspicions, this same Cicero then undertook the defense of P. Cornelius Sulla, a relative of

A representation of the Forum by W. Gell.

the dictator, who was accused of having participated in the conspiracy. There were insinuations that this decision of Cicero's might have been connected to a substantial sum of money, lent to him by the accused and used to purchase a luxurious house on the Palatine Hill.

Many years earlier, P. Sulla had been one of three administrators charged with decommissioning the troops who became the colonists of Pompeii. According to the accusation, he had taken advantage of the native population's

social distress in order to involve them in the conspiracy, apparently with promises of substantial economic and political gain, to the detriment of the colonists, if the plot succeeded. We do not really know how much truth there was to the accusation, although it seems fairly plausible. In any case, in his address, Cicero has given us several useful facts about the situation in the city a few years after the establishment of the Sulla colony, and in particular several details about the institutional system in force at the time:

> As for the accusation aimed at the Pompeiians of having been prodded by Sulla to participate in this conspiracy, I fail to understand how such an infamous crime could have been possible. Do you really believe that the Pompeiians plotted? Who has ever affirmed this and who has ever suspected it? You affirm that Sulla sowed discord between the Pompeiians and the colonists in order to assume control of the city with the help of the former, but first of all, the disagreements between Pompeiians and colonists were all settled through arbitration by the city's patrons when they had already been in dispute for many years; second, the judgment handed out by the patrons was in every way similar to Sulla's; finally these same colonists are convinced that Sulla expressed himself no less in their favor than in that of the Pompeiians, and this can be seen, judges, by the very numbers of colonists who have moved to Rome . . . a similar approval of him has been expressed by the incriminated Pompeiians, who, despite their opposition to the colonists concerning suffrage and the ambulatio, were nevertheless in complete agreement with them regarding the common good.

Thus we learn that one of the principal reasons for the violent disagreement that pitted the colonists against the Pompeiians was the right to vote, which evidently favored the former over the latter in some way. The methods and form of this partiality are hidden within the term ambulatio, which can be understood as closely related to the preceding term, suffrage, in a hendiadys: that is, the meaning must be seen as "suffrage by means of ambulatio."

Ambulatio literally meant "walking," "going" or "promenade," as well as "place where one walks," or, through metonymy, "archway." Given the context, however, in this case we must take it to mean "voting by moving on foot." The expression precisely describes the systems of the Roman *comitia*, in particular the electoral ones, in which the votes of individual citizens had no value; the only votes that counted were those of the electoral units,

A long view of the Forum, seen through one of the honorary arches that adorned its plaza. On the left, the facade of the macellum.

the *tribes* or *centuria*, which had to be expressed simultaneously. Thus the necessity of creating *saepta*, enclosures or corridors separated by stanchions, between which the members of each electoral unity filed one by one to deposit their votes in the urn at the end of the line. When the voting took place in the Forum, these corridors were created by cords that were tightened only on the occasion of an election and later removed to leave the plaza open for its ordinary functions. The majority of the votes of each unity corresponded, then, to a single vote. It thus becomes clear that ambulatio, which can be translated as "line of movement," could well describe such a voting system.

We must conclude that the discord between the Pompeiians and the colonists concerned exactly this system, whether it had been introduced in the city at the time of the colony's founding or had been later modified in favor of the colonists, for example by concentrating the Pompeiians into one or two electoral units. Since there were five such units in Pompeii, as we have seen, this would systematically place them in the minority. Cicero's phrase seems to

throw a ray of light on the political situation at the time of the colony's founding, which would otherwise remain completely in the dark.

New construction in the Forum, as well as modifications to existing buildings, especially

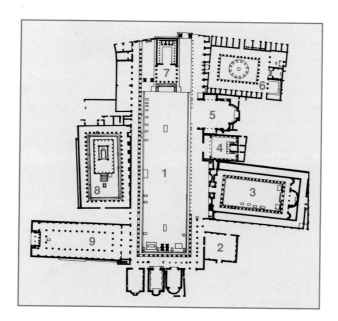

Layout of the Forum

1. Plaza of the Forum
2. Comitium, or Assembly
3. Building of Eumachia
4. Temple of Vespasian
5. Sanctuary of the Lares
6. Macellum
7. Temple of Jupiter
8. Temple of Apollo
9. Basilica

An evocative historic photograph from the Alinari Archive, with a still-active Vesuvius overlooking the ruins of Pompeii.

The Forum area was originally just an open space, bordered by rows of shops along the sides. Indeed, it was only after the second century B.C. that it was modified, adopting the shape of an elongated rectangle, with the two long sides and the southern one enclosed by colonnaded porticoes and with monumental buildings designed for the city's various public functions around it.

in connection with the Temple of Jupiter, seems to confirm this conclusion and ultimately allows us to determine its specific methods.

The intensity of electoral competition is demonstrated by the notable number of propaganda "posters" painted on the plaster facades of buildings facing the principal roads, which were painted over and replaced yearly at every election. This explains why at least fifteen hundred of the twenty-eight hundred inscriptions discovered there were from 79 A.D., the year in which the city was destroyed by the eruption.

The Forum

Pompeii's political and judicial life was concentrated in the Forum, which was also the seat of the city's economic activities. The Forum is not in the geographical center of Pompeii, and this is explained through its connection with the old

city, the "Altstadt," which originally occupied only the southwest quadrant of the urban area in its final expansion. The plaza, oriented from northwest to southeast, had a different form in the beginning from its present one. It had a trapezoidal shape, slanting northward. Its main axis, however, was the western side, which corresponded to the adjacent Temple of Apollo, seat of the principal civic cult, or *poliade*, and to the first expansion of the archaic city, Region VI. The choice of this orientation seems to have been determined by the location of Vesuvius, which dominated the view from the Forum toward the north. The volcano was undoubtedly the seat of an ancient cult, later identified with that of Jupiter, as an inscription at Capua with a dedication to *"Iuppiter Vesuvius"* shows. In the earliest period this would have been a simple open area, closed on its long sides by rows of shops, whose traces were revealed by Maiuri's deep excavations. This aspect is completely analogous with that of the Roman Forum in the age of Tarquinius, which, according to ancient descriptions, had two lines of shops along its sides. These were later called *tabernae Veteris* and *tabernae Novae,* or "ancient stalls" and "modern stalls," and had originally been intended for the sale of foodstuffs. Later still, from the end of the fourth century B.C., after the inclusion of the bureaus of money-changers, they assumed the name of *tabernae argentariae.*

In the late Samnitic era, during the second century B.C., the plaza underwent a radical restructuring and assumed a regular shape, an elongated rectangle 450 feet by 156 feet. The two long sides and the south side were closed by colonnaded porticoes of two stories, and monumental buildings designed for the city's various public functions sprang up all around it. The paving along the borders was of tufa slabs, while the remainder was completed in concrete. Later, probably during the Augustan age, new paving was executed in travertine at the same time that the porticoes were refaced, also in travertine. As in many other cases in Italy, the paving was incised with large letters filled with lead, only four of which have survived. These inscriptions gave the name of the magistrate who completed the work. The absence of much of this paving, as well as of the marble facing from the extremely numerous bases around the forum, and even of the statues, has generally been thought to be the result of supposed delays in finishing the restoration work after the earthquake of 62 A.D. It should be seen, however, as the result of the plundering that took place after the city's final destruction in 79 A.D., when it must have become a veritable mine of materials,

easily reached and exploited. The disastrous condition of many of Pompeii's public monuments, including, for example, the Temple of Venus as well as the Triangular Forum, which was evidently very appealing for its rich marble decoration, can surely be explained by this systematic looting.

We can reconstruct the probable appearance of the Forum from a few surviving illus-

A series of arches behind the Temple of Jupiter.

The Forum's nerve-center was the macellum, located to the left of the Temple of Jupiter; it included a market for meat and fish, as well as for vegetables and other foodstuffs (MANN).

trations, especially the fourth-style paintings in the atrium of the Villa of Julia Felix, which show scenes of daily life near the arches of the plaza, in front of which are two equestrian statues. A relief from the house of Cecilio Giocondo depicts the north side of the Forum, with the Temple of Jupiter and the honorary arches flanking it, at the moment of the earthquake of 62 A.D. The buildings and the statues, expressed in a rough and summary—but very effective—figurative style, appear to be leaning and seem to be on the point of disintegrating.

The Temple of Jupiter, guardian god of political activity in all its aspects, was built in the middle of the north side. In its functions it took the place of the ancient Temple of Apollo, which was then detached from the Forum and given a separate space, enclosed by a four-sided portico in Hellenistic style.

Around the opposite side of the plaza, the south side, were grouped the buildings designed for political and judicial activities: the Basilica, the senate seat, and that of the magistrates, the so-called *Comitium*. It is no accident that in this zone the portico assumes a greater depth, having a double colonnade. On these columns the same word appears many times, painted in large red letters in Oscan—*vaamunim*—which may correspond to the Latin *vadimoinum*, originally "judgment" or "trial." The south sector of the portico seems then reserved for trials, as is confirmed by the similarly important placement of the Basilica, which was designed to house forensic activities, and in particular those of the judiciary, during the winter months. An inscription recovered in this very area shows that the work, begun in the late Samnitic period at the end of the second century B.C., was finished after 90 B.C.: "V(ibius Popidius/Ep(idi) f(ilius) q(uaestor)/porticus/faciendas/coeravit." That is, "Vibius Popidius, son of Popidius, quaestor, was responsible for the construction of the porticos." The use of Latin rather than Oscan in an official document excludes its attribution to the Samnitic city; besides, there is no record in the colonies of such a magistrature as the one mentioned. This makes it possible to attribute the inscription to a precise period between 89 and 80 B.C. when the city, like the rest of Italy after the Social War, acquired Roman citizenship and was constituted as a municipality, which lasted only until the creation of the Sulla colony, around 80 B.C. Another Vibius Popidius, undoubtedly a relative (an uncle?), had built another portico a few years earlier, perhaps that of the

Triangular Forum, as indicated by a Pompeii inscription in Oscan, which also connects it to the Samnitic city.

Facing the Forum on the south side are three parallel halls which, in their current form, built in brick, could be attributed to the middle of the first century B.C., although they actually suggest an earlier phase, of the late Samnitic era. These are surely spaces designed for magistrates and the local senate, even if it is not possible to establish with certainty exactly which is which. According to tradition, the middle one has been identified as the Curia, the seat of the decurions, or local senate, and those on the east and west, respectively, as the offices of the *duoviri*, the high magistrates of the colony, and of the aediles, or building commissioners. Nevertheless, at least one of these should be the *Tabularium*, the city's official archive, whose construc-

tion—or rather reconstruction—is documented in an inscription announcing a spectacle to celebrate the inauguration of the *opus tabularum*, organized by Gneo Alleio Nigidio Maio, an important personage of the period between Nero and Vespasian. Maiuri claimed that this must have been the middle building, usually identified as the Curia, but the center building's dominant position would coincide better with what has been documented in many Roman cities, and we cannot exclude the possibility that the center building is in fact the Curia and that the Tabularium may have been the building just south of it.

The Basilica

The Basilica faces the southwest side of the Forum, as the activities that took place there

The Basilica was constructed in the second half of the second century B.C., and was dedicated, like the plaza of the Forum, to the administration of justice and to commercial activities.

The extremely tall columns of the tribunal at the back of the Basilica, which retains traces of its first-style plaster surfaces. The high tribunal, or platform, where the magistrates sat, was at the top of a flight of wooden steps that could be removed to ensure their safety.

We can establish the dates of the monument with certainty as the last decades of the second century B.C. through the graffiti carved into the walls, many of them in Oscan, even though one of these, in Latin, contains the consular date of 78 B.C. Stamps pressed into the roof-tiles, with the name of a certain Numerius Pupius or Pupidius, have led to this same conclusion.

One reached the building through a sort of vestibule which opened onto the Forum with five openings between pilasters. To the left of these was a large well, furnished with a hydraulic wheel for drawing the water. From here one entered the hall by way of a staircase and five doors. The three central doors, connecting to the nave, were between columns, and the two lateral ones, which closed with gates, between pilasters. The internal space was divided into three naves with enormous columns of brick coated with stucco and then plastered, which had Corinthian capitals of

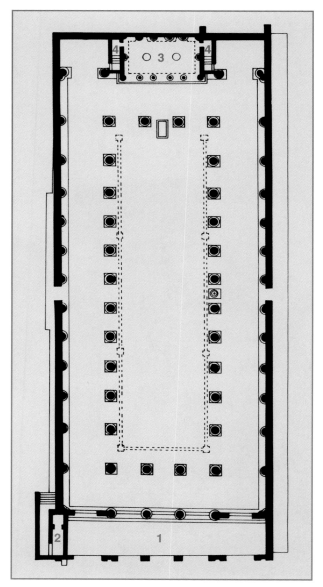

would have required. The building is situated lengthwise from east to west, with the facade opening on a shorter side, and it is oriented slightly differently than other structures in the Forum. This was due to the presence of older buildings, the remains of which have been explored in depth but whose purpose remains unknown. Only the structures standing below the vestibule of the Basilica seem to belong to a series of extremely ancient shops, analogous to those discovered on the opposite side of the plaza, which make it possible to reconstruct a situation similar to that confirmed elsewhere in the Forum of the archaic period.

This is one of the oldest preserved examples of a type of construction that undoubtedly originated in Rome around the end of the third century B.C. Despite its Greek name, the invention is Roman, and was designed—as in the case of the amphitheater—to satisfy local needs. The multiplicity of its functions makes it difficult to translate *basilica* into modern terms: proposals to see it as a stock exchange or a tribunal, not mistaken in themselves, seem nevertheless insufficient. A possible definition is perhaps "covered forum," and it was indeed designed to house during the cold months all those activities, in particular economic and judicial ones, that normally took place out of doors.

Layout of the Basilica

1. Entrance
2. The well
3. Tribunal
4. Staircase to the room below.

66

tufa. This early use of brickwork is notewor-thy, and it is confirmed elsewhere during the Samnitic age, for example in the internal struc-tures of the towers associated with the last phase of the fortifications.

The scarcity of surviving upper portions makes reconstruction difficult, and several dif-ferent hypotheses have been advanced regard-ing them. We can confidently discard that of a roofless central hall. According to more recent studies, the roof, with a single beam and dou-ble slope, would have rested directly on the central colonnade, which would not have had a second floor, and—in the lateral naves—on a double row of half-columns, Ionic below and Corinthian above. Nevertheless, such a hypothesis contradicts what we know about the contemporary style of these buildings, which generally had a hall with double colon-nade, taller on the lateral naves, to allow for light. Besides, the presence of roof tiles of dif-ferent sizes, the largest of them approximately 4½ feet by 3 feet, weighing almost 220 pounds, can only be explained in terms of a more articulated roof.

At the back of the central nave rose the tribunal, with a stage-like facade inspired by Greek architectural models, consisting of two levels of columns, Corinthian below and Ionic above. This was clearly a structure designed for the judges, and for this reason it did not have an approach made of masonry; one must have had to climb up by means of removable wooden steps, which assured the safety of the judges. We already know from Cicero's speeches, for example, how dangerous the reactions of the crowd could be during the course of a trial.

In front of the tribunal we see a large base, intended to support an equestrian statue, undoubtedly that of an emperor, and surely Augustus himself. Starting with the beginning of the Imperial age, as shown for example by Vitruvius' description of the basilica at Fano, tribunals in the basilicas were closely connected to the Imperial cult, and were sometimes in fact turned into Augusteums.

The Comitia and the Temple of Jupiter

The southeast corner of the Forum is occupied by a quadrangle enclosed by a wall with two entrances and furnished with a raised tribunal on one side. This building, completed in the late Samnitic period and restored many times, is often thought to be the *Comitium*, the area that was used in Rome for the oldest popular assemblies, the *comitia curiata*, and where the

seat of the senate and the tribunal of the *prae-tor*, or chief magistrate, were located. But this identification cannot be correct, because already in ancient times, even in Rome itself, the assemblies, especially electoral ones, had been transferred elsewhere, to the Forum or the Campo Marzio. Electoral operations must have taken place in the Forum in Pompeii as well. It is possible therefore that this so-called *Comitium* was designed for vote-counting and was probably then the *Diribitorium*, where votes were tabulated. The tribunal found inside could have been used for communicating elec-tion results to the public. On the front of the tribunal, facing towards the plaza, we find a series of holes, probably designed to attach

A scene of daily life in the Forum. Behind the people, we can see the covered colonnade that ran along three sides of the plaza. From the House of Julia Felix (MANN).

The coins that circulated in Pompeii were the ones commonly used in Rome. This partially-fused handful was found in the city (MANN).

The original bust of Jupiter from the Sulla era is now in the National Archeological Museum of Naples; the one that can be seen in Pompeii's Temple of Jupiter is a copy.

engraved bronze tablets, no doubt recording the law that established the colony, which was usually displayed to the public in the Forum.

As we already know, the "political" temple of Pompeii's Forum was dedicated to Apollo, starting from the very time of the city's founding. During the second century B.C., the situation changed radically: the reconstruction of the plaza, which was straightened and monumentalized by the construction of porticos around the periphery and by a series of prestigious public buildings, resulted in the marginalization of the ancient Temple of Apollo, which was given a separate porticoed plaza and then replaced by a grandiose Temple of Jupiter, which took over the entire northern sector of the plaza. There is no doubt that such a decision was intended to give Pompeii's Forum a uniform shape along the lines of those in Latium, and especially of those in Rome itself. This was an obvious manifestation of the process of self-Romanization that ended a long period of assimilation to the culture of the dominant city, which began at the end of the fourth

The columns of the Temple of Jupiter, which occupies the entire northern sector of the plaza and was built to replace what was then Pompeii's "political" temple, that of Apollo.

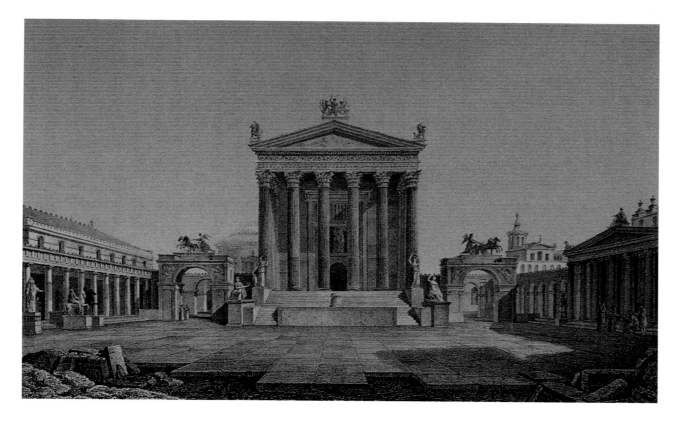

The Temple of Jupiter in a reconstruction by W. Gell.

century B.C., when Pompeii and the other southern Campania cities entered into the Roman-Italic league dominated by Rome.

In its original form the temple had a large frontal staircase, which made it possible to compensate for the considerable slope of the podium, over 10 feet high, from which rose the front colonnade and the *cella*. A large rectangular altar stood in front of the building on the Forum pavement.

This was a large tuscanic temple, approximately 56 feet by 121 feet, with six Corinthian columns along the front and four on the sides. At the back of the cella, which occupied three fifths of the surface of the podium, was a base intended for the god's statue. The underground spaces, or *favissae*, where the offerings and the utensils used in the cult were stored, were divided into three connecting parallel rooms with vaulted ceilings. The original access to them was through two entrances, one in front, opening at the center of the staircase, and the other in back, directly behind the cult statue.

Several decades later the building underwent a profound reorganization coinciding with its transformation into a *Capitolium*, and thus with its dedication to the Capitoline triad of Jupiter, Juno, and Minerva, as we can deduce from the substitution of the cella's original base, designed for a single statue, with a triple base. Only two fragments of these statues have been preserved, the head of Juno and the torso of Jupiter, reworked on the back surface to create a new relief. It appears, therefore, that a workshop of sculptors must have been set up in the area of the temple after the earthquakes that preceded the eruption of 79 A.D. in order to rework marble salvaged from the Forum. This explains the disappearance of most of the marble elements from the square and from the buildings around it, usually—and wrongly—attributed to the slow pace of the work of restoration following the earthquake seventeen years earlier in 62 A.D.

This transformation concluded the long process of Romanization, with the total assimilation of the local cult to that of the dominant city, obviously a consequence of the founding of the Sulla colony.

At this point a series of structural modifications were introduced which cannot be interpreted solely as simple restorations but must surely correspond to a profound transformation of the functions of the building and the plaza facing it. The altar, originally set up in front of the temple on the pavement of the plaza, was now on a spacious frontal platform which took the place of the original staircase, itself replaced by lateral stairs. This eliminated, as well, access to the favissae in the podium of the temple, originally reached from the center of the staircase, which was now replaced by a door on the right side of the podium itself.

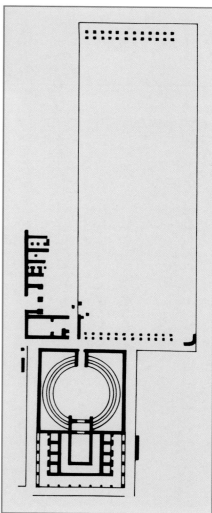

The Forum of Fregellae, in which rope was used to form the corridors needed for the comitia.

The so-called Sanctuary of the Lares, probably Pompeii's Augusteum.

Trimalchio

When I first arrived from Asia, I was no higher than this candlestick. . . . I was my master's companion for fourteen years; there is no shame in doing what your master asks. And I satisfied my mistress as well. You know what I mean . . . but I say no more. I don't like to boast, not me. Then, by the grace of the gods, I acquired my own house, and thus had my master in the palm of my hand. What next? I became his heir, along with the Emperor, and thus received a fortune worthy of a senator. But we are never satisfied, and so I went into business. To make the story short, I built five ships, loaded them with wine, which at that time was worth its weight in gold, and sent them off to Rome. Before you could even say it, all five ships went down. I'm not making this up; in just one day Neptune took thirty million sesterces from me. Do you think that I lost hope? By Hercules! this bad luck didn't make me budge an inch. I built even larger ships, stronger and more fortunate ones. I am truly courageous! You know, a large ship is more sea-worthy. I made a new shipment of wine, lard, beans, perfumes and slaves, and at this moment my wife Fortunata did something very kind: she gave me one hundred gold coins, after having sold all her jewels and clothing. This was the leaven that made my fortune. When the gods wish it, all goes smooth and in a hurry. In just one voyage I made ten million sesterces. Then I bought back all the lands that had been my master's, built a house, and purchased slaves and beasts of burden. All that I touched became sweet as honey. . . . Meanwhile, I built this house, which once was a hovel and is now a temple; it has four dining rooms, twenty bedrooms, two marble porticoes, a suite of rooms upstairs, my own bedroom, the nest that belongs to this viper here, and an excellent lodge for the porter.

Petronius, *Satyricon*

These changes, which we can date to the founding of the colony, can only be explained in relation to functional requirements determined by the new political-institutional situation. They seem connected to the need to have the whole area of the Forum available and to set up a platform at the front of the city's temple that was by definition "political."

It would be hard not to see the connection between these architectural changes and the electoral procedures suggested by Cicero in the passage mentioned above: the introduction of suffrage and the ambulatio, which favored the colonists at the expense of the old Pompeiians. The complete liberation of the Forum and the front platform of the Capitolium seem to have been useful for voting procedures that required the creation of parallel corridors, marked off by ropes and traversed by a considerable number of citizens. We have a relatively accurate idea of how many there were: at least forty-five hundred to five thousand colonists, plus the probably two to three thousand older Pompeiians who had maintained their citizenship rights. Dividing these numbers by the five electoral districts, we can reconstruct lines of at least fifteen hundred persons each. It is possible that this required the entire area of the Forum. As far as the front platform of the temple goes, it was intended to house the structures needed for the voting operations—the urns, the presiding officers, validation commissions, etc.—in a delimited sacred space, the *templum*.

We are thus able to recognize the extent and appearance of the institutional innovations and political techniques introduced following the founding of the colony. These should be understood primarily as the grafting of Roman traditions onto an Italic community, with all that results from it on the level of power relations.

The repositioning of the Forum's layout seems to correspond, on a spatial level, with a polarization of functions, which we can mostly summarize as follows: the southern half was the seat of all political-administrative activities (the buildings designed for the senate and magistrates) and judicial ones (the porticos used for trials—*vadimonia*—and the Basilica). By contrast, the northern half was dedicated to economic activities, such as the weighing counter, with charts of weights and measures on the west, and the *macellum*—food market—on the east. Everything was dominated by the large sanctuary of the "political" divinities, first dedicated to Jupiter, and then to the Capitoline triad, the ideological protectors of all the activities that took place in the area in front, which was functionally unified in the supreme political act, involving the entire community, the electoral *comitia*.

This structure, both functional and symbolic, would remain substantially intact, despite the modifications caused by the progressive and traumatic Romanization, until the end of the Republican era. Only with the advent of the Empire did it undergo a profound restructuring and transformation, which would be concentrated on the eastern side, the area that remained for the most part available after the monumentalization of the Forum in the late Samnitic age.

Here, in the sector between the *macellum* on the north and the entrance into Via dell'Abbondanza on the south, the most ancient situation had been substantially preserved. It consisted of a row of shops, still intended for retail commerce and perhaps for the money-changing activities of the *argentarii*. Beginning with the Augustan age, this situation gave way to profound change, characterized by the founding of the Imperial cult. It is typical that this should take place in an area previously intended exclusively for economic activities. It is noteworthy, in fact, that from its beginnings the Imperial cult was entrusted primarily to representatives of the lower classes, and in municipalities mainly to freedmen—to those ranks, that is, naturally devoted to economic activities, and in particular commercial ones. The hero of Petronius's *Satyricon*, the immortal Trimalchio, appears as the prototype of these classes, more alive and instructive than any sociologic analysis could be.

The Imperial cult was expressed not only in the buildings explicitly dedicated to it, such as the so-called "Sanctuary of the Lares" and "Temple of Vespasian," which occupy the center of the eastern side of the Forum, and in which we find both an Augusteum and a chapel to the spirit of Augustus, but also in structures with an explicitly commercial purpose, among them the *macellum* and—as we will see—the so-called Building of Eumachia, where the predominant side, facing the entrance, seems to have been entirely occupied by chapels for this cult.

This gives us a new and more solid base for investigating the controversial problem of the identification of this last building, which has not had a satisfactory solution until today. In any case, no proposal on this subject can fail to take into account the mixed meaning of this side of the Forum, commercial and ideological at the same time, or to notice the evident symmetry between the *macellum* and the Building of Eumachia, where the latter appears to be dependent on the former, which can only suggest an analogous function.

This reinforces a recent hypothesis that identifies the building as a *venalicium*, or slave market, a structure which could not have been absent in any city of Campania, where such commerce was extremely widespread. It will suffice to once again mention Trimalchio, whose "career" began with his sale, as a youth, in one of these very markets. This episode was depicted in the atrium of Trimalchio's house as a grotesque replica of a Roman history painting: "There was painted a slave market with some inscriptions, and Trimalchio himself with long hair and a caduceus in his hand entering Rome guided by Minerva" (*Satyricon* 29).

Filippo Coarelli

Following pages:
Depicted on the front of the altar of the so-called Temple of Vespasian are the sacrifice of a bull (usual in the cult of an emperor) and various objects connected to the cult. In the background we see a small tetrastyle temple very similar to that of Vespasian.

The temple was built in the Augustan-Tiberian era as a cult site for the emperor. This imposing altar, in white marble, was intended for sacrifices.

71

The Sacred

Temple of Apollo

The large temple complex that occupies the area immediately to the west of the Forum was identified at the time of the 1817 excavation with the principal cult of the city, that of Venus. But the subsequent identification of the cult of Venus with the building immediately to the southwest of the Basilica, between it and Porta Marina, as well as the presence of Apollo's name in the pavement of the temple near the Forum, along with the discovery of a bronze statue of the god inside the portico of that temple, have all led to the definitive identification of the large temple as the Temple of Apollo.

The deep excavations that Maiuri undertook from 1931 to 1932, and from 1942 to 1943, not published until 1986, have shown the extreme antiquity of the sanctuary, the earliest evidence of which goes back to the end of the seventh century B.C. The western walls of the enclosure, the *temenos*, against which the House of Triptolemus was built, belong to this first phase, as do the remains of an altar

and the base of a column, giving every evidence of an open-air sanctuary, similar to that of the House of the Etruscan Column. The first temple building was completed later, during the second half of the sixth century B.C. It was of an Etruscan-Italic type, and its decorative architectural terra-cotta tiles have survived, along with rare pieces of the structure and elements of the altar, which was later rebuilt.

A significant quantity of imported Greek pottery from Corinth, Attica, and the Peloponnese, connected to temples in the archaic era, demonstrates the vitality and wealth of the cult up to 475 B.C., a date which seems to coincide with a crisis in the city.

In this early phase, the sanctuary was the home of a *poliade* cult, and was therefore related to the political structures of the city, concentrated in the nearby Forum. The discovery of *buccheri*, ancient vases of a reddish-black type of clay, with graffiti in Etruscan, datable to the sixth century B.C., and the characteristics of the temple building themselves, lead us to suspect the presence of Etruscans in positions of power, something that is also indicated by literary sources such as Strabo. The cult was obviously of Greek

Facing page:
The statue of Apollo shooting an arrow, found in several fragments and later reconstructed and restored. What we see in Pompeii is a copy; the original is in the National Archeological Museum of Naples.

The Temple of Apollo, on the west side of the Forum next to the Basilica, was begun around the middle of the second century B.C. and later underwent several modifications.

origin, and a connection to Cumae, where Apollo exercised a dominant role from the time of the city's founding, has been proposed. It seems to have been adopted by the Etruscans fairly early, as witnessed by Veio, Pyrgi, and Rome itself.

The monumental reconstruction of the complex began around the middle of the second century B.C. or a little later. The temple was built first, and only later, towards the end of the century, the surrounding four-sided portico. To this phase should be attributed the substitution of the temple building's simple *cocciopesto* floor with a richly segmented one worked in colored stone squares representing cubes in perspective, similar to the contemporary ones in the Temple of Jupiter. On the front band of this floor, decorated in a maze pattern, was an Oscan inscription, now in the National Archeological Museum of Naples and replaced by a copy, which mentions the curator of the work, the *quaestor* O[vius?] Campanius, who had used the resources of the treasury of Apollo. The presence in the *cella* of a tufa *omphalos*, or "navel," the symbolic center of the world, evidently refers to the Delphic cult of Apollo. The temple is a Hellenistic *peripteros* and rises on a typically Italic podium, which at first glance seems to have been lacking a staircase. Located in the center of a four-sided portico with Ionic tufa columns, which originally provided for a second Corinthian floor, it was

certainly inspired by Hellenistic models similar to those which were being constructed contemporaneously in Rome by Greek architects, such as the Portico of Metello—later that of Octavia—built after 146 B.C. It is thus probable that the building at Pompeii was directly inspired by the model in Rome.

At this time the cult was no longer *poliade* but was replaced in its political function by the cult of Jupiter, whose temple was erected contemporaneously at the center of the Forum. This is made evident by the separation of the *temenos* of Apollo from the public plaza, accomplished by means of a series of pilasters of decreasing size from north to south, designed to hide the slight difference in orientation between the two complexes. In a later period even the spaces between the pilasters would be enclosed by walls, completely isolating the temple from the Forum.

At the beginning of the first century B.C. even the altar was rebuilt: the inscription, which is incised on it in two places, notes that the work was created by four magistrates, the *quattuorviri*, one of whom was the same Marcus Porcius who, as *duovirus* of the Sulla colony, would direct the construction of the Small Theater and the Amphitheater. The mention of the quattuorvirate, the exclusive magistrature of municipalities, has generally been explained as alluding to an institution that was not typical of the early years of the colony. This could be a completely isolated fact, and the problem should perhaps be reexamined in relation to the possible existence of

Facing page:
Statue of Artemis found near the Temple of Apollo. The workmanship, especially of the hair and drapery, makes plausible its attribution to the same workshop that produced the beautiful shooting Apollo (MANN).

This column, which had a sundial at the top, was erected during the Augustan age.

Photograph from the turn of the century: the Temple of Apollo without the statue of the shooting Apollo, which was put back on the pedestal many years later.

a municipality at Pompeii in the decade between the end of the Social War and the founding of the Sulla colony.

Doric Temple and the Cult of Minerva and Hercules

Pompeii is the only non-Greek city of ancient Italy in which there was a temple in Hellenic style. Despite a recent attempt to see the Doric Temple of the Triangular Forum as a building based on an Italic model, there is in fact no doubt that we are dealing with a temple built by a Greek architect, even if the decoration of the upper part, in terra-cotta, indicates contact with the Etrusco-Campania world.

This simple realization, added to the fact that the other archaic Pompeii temple, that of Apollo, presents a typically indigenous appearance, must cause us to reflect on the reasons for such an unusual situation, reasons that are surely related to the particular plan of the Triangular Forum, whose nature and function have not been fully clarified. This demands a deep examination of the structures of the temple, beyond the context in which it arose, and of its cult character.

The first thing one notices is the unusual orientation, which is unlike all the other urban plans known in Pompeii. The temple is in fact situated along a northwest-southeast axis, which finds a comparison only in the so-called Via Consolare, the ancient *viu Sarinu* of the Samnitic city. This detail is not without significance: if, as we shall see, it was also dedicated

The Triangular Forum and the Area of the Theaters

1. Quadriporticus
2. *Odeion*
3. Theater
4. Temple of Isis
5. Samnitic Gymnasium
6. Triangular Forum
7. Doric Temple

The Doric Temple of the Triangular Forum was undoubtedly built by a Greek architect, even though the upper part, as the experts have imagined its reconstruction, showed a strong Etrusco-Campanian influence.

to the cult of Hercules, the relationship with the *Salinae Herculeae*, the Herculean Salt Marshes, becomes clear, since Hercules was the tutelary god of salt and of its trade.

The building's terrible condition (it was sacked in antiquity, then prematurely excavated and arbitrarily restored around 1764, and finally struck during a bombardment in 1943) complicates any attempt to reconstruct its original appearance, and this helps explain the almost complete absence of in-depth studies, practically until today. The sloped *crepidine*, with five steps at the point of maximum difference in height, approximately 87 feet long by 55 feet wide, was built of Sarno limestone and faced with blocks of Nucera tufa. This has led to the suspicion that there were two distinct archaic phases, which is further demonstrated by the discovery of two series of architectural terra-cottas, datable respectively to the middle and the end of the sixth century B.C. The oldest of these is striking for its clumsy technique, which suggests the work of local laborers who lacked the skill to execute the models sent from Magna Graecia, possibly from Poseidonia, as we can see from precise comparisons with the archaic Temple of Hera—the so-called Basilica—which extend even to the type of limestone capital, designed with a relief. The shafts of three of these columns, constructed of tufa, were still in place at the time of its discovery. The base, approximately eight feet across, permits us to imagine a building with eleven columns on the long sides and seven on the short ones. This last fact, taken alone, has led to the visualization of a facade with only six columns

and a double space between the central two. This hypothesis is to be excluded, however, both for the technical difficulties it poses (for example, an architrave of disproportionate length) and above all because it would have meant the definitely less acceptable solution of an enclosure consisting of an uneven number of columns on the short sides.

This last solution is not unique, however. It appears in Magna Graecia in at least two contemporary cases: in the ancient temples to Hera at Poseidonia and Metaponto, which have short sides with nine columns. One must wonder, at this point, what brings about such a choice if it cannot be justified by weight constraints.

The only satisfactory explanation is that suggested by the presence in the *cella* of two cult statues, which would have caused a bipolar projection of the architectural structures, with two entrances and, consequently, with an uneven number of columns. In the case of Pompeii, the hypothesis is confirmed by the surviving base of one of the cult statues, distinctly off-center to the right. This would surely have required a second one on the left, which has not survived. Besides, many signs seem to indicate that there was a double cult, of Minerva and Hercules, even though the temple may have been exclusively dedicated to the former, as the sole surviving inscription connected to the temple, which mentions only Minerva, would seem to indicate. The presence of Hercules can be deduced from several clues, going all the way back to the earliest phase of the temple, where a decorative element on the pediment takes the form of a hydra, the mythic monster slain by the hero. When the temple was rebuilt, at the end of the fourth century B.C., a series of antefixes were used which alternately represented Minerva and a young, beardless Hercules.

Of particular interest then is a structure located in front of the temple facade, datable to the time of the colony—but possibly preceded by another similar structure—in the place generally occupied by the altar. This is an uncovered double enclosure, which we can recognize as something

intended for the cult of a hero (a *heroon*). In Rome too, near the extremely ancient *Ara Maxima* of Hercules, there was a sanctuary of similar shape, where the hero's club and cup were housed.

Equally significant is the presence of a well alongside the heroic sanctuary, protected by a small, columned, circular building, a *monopteros*, the importance of which is confirmed, besides its position and the sacred character of its architecture, by the fact that it was built by the highest Samnitic magistrate, the *medix tuticus*, who rarely intervened in the city's building activities, which were usually restricted to the *aediles* and

Antefix of the Doric Temple with the head of Minerva, from about 300 B.C.

79

quaestors. All of this excludes the possibility of a simple well for water and makes plausible a comparison with other similar structures, like those existing in the sanctuary of the *Fortuna Primigenia* at Palestrina, which has been definitively identified as the site of the oracle. We know that both Minerva and Hercules were oracular divinities in ancient Italy, and this permits us to identify the well as an oracular structure, undoubtedly of extremely early origin, even if it was not made into a monument until the end of the second century B.C.

The scant information that has come down to us concerning the cult of Hercules at Pompeii nevertheless makes it possible to specify the central role it played in the city's oldest myths, which, as in nearby Herculaneum, claim that the city was founded by the hero.

The name of Pompeii is supposedly connected to the triumphal procession—*pompa*, from the Greek *pompé*—that the hero would have led with the oxen he had seized from the defeated Geryon. This etymology, false though it is, or perhaps because it is, shows the existence of a myth claiming that the city was founded by Greeks, a myth of great antiquity, from a time that seems to be connected to an ancient temple building.

All of this fits perfectly with the marginal position of the Triangular Forum with respect to the oldest settlement, connected as it probably was with the ancient port at the mouth of the Sarno. We are thus in the presence of a market cult located outside the walls, linked to the presence of Greek merchants since very ancient times, and which must therefore predate the middle of the sixth century B.C.

The association of this architectural complex with the myth of the city's origins would determine its ultimate character: even when the sanctuary was integrated within the limits of the Samnitic city, it retained the characteristics of a marginal structure, and for this reason it would have been particularly suited to host military functions, especially initiation rites required for the admission of the young into the civic body. This explains the Greek-style gymnasium aspect that the Triangular Forum seems to have taken on in its late Samnitic restructuring, as well as the presence of buildings used by the young men of the area, who were organized in quasi-military aristocratic associations known as the *Vereia*, including such groups as the *equites Campani*, or "cavalry" of Campania. Among these buildings were the Samnitic gymnasium and the Large Gymnasium, later used for gladiator games. This is evidently an instance of an Italic structure with a Hellenistic disguise, substantially analogous to the Campo Marzio in

Rome. We should not forget that under the Samnites the functions of Mars were taken over by Hercules, protector of both the economic sphere and the military.

This accords with the presence in the area of foreign cults such as that of Isis and probably that of Aesculapius (the so-called "Temple of the Meilichios Jupiter"), to which we will return below. Even the presence of the theater fits this context if we remember the fundamental role attributed to stage spectacles in ancient Italy by youth organizations, and the very strong connection between the cult and the periodic festive games, during which the local myths—and particularly foundation myths—

constituted the preferred source material for theatrical representations.

In this case, the Triangular Forum's topographic and architectural location, examined as a coherent and functional system, makes it possible to reconstruct a mythic-ritualistic-theatrical context in its entirety, which in other cases can be seen only in fragments.

The close link between the cult and stage spectacles becomes evident, in many Italic sanctuaries and in Rome itself, from the theater's traditional position in front of the temple building and closely connected to it. The most obvious result of such a

Facing page:
Based on comparisons with similar structures, the well built near the *heroon* (sanctuary of the hero) and protected by a small columned circular building (a *monopteros*) was probably the site of an oracle.

The Samnitic Gymnasium, next to the Triangular Forum, was built in the second half of the second century B.C. It has slender columns in delicate tufa stucco, arranged eight on each of the long sides and five on each of the short ones.

Following pages:
Preparations for a satyr play; a mosaic from the House of the Tragic Poet in Pompeii which depicts the actors and musicians with their masks and instruments about to go on stage (MANN).

Facing page:
The great staircase that connects the complex of the Triangular Forum to the Theater and allows for the deep difference in elevation that separates them.

connection is the birth in the late Republican era of an architectural form defined as a theater-temple—although the expression *temple-theater* would be more exact—in which the two buildings were juxtaposed according to a hierarchic scheme along a particular favored axis. There is a general tendency to consider only the formal aspects of such an architectural organization, while it is clear that this was only the last and most recent manifestation of a fairly ancient phenomenon. This phenomenon

and in particular in the previously undiscovered but perfectly recognizable connection between the Doric temple and the theater.

Everyone seems to have failed to notice the existence of a staircase that directly connects the two buildings and makes up for the large difference in level between them. This is not a simple staircase, but a monumental structure, held up by a series of arcades of decreasing size, of the type that we have seen in other buildings of the late Republican era, such as the sanctuary at Palestrina and—in Pompeii itself—the Amphitheater. Today, the ramp comes to an end, incongruously, at a row of shops that close off the northern side of the Gladiator Barracks, but even a superficial observation shows immediately that it actually continued to a lower level, as revealed by the presence of several steps, later obliterated, but whose traces can be seen in the foundation wall of the shops. It is therefore obvious that these shops represent a later restructuring, completed probably after the earthquake of 62 A.D., when the whole area was profoundly changed, transforming what must have been the compound's principal gymnasium into a gladiator arena. Originally, then, the staircase continued along a colonnaded street which ran into the portico still standing along the western side of the Small Theater and from there, turning at a right angle, it opened through a monumental gate, directly onto the stage of the theater.

This monumental structure was surely the route of the sacred ceremonial procession, the *pompa*, that preceded theater spectacles. We know that in this ceremony statues of the divinities to whom the spectacle was dedicated were solemnly carried on litters, or *fercula*. In this way the essential connection was made between the site of the cult and the site of the spectacle, involving the latter in the sphere of the rite.

In this case it is now possible to identify with confidence the procession's point of departure and point of arrival: first the Doric Temple dedicated to Minerva and Hercules— or more accurately, the point of intersection between the temple and the hero's shrine— and then the theater stage. There is thus no doubt that the two complexes are a unitary structure, definable as a temple-theater, nor that the theatrical spectacle was part of the cult activity of the temple itself.

If we had to make a guess as to the "story" that such a procession, and perhaps the oldest spectacles as well, might have told, it would be almost impossible to resist what the myth suggests: that Pompeii was founded as a result of the triumphal pomp celebrated by Hercules

Emblem in the second-style with a mask, from the House of Ganymede (a shop), end of the second century B.C. (MANN).

can be understood through the religious origin of the theater spectacle, which when it began was nothing less than a ritual projection of the cult. If we avoid giving too much importance to the purely formal aspects of this architecture, we will have no trouble understanding that the form of the temple-theater was in fact not late, but goes back to the very origins of the stage games, celebrated from earliest times in close and topographic connection with the site of the cult.

An obvious illustration of this fact can be seen in the complex of the Triangular Forum,

Facing page:
Corinthian capital from the Temple of Venus.

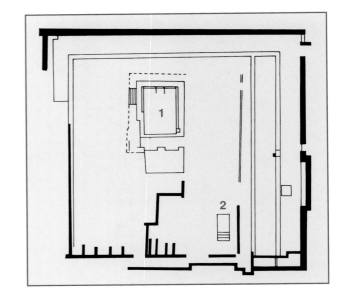

over Geryon. Here, as always, the archetype embodied by the myth would have found its punctual, periodic actualization in the rite that repeated its formalities, rendering it eternal in the sacred realm. The victory of Hercules, mythic founder of the city, thus came to be an ideal model for the young Pompeiians who were preparing themselves in the adjacent gymnasium to acquire the full rights of citizenship through the complex rites of passage of military initiation.

The Pompeiian Physical Venus

Layout of the Temple of Venus

1. Podium
2. Entrance to the lower rooms

The Temple of Venus was a monumental complex made up of an enormous plaza over 40,000 square feet, closed on three sides by a two-story colonnade. The temple itself was over 98 feet long. Today only a few ruins remain.

Beginning with the founding of the colony, the city's principal cult was that of the Pompeiian Physical Venus, which may have taken the place of the earlier *poliade* of Apollo. From that moment on, the city took on the official name of *Colonia Cornelia Veneria Pompeianorum*, a combination of Sulla's name and that of the dictator's personal divinity. This preeminence of the cult of Venus resulted in the construction of a temple dedicated to the goddess, which came to occupy the entire area between the Marine Gate and the Basilica. This was a grandiose complex,

made up of an enormous plaza, approximately 222 feet by 180 feet, which, at least during the Imperial phase, was closed on three sides by a two-story colonnade. In the last phase the temple measured 96 feet by 50 feet and was a pseudo-peripteral temple. Very little remains of the original phase or of its first renewal in the Augustan era; the preserved remains belong

for the most part to the rebuilding following the earthquake of 62 A.D., perhaps not yet finished at the moment of the eruption of 79 A.D. Many of the marble elements were scavenged after the eruption, which makes even just a graphic reconstruction of the complex quite difficult. It was, however, constructed in the typical forms of the large Republican sanctuaries in central Italy, with a temple enclosed inside a triple portico, which had a panoramic view of the port below, the same as the Sanctuary of Terracina, for example, which was also dedicated to Venus. There is no doubt that the goddess acted here as a protectress of navigation and commerce, on a level with the great feminine divinities of Eastern origin.

Representations of Venus in Pompeiian paintings allow us to reconstruct her image, which was completely different from the classical one recurrent in the Greco-Roman religion. Here the divinity is not represented nude, but dressed in a tunic and a blue mantle that covers her to her feet and is decorated with astral symbols such as the moon and stars. A golden diadem, or sometimes the towering crown of ancient protective divinities, covers her head. In one hand she holds a long scepter and an upside-down rudder and in the other a leafy branch that appears to be either olive or myrtle. Next to the goddess is Eros holding a mirror. In one instance, she is carried in procession in a *quadriga*, a two-wheeled chariot, drawn by four elephants.

This is surely an effigy of the cult of the goddess, specially venerated by the common people of the city and in particular by shop owners, as evidenced by her frequent representation on their signs. Her attributes permit us to reconstitute a divine personality that reminds us of the great feminine goddesses of the Near East, rather than the love goddess of the classical tradition. An obvious emphasis was placed on her celestial aspects, as seen in the stars and the color of her mantle, and on her sovereign function, as shown by the scepter and crown, as well as on her connection with the sea, represented by the rudder. The rudder's upside-down position, however, would seem to allude not only to navigation but also to the chthonic valence of the underworld. In her entirety, she is close to the divine figure exalted by Lucretius in the poem *de Rerum Natura*:

Mother of the Romans, descendants of Aeneas, voluptuous to men and gods, vivifying Venus, you who under the errant signs of the

Facing page:
Small idealized head found in the Temple of Venus (MANN).

Venus as she was depicted in Pompeii paintings, with a scepter and crown to indicate her sovereign state and a rudder to emphasize her connection with the sea. Cupid is next to her, holding a mirror. This reproduction was published in the 1950s.

heavens populate the ship-filled sea and the earth rich with fruits, by your works every species of animate being is conceived and at its birth discerns the light of the sun. Before your arrival, the winds and the clouds flee the sky, the industrious earth spreads delicate flowers beneath your feet, the billows of the sea smile on you, and the calmed heavens shine again with soft light (I, 1).

Further clarification is provided by the divine epithet that the goddess took on at Pompeii: *Fisica*. The use of the aspirant *f* rather than the aspirant *ph* precludes an explanation of this term through the Greek *physicòs*, meaning natural, concerning nature. It seems inevitable that it derives from the Oscan *fisios*, connected to the Latin *fides*, which connotes the divinity who guarantees covenants. The Pompeiian Venus, then, would be a goddess of mediation, a guarantor of vows.

This last fact assures us that the cult had a local, pre-Roman origin and was not therefore introduced at the time of the establishment of the Sulla colony, but was recovered from the city's old religious foundation and adapted to the new situation. We must therefore ask ourselves who this local goddess was and what she was called, since the Latin "Venus" could not have been her original name.

Herentas, who was the Oscan equivalent of Venus, would seem to be out of the question, because she was a minor divinity. But perhaps a long-ignored epigraphic detail provides the answer. In the middle of the nineteenth century an Oscan inscription in painted lettering, which later faded away, was visible on the late-Samnitic tufa facade of the House of the Large Fountain. It read "maamiieise.mefitaiiais/ iìkin," which we could render as something like "in the (house) of the Mamii, at the feast of Mefitis . . . " The House of the Large

The same painting in its present condition. The real problem in Pompeii is not how to find what remains of the city, but how to keep what has already been discovered intact.

Fountain could consequently be identified as that of the Mamii, one of the most important families in Pompeii, who seem to have had particular connections to the cult of Venus after the founding of the colony. One of the Mamii in fact was priestess of Venus and Ceres. But above all, we are thus informed of the existence in Pompeii of the cult of Mefitis, one of the most important female divinities among the Samnites and the Lucanians. It seems reasonable to recognize her as the divinity who later took the name of Venus.

There are strong arguments in favor of this hypothesis, beginning with the goddess's name itself. Already in antiquity, this name was explained in connection with the Latin *medius*, corresponding to the Oscan *mefiu*, which means "median, central." Mefitis, then, is the goddess who "stands in the center," who puts the earth in communication with both the underworld and the heavens. She was at the same time a celestial, chthonic, and catachthonic divinity. Her sanctuaries, like that in the Valley of Ansanto, which ancient writers identified as the center, or the "navel" of Italy, are often situated near springs or cavities associated with volcanic phenomena. This, then, is a goddess who "mediates" among these three worlds, and who, as a celestial divinity, also holds sovereign powers. It would be difficult not to recognize in these aspects the perfect equivalent of the attributes characteristic of the Pompeiian Venus, whose iconography seems to directly reflect that of Mefitis.

The decisive argument, however is the epithet *Fisica*, the meaning of which, as we have seen, is probably that of "guarantor of covenants." Not only does this epithet correspond perfectly to the nature of a "mediating" divinity, as Mefitis appears from her name alone to have been, but above all, it was applied not only to the Pompeiian Venus but also to Mefitis alone, as an inscription at Grumentum in Lucania attests (*Mefiti Fisicae* CIL X 203).

Thus we are able to reconstruct in all its phases the transformation of a Samnitic cult into its Latin equivalent, through its "political" use as Sulla's personal divinity, the beginning of a "charismatic" journey that would see it become an Imperial cult.

It is no accident that important buildings of the Marian cult would rise on the sites of several temples to Mefitis. For example, there is

This clay statue of Aesculapius from the beginning of the third century B.C. was found in the eighteenth century in the temple that bears his name, located on Via Stabiana (MANN).

one at Lucania by Rossano di Vaglio, and one in the Valley of Canneto, in southern Lazio, where an important sanctuary to the Black Madonna was built at the Melfa Spring, the original seat of the Mefitis cult. This may also be the case at Pompeii, where the celebrated Marian sanctuary could at last have become the eventual heir and successor, through the Pompeiian Venus, of the Samnitic Mefitis.

Temple of Aesculapius

The small temple located on Via Stabiana, a little south of the intersection with Via del Tempio di Iside, the Temple of Isis, was until a few years ago generally attributed to a youthful underworld divinity of Greek origin, Jupiter Meilichios, the merciful Zeus. The reasons for this identification have been contested recently, with arguments that appear definitive and that are worth examining briefly.

The main document concerning it is an Oscan inscription, found on site at the interior of the Stabian Gate, later moved to the Archeological Museum of Naples and replaced with a copy. The inscription can very probably be translated as follows: "Marcus Suptius son of Marcus and Numerius Pontius, son of Marcus, aediles, determined the limits of Via Pompeiana at a distance of three rods from the Temple of Jupiter Meilichios. This road and Via Decuviare were paved by order [?] of the Pompeiian meddices and these same aediles made the inspection of the work."

The first interpreters of this inscription thought it referred to works carried out inside the city. For this reason, the Temple of Jupiter Meilichios was identified as the one rising on the road that ended at the Stabia Gate, henceforth called Via Stabiana. Nevertheless, when one looks closely, it is clear that this is wrong. The stone with the inscription was in fact just in front of the external arch of the gate, and the text was inscribed on the internal side, and could therefore be read by those leaving the city, not those entering. There is consequently no doubt that all the roads mentioned in the text were exurban roads, not city streets. Likewise, the Temple of Jupiter Meilichios, which was located on one of these roads, could not in any way correspond to the building traditionally identified with it and must be sought outside the city, as would in fact be required by this divinity's underworld nature, which by definition would have excluded him from the urban milieu. One possibility, that of identifying it with the Fondo Iozzino, will be examined below.

The temple on Via Stabiana must therefore be attributed to another divinity, who can be identified, in the absence of any epigraphic evidence, based only on the external elements of the building.

This building, in its current state, seems datable to the first years of the colony, as we can deduce above all from the masonry technique, analogous to that of the Baths of the Forum, the Small Theater, and the Amphitheater, all buildings we can date between 80 and 70 B.C. Nevertheless, several elements appear to be from an earlier period, including the decorated Corinthian capitals connected to the frontal pilasters of the *cella*, the altar, with its serrated decorations and Ionic scrolls, and above all the cult statue in terra-cotta.

This is a shrine on a high podium, preceded by a staircase that takes up the entire width of the building and by an area occupied by the altar. The altar area is closed all around by a high wall, which could be entered through a door that opened onto Via Stabiana, followed by a small colonnaded

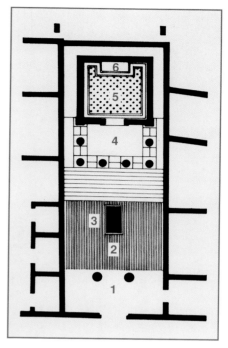

Layout of the Temple of Aesculapius

1. Portico
2. Courtyard
3. Altar
4. Podium
5. Cella
6. Pedestal for the cult statue

Until a few years ago, the Temple of Aesculapius was erroneously attributed to the cult of a youthful underworld divinity of Greek origin, Jupiter Meilichios. Reconstruction by W. Gell.

Originally identified as Juno, this clay
statue was later thought to be Salus,
the Roman equivalent of Hygieia, even
though the features are very generic
and there are no attributes that could
indicate a positive identification (MANN).

portico. The character of the cult undoubtedly
explains why the complex was closed off from
the exterior. It was evidently restricted to a
limited circle of initiates, which may contribute
to the structure's identification. In the absence
of any inscriptions, this identification can be
drawn only from the cult statues. There are
two, in terra-cotta, slightly larger than life-size,
and a bust, and they were discovered still in
place at the time of the excavation in 1766, on
a base at the interior of the *cella*. While the
bust, clearly identifiable as Minerva, is probably a later addition, which may indicate the
prevalence of this divinity, venerated since the
archaic era in the nearby Doric Temple, we
must certainly recognize the other two statues
as a pair of divinities worshipped in this
temple. If we exclude the possibility of the
Meilichios Jupiter and Juno, then we must
turn to the earliest hypothesis, formulated by
Winckelmann, which sees them as Aesculapius
and Salus, and therefore the local equivalents
of the Greek Asklepios and Hygieia. This identification fits perfectly, at least with the masculine statue, while the feminine style is more
generic and difficult to recognize due to the
absence of attributes. The statues can still be
dated to the third century B.C. and the probable first phase of the building, of which no
other traces remain, however. We should note
in this regard that the introduction of the cult
of Aesculapius to Rome occurred exactly at the
beginning of the third century B.C. The temple's cloistered isolation fits this cult, as does
the choice of a "marginal" area of the city, one
well-suited to the installation of a foreign god,
and in particular a Greek god. We see the
same thing, for example, in Rome, where the
Temple of Aesculapius was built on the Isola
Tiberina, facing the Campo Marzio, and thus
in a particularly segregated zone reserved
since very ancient times for foreign cults like
that of Apollo.

Temple of Isis

All across Europe the early discovery in
Pompeii of the Temple of Isis, in 1764,
had broad cultural consequences, which
went beyond even the notable increase in
historical and antiquarian knowledge about
ancient cults. Among the first visitors were
Winckelmann, Goethe, and Mozart, and the
impact on the collective imagination of the
generation that would soon be caught up in
the tempest of the French Revolution can be
seen at various levels: in the birth, for example, of an Egyptianizing style, which inserted
itself into the wider sphere of incipient classi-

cism; and on an ideological level, in the vast repertory of images that became a fund of symbols used by the Masonic lodges, one of which was opened by Cagliostro in Paris in 1784, called the "Mother Lodge of the Adaptation of High Egyptian Masonry." The Temple of Isis must have made an enormous impression on Mozart. He visited it during his voyage to Italy in 1769-70, and the impact was still apparent, as noted, in his composition of *The Magic Flute* in 1791.

The building is located just north of the theater, and its main door opens directly onto Via del Tempio di Iside, in the area between the Samnitic Gymnasium and the so-called Temple of Jupiter Meilichios, in reality probably the Temple of Aesculapius. On the architrave of the entrance portal an inscription was carved (it is now in the National Archeological Museum of Naples and replaced with a copy) recording the restoration work completed just after the earthquake of 62 A.D., which had devastating effects on the temple, such that it had to be completely rebuilt, as the text

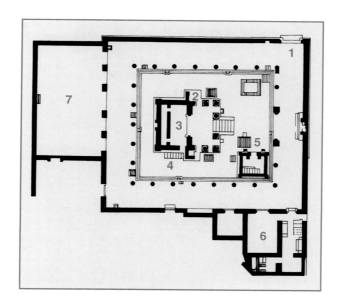

Layout of the Temple of Isis
1. Entrance
2. Square spaces with statues
3. Cella
4. Access stairs
5. Main altar
6. Group of secondary rooms
7. Area probably used for gatherings of the faithful

emphasizes: "Numerius Popidius Celsius, son of Numerius, rebuilt at his own expense from its foundations the Temple of Isis, destroyed by the earthquake. For this munificence the

The Temple of Isis, discovered in 1764, had illustrious visitors like Goethe and Mozart, and its evocative allure influenced the collective imagination of the entire generation that lived through the French Revolution.

decurions accepted him into their order without a fee, even though he was only six years old." The complete reconstruction of the building was thus owed to the extremely young son of a rich freedman, who was compensated for it with membership in the local senate.

The temple was enclosed by a high wall, onto which opened only two entrances. As in the case of the nearby Temple of Aesculapius, we are in the presence of a cult site reserved to a restricted group of the faithful, who could gain access only after having passed a series of trials of initiation. Nevertheless, this complex had a public character, as we can see from the inscriptions cut into the base of several statues that mention the special authorization of the local senate, which was required in such cases.

The structures found on the inside of the enclosure all appear to be contemporary, confirming the comprehensive nature of the rebuilding and the extent of the destruction caused by the earthquake, something that is also emphasized in the inscriptions. The oldest parts of the building, which were reused, are

in fact in different positions from their original locations and on completely new foundations. Everything had been covered with very rich painted and stucco decorations, which appeared to the eighteenth-century excavators practically intact. Today many parts of this decoration, especially the paintings, are preserved in the National Archeological Museum of Naples, and in part replaced by photographs.

The architectural parts belonging to the earliest phase and later reused were executed in tufa from Nucera. This fact, together with the technical characteristics of these elements, again allows us to date them to the late-Samnitic period, and therefore towards the end of the second century B.C. This then is one of the oldest known temples in Italy dedicated to the Egyptian cult.

The actual temple building itself was placed in the center of a porticoed area. This area originally had ten columns on the long sides and eight on the short sides, reduced in the reconstruction to eight and seven, but to only six on the east side, the front, where the central column was eliminated and the two adja-

Facing page:

The Temple of Isis is between the Samnitic Gymnasium and the so-called Temple of Jupiter Meilichios. The fact that it has only two entrances confirms the thesis that the temple was restricted to a small number of faithful, who could gain access only after having passed a series of trials of initiation.

The Temple of Isis in a reproduction by W. Gell.

Statuette of Isis dressed in a transparent tunic, gathered above the waist by a belt with reptile heads. In her left hand she is holding a *crux ansata*, or Coptic cross; in her slightly raised right hand there was probably a *sistrum*, a kind of Egyptian rattle, now lost (MANN).

One of the lovely fourth-style paintings from the Temple of Isis (MANN).

Facing page:
Bust of a woman found in the Temple of Isis and which was part of an acrolith, a sculpture consisting of a cloth-covered wooden support, to which the exposed limbs, made of marble, were attached (MANN).

The only element that could have identified this face as that of Isis was the attribute on her head, possibly a feather; the iconography, however, definitely derives from that of Aphrodite (MANN).

Following pages:

Fourth-style painting of a figure performing a religious rite.

The fresco depicts Io, left on the rocks at Canopus by the river god; here she takes the hand of Isis, who waits for her with a cobra in her left hand and a crocodile under her feet (MANN).

cent ones replaced by half-columns topped with pilasters, in order to leave a broad open space in front of the temple entrance.

This temple, wider than it was long, approximately 27 feet by 21 feet, and facing northeast, is a tetrastyle prostyle—that is, with four columns on the facade—on a high brick podium, which could be reached by a front stairway with seven steps. At the time of the restoration, the Corinthian tufa columns, which were part of the original building, had been covered with stucco molded into a fluted shape. The *cella* was not very deep, and it too was expanded in width. It has a long podium in the back, on which two small bases rest, intended to hold the images of the divinities Isis and Serapis. Another entrance opening on the south could be reached by means of a small side staircase. On the sides of the podium are two projections topped by two square spaces, originally occupied by statues of other divinities, probably Harpocrates and Anubis, whose altars were located opposite, on the plaza pavement. The main altar was located in front of the facade, but displaced toward the left, in apparent relation to a square room from which, by means of a staircase, one could reach an underground space, where excavators found the basin for the purifying water, symbolically identified with that of the Nile and indispensable for the cult.

Behind the temple is a large room, most likely a reunion hall for the faithful, created at the expense of the Samnitic Gymnasium, probably after the earthquake of 62 A.D. It was originally decorated with grandiose fourth-style murals, paintings with large proportions, representing Egyptian landscapes and the myth of Io. To the south of this room one had access to a space possibly intended for initiation ceremonies.

A small group of rooms in the southeast corner of the sanctuary, which we can identify as a kitchen, a triclinium, and a *cubiculum*, or bedroom, was perhaps intended for the priests.

The introduction of Eastern cults into Italy during the late Republic is a phenomenon of extraordinary dimensions, which had its roots in the profound economic, social, and philosophical crisis that overwhelmed the unity of the Roman Empire at the time of its greatest expansion. The transformation of the traditional structures of property and family, and the enrichment of certain classes, which diverted attention from the pauperization of a growing mass of the population, along with the introduction of enormous numbers of slaves, especially from the East, for the growing needs of the new economy and of the

new luxury—all these phenomena combined to cause a profound crisis, which generated new needs and required new ideological solutions. The final triumph of Christianity, which concluded this process, can be explained in fact within such a picture: it was the most reasonable response to the spiritual need of the marginalized lower classes, especially in the big cities, for redemption and salvation—if only in another world. At the same time it furnished an adequate response to the dimensions of the new problems, by then extended to a scale previously unknown. In an absolute, centralized and potentially global empire, religion could only be monotheistic and universal.

It was not accidental then that the religions of the near East—Egyptian, Syrian, Anatolian, and Persian—began to invade Italy proper beginning in the second century B.C. Following the elimination of Carthage and the Hellenic kingdoms, with the exception of Egypt, by then reduced to a protectorate, Rome's dominion extended to the entire Mediterranean. The earliest was possibly the Egyptian cult, whose presence in the Campania region and in Rome itself can be traced back as far as about 150 B.C. We find it documented at Capua before 108 B.C. and in Pompeii, as we have seen, in more or less the same years. Those primarily responsible for this phenomenon were the merchants such as the Alexandrians who settled in the Campania ports and Pompeii and the Italics who swarmed the Mediterranean East—bankers, dealers in agricultural produce as well as luxury merchandise, and slave merchants—all protected by the prestige and arms of Rome. It was not by chance that one of the most important centers for the diffusion of these cults—Egyptian and also Syrian—was the great emporium of the eastern Mediterranean specializing in the slave trade, Delos. Here, under the protection of Apollo, thousands of Italic and Asiatic merchants exchanged not just goods, but ideologies and religions. It was precisely in the Egyptian and Syrian sanctuaries of Delos that the orientalization of the Roman religion took form, the effects of which, through the spread of Christianity, have been carried to the present day.

Sanctuary of the Fondo Iozzino

An important discovery, which took place recently in the Fondo Iozzino, a few hundred yards south of the Nucera Gate, revealed the existence of an archaic sanctuary that survived until the Imperial period. Its oldest phase is documented by numerous ceramic finds, bucchero ware and Greek pottery, from the sixth century B.C., while the visible structures belong to a general rebuilding that we can date to the third century B.C.

There are two concentric quadrangular enclosures, the outer one in limestone and the internal one—rebuilt in the second century B.C.—in *opus incertum* in tufa. This kind of structure reveals the "secret" nature of the cult, which evidently provided for particular ceremonies reserved only to the initiates.

Three chapels were found inside the second enclosure, open towards the north and with various altars between them. This surely involved a complex cult, dedicated to several divinities, whose underworld character is shown by the non-traditional north orientation. The discovery of two female statues, dating from the end of the second century B.C., one life-size and the other half-size, makes the exact nature of the cult clear: these were in fact almost certainly likenesses of Demeter and of Hecate (the three-form underworld goddess of the *trivia*), divinities who were often linked in the Greek religion, which served as the direct inspiration here.

A very similar situation is known in Sicily at Selinunte: together with Hecate, Demeter was venerated there as Malophoros, "bringer of apples," in a sanctuary placed outside the city on a hillside to the west, facing the principal port. An even more interesting fact is that the sanctuary also included a chapel to Zeus Meilichios, the underworld vegetation deity very close to Dionysus. The presence in Pompeii of three chapels, all clearly dedicated to underworld vegetation cults, has a credible explanation: this must have been a sanctuary to Hecate, Jupiter Meilichios and Ceres, the Italic equivalent of the Greek Demeter, located outside the city at an important intersection and near the port at the mouth of the Sarno, like the situation at Selinunte.

There is specific evidence of this reconstruction in an inscription recording road work that was discovered at the level of the Stabia Gate concerning the so-called Temple of Jupiter Meilichios (which should really be identified as the Temple of Aesculapius). The text in question mentions the works of two aediles, who had "limited" the street that exited through the Stabia Gate by the length of ten rods, or *pertiche*, as far as the Stabia bridge—and thus probably as far as the Sarno, which at this point ran close to Pompeii's southern walls. The inscription adds that on the same occasion Via Pompeiana was also limited by the length of three *pertiche*, as far as the "*cella* of Jupiter Meilichios." This makes

one think that this latter road should be identified as a route that separated from the road to Stabia just before the Sarno, turning towards the east, and thus seems to coincide perfectly with the position of the Sanctuary of the Fondo Iozzino, which was located in fact that exact distance to the east of the road to Stabia, evidently on a west-east route, parallel to the walls and to the course of the Sarno.

The identification of the sanctuary as the "*cella* of Jupiter Meilichios" thus seems confirmed, and the mention of it in preference to the other two chapels, probably dedicated to Ceres and Hecate, is probably due to the fact that it was the closest to the Via Pompeiana referred to in the inscription.

Temple of Bacchus

Despite the obvious importance that Bacchus would have had in a city whose principal product was wine, an importance suggested by the frequency with which the god appears in wall paintings and elsewhere, the presence of the cult of Bacchus in Pompeii has only recently been established, following a chance discovery in 1943. That year, in the resort of San Abbondio, 435 miles south of Pompeii, a bombardment revealed the presence of a small temple from the Samnitic era, which would only be excavated and documented years later.

It was a small Doric tetrastyle temple with three columns on the sides, including the corner ones, measuring 49 feet by 27 feet and resting on a low podium. The foundations and the base are of Sarno limestone, the columns of tufa. At its front are two triclinic structures with circular tables, evidently intended for

Facing page:
This ivory statuette found in a house on Via dell'Abbondanza represents Lakshmi, the Hindu goddess of beauty and fecundity, and attests to the existence of more or less direct trade with India (MANN).

Following pages:
Glass cameo panel depicting the initiation of Ariadne into the cult of Dionysus, next to a maenad and a dancing satyr. Objects symbolic of the cult hang in the trees (MANN).

Three-dimensional reconstruction of the Temple of Bacchus.

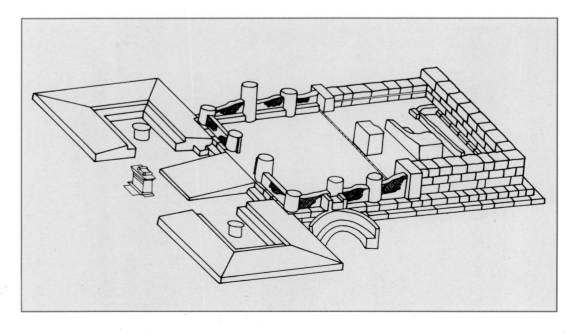

sacred banquets. Between them is the altar, of Nucera tufa, like that of the so-called Temple of Jupiter Meilichios. The Oscan inscription which is carved there in two places, on the front and back sides, honors the magistrate who paid to have it built, the aedile Maras Atinius, the same one who as quaestor had created a sundial in the Stabian Baths with money recovered from fines.

On the sloped ramp that led to the temple is another Oscan inscription created of pebbles in rough mosaic, which reports the names of two other aediles, Oppius Epidius son of Oppius and Trebius Mezius, son of Trebius, who had evidently commissioned other parts of the building.

This temple appears to be quite old, from the third century B.C., although it was restored in the second century and again during the Imperial era, when the triclinia were created, along with the barriers between the columns, evidently intended to create a closed space furnished with seats, as required by the mystic nature of the cult.

The *cella* is occupied by two bases, the front one probably intended to hold offerings, while the one against the back wall was occupied by the cult statues, of which there must have been two or three, judging from its dimensions. The division of the entrance into two parts, by means of a large pilaster, suggests that here too there may have been two effigies.

Without precise indications in the preserved epigraphs, it is possible to identify the cult only through the designs on the pediment connected to the western facade of the temple, built of Nucera tufa, which was discovered almost intact. Represented there are two divinities lying down at a banquet facing each other, separated by a *thyrsus*, the staff tipped with a pine cone and twined with ivy that is carried by Dionysus, Dionysian revelers, and satyrs. The male figure on the left has a panther next to him. In his right hand he holds a *kantharos*, the typical wine cup of the Dionysian cult, and in the left a bunch of grapes. The other, a female figure, is wearing a tunic and mantle, and covers her head with one edge of it, in a typical sacred wedding gesture. At her feet is an image of Eros, holding a *flabellum*, a fan, and followed by a goose. This is an Ariadne-Aphrodite, and the scene represents no less than her wedding with Bacchus-Dionysus.

Facing page:
Fresco from the House of the Centenarian depicting Bacchus as a luxuriant cluster of grapes, with his thyrsus and a panther next to Vesuvius, on whose slopes Pompeiians tended vineyards. The serpent represents the fertility of the soil (MANN).

Bronze statuette from the Villa of the Papyri at Herculaneum (MANN).

Pantheistic hand with images of several divinities and divine attributes; this unusual type of object was probably thought to have magic powers (MANN).

The cult is that of Dionysus and Aphrodite, who were venerated in Rome as Liber and Libera, along with Ceres, in the archaic temple at the foot of the Aventine Hill. On the base of the *cella*, then, there must have been statues of these two divinities, who are also represented together in a famous painted decoration at the Villa of the Mysteries, which may have belonged to a priest or priestess of the divine couple.

The chthonic character of this cult, connected to the earth and vegetation, is seen in the orientation of the temple, whose facade faces west, and in its exurban location, in the middle of countryside planted with grapevines, near the port at the mouth of the Sarno, from which sailed ships loaded with wine. Situated thus, the two divinities could extend their protection and beneficent influence to the agricultural and commercial activities that were the main basis of Pompeii's wealth.

The Imperial Cult

Because of its early disappearance, Pompeii is an ideal observatory for examining the birth and first development of the Imperial cult in Italy before it assumed its definitive and better-known form during the main Imperial era.

The surviving evidence is concentrated in the area of the Forum, within which are the buildings mainly identified today as the Temple of the Public Lares and the Temple of Vespasian. Just north of the plaza—in a zone outside the public property of the grounds—we find the Temple of Fortuna Augusta. Finally, as we have already seen, structures intended to house the Imperial cult were inserted into buildings of a commercial character, such as the macellum and the so-called Building of Eumachia, whose function as a slave market appears probable. It is thus significant, as emphasized above, that the cult was concentrated exclusively in the eastern sector of the Forum, which was largely left out of the grandiose enlargements of the late Samnitic period. This would seem to be directly related to the entirely commercial functions of this area, where the activities of the lower classes, who were by definition less attached to the traditional religion, were concentrated. These groups were the privileged administrators of the new cult of the Emperor, just as they had been, for similar reasons, those primarily responsible for the introduction of the Eastern cults.

The so-called Temple of Vespasian, just north of the Building of Eumachia, occupies the center of the free space to the east of the

The Temple of Fortuna Augusta was built by the duovir Marcus Tullius, who paid for it personally, on land that he owned. The statue of Fortuna was kept inside the sanctuary.

Forum. It consists of an open courtyard, preceded by a small columned portico decorated on the sides by niches framed by half columns. The back wall is occupied by a shrine on a podium, reached by two short side staircases. In front of it is a marble altar decorated with reliefs representing the sacrifice of a bull, the instruments of the cult, and laurels and a civic crown, symbols of Augustan propaganda. Even though the building appears to be largely the result of a reconstruction following the earthquake of 62 A.D., it seems safe to identify it as the temple dedicated to the tutelary deity of Augustus, which is referred to in the oldest documentation of Pompeii's Imperial cult, an inscription from the Imperial period in which the "public priestess" Mamia recorded the construction of the building at her expense and on her own land (CIL X 816).

Immediately to the north of it is the so-called Temple of the Public Lares, also consisting of a courtyard of very pronounced forms, typical of the period of Nero or of the beginning of the Flavian age. It was constructed entirely of bricks, but deep tests have shown the existence on the site of an earlier building with a similar layout. Three niches open onto it, two rectangular ones on the sides and one onto the apse in the back, constituting the true shrine, which housed the statue of an emperor. It might therefore have been Pompeii's Augusteum.

The Temple of Fortuna Augusta, definitively identified from the inscriptions found at the site, is north of the Forum at the intersection of the Forum road and Via della Fortuna. This is a Corinthian tetrastyle prostyle temple on a high podium, reached by steps into which the altar had been set, and its deep *cella*, punctuated by niches, ends with an apse intended for cult statues, typical of temples of the Imperial cult. The inscription, reinserted in the apse in modern times, honors the founder of the temple: "Marcus Tullius, son of Marcus, thrice *duovir iure dicundo*, *quinquennale*, *augur*, and elected military tribune, erected the temple of Fortune at his own expense." We know from another inscription that the little temple was built on land belonging to this same personage. The work, begun in 2 B.C., was completed in 3 A.D., and thus in the main Augustan era. The College of Ministers of Fortuna Augusta was instituted in that same year. They were to lead this cult, which was originally private in nature, and this is why it came to occupy an area outside—but very close to—the public space of the Forum.

Filippo Coarelli

Economics and Industry

Facing page:
A delicate detail of the wall decoration in the triclinium of the House of the Vettii, with a series of references to the tragedy *Iphigenia in Tauris* by Euripides in the lower strip. The wealthy owners of this famous dwelling belonged to the class of *liberti* (liberated slaves) and had become prosperous thanks to their enterprise in commercial affairs.

In this well-known fourth-style fresco from Stabia one can immediately grasp the vigor of the economic and commercial life of a maritime port in the first Imperial age. A harbor beautified by monumental buildings and honorary columns welcomes cargo ships and small fishing boats, successfully evoking the importance in antiquity of such commercial activities, which took advantage of the fastest and least expensive river and sea routes. Although the scene should not be seen as a reproduction of a particular location, the appearance suggests Campania. (MANN).

Following pages:
This beautiful view of the second peristyle in the House of the Faun, with an open perspective onto the exedra where the splendid mosaic of Alexander the Great was located and onto the first peristyle, steeps the viewer in the princely luxury of Pompeii's ruling class during the late-Samnitic era (second to first century B.C.). It exhibits a degree of ease, wealth, and well-being that no other Pompeiian managed to equal, even though the city maintained significant economic and commercial vitality until its tragic end.

There is no doubt that one of the principal factors in Pompeii's socio-economic development was its favorable geographic position. Located in the heart of a territory of volcanic origin, with fertile plains and heavily cultivated gentle slopes, the city ultimately benefitted as well from its proximity to the sea near the mouth of the Sarno. This river was short but important because it was partially navigable, and its outlet to the sea, amid a brackish and partially swampy cove, made an excellent natural port, another favorable element necessary for a trade economy. One should not forget, in this regard, that a large part of ancient commercial traffic was carried out on water, at a much lower operating cost than for trade routes on land, which were important in their own right. Pompeii, in fact, had the additional advantage of being located on important land thoroughfares, at the point where the route from Naples to Nucera split towards Stabia and Sorrento. In a famous passage, Strabo, the Augustan era's skillful geographer, confirms Pompeii's particular economic role as "the port of Nola, Nucera and Acerra, for those who must receive goods as well as for those who must send them." Although we might question the surprising fact that Pompeii functioned as a port even for a relatively distant place such as Acerra, and wonder if perhaps Strabo may have synthesized older facts linked to some unusual historic circumstance, there is no doubt that during the classical era Pompeii was the most important economic center in the entire Sarno valley. It would be naive, however, to explain all the causes for this particular socio-economic development by geographic position alone. Even in a territory

Presumed to be a bronze portrait of Lucius Caecilius Iucundus, possibly an Augustan-era ancestor of the Pompeiian *argentarius* who lived in the Nero-Flavian period and bore the same name (MANN).

On the obverse of this gold piece, coined in Lyon in 9-8 B.C. and found in Pompeii, is a portrait of the emperor Augustus with his official title (MANN).

with favorable physical and natural characteristics, in order for the advantages of location to be realized, the general historic situation must favor the enjoyment of the benefits offered by nature and the geographic environment.

Naturally, this was the case for Pompeii. In the long chronological arc along which the historic events of this city played out, there was in fact one epoch that smiled more than any other on the economic fortunes of its inhabitants. This was the so-called late-Samnitic phase, which encompassed the entire second century B.C. and the beginning of the following century, up to the political-military encounter with the Romans known as the Social War (91-88 B.C.), and culminated in 80 B.C. with the foundation of the Sulla colony and the temporary purge of the Samnitic aristocracy. This period was a true apogee, never again equalled afterwards, with ostentatious shows of personal enrichment, culminating, just to give the most dazzling examples, in the construction of private homes that could have compared favorably in their dimensions and

level of decoration with the residences of the Hellenic kings. In fact, many rich Pompeiians of the time took those sumptuous royal dwellings as models.

All this was possible because Pompeii, and in general all the centers of Italy favored by their positions on transit roads and by their particular products, could take advantage of the energies primed by Roman imperialism as it expanded throughout the Mediterranean. Following the favorable conclusion of the first and second Punic wars—the definitive defeat of Hannibal at Zama, in Africa in 202 B.C. being a determining factor in weakening a powerful rival like Carthage—and the conquests in the Aegean-Anatolian Orient, the Empire was at this point nearly unstoppable. The Roman armies were used not only for the simple territorial expansion of her frontiers, but indeed to guarantee the security of her economic outlets, which were ever more important to Rome's own elites and those of her Italic allies.

In these unusual political-economic circumstances, anyone who owned valuable agricultural lands became increasingly committed to intensive specialized cultivation. Pompeiian agriculture, for example, was known above all for its vineyards, and its famous wines were mentioned in ancient sources and sought throughout the Mediterranean, as we know from discoveries of amphorae with the seals of Pompeiian vintners. Lucrative deals were carried out by *negotiatores*, the most aggressive Roman and Italic merchants, who built commercial relationships of vast importance, choosing as their bases Mediterranean ports with special characteristics, such as the island of Delos, a duty-free port from 166 to 88 B.C. Besides wine and high-priced agricultural products such as olive oil, used in ancient times for many purposes, these merchants enriched themselves by introducing to the most important Mediterranean markets precious fabrics, spices, manufactured products of very refined quality, and above all, the most sought-after economic commodity—slaves, the prime fruit of wars of conquest.

The widespread presence of slaves in various agrarian enterprises and in all the fundamental sectors of economic-industrial activity, was a true motor of production, not just in the figurative sense, but as one of the determining factors that guaranteed the success of investments and enterprises specifically designed to realize a profit. This is very well documented by a number of ancient writers who discussed the subject, among them Cato the Censor, Varro, and Columella. Indeed the phase

apogee, it does not mean that the succeeding phases in Pompeii, the late Republican era and the brief Imperial period prior to the devastating eruption of 79 A.D., were periods of retrenchment or stagnation. The city definitely maintained a significant vitality, as we can see from the numerous public buildings and the still high level of many residential constructions, as well as the very extensive restorations that followed the earthquake of 62 A.D., even if their execution had not always been prompt. Nevertheless, it was no longer possible for any Pompeiian to flaunt such stunning private luxury as the owner of the House of the Faun, from the last quarter of the second century B.C., who put on a grand show with works of art such as the floor mosaic of Alexander the Great, with its obvious political and ideological connotations. Furthermore, in the early Imperial era there began to be seen the first signs of a different economic-productive trend, which tended to favor other areas of the Empire such as Gaul and Spain over the cities of the Italian peninsula. The consumer goods produced in these provinces, especially wine and oil, gradually came to threaten the traditional sources of income from intensive agriculture in territories like coastal Campania.

Beyond these historical considerations, however, it is worth noting that

Among the most typical objects in daily use were terra-cotta vases. At left are two hydrias, used to transport and store water; below is a lovely collection of amphorae from the House of the Chaste Lovers. Amphorae were the containers most widely used in antiquity for transporting foodstuffs of various types: their unmistakable features, such as the double handles and the cap, made them irreplaceably practical and useful.

between the late Republic and the first Imperial era represented the apex of the slave mode of production. This socio-economic order guaranteed the fortunes of the ruling class and continued for some time, despite worrying tremors from several slave revolts and their bloody suppression, as with Spartacus, who was killed in 71 B.C. In the middle and late Imperial age the slave system was replaced by the colonists and, above all, by the spread of the landed estate, not because of moral scruples, the concept of freedom in the ancient world being entirely different from our own Enlightenment-based ideas, but because of several complex historic factors, not the least of which was the legal possibility of emancipation awarded to the most enterprising slaves.

If Pompeii could therefore take advantage of such a favorable circumstance as the larger framework represented by Roman expansionism on a Mediterranean scale, it is easy to understand her economy's vigor, which grew ever stronger as the Roman imperialist thrust became more dynamic. Even if the late Samnitic phase is seen as an

Although they are rarely equal to Greek jewelry, especially because during the Roman era the social class that used precious ornaments was always growing, the numerous jewels found in Pompeii successfully document the love of luxury on the part of its matrons. On this page is a necklace of gold, emeralds, and mother-of-pearl, which came to light in a suburban villa (MANN).

Gold ring with a wide band and a carved oval setting in all probability depicting an athlete, from the Julio-Claudian era (MANN).

Carnelian from the Augustan age, delicately worked, showing a soldier armed with a sword and shield facing an opponent (MANN).

The spiral form of a serpent, a motif very common in Greek jewelry, was also beloved by the Romans for their gold bracelets. Especially noteworthy in this example is the rendering of the scales, obtained through very fine carving (MANN).

These two serpent-shaped bracelets emphasize the propitious aspect that the pagan religions, as opposed to Christianity, saw in these reptiles, usually called "agathodaimonoi," or bringers of good fortune (MANN).

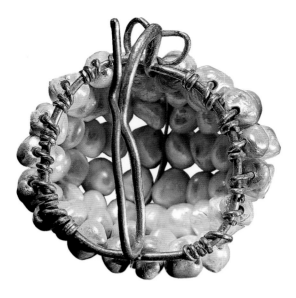

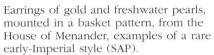

Earrings of gold and freshwater pearls, mounted in a basket pattern, from the House of Menander, examples of a rare early-Imperial style (SAP).

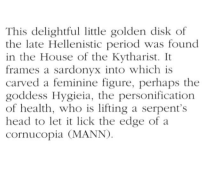

This delightful little golden disk of the late Hellenistic period was found in the House of the Kytharist. It frames a sardonyx into which is carved a feminine figure, perhaps the goddess Hygieia, the personification of health, who is lifting a serpent's head to let it lick the edge of a cornucopia (MANN).

Cameos, or gems worked in relief, were widely used as pendants, and as decorations for rings and pins. Among the stones primarily used for these elegant jewels were agate, onyx, sardonyx, rock crystal, and garnet.

A luxurious diadem of gold and pearls, a lavish ornament to beautify and enrich a coiffure, something to which the matrons of Pompeii already gave a great deal of attention (MANN).

This gold necklace from the early Imperial era, found in Pompeii in two pieces, was made of numerous ivy leaves with five veins in the center. Each gold leaf was connected to the next by a loop hidden under a gold bead (MANN).

119

The oil lamp, an extremely common everyday object, could suggest its owner's rank depending on the material from which it was made and its decoration. Here is an excellent example in gold, found in the Temple of Venus, perhaps donated by Nero and his wife Poppea, who was from Pompeii, on the occasion of their famous travels in the area around Naples during 64 A.D (MANN).

While the above lamp is undoubtedly priceless, even bringing the Imperial couple to mind, this lamp in clay with a sunburst design and a round spout is on the other hand of a style very common throughout the ancient world (SAP).

the particular archeological conditions of Pompeii and its agriculture allow us to quickly comprehend the actual methods that made it possible to sustain the economic life of the city and its inhabitants. If the large farm villas enable us to understand the system for transforming several products of the earth into valued commodities such as wine and oil—although Pompeii was famous also for its cabbages and onions—the numerous factories in the urban center throw additional light on certain basic economic activities, which had nevertheless already been present for centuries. These included a significant phenomenon worthy of note: the establishment shortly before the eruption of craft and "industrial" workshops in several ancient residential houses. Among these activities were the production of bread and flour, and of textiles, a natural outgrowth of the sheep farming widely practiced in the territory. It also included the creation of certain special objects, some of them strictly utilitarian, such as oil lamps, roof tiles, millstones, and olive presses, and others that were more luxurious, such as jewels and lotions, equally important in economic terms.

One final specialty that made the Pompeiians famous was the production of a very flavorful sauce made from a fish called *garum* and greatly sought after by ancient Roman gourmets. This same fish was itself an extremely important resource for the city. In addition, Pompeii certainly did not lack activities that we might define as service industries: its character as a place of transit favored the establishment of numerous taverns and inns, usually located in parts of the city where there was the greatest movement of men and goods. As a further definitive token of Pompeii's archeological value, we must also cite a source of the most direct evidence concerning the city's economic life: for centuries ashes and lapilli had sealed the archives of a banker, similar to so many others in the Roman world, named Lucius Caecilius Iucundus, who was an *argentarius*, or financier. In his house were found over a hundred and fifty waxed tablets, on which he documented his economic transactions and those for which he acted as a broker: loans,

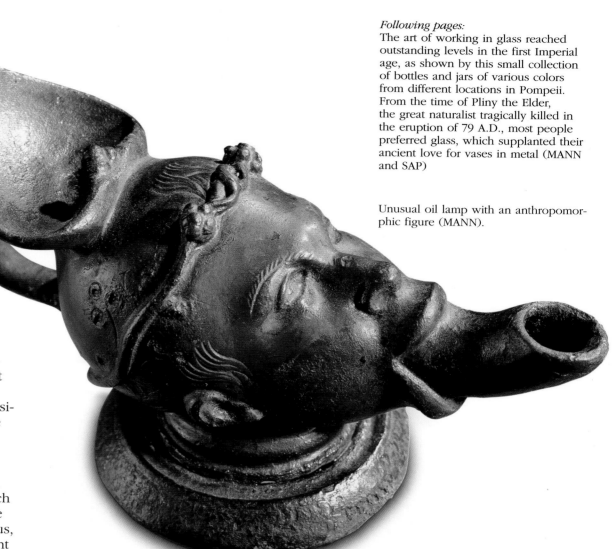

Following pages:
The art of working in glass reached outstanding levels in the first Imperial age, as shown by this small collection of bottles and jars of various colors from different locations in Pompeii. From the time of Pliny the Elder, the great naturalist tragically killed in the eruption of 79 A.D., most people preferred glass, which supplanted their ancient love for vases in metal (MANN and SAP)

Unusual oil lamp with an anthropomorphic figure (MANN).

A group of tools for writing, including a stylus, a pointed instrument with which one etched a tablet that was covered with a thin layer of wax.

A detail of the extraordinary figured frieze, with cupids and spirits occupied in various industrial activities, located in a reception room of the House of the Vettii. This detail illustrates the manufacture and sale of perfumed oils, medicines, and potions.

Facing page:
Detail of a wall painting with two fish, a popular food in Pompeii, which could be purchased at the macellum facing the porticoes of the Forum in line with the Temple of Jupiter.

the buying and selling of lands and other goods, including slaves, the collection of rents, and many others. Surely Lucius Caecilius Iucundus could never have imagined not only the dramatic end Pompeii would suffer, but the surprising circumstance that one day his receipts would become a prized resource for recreating an ancient economy.

The Macellum

The *macellum* was the meat and fish market. Its design was derived from an architectural style probably of Punic origin, but also seen in Greece. In Pompeii it was located very close to the area of the Forum, but still clearly separate from it. This location, which dates back to some time in the second century B.C., fits perfectly with the Forum's urban redefinition in the late Samnitic period, when, for reasons of status and decorum, there was a desire to expel any structures directly connected to commercial activities from the Forum plaza, where they had been for centuries. The

macellum of Pompeii, which compares favorably to similar structures like the so-called Temple of Serapis at Pozzuoli, is of major interest because it enables us to clarify the functions of its various parts, thanks to its preservation and the archeological findings and wall decorations discovered there. Some of these decorations date to the period between the earthquake of 62 A.D. and the eruption of 79 A.D., which took the building by surprise while its restoration was in process. The structure rests on a rectangular court, very probably porticoed, with a circular pavilion in the center, a sort of *thólos*, covered with a conical roof held up by poles resting on twelve bases, arranged in a radial pattern. Inside this thólos was a fountain, and the numerous fish scales found in this fountain's drain canal give us an indication of how it was used.

Once the fish was cleaned, it was sold from a room in the southeast corner of the courtyard with a typical horseshoe-shaped counter, tilted towards the perimeter walls. Half of this counter, connected to a small channel in the floor for water run-off, was obviously reserved for selling fish, while the other half was

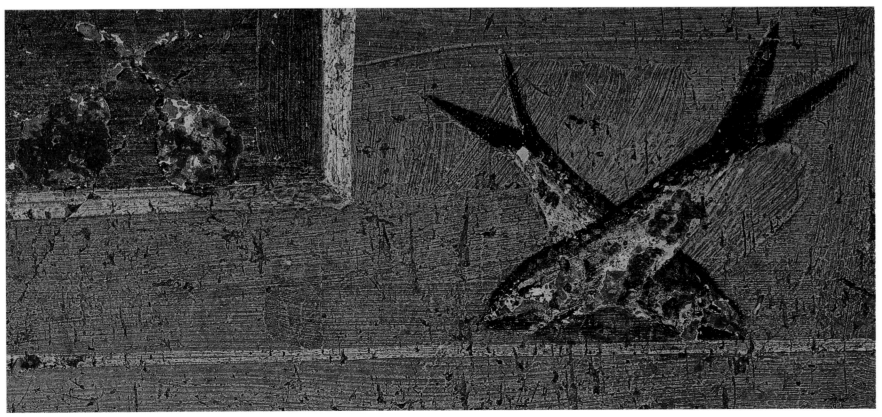

Preceding pages:
Entrance to the macellum, the meat
and fish market, flanked by shops and
harmonized with the Forum by
colonnaded porticoes, which were
originally of two stories and ornamented
with honorary statues, of which only
the bases remain.

The interior of the macellum with, in
the foreground, the remnants of the
central thólos (small circular temple),
in which there was a fountain whose
primary function was to supply the
water needed for selling fish.

intended for meat. Both in the thólos courtyard and around the entire macellum, a well-
stocked series of shops was located, almost
all opening towards the north to keep the
afternoon heat from damaging the foodstuffs
for sale. Amid these were recovered the
remains of figs, chestnuts, plums, grapes,
wheat, lentils, bread and sweets, as well as
sheep and goat bones. Even in the fourth-
style paintings in the arcade of the courtyard
and in other areas of the macellum, valuable
for their style but unfortunately almost completely faded, the images confirm the particular purpose of the structure. Interspersed with
mythological scenes, they depict rare and
unusual subjects such as poultry, fish, and
receptacles for wine and food. Also seen are
the festivals in honor of Vesta, the goddess
who protected millers and bakers, and whose
products were evidently also sold in the
macellum, and even the personifications of
the Sarno and of the fields and the sea, figurative evocations of the origins of the merchandise being sold. After some necessary
reorganization, there was even room in the
macellum for a space dedicated to the
Imperial cult, behind the thólos and aligned
with the entrance to the Forum. Besides the
members of the ruling family, two eminent
local personages received special honors
there for having promoted the building's

Here and on the facing page (bottom) are two magnificent still-lifes in the fourth style from Pompeii, with various pottery vessels and assorted types of fruit.

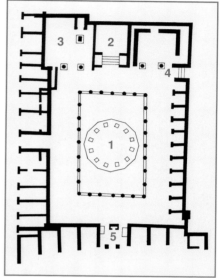

Layout of the Macellum

1. Thólos

2. Sanctuary for the Imperial cult

3. Sales area for meat and fish

4. Entrance from Via degli Augustali

5. Entrance from the Forum

One of the few surviving remains of the fourth-style wall decoration that adorned the interior of the macellum. The episode depicted, taken from Homer's *Odyssey*, is the recognition of Odysseus by Penelope.

reconstruction, but this does not necessarily refer to the restorations following the earthquake of 62 A.D.

The Mensa Ponderaria

The weighing table was located, already in Samnitic times, in a small room facing the Forum plaza, carved out of the wall enclosing the Temple of Apollo. This was the public office responsible for verifying weights and measures, established according to standards that had to be the same for the entire community. This office consisted mainly of two limestone counters, one above the other—of which only the lower one is well-preserved—in which no fewer than twelve cavities of varying widths corresponded to an equal number of standard measures. These cavities were furnished at the bottom with holes to release whatever had been poured into them after verification of the weight, and they were labelled with captions in the Oscan language, only one of which is still fully legible, revealing the names, of Greek origin, for the units of measure that were used, an interesting and final confirmation of the Hellenization of Pompeii in the Samnitic era. The difficulty in reading these signs is due mainly to the fact that around 20 B.C., following a very explicit order from the Emperor Augustus, there was a program to unify the weights and measures in the entire Roman world, with the consequent abolition of the old units of weight in the local areas. To that end, the cavities of the weighing tables were enlarged with the resultant partial erasure of the Samnitic symbols. A

Latin inscription incised on the front of the better-preserved counter attests to this important stipulation.

The Building of Eumachia

Among the most monumental and interesting structures in Pompeii is the so-called Building of Eumachia, which faces the Forum where it meets Via dell'Abbondanza, from which it was in fact possible to enter the building. Even though, thanks to important epigraphic data, we know the chronology (the Tiberian era), the layout, and even the decorative plan, which is mainly concerned with statuary, the problems of interpreting the exact functions of the building have not been completely solved, beginning with its ambiguous public-private nature. This is a building made for civil use, located in an area of the city with a strong official character, but built at the expense of a private citizen who made no attempt to hide her political-ideological ambitions. Thanks to an

nature is likewise seen in the statues that decorated the large apse of the porticoed courtyard, with an image of the Concordia Augusta, unfortunately found without a head, but almost certainly with the features of Livia. A similar gesture is present in at least the two niches of the chalcidicum, where epigraphs were found celebrating Aeneas

Facing page:
Various bronze weighing instruments from Pompeii (Julio-Claudian era): above left, a small balance with identical arms, used to weigh coins; below, a scale with an acorn-shaped weight formed by the bust of a little boy; right, a detail of another acorn-shaped weight with a feminine bust (MANN).

inscription written in two places, we know that Eumachia, priestess of Venus and member of an aristocratic local family devoted to lucrative economic activities, erected in her own name, and on behalf of her son, the vestibule, or *chalcidicum*, a crypt, and a colonnaded portico, dedicating all these building structures to the Concordia Augusta and to the Pietà. This was an explicit homage to the Julio-Claudian Imperial house. The Concordia and the Pietà, having been deified, had been associated with Tiberius and his mother Livia after Livia's serious illness in 22 A.D., and the relationship between this Augustan pair and Eumachia and her son, thus automatically connected to the ruling class, is equally transparent. A gesture of respect of a completely political

and Romulus, the same mythic-historic personages who provided an essential focus for the ideological program of the Augustan Forum in Rome.

It is not difficult to recognize the various structural parts of the Building of Eumachia mentioned in the inscriptions recorded above: the chalcidicum is surely the vestibule, from the interesting detail of being aligned with the porticoes of the Forum and not with the building itself, which is oriented, rather, on an axis parallel to Via dell'Abbondanza and not at a right angle to the Forum. The crypt is the covered horse-shoe-shaped *ambulacrum* surrounding the porticoed courtyard on three sides, which corresponds to the *porticus* of the inscription. This crypt, oddly unpaved, was accessible

A beautiful collection of bottles in pale blue glass from the early Imperial age, found in Pompeii. They must have been used as measures of volume, since each one is exactly half the size of the preceding one (SAP).

through three narrow doorways, which could obviously be locked. It looked out onto the porticoed courtyard through large windows, apparently furnished with grates. Even though it turns out to be easy to identify the various parts of the building, there is still the difficult problem of its significance. A beautiful statue-portrait of Eumachia was recovered in the crypt, in a small quadrangular niche positioned in a direct line with the enormous niche opening onto the courtyard and intended for the statue of the Concordia Augusta. This statue was offered by the *fullones*, the powerful association of wool merchants, dyers, and launderers, and relates to a very significant activity in Pompeii. This has suggested that the Building of Eumachia might have been a sort of wholesale wool market, with the merchandise, visible through the barred windows, exhibited in the crypt, the ambulacrum, which could be prudently locked when necessary.

This long-held hypothesis does not seem tenable, however, in light of other considerations formulated in recent times. Above all, although it is unfortunately not certain, the unusual construction of the crypt, as described

above, so similar to places of forced confinement, suggests that this enigmatic building could have been a slave market like the *venalicium* in Petronius's *Satyricon*. There is certainly no doubt that slavery was one of the major sources of income for Pompeii's economy. It is possible that Eumachia had vast interests in this field that resulted in the enrichment of other economic magnates like the fullones, so that she became a sort of patron honored through comparison to the Imperial house by means of a building of notable structural and decorative refinements, such as the splendid entryway which opened onto the portals of the Forum. Furthermore, the very presence of two small raised podiums in the entrance chalcidicum, useful for auction sales, reinforces the hypothesis that this was an ancient slave market.

Shops, Taverns and Cafes

Retail commerce was entrusted either to ambulatory vendors, whose carts crowded the most populous parts of Pompeii, such as the plaza of the Forum, the area around the Amphitheater, and the main intersections, or to agents who resold their merchandise in the various shops and taverns, called *tabernae*, facing the streets in almost all cities. Many of these shops were directly connected to patrician residences, and it is altogether possible that these same rich householders further enriched themselves by renting the shops or even by entrusting the sale of produce grown on their own allotted lands to slaves or freedmen. Structurally, the shops were made up of one room, sometimes with a back room and a narrow loft called a *pergula*. Many shopkeepers and their families lived, not very comfortably, in these cramped spaces. These shops had large openings onto the street, and thanks to an ingenious system of apposite furrows in the floor and the lintel, it was possible to close this wide opening easily with wooden boards to which was attached, at one of the two ends, a door by which one could enter and leave with ease even when the shop was not open to the public.

Among commercial enterprises of these types, the most common in Pompeii were the *thermopolia*, cafes specializing in the sale of foods and hot beverages, especially wine. In the summer one could also certainly find cold drinks there, among them wine diluted with cold water. The main characteristic of these cafes was a stone counter, almost always L-shaped and fitted with brightly-

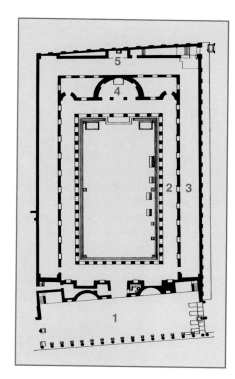

Layout of the Building of Eumachia

1. Vestibule (chalcidicum)
2. Colonnaded portico (porticus)
3. Covered corridor (crypt)
4. Base of the statue of Livia in the robes of Concordia Augusta
5. Base of the statue of Eumachia

Statue of the priestess Eumachia in white marble with traces of the original polychrome. This is from the time of Tiberius (first century A.D.) and emulates, though less effectively, several aspects of Greek art in the late-classical age (fourth century B.C.), especially the extraordinarily gentle and elegant art of Praxiteles (MANN).

Facing page:
The refined marble portal (relocated, according to some scholars, in the wrong place) and the interior of the Building of Eumachia. Alongside the traditional interpretation which saw this structure as a sort of wholesale wool market, a recent hypothesis sees it instead as a slave market.

133

First century A.D. relief in tufa from Vicolo del Gallo in Pompeii, with a depiction of several tools used in the building trade by a mason named Diogenes. There is also room among the tools for a good-luck phallus (SAP).

A lively marble bas-relief from the first century A.D., which was probably the shop sign for a Pompeii coppersmith. We can recognize three different activities in the workshop: weighing the metal, beating it on an anvil, and finishing the end product (MANN).

colored marble frames into which were inserted large terra-cotta jars containing the various foodstuffs for sale. Naturally, these cafes were also furnished with cauldrons and ovens which made it possible to quickly prepare snacks both for those who needed to eat in a hurry and for those housewives, more numerous than one might think, who for one reason or another did not have the necessary equipment in their homes for preparing meals.

The Fullery of Stephanus

The *fullonica* of the freedman Stephanus, situated in Region I in a building opening onto Via dell'Abbondanza, is one of the best examples in Pompeii of a fullery, a private "industrial" workshop which had the respon-sibility both of working fabric and of laundering and removing stains from clothing soiled during normal daily use. One primary operation was scouring, what we properly call *fulling*, to eliminate the wastes that stuck to the fabric during spinning and weaving. Unlike the other three large fulleries in the city, which had previously been patrician residences and were later radically renovated, this fullery was built practically from scratch during the last phase of Pompeii's life. It is thus perfectly legible in all its fundamental elements, allowing us to fully understand the specific methods used in the various phases of the work.

One of the first important operations took place in the peristyle. Three connected vats were found here on descending levels, along with five elliptical basins. Woven pieces of wool were scoured in these basins using a

Bronze bell from Herculaneum in the form of a winged phallus, a typical ornament for shop entrances (MANN).

A fine example of a thermopolium in Pompeii (I, 8, 8), with a stone counter and the jars ready to hold foods and beverages.

In these famous fourth-style frescoes from one of the most important fulleries in Pompeii (VI, 8, 20) several aspects of ancient techniques for working with textiles are documented. Above is a press for ironing wool and felt; below, cloth is hung to dry (MANN).

mixture of water and soda or other reagents such as camel urine, which was rather hard to procure, or that of humans, which was very desirable and which the fulleries collected through various ingenious systems, including, for example, placing the bottom parts of amphorae on street corners. The last phase of this work, which strengthened the fabric, was a final scouring, treating the piece with clay earth (the best came from an island in the Cyclades, Kimolos, but Umbrian clay was also very sought-after), followed by beating, washing and rinsing it in the connecting vats. The next important operation was carding, which removed fibers that had become tangled on the surface, and sulfurization, in which a solution of sulfurous anhydride gave the fabric a sheen. After the last washing, in another vat which Stephanus had placed in the atrium in place of the impluvium, and following other operations like sizing, brushing, and trimming, the fabric was ready to be ironed in the press (*torcular* or *pressorium*), a machine located in the entryway of the fullery, which worked by means of two huge screws. As far as the drying of the cloths was concerned, this workshop could boast of a terrace created above the flat roof of the atrium, an architectural element that was a real rarity in Pompeii.

Workshop of Marcus Vecilius Verecundus

One of the liveliest shop fronts excavated in the early nineteenth century along Via dell'Abbondanza is surely the felt factory of Marcus Vecilius Verecundus. This unusual textile operation, illustrated by scenes in a popular style painted on the front of the building—the only noteworthy archeological element of the structure—involved felting, the production of cloth by means of rubbing or pressing animal hair like rabbit fur, or even clumps of rather rough wool. Under an effigy of Venus, the fresco shows three workers busy carding animal fleece. In front of them is a lighted oven intended for the preparation of the coagulant, perhaps a vinegar solution, which, when ready, would be spread onto the fabric just carded and combed by means of small bowls with spouts, also pictured in the fresco. In this phase the coagulant substance was energetically patted and rubbed onto the fabric by other laborers, who worked naked to the waist, as we can see from the wall painting.

The proprietor of this workshop was the enterprising Verecundus, in all probability a freedman, who is portrayed showing some clients a luxurious heavy brown cloth with vertical red bands. He himself wears clothing and shoes of felt, a textile fiber whose range of uses was rather vast, from high quality cloth for apparel, as described above, to cloth for military use—including horse blankets—definitely linked more to practicality and utilitarian function than to the pompous exhibition of elegant esthetic refinement.

A young employee carding a tunic, and a second worker with a cage made of reeds on which fabric was stretched to be bleached with sulfur steam (MANN).

Facing page:
In this splendid fresco from the tablinum of House VII, 3, 30 in Pompeii is depicted the sale, or even more likely, the complimentary distribution of bread by a baker elected to public office (MANN).

Full view of the bakery of Numerius Popidius Priscus with the oven for baking bread and the stone mills for grinding flour. To operate them, both slaves and donkeys were used.

Bakery of Numerius Popidius Priscus

In the heart of Region VII, a short distance from the meat market and the Forum, one of Pompeii's numerous bakeries is preserved, the property of Numerius Popidius Priscus, who lived in a beautiful house with an atrium and a peristyle located in the area immediately behind his business. This was an establishment dedicated solely to the production of bread and other similar products, sold wholesale and, possibly more important, by itinerant vendors. In the courtyard immediately accessible from the entrance there were four millstones made of volcanic lava from the zone of Roccamonfina, in northern Campania. These stones had a classic structure: on top of the base stood a fixed cone-shaped block, called the *meta*, above which was the *catillus*, an hourglass-shaped rotating element, the upper cavity of which was designed to collect the grain ready to be ground. The catillus was rotated by means of thick wooden beams attached to it. The force required for this heavy task was provided by the muscular arms of slave laborers or, preferably, the slow continuous march of donkeys over a floor specially paved like the streets with basaltic lava. The finely-ground grain, reduced to flour by the friction between the catillus and the meta, fell onto the base, conveniently wider in diameter than the meta itself, where it could be gathered for use in making bread.

Like any such enterprise, the bakery of Numerius Popidius Priscus also had a large vault-like wood-burning oven, furnished with vents to assure adequate air circulation and, as was customary, with an opening made of lava slabs that could be closed with a metal door. Naturally, there was also a water faucet, necessary both for the dough and to cool the paddle and the bread loaves themselves, which were sprinkled with water halfway through the baking to ensure a crisp, shiny crust. The spread of bakeries in Pompeii goes

As this carbonized loaf of bread shows, the baker put his seal on his product and divided it into wedges to make it easier to eat.

Another example of a Pompeii bakery. In the foreground are the millstones made of volcanic lava in the typical manner with a stationary cone-shaped block, the meta and an upper element with an hourglass shape, the rotating catillus.

back to the late Samnitic period, the second century B.C., when this food became an ever more customary part of the diet then common throughout the Roman world. We should note, finally, that during the last phase of Pompeii's life many bakeries in the city were established in what had once been luxurious patrician houses.

A Rustic Villa: the Villa of Pisanella at Boscoreale

During more than a century of archeological activity in the fertile fields around Pompeii, unfortunately not always carried out with rigorous scientific methods, at least sixty farm villas have been excavated. Especially in the territory of what is today Boscoreale, a hilly area north of Pompeii close to the slopes of Vesuvius, extraordinary building complexes have come to light, often reburied, as in the case of the Villa Regina, because it did not occur to anyone until recently to preserve them in the public interest. These structures can provide illuminating details about agricultural techniques, the methods of production, and, more generally, about the many ways the farm was exploited as a favored source of development and income. The farm villas were probably already in existence by the third century B.C., when the ancient agrarian settlements, until then part of what was fundamentally a subsistence economy that consumed its own production, were gradually transformed into large farms based on intensive, specialized cultivation, of wine and oil in particular, but also of prized fruit, aimed at the immense earnings that could be gained by exporting these products. The golden era of this particular socio-economic situation was undoubtedly the phase between the late Samnitic period and the first Imperial era,

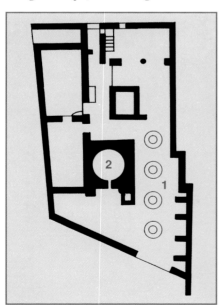

Layout of the bakery

1. Millstones
2. Oven

which corresponded perfectly to the strengthening of Roman rule in the Mediterranean. The rustic villas almost always belonged to the Pompeii nobility, but there are instances of villas belonging to the Imperial house itself and to enterprising personages of the Roman ruling class. They were entrusted to the care of a farmer, the *vilicus*, and a work force of laborers mostly made up of slaves. Over time,

besides the bakery and a stable, a room containing two levered wine presses. The *torcular* went into action after the first pressing of the grapes with the feet, when the crushed clusters, gathered in baskets, were placed under the arms of the press. The liquid thus obtained then flowed through a channel at the base of the torcular towards the *cella vinaria,* or wine chamber, a large

especially during the Sulla era, they were transformed from structures connected to purely agrarian activities into complexes that even included relatively luxurious and comfortable rooms for the more or less temporary stays of their rich owners.

All the characteristics described so far emerge with great clarity in one of the best-known and thoroughly excavated complexes of the areas around Pompeii, the so-called Villa of Pisanella near Boscoreale, explored by Pasqui at the end of the nineteenth century and then reburied. This rustic villa, which dates to the beginning of the first century B.C., has an owner's sector, a *pars urbana*, even furnished with refined private baths, and a *pars rustica*, an extended sector intended for the cultivation and storage of the products of the estate. Among the areas in this large sector we should note above all,

roofless space in which numerous terra-cotta vats carefully set into the ground held the wine for aging. More than eighty-four jugs were found in the villa's wine chamber. Many of these, however, were intended for oil and different types of grain.

Of course, oil was also obtained, using specific techniques with pressing and squeezing instruments placed in designated spaces for working the olives. One should note, however, that in the Villa of Pisanella—and more generally on all Pompeiian farms— the production of oil, though important, was less important economically than wine. Also of interest in this agrarian complex at Boscoreale is a large space called the *nubilarium*, used to hold crops between the harvest and the threshing. Even more significant, however, is the existence of a narrow dormitory for the slave population, the *familia*

A wine press (torcularium) from the Villa of the Mysteries. The beam, decorated with a ram's head, was lowered by a winch onto grapes already crushed by the workers. The juice ran off towards the cella vinaria through a channel at the base of the press.

Following pages:
Another detail of the famous figured frieze, with cupids and spirits employed in various activities of production, from the House of the Vettii. Here we see wine being poured by two attendants from the mouth of an amphora into a cup (right) and the host offering it to a client standing in front of another group of amphorae.

This detailed model created in the 1930s faithfully reproduced the rustic Villa of Pisanella, distinguished above all by the large room with buried terra-cotta jugs in which wine was left to age (Rome: Museum of Roman Civilization).

rustica, whose conditions could reach oppressive levels, as shown by the metal shackles often recovered in farm villas of this type. From these details we can grasp the extremely marked contrasts in Roman society, in which conspicuous groups of unfortunates, forced to work brutally hard with almost no rights, assured the well-being of a privileged few. Two authentic treasures were found in the Villa of Pisanella itself, consisting of a thousand gold coins and over a hundred pieces of silver tableware, today in the Louvre. These are goods that the rich owner certainly could not save from the destructive fury of Vesuvius, which indiscriminately struck the poorest of the poor and the most prosperous of the rich.

Emidio De Albentiis

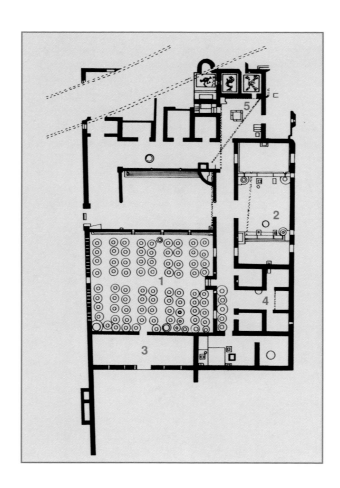

Layout of the Villa of Pisanella

1. Cella vinaria with buried jugs
2. Torcularium (wine press)
3. Nubilarium (grain storage area)
4. Dormitory for the slaves
5. Owner's quarters with baths

Social Life: Spectacles, Athletic Games, Baths

From the earliest years of Pompeii's long history, various socio-cultural elements have been layered one upon the other, leaving behind specific evidence that testifies to the numerous activities associated with the *otium,* or leisure time, as opposed to *negotia,* or work and business affairs, that was considered of primary importance in the ancient world. This important aspect of social life became mingled with the diverse cultural habits of the various populations who originally settled in Pompeii. The city was already open to external influences because of its geographic position along important maritime routes and heavily travelled transit roads. Consequently, a real cultural stratification developed and became solidified over a long period of time, one in which refined Hellenic customs were often mixed with the sometimes coarse and bloody practices of the Italic inhabitants. It would be a mistake, however, to define this unusual plurality in ethnic terms. The co-existence of refined theatrical presentations

Several dice found in the House of Menander in Pompeii. Games of chance were popular among the Romans, even though there were strict laws intended to limit their dangerous consequences. For example, gambling debts were denied legal recognition (MANN).

This lively small fresco painting in a popular style, found in a *caupona,* or inn (VI, 10, 19-1), shows a moment during a game of chance, an episode that surely took place often in real-life in such locales.

with the vulgar gladiatorial spectacles in the amphitheater, however unusual it might seem to modern sensitivities, represents, rather, a sign of social differences marked by varying levels of acculturation and Hellenic influence. Even in this case, however, we should avoid simplistic generalizations, since we cannot deny that even a refined Pompeii citizen who had the benefit of a Greek education might also be fascinated and excited by the bloody fights in the arena that so captivated the masses. Similarly, a particularly beloved habit in Roman times, which spread throughout the entire society, was that of frequent visits to the *Thermae,* or thermal baths, even though the stimulation there was not always particularly relaxing. A famous letter by Seneca, for example, notes, among other details of the baths, that "the noise makes you wish you were deaf." It is also true, of course, that the most well-to-do Pompeii citizens built comfortable and exclusive private baths inside their sumptuous residences. There can thus be no doubt that attention to physical well-being had a central place in the daily life of every citizen, as a well known Latin motto, *mens sana in corpore sano,* asserts and which has become, not without

146

exaggeration, a paradigmatic symbol of the entire Roman civilization.

Athletic activities and gymnastics, thermal baths, theatrical presentations and spectacles in the Amphitheater were certainly some of the principal practices with which the Pompeiians filled their spare time. Of course, we should not forget the more intimate and private pleasures associated with the erotic and the sensual, which they experienced with a thoroughly pagan gaiety, a glimpse of which will be found in the following chapter dedicated to the *Lupanare*. Although some sports activities were undertaken for their own sake, athleticism was primarily connected with the requirements of military preparation and could be practiced in Pompeii within the courtyards of the bathing establishments or in specifically-designed structures such as the Samnitic Gymnasium and the Large Gymnasium. The former was completed in the second half of the second century B.C. as part of an organic late-Samnitic urban project, which also included, among other things, the Large Theater and the Triangular Forum, whose east side was almost certainly used for track meets and for training. It was probably the seat of an aristocratic youth association in pre-Roman Pompeii, as a disputed Oscan inscription on the building seems to confirm. The nearby Large Gymnasium, built close to the Amphitheater, was surely one of the most remarkable structures in Pompeii during the Augustan age. With a rectangular plan, a vast courtyard enclosed by spacious porticos on three sides, along which was planted a shady double row of plane trees, and a centrally-located swimming pool—further proof of the typical Roman inter-relation between athletic exercise and bathing habits—the Large Gymnasium was more suitable and convenient for practicing sports and physical activities, as well as military ones, than the older Samnitic Gym. It seems to be no accident that a building of this kind, principally but not exclusively intended for the youth of Pompeii, was conceived at the time of Augustus, whose special concern for the education of youth is well-documented. This was not simply because of constant changes in the ranks of the primary armed force of the state, the army, but also and mainly in consideration of the authoritarian ideology of the new regime, which was

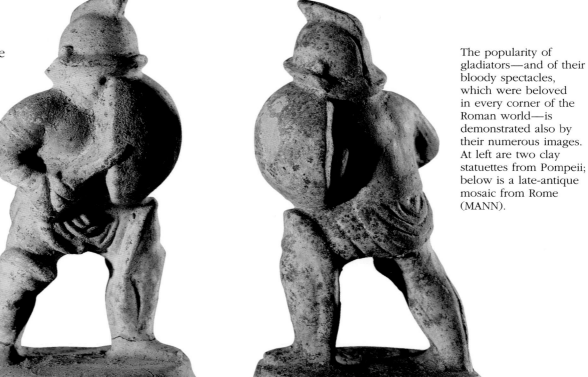

The popularity of gladiators—and of their bloody spectacles, which were beloved in every corner of the Roman world—is demonstrated also by their numerous images. At left are two clay statuettes from Pompeii; below is a late-antique mosaic from Rome (MANN).

Panoramic view of the Large Gymnasium of Pompeii, with porticoes on three sides and a large swimming pool in the middle. It was built in the time of Augustus and was used for gymnastics and sports, as well as paramilitary activities.

Athletes, who were particularly idolized by women, enjoyed a great reputation in the Roman world, especially because their feats showed virile energy. The original ethical and sacred values of Greek athletics gradually faded during the Roman era, as these famous mosaics of a discus-thrower and a javelin-thrower show through their coarse expressions. They are from the Baths of Caracalla in Rome, third century A.D.

now Naples, the city of Greek origin nearest to Pompeii. In the famous Hellenic sanctuary care was taken to inform the public about the Neapolitan games, and even the participants themselves made sure that the inscriptions intended to commemorate their own deeds recorded the final victories of the *Sebasta* games as well.

In Pompeii, a graffito explicitly mentioning the Neapolis competitions was found in the House of Menander. Sports activities included many specialties, from specifically athletic ones such as running, throwing and jumping, and body-to-body combat such as boxing and wrestling, to developments in saddles and horsemanship. In some cases the game rules and techniques were similar to those of today, although they had meaningful differences.

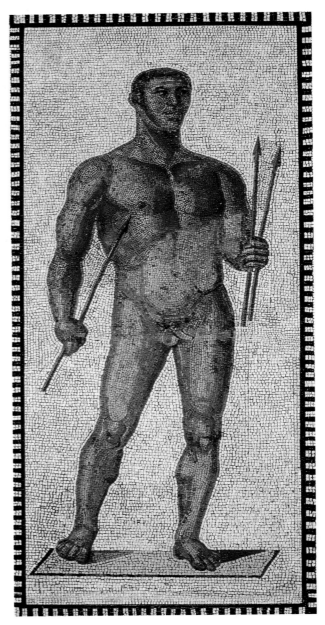

concerned with the rhetorical exaltation, a common imperative in every dictatorship, of the contributions of heroic youth, empha-sized, for instance, in a well-known poem by Horace (III, 2).

With regard to sports activities in Pompeii, we can hypothesize that gymnastics and other sports were modelled on Hellenic examples, developed mostly in the gymnasia. This was one of the most important aspects of juvenile upbringing and became a fundamental factor in social and religious life on the occasion of the Pan-Hellenic games, the best-known of which were the Olympic and Delphic Games. It is interesting to remember, then, that in the second year A.D., the *Sebasta*, which were athletic competitions in honor of Augustus and explicitly inspired by the ones in Olympia, were introduced in *Neapolis*,

The protagonist of this lovely mosaic from Pompeii is a boxer, shown nude in the manner of a hero, with his hands wrapped in bandages held together with leather cords (MANN).

the halteres. In other sections of the decoration there are, on one side, a discus thrower about to throw his device, and on the other, a pair of wrestlers engaged in a struggle supervised by a referee.

Among the equestrian games that we can visualize in the Large Gymnasium, we must mention a sort of fair for young horsemen, the highly regarded *ludus* or *lusus Troiae*, recorded in some very famous verses of Virgil's *Aeneid* as part of the funeral games organized by the Trojans in a town along the western Sicilian coast at *Drepano*, now Trapani, to commemorate the death of Aeneas's father, Anchises (V, 545-602). The great Augustan poet evoked the ludus Troiae, unfortunately with more poetic elegance than descriptive clarity, with the specific ideological aim of establishing a further connection between Rome and its mythical Trojan ancestors. The ludus, whose supposed distant and primordial antiquity is not at all certain, was practiced by thirty-six young knights divided into three ranks, each one made up of twelve individuals guided by an instructor.

Facing page:
Face of a runner found in Herculaneum in the Villa of the Papyri. It is a Roman replica of a Greek original, from the fourth century B.C. A full view is at left (MANN).

Figures in clay with Aeneas fleeing Troy holding his son Ascanius by the hand and in his arms his father Anchises, who clutches a reliquary of the Penates to his bosom; from Pompeii (MANN).

Long jumping provides an excellent example: the athlete used special instruments called *halteres*, a Latin version of a similar Greek term, consisting of two weights that he grasped and which helped him propel himself forward and intentionally control his center of gravity, and at the same time kept him from falling. Naturally, the jumper had to keep the halteres parallel to one another in order to avoid losing his balance. Thanks to several vases, such as a splendid cup with red figures by the so-called Panaitios Painter, an Attic ceramic maker active between the end of the sixth century B.C. and the first two decades of the following one, we can easily reconstruct the way the athlete used the halteres during the jump to enable him to hurl his legs and arms as far as he could. These same dumbbells also appear in a fourth-style Pompeii painting, still largely legible, although it is unfortunately in a precarious state of preservation, located not far from the Forum in a home (VIII 2, 23-24) that was apparently transformed into a bathing complex during the last phase of the city's existence. As a matter of fact, there is a depiction in this so-called gym of several athletes, one of whom is training to handle

Preceding pages:
A magnificent detail of a Pompeii fresco from the *domus* VII, 2, 25 with a quadriga race painted in the midst of the action. Even if not absolutely certain, it is plausible that such races took place in the Large Gymnasium.

View of part of the porticoed courtyard of the Stabian Baths in Pompeii, used from the beginning for gymnastic exercises and beautified with high walls covered by fourth-style polychrome stucco. Figurative scenes on these walls depict the activities that took place in the baths, sometimes with references to mythological stories.

In this small model from the 1930s we can see how the heating worked, especially in thermal rooms. The floor was raised by small widely-spaced brick pilasters (called *suspensurae),* which allowed hot air to circulate freely between them. This invention was soon perfected through the use of special clay tiles (called *tegulae mammatae)* to separate the inner and outer walls, which permitted hot air to circulate there as well (Rome: Museum of Roman Civilization).

It was a real equestrian spectacle with multiple passes that created complicated figures intended to simulate military movements. Indeed, Virgil effectively compares these movements to the sinuosities of the mythical labyrinth of Crete. This particular fair was part of a series of the most significant public Roman games, such as the famous *ludi Saeculares,* and was probably the object of specific training carried out in all the more important centers of the Empire.

In the center of Pompeii's Large Gymnasium there was, as mentioned above, a swimming pool of considerable dimensions, confirming the relationship between athleticism and bathing so dear to the Romans. Although the practice was not unknown to the Greeks, whose habit of taking hot baths is in fact already archeologically documented by examples from the fifth to the fourth centuries B.C., including the thermal structure dug at Olympia near the Kladeos River, in the Roman world bathing gave rise to an architectural style that became highly developed, with thermal establishments often characterized by grand planning and decorative activities. The thermal baths are very well documented in Pompeii from the mid-Samnitic era, the fourth to third century B.C., until the volcanic eruption, with developments that clearly show how bathing locales tended over time to become ever more important compared to structures dedicated to sports activities. They evoke with great immediacy one of the most characteristic aspects of the daily life of the ancients and one of their favorite ways of filling their spare time. Bathing establishments were usually open between the stroke of noon and dusk, but were occasionally also open in the evening, and, except for special cases when a small entry fee was required, access was almost always free of charge. They were real centers of daily life where one could meet people of the most diverse culture and class. The wealthy, who frequented the public baths if their own homes were not furnished with private baths, could be recognized by the large group of servants that accompanied them to provide for all the needs associated with bathing and invigorating massages. The less wealthy, on the other hand, not only went to the baths by themselves, but they also had to make sure someone kept an eye on their clothes, no matter how plain, by paying a small compensation to a specifically appointed guardian. During the long and enjoyable hours spent at the baths customers could satisfy their hunger and thirst with beverages and foods sold in the numerous *tabernae* situated in the immediate vicinity of the complex, as the Pompeii establishments themselves testify. In them we can see the classic division of the baths into two separate sections, one for women, and another, generally better-maintained and equipped, for men. Occasions and opportunities for promiscuity, however, were not lacking.

One of the most important features we see in the Roman thermal complex is a habit almost entirely lost in modern times: the possibility of taking baths in specific parts of the establishments at different temperatures—hot, tepid and cold—apparently inspired by enlightened hygiene and health criteria, combined with the practice of physical activities and games, obviously intended to promote further psycho-physical well-being. Even though they did not follow strictly codified norms, people usually bathed in the cold-water pool only after having properly warmed up their bodies either through a period in the *caldarium*, where one could take high temperature baths, or after a stop in a room called the *laconicum*, reserved for steam baths, or even after a series of intense physical exercises.

The system for heating the water and the environment, which the Romans progressively improved with extraordinary technical skill, is especially interesting. We can get an idea of it both through the descriptions contained in *De architectura* by Vitruvius, written in the second half of the first century B.C., and from archeological data, among which the Pompeiians' own records are particularly valuable. By examining various establishments in Pompeii, including the Stabian Baths, we are able to form an immediate idea of the heating system's main technical and hydraulic characteristics, in which a single big hearth, the *hypocausis*, provided constant hot air and water, functioning as the thermal center for both the male and female sections of the baths. Located in a chamber called the *praefurnium*, this hearth, which burned wood, was continuously

replenished with combustible material by a slave assigned to this service, while in a room not far from the praefurnium other slaves hand-cranked the hydraulic wheel that raised the water from a deep well. Hot and tepid water were produced in three large bronze containers placed next to one another in the boiler room, each at a specific distance from the heat source and all filled with water in a continuous cycle, the cold water being the farthest from the hearth. Pipes made of lead, the material normally used for this purpose in antiquity, carried the three different kinds of water to their destinations. The method of maintaining the water temperature in the caldarium, where the bathtub

Another view of the courtyard of the Stabian Baths, the true center of the establishment, used for both physical exercise and relaxing strolls in the open air, an atmosphere, however, that we must imagine as lively and noisy.

Facing page:
Detail of the splendid fourth-style fresco depicting the Cycle of the Muses, noteworthy for the quality of its colors, from the suburban baths at Murecine, a few hundred yards from the Stabia Gate (MANN).

A detail of the prized terra-cotta decoration from around 80 B.C. that ran along the walls of the tepidarium in the Baths of the Forum: a series of telamons set between display niches held up the architrave on which the barrel vault of the room rested.

Although they were not finished at the time of the eruption, the Main Baths were certainly the most technologically and architecturally advanced thermal establishment in Pompeii. In this view of the courtyard we can see the series of large windows intended to brighten the adjoining thermal rooms.

The Noise at the Roman Baths

All around me there is a tremendous racket: I live right above the thermal baths. Imagine that your ears are bombarded by all kinds of voices. I hear the groans of the athletes when they strain themselves lifting weights (or at least when they pretend to do so), and every time they let out a breath I hear the hissing sound of their labored breathing. When one of the more lazy ones wants only a rubdown, I hear the hands that massage the back and make sounds according to whether it is tense or relaxed. And if the ones who play ball and discuss the score in a loud voice arrive, it's all over. Then there is the troublemaker, and the thief caught in the act, and the one who delights in the sound of his own voice while taking a bath. Not to mention those who dive into the pool. Besides all these who, all things considered, have normal voices, think of the one who plucks out his hairs and, to make sure that he is noticed, says everything twice and never shuts up, except when he removes the hair in his armpits and obliges someone else to yell for him. There is the refreshments seller who calls out in ever-different ways, the sausage vendor and the baker and all the shop boys who use their voices to sell their products.

Seneca, *Letters to Lucilius,* 56

was usually made of marble, a material not particularly well suited for heat preservation, involved several ingenious systems. The problem was resolved by recycling the hot water, which ran into the tub from a semi-cylindrical metal container kept in close contact with the hot air circulating through ducts specifically designed to carry heat to the rest of the environment. Constant recirculation of the recycled water was assured by positioning the bottom of the semi-cylindrical container about six inches below the bottom of the tub.

The heating system guaranteed more than just the pleasant opportunity to take tepid and hot baths; the spacious rooms intended for those functions, the caldarium and tepidarium, were conveniently heated by means of a technical development of ingenious simplicity, created in the beginning of the first century B.C. by Caius Sergius Orata, an enterprising character probably from Puteoli (modern day Pozzuoli), who, according to the sources, was famous for having become extremely rich cultivating oysters and was remembered as well, in fact, for having invented a system of so-called hanging baths. The idea behind the device was to heat the floor of the thermal rooms by raising it, by means of small lateral pillars, or *suspensurae,* with spaces between them. In this way, hot air coming from the hearth could freely circulate in the cavity thus created below the floor, and the rooms above could enjoy its beneficial effects. The invention of the suspensurae was soon perfected

with an additional improvement: the circulation of hot air was extended to the walls of the *caldari* and *tepidari* thanks to the so-called *tegulae mammatae,* special quadrangular clay tiles endowed with breast-shaped protrusions—hence the name—which were the only points touching the outside walls, thus permitting the free passage of the heated air along the sides of the rooms. Air holes located at the top of the walls, perfectly recognizable in archeological discoveries in Pompeii, provided the necessary circulation. Naturally, the difference in temperature

between caldari and tepidari depended on the difference in distance of these rooms from the source of heat. The clever devices of the suspensurae and the tegulae mammatae were conceived in the late-Republican era: before that time the air was heated by means of braziers situated in the middle of the rooms, a system that was also used in some cases during the time of the Empire, as in the tepidarium of the thermal baths in the Pompeii Forum, which were quickly restored after the earthquake of 62 A.D., although without renovating its heating system, which was based on hot air circulation.

If a visit to the thermal baths can unquestionably be regarded as an almost daily habit, the possibility of taking part in spectacles at the theaters and amphitheaters was less certain and depended on specific organizational contingencies. Many factors contributed to a calendar of events that was necessarily rarefied and, probably because of this, produced great collective expectation. First, enormous funds were needed, and these were usually controlled by the ruling magistrates, whose munificence in this particular matter, we should not forget, was considered an essential requisite for aspiring to public office. Second, the traveling companies specializing in the various types of *ludi*, or games, were required to be registered, and finally, the spectacles' original connection with sacred and religious rituals had to be considered, although, especially in the Roman world, these particular ceremonies were progressively secularized and had become almost entirely profane. Even though popular favor went to the coarse spectacles in the amphitheater, it cannot be denied that in antiquity a more or less vast public greatly enjoyed these theatrical presentations.

The birth of theater and its genres in the Mediterranean world, among which tragedy and comedy stand out, we owe to classical Greece. Intimately connected with the cult of Dionysus, the spectacles were essentially solemn and sacred rituals that caused the people to reflect on the moral lessons of their mythical and religious tradition, with its ancestral heritage of stories and legends, as well as on contemporary social customs. The influence of the great Greek dramatists began to manifest itself in a major way in the Italic Roman world as early as the first Hellenistic era, especially in the third century B.C., when even in Greece the original connection between theater and religion had begun to weaken. One thinks, for example, of a key figure like Livius Andronicus. It is not surprising then that in Pompeii, a city that had been

Fourth-style marble bas-relief from the peristyle of the House of the Gilded Cupids, with a collection of tragic, comic, and satiric masks, among which we can also recognize a kithara and a syrinx (Pan-pipe), instruments used to accompany the actors on the stage (MANN).

Frescoes in Pompeii did not lack scenes of theatrical inspiration: in this image, an actor is portrayed while he is waiting to go onstage and perform a tragic part, as we can see from the type of mask being handed to him.

A beautiful theatrical mask, painted in fresco in the second style and belonging to the oldest phase of the Villa at Oplontis, part of the property of Poppea, Nero's wife.

The imposing ruins of the Large Theater of Pompeii, with the traditional division, of Greek origin, into the cavea (the steps for the public), the orchestra (the area intended for the movements of the chorus, later radically transformed even in its function), and the stage structure.

in contact with the major centers of Magna Graecia along the Gulf of Naples for years, a masonry theater was built in the middle of the Samnitic era, whose first phases appear to date as far back as the first half of the second century B.C. This means that Pompeii, like other cities in the Samnitic area of Campania, had a permanent theater long before Rome, one based on a historical and ideological model perfectly traceable to what occurred in amphitheaters. For complex reasons, in fact, the ruling class in Rome obstructed for a long time the erection of permanent structures for spectacles. The all-important political and ideological need to maintain respect for the austere *mos maiorum*, the traditions of the ancestors, at least in appearance, made it possible for them to resist Hellenistic influence. But even in Rome, where for centuries presentations took place in precarious structures that were demolished right after

the *ludi*, the love of theater soon took root. It was not until 55 B.C. that Julius Caesar's antagonist, Gneus Pompeus, made possible the construction of the first stone theater, whose stairs were also crowned by a temple for religious occasions.

Access to the spectacles was generally free of charge, although the privilege of watching presentations from the first rows was especially sought-after. This honor was reserved for the members of the aristocracy who, as the Large Theater of Pompeii effectively attests, could claim their right through epigraphs carved into the very steps. This particular custom reflects very well the desire for recognition felt by the majority of the people in antiquity, who gave great symbolic value to this particular show of power.

A comic mask, framed by rich vegetation, depicted in a lovely polychrome mosaic from the House of the Faun, the most luxurious Pompeii dwelling of the late-Samnitic era (MANN).

In a niche at the back of the peristyle in the refined Pompeii *domus* that takes its name from this fresco, this portrait of the Athenian comedian Menander (end of the fourth Century B.C.) was painted during the late Julio-Claudian era. The Greek playwright sits in a meditative pose with his hand on a scroll. The painting attests to the lasting interest that the Romans of the early Imperial era had in Greek theater, which was already a source of inspiration during the time of the Republic for Latin authors such as Plautus and Terence.

Facing page:
Another superb example of a theatrical mask, in this case a tragic one, from the Villa at Oplontis, which was close to Pompeii and more or less on the site of modern-day Torre Annunziata.

Bronze cymbals from Pompeii: these instruments were used primarily in the Asiatic cults. (MANN).

This bronze sistrum comes from the shrine to Isis in Pompeii. It was typical of this Asiatic cult, which was fairly widespread in the Roman world. By shaking the instrument with the hands one produced rhythmic sounds of hypnotic intensity (MANN).

Facing page:
Detail of a Pompeii fresco with two cupids playing a lyre.

Bronze wind instrument called a syrinx, found in Pompeii, with a decorative frieze possibly representing the stage front of a theatre (MANN).

In fact, everything, from precious clothes to the comfortable and luxurious seats where they took their places—ample seats called *bisellia*, even represented in sepulchral monuments, rendering eternal the prestige they enjoyed in life—granted them what we would today call a "return on investment," to be freely spent in political life. It is useful to remember, in this regard, an informative verse by Ovid, which referred specifically to women but seems fitting here: at the theater, the disillusioned Augustan poet recalled, "they come to see and be seen" (*Ars Amatoria*, I, 99). The common people, on the other hand, crowded the highest stands farthest from the stage. Because spectacles took place mainly during the day and were quite long, there were people who arrived the night before the performance to occupy the seats that permitted a better view. In order to give the public some protection from the sun, the best-equipped theaters, as in the case of the Large Theater in Pompeii, were equipped with a gigantic tent, called a *velario*, mounted on wooden poles at the highest point of the tiers and operated by specialized personnel. In case of sudden bad weather, one

could find refuge under the porticos of a big quadrangular courtyard located behind the stage structure, the *porticus post scaenam*. The fascination with theatrical spectacles was based not only on the actors' interpretative skills, but also on the painted scenery and on the use of particular mechanisms to create realistic special effects that would capture the audience's imagination. As the Pompeii theater building well documents, even in antiquity there was a curtain, the *aulaenum*, but it was activated exactly the reverse of the way it is in modern times: at the beginning of the show, the curtain fell into a special slot in the stage floor, and it was raised at the end of the performance.

Despite the lack of epigraphic evidence about the theatrical programs, it is likely that both tragedies and comedies were performed in Pompeii, perhaps even involving an intentional mixing of genres, in which the popular Campania tradition known as Atellan farce might also have found a convenient venue. The existence of various genres seems to be attested by a group of wall paintings in several Pompeii dwellings, such as the House of the Centenarian, where several scenes are depicted one next to the other, some with tragic subjects and others with a comic attitude. Among the authors most beloved by the Pompeiians, the Athenian Menander, who lived during the end of the fourth and beginning of the third century B.C., enjoyed particular admiration. He was the witty founder of the New Comedy, later revived by the Latin playwright Terence. In a rich and noble Pompeii house, not far from the Large Theater, Menander is portrayed sitting on an Attic seat, his head crowned with a laurel wreath. Although their profession was generally regarded with disapproval, even actors could achieve great celebrity. A certain Paris provides an excellent example; an epigraph testifies that this successful actor, who was known to Tacitus, actually had a fan club in Pompeii! Musical performances also took place, especially including declamations of poems accompanied by the sound of a kithara. The *Odeion*, or Small Theater, was built next to the Large Theater during the time of Sulla especially for musical productions.

There is no doubt that for the inhabitants of Pompeii, and for ancient Italic and Roman populations in general, the most enjoyable entertainment by far was watching the bloody and spectacular games organized in the Amphitheater, which, significantly, was the only monument in Pompeii completely restored after the earthquake of 62 A.D.

The proverbial expression *panem et circenses*, bread and circuses, which we owe to Juvenal's polemic verve, concisely and effectively captures one of the most profound socio-political mechanisms of the Roman world, created by the inseparable link between autocratic power and demagoguery, used to gain consensus and also to offer a controlled escape valve for the tensions in the social body. The main forms of performance staged in the amphitheaters were gladiatorial contests and hunts—that is, duels between men and beasts or between ferocious beasts and domestic animals—and most likely were derived from Etruscan rituals, yet it seems mainly in the Samnitic Campania that they were affirmed as the favored form of collective entertainment on a vast scale. It is meaningful that the most ancient architectural examples of amphitheaters were found in Campania, at Capua, parts of which were built as early as the second century B.C., and also in Pompeii, whose first-century building is exceptional for its optimal state of preservation. Rome, for reasons previously mentioned, would not develop a permanent structure for this kind of spectacle until the Augustan age with the

167

Facing page:
This third-style Pompeii fresco from the time of Tiberius, discovered in the eighteenth century, was so greatly admired by the Bourbons that it was reproduced in an "antique style" room in the Royal Palace of Capodimonte. It shows a young woman sitting on a *kline*, or couch, tuning a small harp and holding a kithara in her other hand. The other women seem to be waiting for the music to begin (MANN).

Interior view of the Small Theater (*Odeion*) of Pompeii in a lovely nineteenth-century watercolor drawing by T. Duclère, published in installments in the massive work *Le case e i monumenti di Pompei disegnati e descritti*, edited by Fausto, Felice, and Antonio Niccolini.

amphitheater of Stanlius Taurus, the illustrious predecessor of the Coliseum.

It is in fact thanks to Pompeii, to its epigraphy, reliefs and paintings, that we can confidently claim to have acquired a better understanding of the world that gravitated to these cruel arena exhibitions. Among the inscriptions, we must mention numerous graffiti that testify to the enormous primacy the gladiators enjoyed, especially among the female audience. We must also recall a valuable inscription, almost illegible today, of two detailed programs for a day of contests in the Pompeii amphitheater that mentions pairs of gladiators with different kinds of armor as well as a *curriculum* indicating the losses and victories they had acquired during the previous exhibitions. The anonymous Pompeiian who wrote those texts also added the final results of the combats, naming the losers, who

were allowed to live in certain cases, when the majority of the audience waved little flags, while others were sentenced to suffer the *coup de grace*, which the spectators requested with the famous thumbs-down gesture. A stucco relief in a tomb in the necropolis of the Herculaneum Gate, called the Tomb of Aulus Umbricious Scaurus, portrayed gladiatorial scenes of great documentary value. Unfortunately, this plaster work has not survived, although it is known through nineteenth-century drawings. Even in the great simplicity of its representations we see a dramatic depiction of the ruthless dialectic between skill in combat and the constant threat of death, a hard fate that gladiators, almost all of whom had been slaves, could not escape. The frieze is also interesting for the diverse typology of the gladiators and their equipment: among some, we can

Frieze with various gladiator scenes from the Tomb of Aulus Umbricius Scaurus in Pompeii. This important stucco decoration, now lost, is known to us from nineteenth-century drawings like this one by G. Genovese

Preceding pages:
Detail of an exceptional polychrome mosaic of strolling musicians, signed by Dioskourides of Samos, from the Villa of Cicero in Pompeii. The painted original could date from the third century B.C., while the surviving mosaic copy is possibly from the end of the second century B.C. (MANN).

From the tomb of Caius Vestorius Priscus, of the Flavian era, comes this interesting picture with bloody gladiator clashes.

distinguish the *Tracis*, lightly armed with a small round shield and a curved sword; the *Oplomacies*, covered with heavy suits of armor; the *Reziarii*, with net and trident; and the *Essedaries* and *Equites*, who fought, respectively, on carts and horses. Finally, the animals employed in the hunts, or *venationes*, such as bulls, bears, lions and wild boars, were also depicted in this tomb.

From a house in Pompeii that belonged to a gladiator (I 3, 23) comes a lively painting in a folk-like style representing the famous episode of 59 A.D., also known through Tacitus, of the brawl between Pompeiians and Nucerians, a result of municipal rivalries with important political implications, that took place in the city's amphitheater and

its immediate surroundings. The painting, with its bird's-eye view of the bloody clash, shows the Amphitheater in great detail with its unfolded velario and the various stalls clustered around the building on the occasion of the gladiator games. The clash resulted in a ten-year suspension of contests in the Amphitheater, an imperial decree that was surely very distressing for the majority of the citizens. It was revoked, however, just three years later, in 62 A.D., thanks both to the intercession of Nero's wife Poppea and to the disastrous earthquake that devastated the city, a sinister premonition of the terrible volcanic catastrophe that would cover Pompeii with ashes and lapilli less than twenty years later.

A Riot in the Amphitheater of Pompeii

At that time there was a bloody massacre between the Nucerians and the Pompeiians, caused by some petty incident during the gladiator games announced by that same Livinius Regulus who, as I have already said, was expelled by the Senate. At first, they exchanged insults with the insolence that is typical of provincials. Then they threw stones. And finally they took up arms. The citizens of Pompeii, where the spectacle took place, prevailed. Thus many were taken back to Nucera with bodies mutilated by wounds, and in that city many wept over the deaths of sons and fathers. Emperor Nero referred the matter to the Senate and the Senate entrusted it to the Consuls. Then, when it passed back to the Senate again, the Pompeiians were forbidden to hold gladiator games for a period of ten years. It was further ordered that all associations formed contrary to the law be disbanded. Livinius and all those who took part in the riot were condemned to exile.

Tacitus, *Annals*, XIV, 17

This eighteenth-century painting by G. Cel vividly and meticulously reconstructs a scene of the *venatio*, a bloody spectacle centering on the hunt for ferocious animals in the arenas of the ancient amphitheaters. A favorite source for the artist was above all the frieze painted in the Amphitheater of Pompeii, which was still visible in the nineteenth century but has since disappeared.

The Triangular Forum

The urban systems created in Pompeii throughout the second century B.C., in the last phase of the Samnitic dominion over the city, were essentially inspired by models of Hellenic taste and culture: an outstanding confirmation of this is the monumental complex referred to in modern times as the Triangular Forum for its unusual geometric shape. It occupies the summit of a lava slope that falls straight to the countryside below, in the southern section of the plateau where Pompeii rises. This historic Forum, which also enclosed the ancient Doric Temple, was adorned with elegant Doric porticoes with slim tufa columns, arranged along two of the plaza's three sides; the third side was left free of any architectural elements so that one could admire a beautiful, undisturbed view of the nearby plain and the Sorrentine mountains towards Capri. This specific detail gives an indication of a Hellenistic sensibility, expressed through an enthusiastic integration of architecture and landscape.

The monumental vestibule that provides access to the Triangular Forum on the northern side also reveals an important attention to scenic effect: there is an elegant and slender facade with six columns and two Ionic half-columns, alternating deliberately with the Doric order used in the arcades, in a typically Hellenistic style. It has been suggested quite convincingly that this forum plaza was used as a gymnasium, particularly considering the long east portico, bordered by an uncovered walkway of equal length. These structures also seem to have been created to function as running tracks, as suggested by the contiguity of the Forum and the Samnitic Gymnasium.

A full view of the Triangular Forum of Pompeii, with its monumental portico arrangement with Doric columns of Nucera tufa, erected in the late Samnitic era. It is possible that the longest side of these porticoes, the west one, was used as a track where one could practice for races.

This replica of one of the most famous statues of antiquity, the *Doryphoros* of Polyclitus, comes from the Samnitic Gymnasium of Pompeii, of which a section of the porticoed court-yard is visible below (MANN).

Nonetheless, from another perspective, the Triangular Forum, which contained a statue dedicated to Marcellus, a nephew of Augustus who died prematurely and who for a short time held the office of *patronus* of Pompeii, a kind of guarantor of the city's interests at the imperial court in case of controversies, was definitely initially conceived to allow more comfortable and convenient access to the adjacent Large Theater.

The Samnitic Gymnasium

In the course of the redesign of the Triangular Forum and its surroundings, completed in the second century B.C., a structure for athletic activities, the Samnitic Gymnasium, was created,

accessible from both the adjacent path and the Forum plaza. It consists of a courtyard with modest-sized arcades and Doric tufa columns, whose proportions are more slender than those used in Greece during the classical era. The east side of the portico was eliminated after the earthquake of 62 A.D., in favor of the new plan for the adjacent Temple of Isis, rebuilt with a larger floor space after the quake.

The identification of this structure as a gymnasium is further validated by the discovery of a copy of the *Doryphorus* of Polyclitus. Another indication is the base, earlier consisting of a sort of platform and a flight of stairs at the back, located in the courtyard in front of the main entrance. It has been suggested that the base held a statue of Hermes, the protector-divinity of athletic activities, and that it was customary to put the crown intended for the winners on top of the platform. The winner would then ascend the stairs and consecrate the victory he had attained by placing the crown on the divine effigy. The chambers located on the western

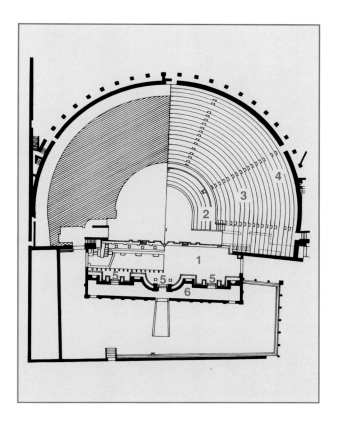

Greek architecture, we shall see that the very existence of the previously-mentioned large courtyard with arcades behind the stage building, the porticus post scaenam, confirms what we already know from a passage by Vitruvius (V 9, 1) that recalls similar solutions in certain Greek cities. In the same passage, the architect, who lived in the time of Caesar and Augustus, mentions the contiguity, in the classical Athens of the fifth century B.C., between an open-air theater for spectacles and a covered theater, or Odeion, exactly as would be proposed for Pompeii in the urban plan conceived in the late-Samnitic era and finally completed with the arrival of the Sulla colonists. Furthermore, even in nearby Neapolis, two similar theaters adjoined one another, as we know from a verse by Statius that has also been validated by archeological discoveries.

Not much is left of the original building phase of Pompeii's Large Theater, which underwent a remarkable renovation in the Augustan era, and which is marked by significant further interventions conducted after the

Layout of the Large Theater

1. Stage
2. Ima cavea
3. Media cavea
4. Summa cavea
5. Doors connecting the stage and backstage
6. Backstage area

Fourth-style marble bas-relief found in the peristyle of the House of the Gilded Cupids. It shows a group of theatrical masks which are interesting because of the sophisticated interplay of perspectives among the different depths of the surfaces (MANN).

part of the Gymnasium were useful for various athletic practices. The *destrictarium* is particularly interesting; this is where the youths would first spread firming ointments on their bodies and later remove the oil and dust with an instrument called a *strigil*, an activity that has been immortalized forever in a famous sculptural masterpiece of the late-classical period, the *Apoxyomenos* by Lysippus (late fourth century B.C.).

The interpretation of an inscription in Oscan discovered in the Samnitic Gymnasium is controversial, especially concerning the expression *vereiiai*, an enigmatic term that seems to allude to some sort of aristocratic political and military organization in pre-colonial Pompeii. It does, however, give us a further indication of the date of the structure, which goes back to the second century B.C.

The Theaters and the Gladiator Barracks

Despite extensive periods of construction and the constant transformations and repairs that occurred under Roman rule, the monumental theater complex in Pompeii immediately reveals its Greco-Hellenistic matrix, thanks partially to a natural declivity in the terrain. Besides the specific details of the Large Theater that are comparable to elements in

Partial view of the orchestra and the steps of the Small Theater (Odeion) in Pompeii, created during the time of Sulla by two magistrates of the colony that was founded in 80 B.C. The building, which was originally covered, was used for musical performances such as declamations of poetry accompanied by a kithara.

One of the two dynamic kneeling tufa telamons placed at the ends of the walls that marked off the *cavea* of the Odeion.

earthquake of 62 A.D. Nonetheless, its affinity with Greek models is indisputable. This is attested not only by the traditional partition of the space into the *cavea* (the steps for the public, divided into five *cunei*, or sections, by staircases radiating outward), the orchestra (the area at the foot of the cavea intended for the movements of the chorus), and the stage structure itself, but also by several specific features of these elements. Let us consider, in particular, the horseshoe shape of the cavea, which is absolutely typical of Greek theaters, and certain peculiarities revealed by the strati-graphic studies and analyses of the walls. The earliest stage, for instance, was organized as a rectilinear proscenium with columns. The proscenium was the side of the relatively low podium facing the orchestra and the cavea, and on which the whole stage structure was set up. On it were also arranged a stage punctuated by matching oblique, lateral wings called *paraskenia*, provided with passage-ways, and by a wall structure onto which opened three doors. These doors and the openings of the paraskenia allowed the actors to go backstage, where they had a dressing room and could store their costumes and props.

This particular setup of the stage structure, with its strong perspective and scenic effects, correlates perfectly with the Greek theater at Segesta. Even the primitive arrangement of the vast lateral corridors, the *parodoi*, for access to the orchestra and stage are Hellenic in taste and are derived from Greece. During the major renovations that took place after 80 B.C. and were mainly completed in the Augustan era, the Large Theater thoroughly changed its appearance. In addition to an intense Neronian restoration, to which we owe the present-day shape, with a regular proscenium and a fore-stage punctuated by an interesting interplay of uneven indenta-tions and protrusions, the stage was modified, the paradoi were closed off to create more space for spectators (approximately three thousand seats), and the orchestra was rearranged, losing its original function as a choral space in order to accommodate a basin filled with scented water. The wealthy Holconii brothers, leading Pompeiians at the time of Augustus, financed the majority of these transformations, for which they were granted the right to the *bisellium* seat men-tioned above. An epigraph also records a very rare piece of information, the name of the architect who supervised the work, the freedman Marcus Artorious Primus.

The elegant Odeion, next to the Large Theater and known today as the Small

Facing page:
Panoramic view of the quadriporticus located behind the Large Theater. Originally conceived as a structure where spectators might gather during the intermissions, it was transformed into quarters for the gladiators who performed in the Amphitheater.

Theater, was instead financed by two high magistrates of colonial Pompeii during Sulla's rule, whose names were carved into the marble. These were the same two who, years later, made possible the construction of the Amphitheater. The most significant of the two is certainly Caius Quinctius Valgus, a land owner famous from literary sources, whose

by several decorative details, such as the kneeling telamons sculpted at the bottom of the containment walls of the cavea, as well as by certain structural details. The orchestra, for example, is significantly smaller in size and perfectly semicircular in form; the front stage, rectilinear in shape and distinguished by doors opening backstage, is furnished with

Detail of a Julio-Claudian marble relief from a Pompeii tomb. The two figures on the right are gladiators involved in combat, a *hoplomachos* (heavily-armed fighter) and a *mirmillo* (fighter armed with a small round shield and a dagger).

economic interests extended to areas far from Pompeii, the city where his political career began after he allied himself with the Sulla party during one of the first devastating internecine battles of the late Roman Republic. Substantially similar to the Large Theater, the Odeion, which could house about a thousand spectators, is distinguished

openings that are offset with respect to those at the front. This particular device facilitated suggestive illusions of perspective which we can more or less appreciate in the vogue of the time for similar effects in painting. The structural characteristics of the covering, most likely a double-slope roof, are not entirely certain. Nonetheless, we must note that the

178

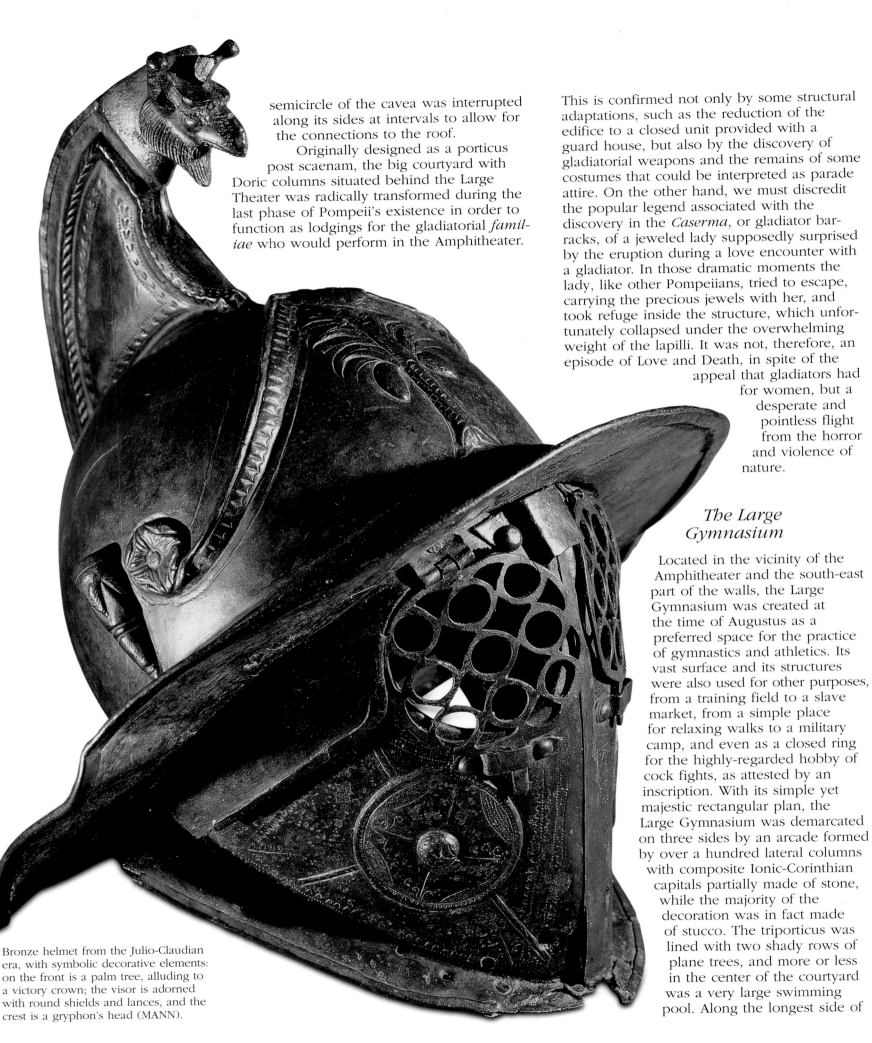

semicircle of the cavea was interrupted along its sides at intervals to allow for the connections to the roof.

Originally designed as a porticus post scaenam, the big courtyard with Doric columns situated behind the Large Theater was radically transformed during the last phase of Pompeii's existence in order to function as lodgings for the gladiatorial *familiae* who would perform in the Amphitheater.

This is confirmed not only by some structural adaptations, such as the reduction of the edifice to a closed unit provided with a guard house, but also by the discovery of gladiatorial weapons and the remains of some costumes that could be interpreted as parade attire. On the other hand, we must discredit the popular legend associated with the discovery in the *Caserma*, or gladiator barracks, of a jeweled lady supposedly surprised by the eruption during a love encounter with a gladiator. In those dramatic moments the lady, like other Pompeiians, tried to escape, carrying the precious jewels with her, and took refuge inside the structure, which unfortunately collapsed under the overwhelming weight of the lapilli. It was not, therefore, an episode of Love and Death, in spite of the appeal that gladiators had for women, but a desperate and pointless flight from the horror and violence of nature.

The Large Gymnasium

Located in the vicinity of the Amphitheater and the south-east part of the walls, the Large Gymnasium was created at the time of Augustus as a preferred space for the practice of gymnastics and athletics. Its vast surface and its structures were also used for other purposes, from a training field to a slave market, from a simple place for relaxing walks to a military camp, and even as a closed ring for the highly-regarded hobby of cock fights, as attested by an inscription. With its simple yet majestic rectangular plan, the Large Gymnasium was demarcated on three sides by an arcade formed by over a hundred lateral columns with composite Ionic-Corinthian capitals partially made of stone, while the majority of the decoration was in fact made of stucco. The triporticus was lined with two shady rows of plane trees, and more or less in the center of the courtyard was a very large swimming pool. Along the longest side of

Bronze helmet from the Julio-Claudian era, with symbolic decorative elements: on the front is a palm tree, alluding to a victory crown; the visor is adorned with round shields and lances, and the crest is a gryphon's head (MANN).

the arcade there was a rectangular chamber with two columns on its facade, most likely intended for the imperial cult.

The Amphitheater

One of the few monuments in Pompeii to remain partially visible throughout the Middle Ages, the Amphitheater was established in a peripheral area in the southeast corner of the boundary walls. It provides excellent evidence, thanks to its optimal state of preservation, not only of its builders' engineering expertise—which was, however, not always impeccable—but also of an atmosphere full of overwhelming excitement typical of a time when a handful of desperate poor people, greatly admired and even at times fanatically popular, would risk their lives in the cruel arena contests staged for collective amusement. The Amphitheater was built around 70 B.C. through the efforts of the high magistrates of the Sulla colony, Caius Quinctius Valgus and Marcus Porticus, who had previously financed the construction of the Small Theater. Of particular interest is a term used in an epigraph to define the building, *spectacula*, literally meaning a building for spectacles, which places semantic emphasis on the content—the spectacle—over the container—the building. As a matter of fact, the Latin term *amphitheatrum* was invented only a few years later, in 53-52 B.C., as testified by a famous passage of Pliny the Elder. It derived from a peculiar contrivance invented in Rome, of two mobile semi-circular wooden theaters placed alongside one another. In the side-by-side position they were used for theatrical presentations, but for gladiator games, the two semi-circles were rotated until the two extremities touched, and once the stages were removed, the result would be an arena. The word *amphitheater*, in fact, means construction in the round.

With its elliptical shape, the Amphitheater could accommodate about twenty thousand spectators, who could be sheltered under the shade of a velario. This statistic shows the extent to which the spectacles attracted crowds from nearby places, as the previously-mentioned brawl between Pompeiians and Nucerians confirms. The Amphitheater arena is situated at a lower level than the footpath of the surrounding area. This is explained by the great excavation effort that was begun expressly to erect the building: the earth that had been removed was used to create an artificial embankment as a base for constructing the tiers of seats intended for the

Detail of a bronze greave from the Gladiator Barracks with a Dionysian head, thyrsi, and other symbols related to the god of inebriation and excess (MANN).

Facing page:
An enlarged detail that shows all the refinements of a bronze helmet from the Flavian era found in Pompeii in the Gladiator Barracks and reproduced in full view below. The subjects all relate to the Trojan War and the bloody night when the Achaeans invaded the city. The groups of figures on the crown can be recognized as Ajax and Cassandra on the left and Neoptolemus in the act of killing Priam on the right.

Among the gladiatorial weapons found in Pompeii in the Gladiator Barracks were this round shield bearing a head of Medusa in the center, around which runs a double wreath of olive branches, and this iron dagger with a bone handle, a typical weapon of the *reziari*, lightly-armed gladiators (MANN).

spectators. In order to guarantee the integrity of such an embankment, an escarpment wall with stout radial buttresses was erected. Because care was taken to locate the Amphitheater where it would partially lean against the city walls, it was not necessary to build a boundary wall on the east side of the building. The buttresses mentioned above were connected by blind arches made to support the ambulacrum that permitted access to the upper part of the seats, the *summa cavea*. To reach the ambulacrum the spectators had to use one of the six ramps of stairs located on the exterior of the buttresses and supported by blind arches of different heights, of a type similar to the blind arcades arranged radially between buttresses. The people who wanted to go to the *media* and *ima cavea*, the sections where the privileged seats for the managerial class of citizens were located, had two possibilities: either to choose one of the two corridors accessible from the exterior at street level, which went to a covered upper corridor ring with access to the stairs, or to use the same entryway as the gladiators. This entrance, in fact, led directly into the arena from the large

exterior plaza through two large passages with vaulted ceilings, situated along the building's main axis. One of the two passages had an elbow turn made necessary by the presence of the urban walls on that side. Once inside the arena, the spectators could still reach the covered corridor ring mentioned above.

We must mention in particular a dark and narrow corridor along the minor axis of the Amphitheater, an additional passage connecting the exterior to the arena. It has been thought that the small door that opened onto it was the *Porta Libitinensis*, from the name of the funeral divinity, the goddess Libitina, through which the dead bodies of the men and beasts killed in the cruel combats were carried out. The presence of a small room in the immediate vicinity of this door seems to reinforce this conjecture, since it could have been used as a mortuary chamber or even as an emergency

182

Preceding pages:
A panorama of the Amphitheater of Pompeii, built during the first years of the Sulla colony, with its arena and its steps only partly preserved.

Facing page:
The southern part of the men's caldarium in the Baths of the Forum, from the early colonial era in Pompeii. Note the marble tub (labrum) in the center, which spurted jets of cold water.

Layout of the Baths of the Forum

1. Entrances
2. Courtyard Gymnasium
3. Men's apodyterium
4. Laconicum, later men's frigidarium
5. Tepidarium
6. Men's caldarium
7. Women's apodyterium
8. Cold-water tub
9. Tepidarium
10. Women's caldarium

Detail of the tepidarium of the Baths of the Forum, with terra-cotta telamons and delicate polychrome stucco in the vault.

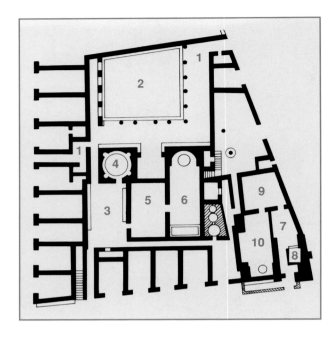

room for the curable wounded. However, there are two similar rooms adjacent to the two main vaulted passages, a circumstance that makes it less clear which of them was in fact the Porta Libitinensis of the Pompeii Amphitheater. The arena was divided from the stairs of the ima cavea by a six-foot-high bulwark, onto which a metallic fence was almost certainly fixed to further protect the public against possible leaps by the beasts. This parapet was originally decorated with interesting pictures of gladiatorial subjects, which no longer exist today but were reproduced in nineteenth-century watercolors. One of the most significant of these depicts two gladiators preparing for combat. The two contestants, assisted by servants and not yet fully armed, face each other in the presence of a supervisor who traces in the sand the area intended for the combat, while the effigies of two Victories appear in the background with crown and palm leaf.

Promptly restored with brick fillings after the damage from the earthquake of 62 A.D., the Pompeii Amphitheater is undoubtedly a milestone in our understanding of an architectural type so characteristic of the Italic and Roman world. Nevertheless, we must note that the structural solutions used in the building were not always the best. The external ramps that provide access to the ambulacrum of

the summa cavea, for instance, are somewhat graceless, and in the arena there are none of the subterranean spaces that one sees in the large amphitheaters of the most important cities, and which made possible prodigious scenic effects that would excite the public. Even from this detail we can see that Pompeii was in fact a provincial center that became, only because of a tremendous catastrophe, one of the most important sources of knowledge for anyone who wants to acquire a vivid picture of antiquity.

The Thermal Baths

The Baths of the Forum were of modest dimensions, but they were centrally located in the heart of a residential urban neighborhood, close to the Forum and to several important patrician villas. They belonged to a group of buildings planned by a new executive class in colonial Pompeii around 80 B.C. and were organized into two distinct sections, a male section and a smaller female one. The interior of the Baths of the Forum was arranged primarily along the lines of the standard designs for this type of system. Among the most significant elements is the *laconicum*, a term associated with the possible Spartan origins of this particular thermal design, which was modeled on similar settings present in the Greek gymnasia, consisting of a space with a circular floor plan and four apsidal niches. It is covered by a cone-shaped dome with a windowed opening at the top that has an additional square extension built expressly to face south. The

Detail of a famous erotic frieze, probably painted during the time of Nero, in the apodyterium of the Suburban Baths of Pompeii: a true illustrated manual of various sexual positions, it appears to have been inspired by literary works on comparable subjects such as Ovid's *Ars Amatoria*.

Two of the four semi-circular niches in a room in the Stabian Baths with a cupola ceiling, originally used as a laconicum (room for steam baths) and later turned into a frigidarium.

room was used for *sudationes*, hot and warm-air baths that were predecessors of the modern sauna. Its characteristics correspond almost exactly to a specific passage in *De Architectura* by Vitruvius regarding designs with circular floor plans, which were practical for even heat distribution. Like the similar setting of the Stabian Baths, the laconicum of the Baths of the Forum was later transformed into a *frigidarium*, probably because of the inadequacies of its heat regulation system.

The caldarium of the men's section is extremely well preserved; it has a barrel vault decorated with stucco, and the walls were painted with an elegant combination of complementary hues like yellow and purple. In the chamber there are still, on the north side, the rectangular marble tub, where one could sink into a warm bath, and on the opposite side to the south, the so-called *schola labri*, an apse with a circular basin, or *labrum,* equipped with spouts gushing cold water for those who wished to cool their overheated bodies. This particular device was created by two five-year *duoviri*, the civic magistrates of highest rank, as announced by an inscription in bronze letters along the same marble basin. The room with the most refined ornamentation in these thermal baths, however, is the men's *tepidarium*, which has a barrel vault with ornate coffers of various shapes, in polychrome stucco, decorated with lively mythological subjects. A notable effect is also created by the telamons that support the architrave upon which the vault rests; located between a series of niches, these clay statues recall the similar telamons of the Odeion, implicitly confirming that the Baths of the Forum go back to the time of Sulla.

Like the Stabian Baths, which were located close to the most important structure in Pompeii dedicated to the business of love, the *Lupanare*, this building, being situated next to the plaza of the Forum, was also certainly one of the places where many amorous and fleeting erotic adventures were consummated for a fee. This is indicated by the back room of a shop in the inn opposite the Baths of the Forum, which was transformed into a brothel, and especially by the facade of the House of the Tragic Poet, also in the immediate neighborhood, which was covered with graffiti suggesting the not-so-remote possibility of casual encounters, adding further evidence to the many allusions by Latin writers to the licentious pleasures, sometimes considered reprehensible, of days spent at the baths.

The largest and oldest thermal baths in Pompeii are the famous system today called the Stabian Baths, for their location next to the important road that crosses the city diagonally from north to south in the direction of ancient Stabia. Although there still remain some archeological questions, such as the supposed existence of an underground tomb from the fourth century B.C. beneath one of the rooms—tangible proof, according to some researchers, of the early eastern border of pre-Samnitic Pompeii—or the very date of the thermal system's first phase (the end of the fourth century B.C.?), the Stabian Baths undoubtedly represent one of the best examples of this particular architectural style. The heart of the structure is the grand porticoed courtyard with its trapezoid layout, usually used as a gymnasium for athletic exercises. It seems evident that this athletic purpose was originally more important than the thermal one; in fact, when the system was established, only small chambers with tubs large enough for one person at a time were available for baths. During the second century B.C. it was decided to build real structures for thermal baths, divided in two distinct sections for men and women, with a common heating system. In the beginning these sections were not connected, and the use of the gym was restricted to men. We can definitely date this particular enlargement to the late-Samnitic era, not only through specific building details, but especially because of the large travertine sundial, one of the oldest known, which bears an Oscan inscription with the name of the magistrate who had it built, using money from fines assessed by the public administration.

A final stage of the building history of the

Stabian Baths was promoted by the Sulla colonists around the middle of the first century B.C. As we know from an important epigraph, the five-year duovirs Caius Uulius and Publius Aninius provided for the construction of several new rooms, such as the laconicum, later transformed into a frigidarium as in the Baths of the Forum, and the destrictarium, the room where athletes cleansed themselves with the strigil. The same magistrates saw to the restoration of the gymnasium and its porticoes, further proof of the existence of the basic elements of the thermal system during the time of the Samnites. Another important building intervention goes back to late-Republican times: the construction of a great uncovered pool, the *natatio*, in an area of the gym appropriately restored. Bathers could enter this pool only after they had rinsed their feet in special tubs located in rooms adjacent to the natatio. Despite their largely traditional structure, the Stabian Baths present a peculiarity not always found in Roman thermal systems: the tepidarium is in fact provided with a special tub specifically for baths with tepid water. Finally, the decorations of the various rooms in these baths are of very high quality. We point out especially the paintings in the laconicum/frigidarium, which represent a

Another detail of the erotic frieze in the Suburban Baths of Pompeii: the protagonists of the scene are a half-reclining man and a woman seated on top of him, making love in a position commonly depicted in Roman painting and sculpture.

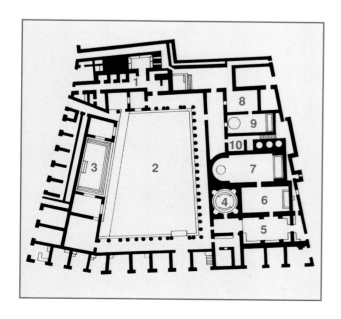

Layout of the Stabian Baths

1. Entrance corridor off Vicolo del Lupanare
2. Courtyard-gymnasium
3. Natatio
4. Laconicum, later men's frigidarium
5. Men's apodyterium
6. Men's tepidarium
7. Men's caldarium
8. Women's tepidarium
9. Women's caldarium
10. Praefurnium

Wide colonnaded courtyard of the Stabian Baths in Pompeii, laid out in this form towards the end of the second century B.C., and inspired by Greek architecture. Restored many times, even after the earthquake of 62 A.D., it was given a heavy coat of stucco that altered the original delicacy of the columns.

Following pages:

In this view of the tepidarium and the caldarium of the men's sector, we can appreciate both the massive brickwork vaults and the system for heating the rooms, effected by elevating the floor with brick pilasters (*suspensurae*), around which hot air coming from the boiler room circulated.

View of the courtyard in the Main Baths of Pompeii, with large windows framed by half-columns, designed to provide air and light to the thermal rooms, in keeping with building techniques that were innovative compared to earlier systems.

One of the splendid Muses, frescoed in the fourth style, found in the complex at Murecine, not far from the Stabia Gate (MANN).

garden on the walls and a starry sky on the dome, calculated to create the illusion of a much larger room. The stucco decorations in the *apodyterium,* or changing room, of the men's thermal baths, where various motifs appear between the coffers, are also famous, as is a wall in the southwest corner that is covered with fourth-style polychrome stucco works predating the earthquake of 62 A.D., and depicting lively subjects of a mythological and athletic character.

Planned after the earthquake of 62 A.D., the Main Thermal Baths were meant to provide the northeast neighborhoods of Pompeii with a newer and more satisfactory bathing system. The funding was certainly not inadequate, and great care was taken to set up the thermal system according to the most functional and up-to-date technological and architectural methods, following models already operating at least in part in the fairly new Stabian Baths. This gives an interesting indication that the socio-economic vitality of the city had not been weakened by the quake, even though we must remember that these impressive works were still under way at the time of the eruption seventeen years later. In order to avoid costly duplication and to allow for the construction of larger rooms, the division into two distinct sections was abolished, and one single structure was created in the form of a large arcaded gymnasium. We cannot be absolutely certain about the eventual mixed use of the system, but it is a more likely scenario than a gym used only by men.

The capitals of the porticoes were still at a rudimentary stage, and next to the thermal rooms there was an uncovered natatio, not quite finished in time. These rooms reveal the most significant innovations. Unlike the oldest thermal systems in Pompeii, these are imposing, light-filled chambers with very high walls punctuated by many windows. The obvious pursuit of architectural rationality called for the various side-by-side rooms to be connected to each other with doors intentionally situated on different axes in order to prevent unnecessary loss of heat. Behind the tepidarium was a circular laconicum, ideally equipped for steam baths as well, thanks to a special oven and ducts along the walls. Unfortunately, no Pompeiian ever had the pleasure of bathing in these magisterial unfinished baths. Nevertheless, the Main Thermal Baths can be included in the technical and evolutionary lineage that would culminate in the ingenious thermal creations of the Imperial era, which are also embodied in the majestic establishments in Rome.

The Suburban Thermal Baths, completely excavated in recent years and datable to the first Imperial era, are situated outside the city in the immediate vicinity of Porta Marina. They were very innovative in their architectural conception, having improved their bathing structures over older models, as in the case of the laconicum, and abolished the division into men's and women's sections, all features that would soon be adopted in the Main Thermal Baths. The Suburban Baths are distinguished by their scenic integration with the landscape, with rooms whose large windows open towards the nearby coast.

It is actually probable that the thermal plant extended to the sea, if we are to believe a hypothesis that connects it to a Pompeii epigraph recalling thermal baths that used sea water and were built by an important member of the Roman ruling class, Marcus Crassus Frugi, who was consul in 64 A.D.

and was later killed by Nero. Yet the most remarkable and distinct feature of the Suburban Baths is the splendid pictorial decoration of the apodyterium, with an erotic frieze of sometimes rare iconography, including a scene of Sapphic love. It is a sort of illustrated handbook inspired by literary texts such as Ovid's *Ars Amatoria*, further testimony to the joyous and utterly pagan sexuality implicitly connected with the almost daily habit of visiting the baths.

The exceptional archeological wealth of Pompeii and its countryside has very recently received yet another extraordinary affirmation: in the course of work to widen the highway between Naples and Salerno, the remains of an extremely ancient *hospitium* were discovered in Murecine, a few hundred yards from the Stabian Gate. This was a true hotel, provided with every comfort, such as small, delightful, private gardens and individual baths built with considerable care. Several of its beautiful paintings, representing the cycle of the Muses and dating from the last building phase of Pompeii, are historically and artistically valuable and provide another indication of the cultural ferment that was interrupted only by the terrible volcanic catastrophe of 79 A.D.

Emidio De Albentiis

The Lupanare *(VII 12, 18-20)*

One of the rooms in the Lupanare. Through the door we see a stone pallet, which was usually covered with cushions and fabric to make it more comfortable. Above the door jamb is one of the various frescoes that adorned the brothel walls.

Bi-phallic Priapus on a pedestal; a fresco from the brothel's north wall.

The brothel was built on the corner of a trivium, at the intersection of Vicolo del Balcone Pensile, or Hanging Balcony Lane, and Vicolo del Lupanare, or Brothel Lane. The building, on two floors, appears to have been expressly conceived for this function; furthermore, it was in a location typical for establishments of this type, and its layout took maximum advantage of the limited space it had available. Five small cells were arranged on each floor, even though perhaps only those of the lower floor were actually used for prostitution.

One reached the rooms of the upper floor by means of a wooden staircase that opened directly, with its own entrance, onto Vicolo del Balcone Pensile at number 20. These rooms were more spacious and were unconnected on the inside, thanks to a covered gallery that jutted out over the sidewalk below, following the building's elbow-curve. Along it, windows corresponding with each cell let light and air into the individual rooms. It seems apparent that these rooms were used as private lodgings for those employed in prostitution on the lower floor. The excavation of the complex, carried out in 1862 with the methods approved at the time, has unfortunately not made it possible to recover either the decoration or the graffiti that could help us better understand the exact function of these rooms.

The cells on the lower floor, on the other hand, were located to the left and right along the long arm of a wide L-shaped corridor, which at the same time served as a waiting room, linked as it was to the two brothel entrances, the main one at number 18 on Vicolo del Lupanare, and the secondary one at number 19 on Vicolo del Balcone Pensile. These very narrow cells were furnished with a bed and bolster in masonry. Obviously, mattresses, pillows and sheets were placed on them to offer some comfort for the embrace. To ensure a minimum of privacy

Bronze *tintinnabulum* from Herculaneum depicting a gladiator fighting with his phallus, which is in the shape of a panther (MANN).

Another example of a sexual position. These small paintings with erotic subjects fairly often decorated the houses of the higher classes and served both to excite the libido and to suggest new sexual games and positions (MANN).

A couple in an embrace; a fresco from the east side of the brothel's south wall (MANN).

Following pages:
Banquets were an occasion for encounters that often had a sexual outcome; food and wine encouraged guests to relax and enjoy life's pleasures to the fullest. This fresco comes from the *Insula* of the Chaste Lovers.

195

the cells were closed with a wooden door as the client entered. A latrine was located on the wall at the end of the corridor, making use of a space under the stairs leading to the upper floor, and a low staggered wall protected it from the view of anyone coming in the main entrance.

The building seems to have been designed and built in this form only in the last period of the city's life. What is certain is that its decoration, as we see it today, dates from after 72 A.D., as attested in the first small cell to the left of the main entrance by the imprint of a coin, actually dated in that year, that was placed on the plaster when it was still fresh.

The decorative cycle still visible in the complex is very interesting. Paintings in an unrefined popular style are found on the walls of the corridor, above the cells in fact, reproducing various sexual positions undoubtedly inspired by those manuals that, as ancient sources well illustrate, discoursed on the positions to assume during amorous relations.

Two paintings stand out from the others. The first, located just to the right of the main entrance, depicts a biphallic Priapus in the shade of a fig tree, who is holding his duplicate attributes in both his hands, pointing them in different directions. The figure is surely apotropaic, intended to keep away evil spirits, no matter what direction they might come from, a prudent precaution in a brothel, since it was believed that one was more liable to be prey to them when nude. The second, located above the latrine, facing whoever came in through the main door, or first on the left for those coming in the secondary door, is the one that can perhaps explain the significance of these paintings. It shows a man lying on a bed. Standing next to him is a still-dressed woman, portrayed as a hetaira. He points out to her on the wall facing them a *pinax*, a small painting with a window on it through which another man and woman can be seen copulating, perhaps instructing her on what she should do with him.

Literary sources give ample accounts of the fashion common among the society's upper classes of furnishing several rooms of their own houses with these precious *pinakes* whose erotic subjects were intended to excite the libido as well as provide inspiration for sexual games and positions (Ovid, *Tristia* II, 521-4 and *Ars Amatoria* II, 679-681; Tibullus II 6, 29s; Suetonius, *Life of Tiberius* XLIII 2 and XLIV 2). Indeed, Suetonius gives us to understand that Tiberius used them almost as a catalog for the benefit of the young girls and

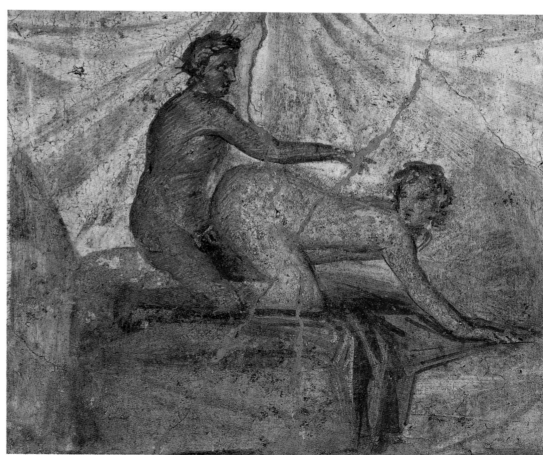

Preceding pages:

Marble bas-relief from the first century A.D. with the so-called *Venus Pendula*, or *Hesitant Venus*, from the triclinium of the *Caupona*, or "Mistress of the Inn" (VII, 7, 18) (MANN).

Two small paintings from Pompeii with erotic scenes (MANN).

boys that he recruited, "so that no one would lack a model for whatever position their duties required of them."

Besides characterizing the functions of the locale and boosting the erotic impulse, inviting and predisposing the client's psyche to passionate pleasures, these paintings also served to ennoble the surroundings, showing the consummation of amorous embraces in an opulent setting and making the clients feel in

by a *puer* (CIL IV 2258 a), wrongly interpreted and compared to other inscriptions (CIL IV 817, 818), gave many the false notion that the Lupanare was run by a certain Africanus and a Victor.

Since these were slaves who enjoyed no legal rights, all proceeds from the activities went to the owner, or to the pimp who made the arrangements, and who, according to a decree by Caligula, had to pay a daily tax for

A cameo representing a *pinax* (a painting with a view through a window) with an erotic scene consummated on a bed adorned with fabrics and pillows (MANN).

Facing page:
Even the furnishings of the most modest houses sometimes reproduced amorous scenes, as in this detail from the bottom of a bronze basin with an explicitly erotic bas-relief (MANN).

some way invited into the cozy world of the aristocracy.

In reality, the clients belonged to the lowest ranks of society. The numerous graffiti found on the walls of the cells display their names and habits. Even the prostitutes were generally from servile backgrounds and most often had names of Greek or Asiatic origin. There is also no lack of names of young boys, or *pueri*, who were requested by those who wished to *paedicare*, that is, to join with them in sexual relations, a custom that at the time was considered completely normal and in no way reprehensible. Indeed, an inscription left

every prostitute, equal to a single client's fee. The prices for these mercenary encounters were very low, varying from two to sixteen assi, according to the charms the prostitute was able to offer. Two assi were about the price of a loaf of bread or a good tankard of wine, and even this shows us that the services were essentially meant for the most modest classes.

Antonio Varone

200

LEGEND

Unless otherwise indicated, all images are on site
or from Pompeii.

MANN = National Archeological Museum of Naples

SAP = Archeological Superintendence of Pompeii

Private Life

The House

"Our city consists of 10,000 houses, and it is really difficult to be concerned with so many families at the same time." The words that Xenophon has Socrates speak in the *Memorabilia* (III, 6, 14), referring to the needs and expectations of the blossoming and articulate political community that was Athens in the fourth century B.C., could serve as an epigraph to describe the complex situation of private housing in any archeological site. This is true because in the ancient world, and in a

private complexes of various types, including rented houses, commercial enterprises, reception and meeting places, and workshops of every kind. Paradoxically, very few specific studies of those houses have come to light in over two hundred fifty years of excavation. Furthermore, recent editions of the city's real estate registries differ considerably on the

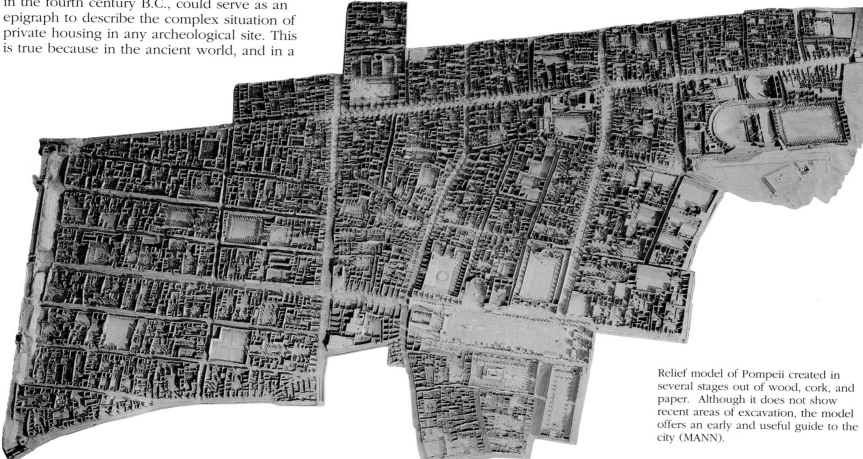

Relief model of Pompeii created in several stages out of wood, cork, and paper. Although it does not show recent areas of excavation, the model offers an early and useful guide to the city (MANN).

particular way in Roman society, the house, more than any other kind of building, reflected the class structure, the relationships, and the very social identity of the members of the community to which it belonged. This was especially true for a city like Pompeii which had a very high number of habitations and

actual number of habitations: 413 according to L. Eschebach, but 818 in the registry published in *Pompei: L'informatica al servizio di una città antica*, the title of which can be translated as "Pompeii: Information Technology in the Service of an Ancient City." It is especially difficult, because of our way of perceiving an

Following pages:
Detail of the famous fresco called *The Aldobrandini Wedding*, now in the Vatican Museum.

A housing block in Ostia, a sign of the intense building activity during the second century A.D.

century. There have been publications of large scientific works like the four volumes on the monuments of Pompeii edited by F. Mazois between 1824 and 1838; descriptions or guides to the ruins, the best-remembered being those of W. Gell (1817-1819) and of E. Breton (1855) because of the impact they had on the authors' own nations; and works of pure fantasy, such as the most famous novel set in Pompeii, written by E. Bulwer-Lytton in 1834. These works made the exceptional nature of the Pompeii excavations known, rescuing them from the myopic monopoly of scholars at the Herculaneum Academy and from the almost exclusive enjoyment of the Bourbon monarchy. Faced with the perfectly preserved houses of Pompeii, Madame de Staël may have been unable to hide her disappointment at the absence of the sense of decay that ruins were supposed to stir in the romantic sensibility. Nevertheless, the wonder of finding oneself in front of a sort of gigantic photographic plate, on which are imprinted the latest photograms of a living Roman city, has permitted visitors up to our time to enjoy the illusion of sharing for a moment in the daily lives of the ancient inhabitants and has furnished the archeologist with complete sequences of materials and the products of artists and craftsmen, without which our understanding of the Roman world would be quite different today.

For example, without this copious documentation, most of which comes from private dwellings, the history of Roman painting, with

ancient city, to definitively determine a building's function when it includes elements that do not fit the norm.

The Roman house, or more precisely the Pompeii house, has enjoyed particular attention from both experts and ordinary visitors ever since the first half of the nineteenth

House of Venus on the Shell in Pompeii; detail of the painting in the garden.

all its debts to and improvements on earlier classical Greek and Hellenistic works, would have been founded entirely on relevant but widely isolated artistic artifacts. Among these would be the fresco known as *The Aldobrondini Wedding,* produced by a large urban atelier at the end of the first century B.C. and discovered in Rome at the end of the sixteenth century, as well as the decorations of Nero's *Domus Aurea,* which greatly influenced painting in the late Renaissance. Because of everything we have

learned from the excavations of the Vesuvian cities, it was possible in fact for scientific archeological studies based on A. Mau's important 1882 work on painting not only to distinguish specific phases and chronologies of Roman wall and floor decorations—and of their Greek origins—but also to develop an enormous iconographic repertory and to propose a system for reading iconography. This made it possible to recreate the cultural climate in which those who commissioned the art lived, along with

Foreshortened view of the city of Herculaneum.

Housing and Landlords

1. Once having considered the layout in relation to the points of the compass, one must take into account the different requirements for the design of rooms meant for the owners and those meant for persons who are not part of the family. In fact, those who are not invited to do so may not enter the private areas, and the same is true for the bedrooms, the triclinium, the baths and other similar rooms. In those spaces considered public areas, like the vestibules, the courtyards, and the peristyles, anyone may enter without a specific invitation, even ordinary persons. For those who are accustomed to render homage to others, and not receive it, it is not necessary to have a tablinum, vestibules or splendid atriums.

2. He who has income from agriculture must create sheds and store rooms in the vestibules and in the house he must put cellars, granaries, warehouses and other rooms more suited to the preservation of crops than to the pursuit of elegance. Obeying at all times the need for functionality, bankers and tax collectors must have rooms that are welcoming, spacious, and safe, while lawyers and men of letters need elegant spaces large enough to accommodate many people at the same time. In order to perform their administrative and judicial duties, persons of rank require vestibules of great height and nobility along with airy peristyles and atria, as well as gardens and promenades that are broad and spacious. Necessary as well are libraries, art galleries and assembly halls that can draw attention to the riches of public institutions, because in these houses public councils are often held and private lawsuits argued.

Vitruvius, *On Architecture,* VI, 5,1

207

Decorative element of a wooden fitting shaped like the head of a woman, and a statuette of a cupid with a dolphin, a Roman copy of a late-Hellenistic work (MANN).

the system of values they intended that art to communicate to those who entered their homes.

Roman archeology owes an even greater debt to the Vesuvian cities for all the information these dwellings have furnished, and continue to furnish, about the history of private architecture. This information allows us to draw a fairly accurate picture of Roman

housing systems in use between the third century B.C. and 79 A.D. Entire chapters of the book of Roman civilization would have been lost if the eruption of Vesuvius had spared Pompeii and Herculaneum. With the exception of isolated and extraordinary monuments like the Oppio Hill pavilion belonging to the *Domus Aurea* and the Imperial residence of the Palatine, documentation on private building in Rome is actually extremely scarce. Its best evidence is perhaps represented not so much by buildings and building complexes as by a fragment of a marble map from the age of Severus, a *Forma Urbis*, on which are reproduced houses with atriums, facing the *Vicus Patricius*, or Patrician Quarter, very similar in layout and distribution of space to dwellings documented in Pompeii during the first Imperial age. Except for what we can learn from surviving documentation, the great urban and construction developments in Ostia during the second century A.D. would be almost incomprehensible to us. Ostia's housing blocks, an important innovation in popular housing, inserted into planned urban spaces already formalized by Nero's architects immediately after the disastrous fire of July 19, 64 A.D., might be nothing but mute boxes if we could not compare them with what we know about the various living situations of Pompeii.

Nevertheless, our knowledge of the houses and living styles of Pompeii still includes gray areas and uncertainties. The widespread antiquarian trend, especially during the first decades of the excavations, and the classicist distortion that colored the archeological research for a good part of the nineteenth and twentieth centuries have, on the one hand, favored the attempt to find confirmation in the field for notions handed down by literary sources; on the other hand, they have generally focussed the investigations on dwellings that showed signs of carefully considered

planning and promised works of art likely to be beautiful. These two different aims, sometimes also intertwined, have resulted in a great deal of attention to a few large houses, considered exemplary not only for their architectural aspects, their decorative apparatus, and the richness of their furnishings, but also—in a crescendo of ever more specialized disciplinary threads, showing a strong positivist trend—for the engineering systems, construction techniques and an ever more precise definition of absolute chronological sequence.

It would be reductive, however, to accuse only these approaches to Pompeii studies of a sort of unconscious suppression of a significant number of the buildings brought to light in the city, since much of the responsibility rests with the management and with the direction given to the excavations for almost all of the

Following pages:
Detail from a fresco in room 32 of the House of the Golden Bracelet in Pompeii. Depictions of gardens are an important part of fresco painting in the Vesuvius area.

Mosaic in vitreous paste from the summer triclinium of the House of Neptune and Amphitrite in Herculaneum, an excellent example of this type of decoration, which was very widespread in the area around Vesuvius in the first century A.D.

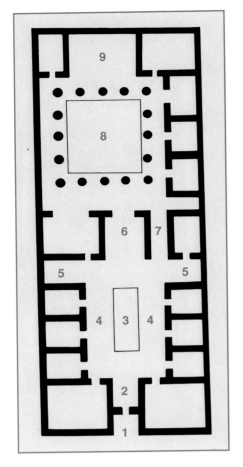

*The Roman House
according to Vitruvius*

1. Vestibulum

2. Fauces

3. Impluvium

4. Atrium

5. Alae

6. Tablinum

7. Andron

8. Peristylium

9. Exedra

Polychrome mosaic floor with a three-dimensional geometric design, from Niccolini, *Le case e i monumenti di Pompei.*

Facing page:
A lost painting from the House of Queen Caroline (VIII, 3, 14) with Hercules and Deianira, from Niccolini.

Peristyle of the House of Venus on the Shell.

The first fruits of these changes became manifest shortly afterwards. In this case too, we must recognize, more than a century after their publication, the enormous debt that every scholar today still owes to the great archeological summaries of A. Mau, R. Schöne, H. Nissen, and J. Overbeck, who, we should note, did not visit Pompeii for the first time until seventeen years after his book was first published. In all these works the house takes on a central role in describing the living systems of Roman cities in general and those of Pompeii in particular. But the new impetus given to the excavations, which the political and cultural forces of the time wanted to use as a sort of window onto their new institutions, made continuous and critical updates on the discoveries progressively more difficult. It was very late when a complete report was made of all the private buildings that had come to light during the great excavation effort in part of Region I, an endeavor promoted by V. Spinazzola using excavation and reconstruction methods that were completely innovative at the time. As often happens, A. Maiuri's intense excavations, to which we owe the discovery of a good part of the southeastern quadrant of the city, were often revealed in preliminary reports, which were substantiated later. All these complex affairs, briefly recapitulated here, have caused what we can call the "Pompeii paradox": the excavation of two-thirds of the city did not in fact produce a greater understanding of the arrangement of monumental and living spaces in Pompeii, but only a greater number of buildings not yet studied and greater burdens for conserving monuments that, we should always remember, were not planned and constructed to function as empty ruins or shells, but to be lived in, remodelled, and torn down, like the fibers of that vital fabric that the houses of a city weave in every epoch.

In general, to best exemplify the model dwelling, almost every introduction to Pompeiian or Roman houses begins by citing more or less exactly a famous passage from the Roman architect Vitruvius, in which he gives the reader the construction norms for the "perfect aristocratic house," and then provides the plans of two famous Pompeii dwellings, the Pansa House and the House of M. Trebius Valens. The first of these is an example of an aristocratic house with an atrium and the second of a standard home of the city's upper-middle class. Nevertheless, an awareness of the extreme variety of living solutions found in Pompeii, even within a generic typology of reference represented by houses with atriums, persuades us to avoid

nineteenth century. In fact, only after the formation of the Kingdom of Italy did we see a flowering of works, still essential today, that tried to organize into a coherent whole what the great excavations of the Bourbon era had discovered in a disorganized and superficial way, with the sole and avowed scope of adding prized pieces to the collections of the Royal Museum of Naples. It was no accident that the first organic description of the Pompeii excavations, which took shape at the same time as a proper registry of all the discovered buildings, should have been written by Fiorelli at almost the same moment that he published the disorganized excavation reports contained in the notebooks of the directors of operations from the Bourbon period (the invaluable *Pompeianarum Antiquitatum Historia*). Along with the first attempts to turn the excavated houses into museums on site in Pompeii, which would result in the complete roofing of dwellings such as the House of the Silver Wedding and the House of the Vettii at the end of the century, these editorial undertakings created solid bases for all future studies.

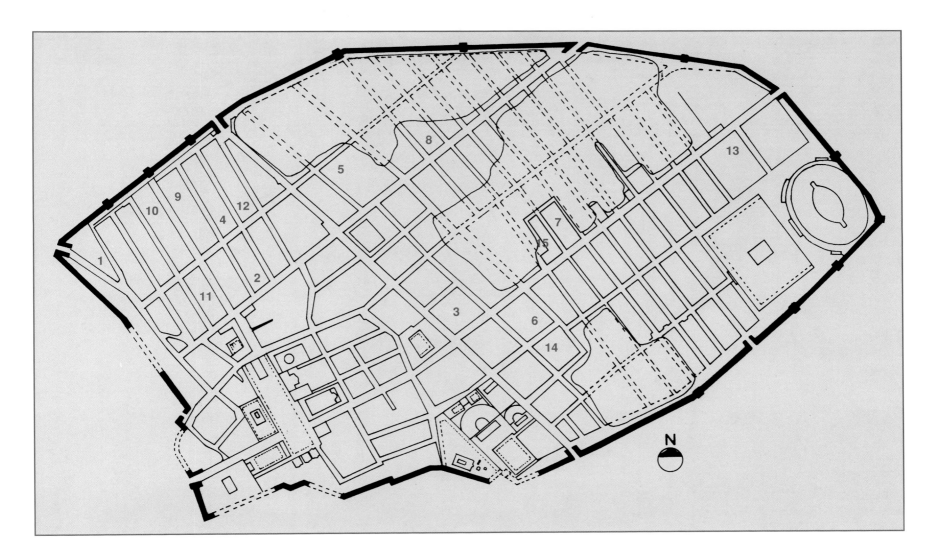

this easy distortion of archeological reality and lean toward an explanation perhaps less didactic but closer to the state of documentation. The following pages refer to Vitruvius, not for the "normative" sections concerning the construction of the ideal *domus*, but for the definition, much closer to reality, of the house as a tangible expression of the social stratifications inside the city. This is intended to show the reader the development and the modifications that several of the most significant houses in Pompeii underwent between the third century B.C. and August 24, 79 A.D., using as chronological indicators the four types of pictorial and mosaic decoration documented primarily in the dwellings discussed and synthesizing the consequent results of the most recent archeological research.

Maria Paola Guidobaldi
Fabrizio Pesando

Note to the reader

The extent of the Pompeii excavations makes immediate topographic identification of public and private buildings particularly complicated. In 1858, Giuseppe Fiorelli established a registration system which has become standard for the site of Pompeii and whose criteria have subsequently been applied in the archeological area of Herculaneum as well. To avoid confusion among the hundreds of conventional names given to the houses and shops of Pompeii at the time of excavation, he divided the city into nine regions or sectors (*regiones*); each one of these is made up of blocks (*insulae*), within which are the houses and shops, each identified by an actual municipal number. In this way, it is always possible to identify a building referred to on a map of the city. For this reason every habitation in this text is specified both with its best-known conventional name and with its registry numbers: House of the Faun, VI (region), 12 (block), 2–5 (municipal number).

First Style

1. House of the Surgeon
2. House of the Faun
3. House of the Diadumeni or of Epidius Rufus

Second Style

4. House of the Labyrinth
5. House of the Silver Wedding
6. House of the Cryptoporticus and of the Ilion Sanctuary

Third Style

7. House of Julius Polybius
8. House of Marcus Lucretius Fronto

Fourth Style

9. House of Meleager
10. House of Apollo
11. House of the Tragic Poet
12. House of the Vettii
13. *Praedia* of Julia Felix
14. House of Menander
15. The *Insula* of the Chaste Lovers

House of the Surgeon (VI, 1, 10.23): First to Fourth Style

The House of the Surgeon on Via Consolare is distinguished from the surrounding buildings because it is higher than the level of the street and is built of regular limestone blocks.

The House of the Surgeon is visually imposing both for its facade, built of regular limestone blocks, and for its higher elevation relative to the other buildings facing Via Consolare at its northern end. For a long time, because of its building techniques, also used for many of the interior walls, this dwelling was used as a model for understanding the oldest Roman and Italic houses, and for this reason it was dated to the fifth century B.C. Limited excavation tests conducted by Maiuri in 1926 made it possible, however, to establish that its currently visible state is the result of two renovations completed in the Samnitic era; these involved raising the floor considerably, as occurred in other documented cases like the House of the Faun, the House of the Diadumeni and the House of the Centaur. In 1990 a reexamination by Chiaramonte Treré of the data which came out of the excavation confirmed that, contrary to what was believed, the house probably had an *impluvium* in the center of the atrium from the beginning, and that the date of its original construction should thus be put in the third century B.C.

Research carried out in the last ten years attributes to this period several of the oldest Region VI dwellings still visible in this quarter today. They can be recognized from their plain facades in square-worked limestone masonry or from the delicate monumental

portals in Nucera tufa with pilaster strips or half-columns crowned with Corinthian-Italic or figured capitals. Between the end of the fourth and the first decades of the first centuries B.C., these houses took the place of earlier public and private buildings, whose structures, often very simple in building technique and decorative level, are regularly found every time stratigraphic excavations are undertaken in this sector of the city.

The House of the Surgeon has a regular floor plan, with the most important spaces arranged around the atrium. The decoration that was seen at the time of the excavation has survived in only a few places. In the left *ala* the entrance threshold of the space is emphasized by a prized box-motif, going back to the first Imperial era. Of great interest is a windowed room, facing a small garden situated at the back of the house; the exterior wall shows a

In this fourth-style fresco from the House of the Surgeon a young woman is painting a herm of Priapus on a tablet held by a small boy (MANN).

first-style painting from the second century B.C., which was chipped so that a new layer of white plaster would adhere. The interior of this space is decorated with a fourth-style painting completed shortly after the middle of the first century A.D., while the floor, created from fragments of ceramic and travertine, is still from the Samnitic era. In the center of the right wall is a small painting, almost vanished by now, representing a poet; on the wall opposite the entry, in the middle zone, at the center of the niche, was a painting, now in the National Museum of Naples, first described in the report of the discovery, on June 22, 1771: ". . . one sees there a well-draped woman who is helping someone paint, holding a brush in

Facing page:
Detail of a fourth-style fresco from the House of Siricus which shows the doctor Iapygius removing an arrow from the leg of Aeneas.

Surgical instruments, all from the first century A.D., found in the House of the Surgeon. Counterclockwise from bottom left: a *speculum ani*, a *speculum uteris*, a container for medical instruments called a *theca vulnuraria*, a case for medicines, and a pincer for extracting teeth or removing foreign objects from wounds (MANN).

her right hand and in the act of dipping it in several *albarellos. . . ."* The scene, in exquisite Hellenistic taste, in fact represents a female painter intent on reproducing an urn of Priapus, while two women, elegantly dressed, observe her thoughtfully. Below this painting two visitors left signs of their presence: the first, named Tullio, visited the house in 1799, and the anonymous second added the date 1802 next to the first.

The house's conventional name comes from the more than forty surgical instruments "found wrapped in something completely rotted." It was April 21, 1771, and the discovery of these complex instruments, very similar to those still in use today, such as dilators for gynecological use, caused great amazement among contemporaries, since their modernity and formal complexity revealed the existence of a surgical practice far more advanced than was thought.

Maria Paola Guidobaldi

House of the Faun
(VI, 12, 2-5): First Style

Amazement at the grandiosity of the architecture and admiration for the refinement of the decorations recur in all descriptions by the researchers, antiquarians, and travellers who were able to see the House of the Faun as it looked when it was excavated. Very little of those impressions is perceptible today to those who enter what was the most sumptuous dwelling of the late-Samnitic era in Pompeii. The decision to transfer the rich mosaic apparatus to the Museum of Portici almost immediately—virtually obligatory according to the aesthetic notions of the time—and the damage caused by the bombardments of the summer of 1943 and by long exposure to atmospheric agents have in fact left incomprehensible gaps in the rooms and caused the disappearance or destruction of the ancient first-style paintings that the owners so carefully preserved right up until 79 A.D. It is almost as if the house constituted a sort of museum of local identity for all

Pompeiians, important for inspiring the architecture and decoration of other slightly more recent great dwellings, such as the House of Pansa, the House of the Labyrinth, the House of Menander, the House of the Silver Wedding, and the House of Obellius Firmus. This description will attempt to bring space and decoration back together, so that the house may be seen as it appeared to the ancient visitor who was invited inside.

A House like a Palace

Stratigraphic excavations undertaken after 1960 have made it clear that around the first decades of the second century B.C., the block on which the House of the Faun rose had begun to take on the appearance that it kept until the eruption. All the modest houses of the preceding period, partly visible today under room 10, were systematically

Detail of the house's beautiful garden, arranged with geometrically-placed flowerbeds.

Imposing entrance to the House of the Faun, formed by two square Corinthian pilasters.

dismantled and in their place was built a single dwelling that then occupied the entire block. The house was organized around two atriums that were unusual for their large size and architectural style, the main one being tuscanic and the secondary one a tetrastyle, and it had only one peristyle. But the most obvious difference compared to what we can see today is that there was no connection between the tetrastyle atrium and the street and there was a vast garden in the back.

This arrangement did not last long; at the end of the second century the house underwent an intense renovation that added so

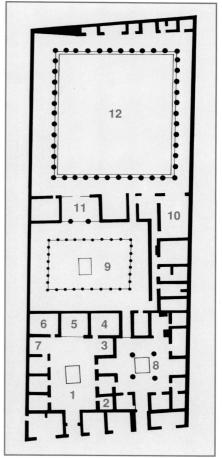

Layout of the house

1. Atrium

2. Master bedroom

3. Ala

4. Triclinium

5. Tablinum

6. Triclinium

7. Ala

8. Tetrastyle atrium

9. Secondary peristyle

10. Triclinium

11. Exedra of Alexander the Great

12. Large peristyle

The entrance and the atrium of the house, as they were reproduced in the book *Le case e i monumenti di Pompei*. Note the position of the faun, which is placed on a small pedestal at the edge of the impluvium.

221

greatly to the opulence of the floor plan and the richness of the decoration that it was never again necessary to touch it except purely for conservation. It was in this period that the tetrastyle atrium—whose private but hardly modest nature is shown by its essentially sober decoration and by its proximity to practical rooms like the bath and kitchen—was provided with a separate entrance from the street, and an exedra was built on the north side of its peristyle, which was intended as the architectural and decorative pivot of the entire house. But the most extensive alterations centered on the area till then occupied by the garden, where a second, larger peristyle arose, lined with forty-three brick columns and with living rooms opening on its south side and a series of rooms of decreasing size on its north side. Among these, in an important position, was a room occupied almost entirely by a podium, almost certainly intended to display a statue.

Detail of mosaic emblem reproduced in its entirety on a following page.

This alteration completed the monumentalization of the House of the Faun, which then became comparable, not only in size, but also in its use of internal spaces, to the most vast palatial complexes of the Hellenistic East, such as the large residences of the Macedonian king and nobility, seen in Pella, *Aigai* and Tolemaide, where the traditional distinction between the different building sectors—corresponding, according to a passage by Vitruvius, to the *andronitis*, or "men's sector" and the *gynaeconitis*, or "women's sector"—can be seen as a possible model for the strongly hierarchical structure of the spaces of this dwelling.

The expert re-elaboration of the most prestigious Hellenistic housing models in the forms of Roman domestic architecture is fully represented in the House of the Faun, where the spaces are arranged at the disposal of *clientes* and *patronus* (the tuscanic atrium), friends (the two peristyles), and family (the

Following pages:

Emblem with marine life from the triclinium to the left of the tablinum (MANN).

Mosaic in the triclinium to the right of the tablinum depicting a Dionysian guardian spirit drinking from a large transparent container while riding an animal resembling a tiger (MANN).

Detail of the face of the animal.

tetrastyle atrium and the rooms connected to it), which could be reached by different and alternate routes. The example of the House of the Faun would serve as a model for the layout of aristocratic dwellings in the late Samnitic era and would be applied in other homes with double atriums built between the end of the second and beginning of the first century B.C. As has already been noted, the architectural reconstruction was accompanied by an almost complete redecoration of the walls and especially of the floors, designed to emphasize the different uses of the spaces and at the same time provide a system of functional symbols for the image of himself the owner wished to convey to anyone who came into his home.

A Hall of Images

The walkway that connects to the vestibule of the tuscanic atrium has a lava-floor panel, similar to the floor of the atrium, a sign of the contemporary execution of both surfaces. The panel is unusual in that a series of colored limestone tiles is imbedded in it on edge, forming a phrase of welcome, "*have*," written, not in Oscan, the language used in Pompeii at the time for public and private inscriptions, some of them actually discovered in the House of the Faun, but in Latin. This preference signals the owner's desire to let his visitors know of his perfect adherence to the tight web of economic, social, and political relationships of which Rome was the center, by using a greeting expressed in a sort of international language known to all. Just past the vestibule, the *fauces*, an entrance or passage, provided the first introduction to the majesty of the atrium. On the upper part of the side walls, painted in first style and absolutely the most important example in all Pompeii, are two small symmetrical temples in relief in tufa coated with colored stucco. These can be seen as public shrines for the household gods, perfectly inserted into an entry corridor that, with its floor of colored-limestone triangles and the motif of cubes in perspective reproduced along its base molding, duplicated flooring types and decorative choices documented during that time only in the Temple of Apollo.

The passage between the fauces and the tuscanic atrium was indicated by a threshold of minute tiles in *opus vermiculatum* representing tragic masks amid grapevines and fruit. The first image encountered on the interior of the house referred, then, to the theater and its consecration to Dionysus, the divinity

directly or indirectly alluded to by other decorative elements concentrated in the atrium and the rooms facing it. Among the decorations with Dionysian subjects the best-known is undoubtedly the bronze statuette that gave the house its conventional name, discovered at the time of the excavation on the edge of the *impluvium* whose pool was decorated with polychrome limestone lozenges. As nineteenth-century drawings have shown, the statue may originally have been placed atop a small base on the northern edge of the pool. The figure is slightly off-balance, creating the effect of a dance step taken in a state of drunkenness, and it does not represent a faun, as was suggested at the time of the first excavation report, but rather a satyr, and in particular the *Skirtos*, or "leaping satyr" (Moreno, 1994). A life-size statue of this satyr appeared both in a Pergamon temple from the beginning of the second century B.C., the work of Thoinias, and in the funeral monument of Sositheos, one of the greatest authors of satyr plays, active in Alexandria in the third century B.C. Two other replicas of the statuette, from the second century B.C., found at Tanis and in the Nile Delta area, suggest that its probable archetype was created in that Egyptian metropolis. Equally elevated expressions of Alexandrian artistic crafts are recognizable in many

White marble trapeziform from the Augustan era in the shape of a sphinx, with a woman's head and a basket decorated with bas-relief palm leaves on its shoulders (MANN).

Facing page:
Polychrome mosaic emblem depicting the amorous overtures of a satyr and a nymph, from bedroom 2 (MANN).

of the mosaics that decorate the rooms facing the atrium, created by an atelier active in Pompeii between the end of the second and the first decade of the first century B.C. The master bedroom (2) showed an emblem in opus vermiculatum representing a satyr copulating with a maenad. This is yet another subject pertinent to the followers of Dionysus, to whom the mosaic of the triclinium, located to the right of the tablinum (4), was connected even more explicitly; it depicted a sort of tiger with a Dionysian spirit astride it, drinking from a large transparent receptacle. The position of these Dionysian

Atrium of the house, with the beautiful impluvium in *opus sectile* of polychrome rhomboids. Note that the bronze statue of the dancing faun is today erroneously placed in the center of the pool, while it was originally located on the marble ledge of the short side at the back.

subjects—festoons with masks, copulation between satyrs and maenads, Dionysian spirits, and the statuette of the *Skirtos*—in the most representative rooms of the home, including the tuscanic atrium, the master bedroom, and the triclinium, seems to indicate a deliberate decorative program, clearly based on the specific wishes of the one who commissioned these works, someone who, as we know from nearly contemporary Roman sources like Cicero's *Letters to his brother Quintus* (II, 5; III, 1), often intervened directly in the design and supervision of the work in the crafts shops responsible for the decoration of his property.

The mosaics decorating the alae (3 and 7) and the triclinium located to the left of the tablinum (6) seem more in keeping with the

Historic late nineteenth-century photograph from the Alinari Archive which shows clearly that there was originally no statue in the center of the pool.

Following pages:
Detail of two ducks typically found along the Nile, as shown by the lotus flower in the beak of one of the animals.

functions of the rooms for which these works were created. In the right ala (3) the central panel depicted a cat caught stealing from a pantry with two shelves, one above the other, where the delicacies intended for the guests were stored: partridges, fish, and two ducks. Here too we recognize an explicit reference to the Egyptian world, both in the iconography of the cat, documented from a tomb of the Ptolemaic period, and in the type of duck, a Nile species clearly indicated

stealing a necklace from a drawer. It is unlikely that the choice of similar subject matter for these mosaics was a coincidence. Most likely, in the same way that the decorative scheme for the floor was used to indicate the space as a banquet room (polychrome benches along the walls and a central panel), there was also a desire to recognize that the primary function of this type of room in a Roman house was to store the family's valuables, as the visible

Mosaic emblem with a cat stealing from a pantry with two shelves, with partridges, fish, and two ducks (MANN).

by the lotus flower in its beak. In the opposite wing (7), the poorly executed emblem, possibly substituted during the Imperial era for a similar panel that had been destroyed, shows instead a pair of doves in the act of

indentations for shelves and bases for cupboards in the alae of many dwellings suggest.

The mosaic of the triclinium (6) is also connected to the function of the room. Here the subject, notable for a conspicuous series of representations that carry us right up to the threshold of the Christian era, consists of a sea in which various types of fish are swimming. At first glance, the mosaic must have suggested to the dinner guests how much would be served in the banquet room and, therefore, the favor accorded by the gods of the household in which they were received. A more attentive eye, however, would have lingered on the central image of a battle between an octopus and a lobster,

with the fauces. Because of the complex social relationships in Roman society, this space, which constituted the point of contact between the *dominus*, or resident lord of the house, and the mass of persons tied to him by family connections, hospitality, and social dependence, the *clientes*, is slightly higher than the level of the atrium and is decorated with a refined floor of colored limestone cubes in perspective, a *scutulatum*. The proprietor, seated in the center of the room,

observed with particular interest by an aggressive moray eel, and certain of the guests would have been reminded of a passage in Aristotle's zoological treatise that reconstructed the food chain, pitting crustaceans against mollusks and mollusks against fish (Aristotle, *The Generation of Animals*, 8, 2, 590 a-b). The mosaic must have originally been intended to illustrate this treatise, and was perhaps made into a painting for the use of the great scholars gathered in the Museum of Alexandria.

The real architectural focus of the tuscanic atrium was the large tablinum (5) aligned

must have seemed like a sort of living effigy, an image no doubt reinforced by both the slight elevation and the type of floor, also created in Pompeii in those same years and by the same skilled workers in the cella of the Temple of Apollo, on the model of the Temple of Jupiter Optimus Maximus in Rome. The tablinum, as the client's final destination inside the house, was therefore designed as a sort of temple cella, reinforcing the majesty and sanctity of the proprietor, already established by the two little temples placed as decorations in the entryway.

The most important figurative mosaic of the ancient world comes from the House of the Faun. It represents the battle between Alexander and Darius. Composed of about a million and a half tesserae, it covers an area of around 200 square feet (MANN).

Following pages:
Detail of the face of Darius who, aware of his defeat, turns his chariot toward the enemy, followed by his army, which is already unable to resist.

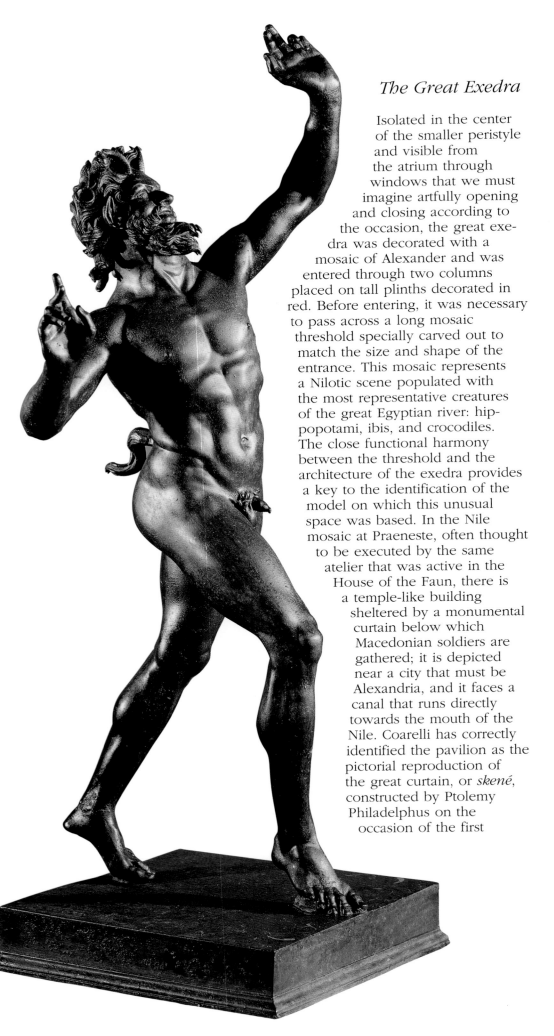

The Great Exedra

Isolated in the center of the smaller peristyle and visible from the atrium through windows that we must imagine artfully opening and closing according to the occasion, the great exedra was decorated with a mosaic of Alexander and was entered through two columns placed on tall plinths decorated in red. Before entering, it was necessary to pass across a long mosaic threshold specially carved out to match the size and shape of the entrance. This mosaic represents a Nilotic scene populated with the most representative creatures of the great Egyptian river: hippopotami, ibis, and crocodiles. The close functional harmony between the threshold and the architecture of the exedra provides a key to the identification of the model on which this unusual space was based. In the Nile mosaic at Praeneste, often thought to be executed by the same atelier that was active in the House of the Faun, there is a temple-like building sheltered by a monumental curtain below which Macedonian soldiers are gathered; it is depicted near a city that must be Alexandria, and it faces a canal that runs directly towards the mouth of the Nile. Coarelli has correctly identified the pavilion as the pictorial reproduction of the great curtain, or *skené*, constructed by Ptolemy Philadelphus on the occasion of the first presentation of the games named after his dynasty, the *Ptolemaia*, and described in great detail by Callisthenes of Rhodes (*Atheneum* 5, 196a-197c). Particularly relevant is the shape of the columns that delineate the entrance to the building, protected by a tent, possibly part of the sovereign's palace. These columns are set on a high podium, almost identical to that which supports the columns in the exedra, the color of which recalls the material metaphorically connected with the exercise of power in Egypt, porphyry.

Egypt appears prominently again on this patron's cultural horizon, and it is perhaps Egypt, or at least the figurative culture of that world, that is recalled in the most precious art work found in the house, a mosaic which reproduces the battle between Alexander and Darius, absolutely the most significant mosaic yet known representing the ancient world. Extending over an area of about 200 square feet and created using about a million and a half *tesserae*, this mosaic probably reproduced only part of a much larger easel painting, whose central area was almost entirely taken up with the direct encounter between the two rulers, protected by their respective elite militias. Our mosaic is a copy in stone of an original painting whose creator intended to render in images the pathos beloved by early Hellenistic historians, capturing the climactic moment of the entire Asiatic campaign. A furious, helmetless Alexander, charging the enemy with just a few companions, is contrasted with the disorientation and chaos of the overwhelmed Persian troops, unable to resist or to protect their own king, who is turning his huge battle chariot towards what the viewer already knows is a fate of solitude, betrayal, and death. The sources record two artists active at the end of the fourth century B.C., Helena of Alexandria and Philoxenus of Eritrea, whose fame was connected to the reproduction of the clash between Alexander and Darius. Following H. Fuhrmann's essential 1931 study, modern research generally agrees in attributing the original painting to Philoxenus. Nevertheless, even in recent years there are those who have just as persuasively argued for Helena as the author of the original painting, by pointing out a certain resemblance between the most recognizable of Alexander's companions and the first king of Egypt—Ptolemy Soter, who might possibly have commissioned the painting from Helena—and by noting the entirety of the choices made by the owner of the House of the Faun. He had a predilection, as we have seen, for subjects of Alexandrian inspiration executed by an atelier which was most likely also responsible for a cartoon of the original painting (Zevi, 1998). There are, in fact, some second-thoughts on the attribution of this isolated echo of great Hellenistic painting, which refer with equally plausible arguments to the formal innovations of Philoxenus (Moreno, 1987) or to the hand of Apelles, who was Alexander's official painter (Moreno, 2000).

The name of the painter is not the only uncertainty about the original work. The episode itself is not clear. Is it the battle of Issus, as the barren landscape and dead tree would seem to indicate? Is it Gaugamela, the decisive moment of the clash between the Macedonians and the Persians? Or is it, rather, a conflation of several battles, as the portraits and the military garb of the two rulers would suggest? Finally, there could have been several motivations for commissioning the painting: a celebration of the regency of Cassander over the young Alexander IV, if the painting is by Philoxenus; Ptolemy Soter's assumption of the title of *basileus*, if it is by Helena; praise for the heroism of one of the Persian nobles, as a suitable framework for the mixed marriages between Macedonian nobles and Persian princesses celebrated in 324 B.C. at Susa; or an official painting executed at the request of Alexander himself. The only reliable fact is the mosaic itself, which reveals in its few imperfections the artisans' perfect adherence to the painted model and in its subject the propensity of the great "painters in stone," as Pliny called them, to reproduce noble themes, a tendency ever more documented today thanks to studies of the splendid pebble mosaics at Pella and of the polychrome mosaics produced in Alexandrian territories up until the high Imperial era.

Prophetically, when Goethe saw a reproduction of the large mosaic, he predicted in a letter of March 10, 1832 that it would be vain to try to fully explain and interpret its subject. If, as we have seen, there are strong doubts about the analysis and attribution of the

original, even greater uncertainties present themselves if we try to understand what inspired the owner to make the large exedra the architectural and decorative center of his house and what imaginary thread seems to link the whole undertaking to the Macedonian king. The strong adherence to royal models elaborated in the Hellenistic East emerges not only from the house's overall floor plan, but

Facing page:
The original statue of the dancing satyr (a copy is now in situ) which shows its great refinement and overwhelming expressiveness (MANN).

Alexander the Great in a late-Hellenistic statue from Herculaneum made of bronze inlaid with silver (MANN).

Carnelian decorated with the head of a military commander, probably Alexander the Great, found in the House of the Faun on March 4, 1831 (MANN).

also from objects the owner most likely acquired on the antiques market, such as a carnelian decorated with the head of a Hellenistic ruler, possibly, as has been conjectured, Alexander himself, and found in an unspecified location in the house during the excavation of March 4, 1831.

A direct connection has been posited more than once between the choice of subjects and the family's history. One hypothesis, identifying the original as Philoxenus' painting executed for Cassander, is that the person who commissioned the work wanted to commemorate some ancestor's participation in the Third Macedonian war, fought between 171 and 168 B.C., through a reproduction of one of the most significant works of art carried to Rome as spoils of war (Fuhrmann). Nor has the possibility of a direct reference to the age of Alexander itself been excluded. Such a reference might claim a role for the family at the forefront of the Italic elites received in delegation by the Macedonian king in Babylon in 324-323 B.C.—an episode whose veracity has been seriously questioned by modern critics—or could claim a link with Alexander of Molossus, brother-in-law of Alexander the Great. Called to Italy by Tarantum in 334 B.C. to counter the threat of the Bruttians and Lucanians, and referred to in clever propaganda as "The Other Alexander," he stirred up the Italiote Greeks and their allies with a series of military campaigns that brought him to the walls of Paestum (Zevi, 1997).

The close correlation between the architecture of the exedra and its decoration also suggests another explanation. If we recognize in the layout of the room a reference to the great tent of Ptolemy II, which Callisthenes records as an actual exposition space for statues and paintings, and if we see in the reproduction in mosaic of a famous painting the persistence of an artisanal tradition going back to early Hellenism, we must not rule out the possibility that the owner wished to evoke the pomp of the Alexandrian court, famous for the refinement of its buildings facing the city of Canopus, east of Alexandria at the mouth of the Nile, and to explicitly recall it to the minds of his guests by means of the luxurious Nilotic scene on the threshold of the exedra. The multiple references to Alexandrian art and culture indicate that the person who commissioned the House of the Faun was an attentive connoisseur of that world. It is perhaps not far-fetched to see him as one of those very rich Italic and Roman merchants active in Alexandria who are recorded in two dedicatory inscriptions in Delos, dated between 127 and 99 B.C.

The reconstruction of the owner's complex personality, to the degree that we can discover it through the vestiges of his house, stops when we try to assign him a name among the eminent candidates in late Samnitic Pompeii. From what we know now, we can only offer a suggestion. As we have seen, the figurative repertory of the mosaics created for the

tuscanic atrium refers for the most part to the Dionysian world, and the bronze statuette of the *Skirtos*, the real emblem of the house even at the time of its original establishment, belongs to that same sphere. Among the discoveries in this house several inscriptions in Oscan characters, both public and private in nature, stand out. Among those of a public character there is a cornice in tufa, perhaps belonging to a larger base, for a statue in honor of a person named *V. Sadiriis*, who held the position of aedile. Whether the statue was part of the dwelling's original furnishings, being located logically in the north peristyle's display room, or was brought into the house at a later period, one is struck by a strong assonance between the Oscan name of the magistrate, *Sadiriis* (Latinized *Satrius*), and the Greek name of the companion of Dionysus, *Satyros,* who appears both in the mosaic of the cubiculum and on the statuette placed in line with the entrance. We do not know whether the *Sadirii*, like many Roman and Italic families, had elaborated a myth of origins using a pseudo-etymology based on a link between the family name and that of some mythic personage. One is reminded, for example, of the House of the Marcii, who claimed to be descended from the Marsian Silenus.

Nevertheless, what we know about the definitive arrangement of the principal atrium takes on much sharper outlines if we look at it as part of a family legend beginning with a mythic ancestor whose memory the family retained in their own name. With the two temple-shaped shrines to household gods placed in the entrance, and with the tablinum, which reproduced a temple cella in a domestic space, there was an obvious intent to strongly emphasize the sacredness of a dwelling belonging to a family that might boast a semi-divine origin and close ties to a great divinity like Dionysus, whose power was evoked explicitly in one of the large mosaics in opus vermiculatum. The tragic masks, which probably recalled a contract for the funding of a theatrical production during the magistrature of one of its members, immediately evoked the world of the theater dedicated to Dionysus, whose origin was directly connected to the god's companions. Finally, by setting the refined statuette of a dancing satyr right in front of the tablinum and displaying a satyr copulating with a maenad in the mosaic of the matrimonial chamber, the *Sadirii* placed in front of everyone images that would remind them of the myth of the family's founding.

Fabrizio Pesando

Mosaic with tragic masks from the main atrium (MANN).

House of the Diadumeni or of Epidius Ruffus (IX, 1, 20): First to Fourth Style

This dwelling, named after the two freedmen who dedicated a splendid marble *lararium* in the east wing of the atrium to their patron Marcus, opens onto Via dell'Abbondanza with an uncommon architectural element, an extremely high podium reached by means of two staircases located at the ends of the facade. The facade was set back in relation to the houses around it, and the building's isolation from the street was completely contrary to the habit of placing masonry benches along the facades of aristocratic houses— where the *clientes* could sit while waiting to be received by the patron of the house— or of greeting visitors with welcoming inscriptions. It has few parallels in the Pompeii area. Among the exceptions are the Gladiator Barracks, organized around a large peristyle with a complicated building history, and the House of the Mosaic Doves, a sort of urban villa, built across a section of the city's south walls.

Traces of an earlier habitation are still quite visible along the facade to the right and the left of the entrance, where two tall portals, framed by jambs of limestone ashlar masonry, have been walled-up. Furthermore, limited excavations made in the area of the servants' quarters, opening onto the *andron*, a men's chamber or dining hall, leading to the garden, have brought to light earlier structures originally belonging to the adjacent house (I, 1, 12). Among these one finds part of a room decorated with a floor of inlaid colored limestone dating to the end of the third century B.C. The construction of the house in the form we see today goes back to the last years of the second century B.C. This can be seen from the remnants of first-style decoration inside a later fourth-style painting, the decorated capitals crowning the entrance portal, and the pilasters at the entrance to the exedra facing the atrium, as well as from the floors in the residential rooms, made of *cocciopesto* in the bedrooms and in the exedra and of white tesserae in the oecus and the tablinum.

Compared to traditional Pompeii housing styles, the House of the Diadumeni is an extreme anomaly, illustrating a rare type of dwelling with a Corinthian atrium recorded by Vitruvius, the model for which was the aristocratic house common throughout the Hellenistic world. Among the spaces that deviate from the normal organization of Roman houses, the one that stands out above all is the entrance, where we can recognize an unusual vestibule, called a *prothyron* by Vitruvius (6, 7, 5). In general the arrangement of the entryway in most houses in Pompeii was fairly simple: from the sidewalk, one entered single or double doors into a long corridor, the fauces, which opened at the end onto the atrium. Other cases have been documented in which actual vestibules occupied the front part of the fauces, indicated by two jambs on the lateral walls framing the entrance threshold and set back with respect to the perimeter wall. By contrast, in the House of the Diadumeni and a dozen others as well, the entrance has a much more complicated design, with two doors of different widths placed at right angles, which afforded access to the fauces by different passageways. From a functional viewpoint, this kind of entrance guaranteed more privacy, keeping the house interior from public view. This is in contrast to the rule often observed in Roman homes, where considerable care was taken to favor the visual axis between the fauces and the tablinum, which was usually located just inside the entrance.

Facing page:
Marble lararium in the east ala of the atrium, dedicated to their patron, Marcus, by the two freedmen to whom the house owes its name.

Detail of one of the figured capitals placed as decorations on the entrance portal and on the square pilasters of the exedra facing the atrium.

View of the Corinthian atrium from the tablinum.

Facing page:
Group of the *Ludovisi Ares* in a reconstruction proposed by Filippo Coarelli (Roman National Museum in Palazzo Altemps, Rome).

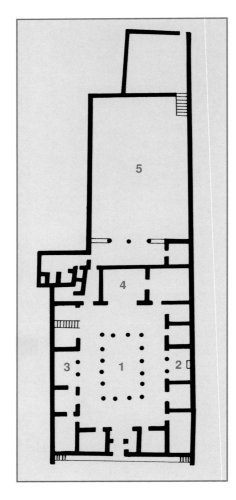

Layout of the house

1. Corinthian atrium
2. Ala with the lararium
3. Ala
4. Tablinum
5. Hortus

Closing the house to the exterior, on the other hand, was characteristic of Greek architecture. In homes of the classical age at Olynthus and Athens, for example, the entrance was never along the middle axis of the dwelling, and residential rooms like the andron and the *thalamos*, which was a chamber or woman's bedroom, were almost always hidden from the view of visitors. And in the most refined Hellenistic houses of Delos, the presence of a closed vestibule with a door at the point where it opened into the *aulè*, or forecourt, was the norm. This is therefore quite different from a rich Pompeiian *domus* of the late Samnitic period such as the House of the Faun, where, as we have seen, the owner used the atrium of the house and in some cases the vestibule itself as a backdrop for his self-aggrandizement.

Past the entrance, the House of the Diadumeni has a sumptuous colonnaded atrium. Considered by Vitruvius one of the five types of courtyard found in Roman houses of the Republican period, the Corinthian atrium betrays its Hellenistic origins in the arrangement of numerous columns around the pool of the *impluvium*, faithfully following the appearance of peristyles in Greek dwellings. The choice of a Corinthian atrium as an architectural focal point reveals the owner's desire to redefine himself explicitly by emulating the most sumptuous Greek urban residences. The impluvium was surrounded by sixteen Doric tufa columns, six on the long sides and four on the short ones. Despite being located on an axis with the most interior part of the fauces, the tablinum of the house was partially hidden from this observation point by the two central columns of the north portico and, because of the distance between the two spaces, must have given the impression that the tablinum, corresponding to an exedra, was furnished with two columns *in antis*.

Arranged at the center of the main axis of the atrium, according to a pattern documented in few other dwellings in Pompeii, the two alae had the form of Ionic distyle exedras. Both wings had low openings which communicated with the adjacent bedrooms. At the time of the eruption, the only one of these passageways which had been preserved was the one connecting the first bedroom to the west and the exedra; the other three had been closed off during the dwelling's last building phase. An architectural scheme that projects a colonnaded exedra, onto which smaller spaces open at the sides, seems to recall an organization of residential space characteristic of palatial Macedonian architecture as documented in the Palace at Vergina. Here, however, it is

seen on a reduced scale and with the variant of direct communication between the smaller rooms and the peristyle. This scheme is also seen in peristyle I of the Palace of Pella and in the organization of the west side of the main peristyle of the Palace of the Columns of the Ptolemies.

The impression that this is a reduced-scale replica of a Hellenistic palace was finally emphasized by its exuberant architectural decorations, not limited, as in other cases, just to the facade. In fact, figured capitals decorated both the pilaster strips framing the prothyron—one of which has representations of a sphinx and a gryphon—and the corner half-pilasters of the two exedras. On the capitals of the exedra, as in other rich houses of the late-Samnitic city, there are figures representing satyrs and maenads. Only the scene on the south capital in the west wing does not belong to the Dionysian world. On it, in fact, is sculpted a couple accompanied by a cupid. Normally these figures would be identified as Mars and Venus, but the extraordinary resemblance between this small relief and the group of statues that according to Coarelli decorated the Temple of Neptune near the Circus Flaminius in Rome, the statues called the *Ludovisi Ares* and Thetis, opens the possibility that the scene represents a melancholy Achilles, whose mother, accompanied by Eros, has just given him the weapons forged by Hephaestus for his last, fatal battle with Hector.

Organized as it was around a large Corinthian atrium and provided at the back with a vast private area without architectural ornamentation, where a vegetable garden was planted, the House of the Diadumeni betrays more than any other dwelling in Pompeii the decision of the original owners to choose the best possible example of a private Hellenistic building as the model for their lifestyle. If they—as we have good reason to suppose—belonged to a branch of the Nucera *gens Epidia*, who claimed their origins from an ancestor deified through the intervention of a local divinity—the River Sarno—it is not surprising that they would choose to build a house inspired by the royal Hellenistic palaces, very near the heart of the civic center.

Fabrizio Pesando

House of the Labyrinth
(VI, 11, 9-11): First to Second Style

The House of the Labyrinth stands out amid the panorama of rich homes of this period. Its architectural elements are of high quality, and it represents one of the few houses in which it is possible to follow the changes in the design of living spaces that took place among the local elites in the city just after the settlement of the Sulla colony. It is also possible to identify the owner who was primarily responsible for the appearance that the house retains today.

In fact, very few urban dwellings show extensive signs of construction and decorative renovations during the delicate phase of institutional passage from an autonomous city to a colony. From the documentation in our possession, it seems that the new citizens of Pompeii, regardless of rank, generally chose to live in the agricultural properties assigned to them. This meant, in the case of members of the higher social classes, very rich villas like the villas of the Mysteries and of Diomedes, and villas at Boscoreale, Terzigno and Oplontis. In the case of the lower classes, it meant modest farms such as Villa Regina, the rustic villas of Terzigno, and the Villa of the Prisco Estate. Beginning in the sixties B.C., as an alternative to the large residential complexes and modest structures situated within agricultural properties, there was a return to building activity inside the city. Instead of the traditional living spaces located close to the main public areas like the Civic Forum and the Triangular Forum, this phase seems to have favored the peripheral zones, especially the south and west borders of the lava plain stretching out toward the sea (Blocks VIII, 2 and VI, 17). There, reinforcing a tendency already seen in the late second century B.C., multistoried residential complexes were built on top of the city walls. No longer needed as bulwarks, the walls now served as the substructure for quiet, calm living spaces.

In this situation, with so few examples, the identity of the house's owner takes on more significance. During an excavation completed in 1980 in an underground room, a sort of

Detail of a second-style decoration in the opulent Villa of Poppea at Oplontis.

cellar that had not been explored during the nineteenth-century digs, a 50-libra travertine weight (about 37.5 pounds) was discovered, bearing an inscription with the name of the house's owner, P (ublius) Sex(tilius) (Rufus). This person, very well-known in the city during the age of Nero, when he twice held the position of aedile and was then elected to the office of duovir quinquennalis, descended from one of the first magistrates of the colony, that very L. Sextilius P. F. Rufus who, together with his colleagues in office, appears in the dedicatory inscription for the altar of the Temple of Apollo (*CIL* X, 800). The social position and political role of L. Sextilius Rufus are perfectly mirrored in the layout that the House of the Labyrinth assumed between 70 and 60 B.C., thanks to work undertaken primarily in the residential quarters facing the peristyle.

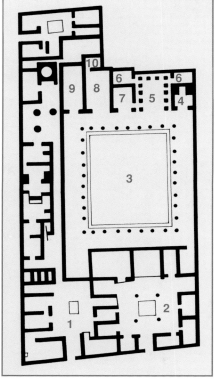

Layout of the house

1. Tuscanic atrium
2. Tetrastyle atrium
3. Peristyle
4. Bedroom
5. Corinthian oecus
6. Sitting room
7. Master bedroom
8. Exedra
9. Oecus
10. Small room

Atrium of the monumental tetrastyle type. As the layout of the house shows, this dwelling had a secondary atrium of the tuscanic type.

The house as it appears today has the form of a double atrium, the main one a monumental tetrastyle and the second one tuscanic, with a peristyle in the back and an independent servants' quarter accessible through a long corridor, which also led directly to a small bath. As demonstrated by both the type of Corinthian-Italic capitals on the columns in the main tetrastyle atrium and the preservation of almost all the first-style paintings in the large tablinum, this dwelling dates from the Samnitic

period. An analysis of the wall structure has confirmed that the first construction phase goes back to the end of the second century B.C., when an earlier garden was enlarged at the expense of at least two bordering dwellings, with a surface area corresponding roughly to that of the small house (VI, 11, 8) which was also absorbed by this large patrician residence and used from then on as lodging for the *procurator*, or estate manager. During the time of the large peristyle's construction, the triclinium and tablinum of the tetrastyle atrium were also rearranged, and the tablinum was furnished with a large window looking out on the garden. From this construction phase we can recognize only parts of the old first-style decoration under the more recent paintings in the small room (10) and the bedroom (7), while the floor of the oecus (9) was preserved without alteration. It is of cocciopesto decorated with small black-and-white crosses and dates from

Facing page:
Corinthian-Italic capital from one of the columns in the main tetrastyle atrium.

An early building phase of the peristyle dates from the end of the second century B.C. and involved the annexation of land once occupied by at least two adjacent houses.

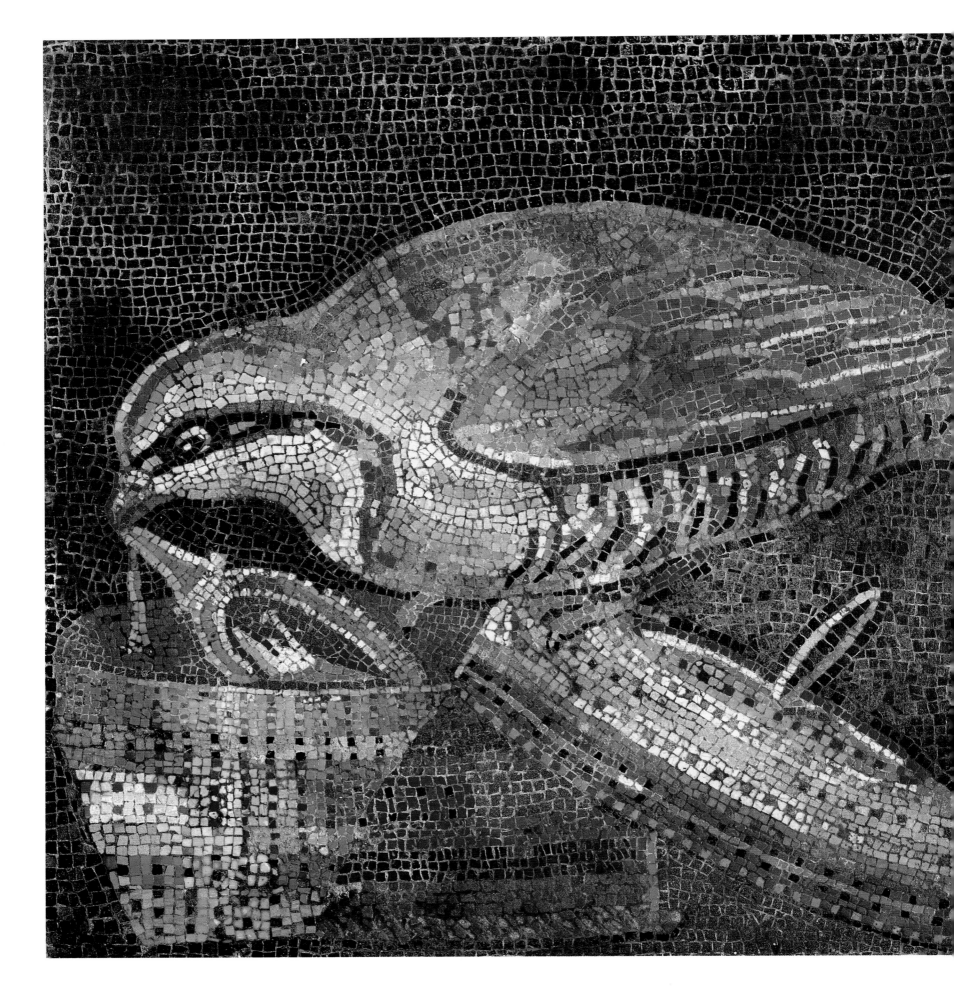

Preceding pages:

Polychrome mosaic emblem depicting a partridge stealing a mirror from a wicker basket; from one of the two rooms connected to the Corinthian oecus (MANN).

Another polychrome mosaic emblem with a cock fight, an obvious reference to struggle and victory. The fight takes place in the presence of two youths (MANN).

Facing page:
Detail of labyrinth motif mosaic with Theseus and the Minotaur.

Labyrinth motif mosaic in the master bedroom; in the center is a square depicting the fight between Theseus and the Minotaur.

100-80 B.C., the oldest example of this type of ornate pavement in the area.

Almost certainly because of the serious damage caused in this part of the house by projectiles launched by war machines during the Sulla siege, it was necessary to make drastic repairs to the peristyle, where new columns replaced the damaged ones, and to almost all the open areas on its north side, which were decorated around 70 B.C. with paintings and floors with emblems in opus vermiculatum and in second-style tessellated polychrome. The structure of this residential section was particularly opulent and innovative; the architectural focus was a rare Corinthian oecus (5) which communicated with two small rooms, and next to which two large master bedrooms were arranged symmetrically. Two other rooms, an exedra (8) and an oecus (9), enclosed the northwest corner, giving the whole space the characteristics of a true residential suite. This would become a genuine model for rich houses in Pompeii; in an almost identical form, it would be imitated in the middle of the first century A.D., more than a century later, in the House of Meleager.

Particular attention was paid to the floor and wall decorations in these spaces, true jewels of the early second style. In the two small rooms that communicated with the Corinthian oecus were emblems in polychrome mosaic representing, respectively, a cock fight in the presence of two youths and a partridge stealing a mirror from a basket, iconographic variants of one of the mosaics in the House of the Faun. This last subject is well suited to a woman's bedchamber, while that of the room opposite, with its reference to struggle and victory, seems appropriate for a masculine room. According to a recent hypothesis, these emblems may have been moved from an earlier location in the house. The large Corinthian oecus, held up by ten Corinthian stucco-coated brick columns, is notable primarily for the ornamental richness of its paintings, real architectural scenes behind which open foreshortened views of sacred buildings and princely palaces. The sobriety of the simple white tessellated floor, separated from the columns by a refined polychrome maze motif, helps direct the spectator's gaze towards the painted walls; the sole sign of luxury is the precious emblem of colored marble arranged in a basket-weave pattern, put in place here fifty years after the execution of the rest of the decoration, perhaps to replace an earlier one that had been destroyed.

In the room to the east of the Corinthian oecus, a bedroom (4) distinguished by an antechamber and alcove, the second-style decoration is more sober in its reproduction of architectural elements and is enlivened only in the fake ashlar of the alcove's central zone by a series of divine figures and personifications of benign demons. In the eyes of those who discovered the house, however, the most representative room seemed to be the large west master bedroom (7), where they found a splendid mosaic with an emblem in the center representing the battle between Theseus and the Minotaur, framed by the labyrinth motif that gave the house its conventional name. The person who commissioned the work must have intended for the subject represented in the center of the floor to be integrated with the painting on the side walls, where two giant Tritons standing on the prows of ships, one with an oar in his hand and the other blowing into a shell used as a bugle, were silhouetted against an architectural background.

An interesting reading suggests that the emblem may commemorate the victory of the Romans, symbolized by Theseus, over the

Samnites, whose animal-totem during the Social War had been a steer. Others have seen in the painting an allusion to the occupation of the patron, who may have been an arms manufacturer or an official of the military fleet. The first interpretation is problematic because of the frequent appearance of this subject, of which there are many replicas, and above all by the relative obscurity of the message, for few visitors are likely to have grasped the allusion to the Roman victory over the Samnites. The possible reference to the owner's economic or military activities in the figures of the marine monsters may have a stronger basis, especially considering that in that same period parts of ships appear in pictures and mosaics found elsewhere in Pompeii. Among these are pictures of ship prows seen in the house of N. Popidius Priscus, those represented in the atrium floor of another house (VI, 17, 10), and finally, a splendid mosaic in the *caldarium* of a house in Cirta, dating from the middle of the first century B.C. and attributed to Campania workmen, where heaps of weapons appear displayed as trophies alongside the bows of ships.

Events contemporary with the decoration of this space could provide a frame within which to view the choice of subjects: the years from 70 to 60 B.C. were in fact dominated by the insecurity of the Italic coasts because of frequent incursions by pirates, who managed to brutally attack flourishing urban centers such as the ancient Latin colony of Cosa and to destroy a military fleet moored at Ostia, which was the port for Rome. It is no coincidence that one of the four triumphs celebrated in Rome by Pompeius in 61 B.C. was the victory over the pirates, which guaranteed the safety of commercial traffic and, above all, the steady availability of wheat for the populace. These two works of art, in which the valor of a hero like Theseus overwhelms monsters such as the Minotaur or reduces them to gigantic helmsmen in the form of Tritons, would therefore have marked the path to a tranquil and civilized world, in which one could lead a peaceful life.

Fabrizio Pesando

House of the Silver Wedding (V, 2, 1): Second to Fourth Style

Fourth-style fresco decoration in the House of the Silver Wedding.

The large tetrastyle atrium with a rectangular impluvium and four Corinthian columns in grey tufa, onto which at least eight rooms opened.

The House of the Silver Wedding, which opens onto an irregular street parallel to the large *decuman*, or main east-west axis, of Via di Nola, is one of the most remarkable examples in Pompeii of a dwelling with an atrium and a double peristyle. The enormous space occupied by the dwelling is in fact organized into three distinct sections of roughly equal size: an atrium, a peristyle in

the Rhodes style, and a *xystus*, or garden. Each of these represents a complex elaboration of a certain architectural type. In its present state, the house has the form it assumed after a series of renovations conducted between the middle of the first century B.C. and the middle of the first century A.D., but more thorough study has made it possible to reconstruct the original appearance of the dwelling, going back to the last years of the second century B.C.

The atrium is of the tetrastyle type. Originally opening onto this atrium were the large alae, the tablinum, two *triclinia* flanking the tablinum, and eight additional rooms, one on each of the short sides of the fauces and three on each of the long sides. The width of the atrium and the presence of very tall Corinthian tufa columns supporting the roof beams present an extremely valuable example that allows us to imagine the appearance of those patrician Roman dwellings in which the large atrium columns—in Rome made of marble from Asiatic quarries—were considered the most impressive sign of the wealth of the house's owner, because they were displayed in the place traditionally intended for greeting clients, which was thus transformed into a sort of royal hall. Detailed analyses of the walls of the open spaces on the east side of the atrium have made it possible to reconstruct the most unusual aspect of the original plan of the House of the Silver Wedding, altered in part by the renovations mentioned above. For example, on entering the first room, which was near the atrium and had the traditional appearance of a bedroom, a visitor actually found himself in a sort of exedra, which opened into a garden on the other side. The result of this architectural solution was the insertion of a powerfully Hellenistic element—a garden with one or more exedras, evoking the atmosphere of a gymnasium—into an apparently conventional house plan with a tuscanic atrium.

There is probably no more important evidence in Pompeii of the cultural compromise the late-Samnitic aristocracy made between tradition and innovation in their way of life within the domestic space. These aristocrats managed both to cultivate the ancient institution of patron and client, which relied on the scale and hierarchical arrangement of the spaces located around the atrium, and to evoke, with the peristyle and gardens, the cultural model of a lifestyle by then recognized as superior and more refined. In the form visible today, this refined projection is scarcely perceptible. Between the late Republican era and the first century A.D., the elimination of many rooms facing the atrium, the creation of a second floor above the open

The oecus with its four octagonal columns on square bases which support a coffered barrel vault. The room is decorated with second-style frescoes.

Peristyle in the Rhodes style. In the background can be seen the columns of the north portico, which are taller than the others to create a greater separation from the spaces facing it.

spaces on the long side of the atrium, and the transformation of the ancient impluvium into a pool with a fountain, did in fact profoundly transform this sector of the house, making it into a sort of gigantic vestibule for the peristyle behind it.

This is a peristyle in the Rhodes style with a portico facing south, punctuated by Doric tufa columns, and it is taller than the other rooms, in order to create a greater isolation from the spaces facing it. This type of peristyle, obviously of Hellenistic origin, is extremely rare, not only in Pompeii, but even in Greece itself. It has been documented only in this house, the House of the Golden Cupids, the House of the Dioscuri, and *domus* V, 2, 10. It probably represents an architectural element confined to and typical of houses in Rhodes, which spread to the West perhaps because the Romans of the late Republican era knew the island directly as the seat of one of the most famous schools

of rhetoric in the ancient world, frequented by many members of the Roman aristocracy. The large open oecus in the southeast corner of the peristyle and the large garden that occupies all the space east of the atrium and peristyle contribute to the strongly Hellenistic appearance of this part of the house. The oecus is divided into an antechamber and a room in which four octagonal columns on square bases support a coffered, barrel-vaulted ceiling. Here we have another, rather unusual architectural style, the *oecus tetrastylus*, a sort of smaller version of the richer Corinthian room, in which more columns ran along three sides of the room. In this part of the dwelling, too, around the middle of the first century B.C., a rather important series of renovations took place, which, unlike what we have seen in the atrium, did not measurably alter the original plan. In fact, the main renovation consisted of redecorating almost all the rooms with lavish second-style paintings, which are among the most noteworthy found to date in the city. The only structural intervention that stands out can be seen in the addition of baths along the western side. The last modification of note had to do with the columns and the porticoes, which were refurbished with paintings in the fourth style. We can date this renovation with certainty as having taken place before the rebuilding in the house following the earthquake of 62 A.D., because of a graffito written on the central tufa column in the north portico listing the names of the consuls elected in 60 A.D.

The only decorative element in the large garden worthy of note today is a summer triclinium built of masonry located at the center of the west side, in front of which is a pool with a water jet. This little leisure spot, very characteristic of houses in Pompeii after the middle of the first century A.D., took the place of an earlier four-sided portico punctuated by octagonal columns of concrete stuccoed in red and very similar to those of the tetrastyle oecus. The close affinity with the columns of the tetrastyle oecus allows us to date the enlargement of the garden as 40 to 30 B.C., placing this building within the large renovation in those years which altered the original architecture of the dwelling in many places. The complete absence of spaces directly facing this sector and its structural affinity with similar floor plans in suburban villas such as the Villa of the Papyri in

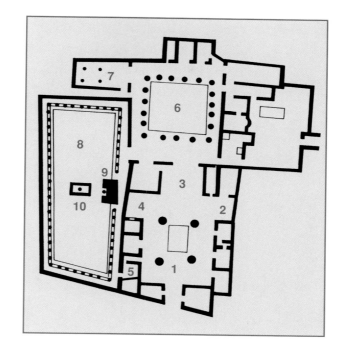

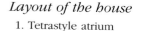
Layout of the house
1. Tetrastyle atrium
2. Ala
3. Tablinum
4. Ala
5. Room with lararium
6. Rhodes peristyle
7. Tetrastyle oecus
8. Porticoed garden
9. Summer triclinium
10. Fountain with water jet

Herculaneum and the Villa of Poppea at Oplontis argue for considering this garden to be a xystus, which reproduced the appearance of that part of a Greek gymnasium that was a covered promenade. Beginning at least with the early Imperial era the small house (V, 2, *e*) also belonged to this dwelling. Based on what has been documented in the House of Menander, this was probably the residence of the *procurator*, or estate manager.

Maria Paola Guidobaldi

Around the middle of the first century B.C., the entire House of the Silver Wedding was rebuilt and beautified with second-style paintings in almost all the rooms.

House of the Cryptoporticus and of the Ilion Sanctuary (I, 6, 2 and 4): Second to Fourth Style

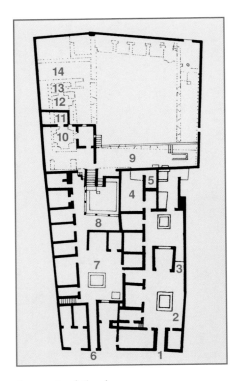

Layout of the house

1. Entrance to the House of the Ilion Sanctuary
2. Atrium
3. Room of the Ilion Sanctuary
4. Room of the Elephants
5. Red bedroom
6. Entrance to the House of the Cryptoporticus
7. Atrium
8. Interior courtyard
9. Cryptoporticus
10. Caldarium
11. Tepidarium
12. Frigidarium
13. Apoditerium
14. Oecus

These two adjacent houses have a troubled building history. Over the course of three centuries they were frequently separated and combined, depending on changes in ownership, until a final change in function a little before the eruption of 79 A.D.

In the late second century B.C., two originally independent houses facing Via dell'Abbondanza were unified into a single living complex, extending to the southern edge of the block with a porticoed garden on the north, west and east sides. The garden, the width of both houses, presented a unique architectural solution to the problem of a difference in level between the north and south sides of the block: the north portico acts as an elevated loggia, which creates both a direct passage between the two dwellings and a

On this page and opposite:
Small fresco paintings with parts in stucco illustrating episodes from the Trojan War. The choice of such subject matter shows the strong interest in the story of Troy that developed a short time after the publication of the *Aeneid*.

pleasant vista onto the garden below. The paucity of decoration in the atrium belonging to the entrance of number 4, which remained a common feature of this part of the house even in successive building phases, gives a strong indication that this part of the dwelling was intended as the service sector, while the area surrounding the adjacent atrium must have from then on represented the residential quarter.

Around 40 to 30 B.C., the porticoes of the garden were transformed into a large *crypto-porticus*. The main access to this new sector of the dwelling was through a door in the long south wall of the house, followed by a vestibule guarded by a porter's lodge, an obvious sign of its autonomous function in relation to the rest of the dwelling. The construction and decoration not only of

257

Fresco decoration from the House of the Ilion Sanctuary.

the cryptoporticus, but also of the new rooms facing it, among which those concentrated on the east side stand out, belong to the same renovation phase as this zone. Here we find the thermal system, including the *apodyterium*, the *frigidarium*, the *tepidarium*, the *caldarium*, and the large *oecus*, which closed off this side from the vaulted corridor. On the other hand, what was probably the *laconicum*, built at a later time, was near the entrance.

Of the rich late second-style decorations in these spaces, only a few pictures survived up to the time of the eruption. In the apodyterium, or dressing room, panels representing Mars, Venus, and a scene referring to the feminine world were inserted within an architectural framework on the south wall, while a rural scene occupied the wall opposite. In the frigidarium two large identical architectural backdrops on the south and north walls set off panels in the lower section representing a maenad, a rural cult scene and a satyr, and in the upper one paintings with scenes from feminine life. The walls in the large oecus are punctuated by herms with garlanded satyrs and maenads. In the upper registers are a series of still-lifes, or *xenia*, and scenes that may refer to the Dionysian world in general or, more likely, to rites of initiation. Polychrome and black-and-white mosaic floors were coordinated with the paintings in these rooms, and one that stands out in particular is the floor of the oecus, which involves two different designs, separated by a threshold of polychrome

squares. The one near the entrance is a mosaic with a black ground into which colored stones have been inserted, and the one in the other part of the room is of travertine chips on a black ground. In the cryptoporticus, above a large center strip of red panels separated by herms with satyrs and maenads, were scenes with captions in Greek illustrating the events of the Trojan War. These must have been read like an ancient scroll, beginning from the left wall as one entered from the south entrance of the house. This cycle reveals a strong interest in the events of Troy in the years immediately preceding the publication of the *Aeneid* and takes its themes from the *plurimae tabulae* representing episodes of the Trojan War, written by Theoros and placed in Rome in those same years by L. Marcius Filippus, Octavian's half-brother, in the *porticus* that took its name from him.

In the residential sector of this new arrangement of the house there was also a separate and especially sumptuous area, which allows us a close look at the Roman notion of an "ideal living space" so often sketched in literary sources. It is a series of rooms decorated with second-style paintings and floors, situated near the interior courtyard of the owner's sector, originally open at that time onto the loggia of the garden, and including an antechamber, a large oecus with a megalograph, called the Room of the Elephants, and a bedroom connected to it which, because of the color of its paintings, was called the Red Bedroom. The isolation of

Fresco near the entrance of two elephants with cupids holding reins of myrtle, the plant sacred to Venus. Unfortunately, the frescoes were already severely damaged at the time of their excavation.

these rooms and their scenic opening onto the garden below show strong affinities with what we know about spaces reserved for study and reading, both in residential villas of the late-Republican era and, in Pompeii itself, in several of the so-called urban villas built during these same years over several sections of the city walls, among them the House with the Library (VI, 17, 42), which shows significant architectural and decorative similarities with this house. The impression that this was an area in which the owner's cultural activities took place and were celebrated is reinforced by the decoration found in the Room of the Elephants. The vast space was divided in two parts by a mosaic threshold in a scroll motif and by wide pilaster strips painted on the walls to mark the passage from a zone characterized by more simple decoration, close to the porticoed loggia, to a much more elaborate zone of the same quality as the entrance to the room from the

immediately fell on two gigantic elephants in heraldic postures on either side of a candle-stick and led by two cupids using branches of myrtle, the plant sacred to Venus, as reins. This leads us to interpret the scene as an allegory of the power of Venus, who was defined by Lucretius in almost the same years as the execution of this fresco as *sola gubernatrix rerum naturae*, or "sole ruler of the things of nature," (Lucretius, *De Rerum Natura*, I, 22). The intellectual life is represented in the part that decorated the north wall, unfortunately found in the worst possible state of preservation: in the presence of a muse identified as Urania, two robed figures, seated on chairs, are deeply absorbed by a celestial globe. Although the overall reading of the painting is clear, it is difficult to establish the identity of the two figures meditating on the secrets of the cosmos. Because of the absence of a beard, the smaller figure seated to the left of Urania is probably a poet and,

Detail of the oecus in the House of the Cryptoporticus, frescoed with herms of maenads and, in the upper section, with small still-life paintings *(xenia)*.

internal courtyard, where a rich box-motif floor contrasted with the megalograph painted on the walls.

The terrible state of deterioration in which the paintings were found at the time of the excavation made it difficult to recognize the figures that made up the megalograph, which we can still assume must have been read as parts of a single theme. In front of the entrance to the room the spectator's eye

in particular, a poet famous for having drawn his inspiration from the study of the cosmos. He is obviously Aratus, the author of *Phaenomena*. The larger figure, also clean-shaven, is harder to identify. It may well have represented the owner himself, absorbed in one of his favorite intellectual activities and presented in the guise of a scholar alongside the high priest of the cosmos, Aratus, whose renown in the Roman world at the time is demonstrated by the numerous Latin versions of his work, translated by such exceptional members of the nobility as Cicero, Varro, and Germanicus. The intent of this juxtaposition would have been to characterize the owner as a member of the Alexandrian "Pleiades," the most refined cultural circle in the Hellenistic world.

The hall's west wall, which was shorter because of the space taken up by the entrance to this room and to the bedroom,

Lararium in the peristyle of the House of the Cryptoporticus, with a bust of Hermes in a niche and an agathodaimon, or good-luck serpent.

contained a painting of which only one large figure remains, a seated muse with a scroll in her hand. She is surely Clio, the muse of history. It seems possible, therefore, to identify two related themes in the megalograph: the house owner's representation of himself as a scholar of earthly and heavenly subjects—history and astronomy—and the subordination of creation and of human acts to the dominion of Venus, who in the very years when this hall was decorated was becoming ever more visible in the new world order inaugurated by the most famous descendent of the Julian family. The rich floor decoration in red hexagons and the walls in large panels of the same color suggest that the small bedroom connected to this hall by means of a narrow door was the most important resting place in the house. The two small, erotic Dionysian scenes that decorate the upper part of the alcove on a level with the foot of the

bed clearly indicate what other function this space performed.

After the earthquake of 62 A.D., the houses were separated again, creating the two living spaces known as the House of the Ilion Sanctuary (4) and the House of the Cryptoporticus (2). On many of the walls the evidence of these modifications is still visible today. Separating the two houses meant that in the house whose entrance was at number 4 the original opening to the loggia above the cryptoporticus from a group of rooms to the south had to be closed off. All of these spaces were then added to the House of the Cryptoporticus, enclosing a large masonry triclinium intended for summer banquets. The small atrium belonging to number 4 was completely rebuilt in the form of a tetrastyle atrium, no doubt because of the serious damage it had sustained. Many rooms in the House of the Ilion Sanctuary were redecorated with fourth-style paintings. Finally, the cryptoporticus was transformed into a cellar, where the paintings that until then had been the pride of the late Republican-era renovation were left to deteriorate. Nevertheless, at the time of the eruption, the work in both houses was still far from finished. Except for a large lararium and the summer triclinium, all the rooms in the House of the Cryptoporticus still had unpainted walls. In the House of the Ilion Sanctuary a small brick-kiln, set up in a large room that opened onto the interior courtyard, testified that here too the decorative renovations remained unfinished.

Even after the separation, the two houses maintained the different levels of opulence that had been a constant in all the preceding periods. The most important rooms are still in House I, 6, 4. There, next to a deep tablinum, is the small room transformed into the so-called Ilion Sanctuary, which very probably already existed in a different form in the preceding period. Here, one of the paintings from the Trojan cycle in the cryptoporticus was replicated in an abbreviated form on a fourth-style stucco frieze. It is the scene representing the preparation and final outcome of the duel between Hector and Achilles, a probable sign that the last descendants of the owners of the entire complex lived in this house. A representation in stucco of a lunette with Selene's visit to Endymion, a medallion located at the center of the vault depicting the abduction of Ganymede—a clear allusion to the attainment of immortality—and a tiny flock of alabaster doves discovered in the sanctuary all give sufficient evidence that this space functioned as a *sacrarium* dedicated, at least in the last phase of the house's life, to the cult of Venus. All these themes taken together, evoking immortality in their mythological subjects and the heroic cult in their celebration of Hector, the divinity chosen to protect the house, in addition to the small room's probable function as a sanctuary for the celebration of the family cults, could have alluded to the mythic origins of the inhabitants of the house, who may have belonged to one of those *familiae Troianae* that arrived

celebrated in front of everyone, in fact, through the learned references to Homer and Troy. Subjects of mysterious character that, as such, appear to have been connected to the feminine sphere were relegated to the more private rooms, the baths and the oecus that connected to it. Finally, in the Room of the Elephants, open to few guests, the large mega-lograph indicated the cultural foundations of the owner's piety. Among the few dwellings in Pompeii endowed with a cryptoporticus,

Frieze and barrel vault in stucco in the Ilion Sanctuary.

in Latium with Aeneas after the destruction of Troy, and whose complex genealogies were reconstructed by scholars of the Augustan age like Varro, Atticus and Hyginus.

Despite the intense renovations that greatly altered the structure of the house, the appearance it took on during the second-style phase seems to have been intended to suggest to visitors a microcosm enclosed in a few hundred square yards. In the cryptoporticus and in the sacrarium—if we assume that this was always the function of what we call the Ilion Sanctuary—the antiquity of the family line was

an architectural feature widespread in the grand noble villas of the period, House I, 6, 2–4 thus bears witness to an ambitious decorative program subordinate to the functionality of the spaces, in which it is possible to discern references to the occupants' piety, the exaltation of their presumed origins and their celebration of the spiritual.

Fabrizio Pesando

The Third Style: c. 20 B.C. to c. 50 A.D.

House of Julius Polybius (XI, 13, 1-3): First, Second, and Third Style

During the last phase of the city's life this house belonged to the descendants of the Imperial freedmen C. Julius Polybius and Julius Philippus. It contains many striking elements of interest: its unusual organization, unique to date, even amid the many examples in Pompeii; the great expanses of its oldest decoration that have been preserved; and finally, the extraordinary amount of

Facade of the house on Via dell'Abbondanza

Facing page:

Fresco of Mars armed with sword, helmet and shield in the center of the west wall in the bedroom at the back of the south portico.

Detail of the large fresco *Punishment of Dirce*, a theme from Euripides that was very popular in the Julio-Claudian age.

Atrium of the House of Julius Polybius showing the impluvium and the floor made of river stones. In the background is the peristyle.

Faux double door painted to correspond to an earlier opening that was later walled over.

information regarding various aspects of domestic life that surfaced during the excavation, which was completed between 1964 and 1977 using sophisticated modern methodologies. The floor plan of this house, built on a plot that had remained vacant until then, dates from the years between the third and the second centuries B.C., and it is therefore contemporary with those of other dwellings built along the stretch of Via dell'Abbondanza between Via Stabiana and Via di Nocera. Furthermore, in its front section the house mirrors the look, though not the proportions, of dwellings found in this part of the city. This section turns out to have been created by combining two vaulted atriums of almost identical dimensions, with the long side parallel to the front on the street side and open spaces only along the *fauces* and in the back. To increase the number of rooms available for reception and services, two more courtyards were interposed, each with an *impluvium*, between the vaulted atriums and the three-armed peristyle at the end of the house. Following the reconstruction already completed during the second century B.C., the dwelling also boasted an upper floor that almost doubled its area.

The house's plain facade, decorated in first-style ashlar, was originally interrupted

263

Facing page:
Detail with a flying *Victory* in the bedroom at the back of the south portico.

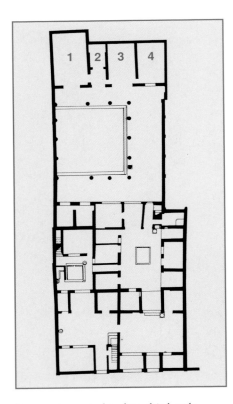

Rooms decorated in late third style. Several of these rooms had ceilings with pronounced coffers and *specchiature*, frames of smooth or carved wood (1, 2, 3, 4).

only by two entrances crowned with elegant cornices. The east entrance (number 3) led to the entertainment area, made up of two atriums located in a row, which were larger and more lavishly decorated than those accessible from the west entrance (number 1). Despite a number of structural and decorative changes that took place in the home during its long occupation, a good part of the first-style decoration is still visible in the vaulted east atrium, only partially nicked on the lower part by restoration work, which had barely begun at the time of the eruption. In fact, the old painting is preserved both in the high part of the fauces, originally flanked by two rooms that opened toward the interior, and in that of the atrium, presenting in this area several compositional characteristics that can be associated with a renovation

completed only a few years after the dwelling was built, adding a habitable floor.

As in other Samnitic-era dwellings of a certain tone, the passage from first to second style was marked in this house by a small but significant change in the function of the atrium. Because it had another space of the same type behind it, it apparently then took on the appearance and function of a large vestibule. In fact, the faux two-panel door painted on the north-west stretch of the wall belongs to this same period; it originally opened onto a room whose entrance was then rotated 180 degrees, and whose internal walls were then decorated with simple second-style painting.

The center room at the back, which was at a higher level than the atrium and had a floor decorated in first-style cocciopesto placed on a slight incline, created a passageway

East side of the peristyle with columns stuccoed in yellow.

between the two atriums in the entertainment area of the house. Living and sleeping rooms, almost all redecorated with rather ordinary third-style painting, were arranged around the small interior courtyard, in which several traces of the old first-style decoration are still visible. The peristyle was finally reached through a narrow andron bordered by a lararium niche. On the west side it had a false portico composed of stucco half-columns attached to the wall, following a decorative technique that has also been documented in the late second century B.C. in the House of the Figured Capitals (VII, 4, 57). The rooms most representative of the dwelling (1, 2, 3,4) were located at the end of the garden, which at the time of the eruption was planted with fruit trees. These rooms document a coherent third-style decorative renovation in the middle of the Claudian era, which it seems reasonable to attribute to the house's acquisition by descendants of rich Imperial freedmen like C. Julius Polybius and C. Julius Philippus. In several of these rooms, careful excavation has also made it possible to reconstruct the ceilings, which were coffered and had pronounced *specchiature*, frames of smooth or decorated wood. Although the overall quality of the painting was not very high, the decoration of the large winter triclinium (1), in the midst of renovation at the time of the eruption, was distinguished by great refinement. Rough plaster had already been spread on one section of the walls, in fact, while part of the earlier third-style decoration had been intentionally preserved, above all the central painting with various episodes from the *Punishment of Dirce*, a theme from Euripides which had become very popular in the Julio-Claudian period, especially because of its translation into statuary in the famous group known as the *Farnese Bull*, today exhibited in the National Museum of Archeology in Naples.

The owner's desire to display his own sophistication to his guests had even pushed him to frequent the antiques market, acquiring objects that would elicit admiration and amazement. In the large triclinium (1), in fact, were found, carefully hidden, a bronze statue of Apollo used as a lamp-base, a beautiful second-century B.C. krater with mythological images, and a very interesting bronze hydria with a dedication to the Argive Hera dating from 460-450 B.C., probably adapted earlier as an urn for ashes.

The west sector of the house was much more modest. A large room located to the left of the fauces had been used in the oldest

Facing page:
Detail of the face of the bronze statue of Apollo found in the large triclinium along with numerous other furnishings of refined workmanship.

Bronze statue of Apollo, used as a lamp holder (MANN).

Bronze krater from the second century B.C. with mythological images (MANN).

period as a shop open to the street and made its commercial function apparent even from the outside. In this vaulted atrium, illuminated only by tiny windows on the western street side, closed with iron grates, there was the foundation for the stairs to the upper floors. Thanks to a wooden gallery, these floors faced not only the arched east atrium, but also the rear courtyard with its impluvium. The second service atrium, reached on the ground floor through an andron created on the left out of a sort of tablinum, represented the heart of the domestic activities, with a big kitchen, preceded by a painted lararium whose paint had been restored shortly before the eruption. It represents a sacrificial rite being celebrated in the presence of two large *Lares* by a bearded old man in the guise of a *genius*, or household

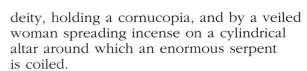

deity, holding a cornucopia, and by a veiled woman spreading incense on a cylindrical altar around which an enormous serpent is coiled.

Fabrizio Pesando

266

House of Marcus Lucretius Fronto (V, 4): Third to Fourth Style

Atrium and tablinum of the House of Marcus Lucretius Fronto.

Located in a marginal sector of the city, the House of Marcus Lucretius Fronto opens onto an eponymous lane, not yet fully excavated, perpendicular to Via di Nola. Although the dwelling's architectural layout, whose overall dimensions seem rather modest (about 5,000 square feet), does not demonstrate particu-

larly noteworthy techniques, the wall decorations, on the other hand, catch our attention as some of the most refined examples of the late third style, which recent studies attribute to the Claudian era. The owner of the house, identified thanks to four electoral advertisements painted on the exterior and to a

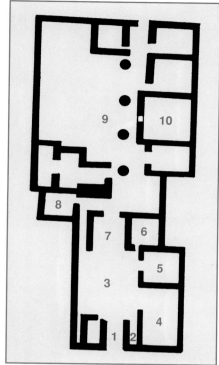

Layout of the house
1. Fauces
2. Storeroom
3. Atrium
4. Winter triclinium
5. Bedroom
6. Bedroom
7. Tablinum
8. Room
9. Peristyle
10. Exedra

Fresco with Mercury, recognizable by his wide hat and the caduceus.

graffito with his name written in the garden, was an important personage during the age of Flavius: a candidate for *aedile* and for *duovir quinquennalis*.

The first building phase we can document with certainty is from the second century B.C. Among the few materials belonging to the preceding period and found during stratigraphic tests conducted by the Dutch School, fragments of Attic ceramics and of bucchero ware and a terra-cotta votive apple stand out. This would seem to suggest the presence of a rural sanctuary in this zone of the city, similar to the one that preceded the establishment of the House of the Etruscan Column (VI, 5, 17), or to the one we can locate between the annexes of House VI, 14, 12,

documented to date only from one limestone votive column imbedded in a later wall.

The floor plan we observe today is the result of transformations verified over time, traces of which remain evident in the wall strata. In fact, in the second century B.C., the house probably consisted only of what is today the west sector, the one arranged around the atrium (3), which also seems to have been planned with rooms on its north side. Construction of the east side, centering on the peristyle (9), seems on the other hand to have begun only during the early Imperial age, perhaps at the expense of a housing unit behind the House of Marcus Lucretius Fronto which opened onto Via dei Gladiatori. The raising of the floor in several rooms in the

Following pages:
South wall of the tablinum, in which the typical arrangement of third-style painting is easily recognized.

Details of small paintings of seaside villas.

269

west zone of the dwelling would also date from this same period.

A series of more or less extensive reconstructions recognizable in the walls can be attributed to activity following the earthquake of 62 A.D., while an amphora full of limestone stored under a stairwell gives evidence of work in progress in the garden area at the time of the eruption, seventeen years later.

As noted above, the paintings, with few exceptions, all belong to the late third style and have been identified as the production of a single workshop, which aimed for and obtained decorative variations in the different spaces that were appropriate for their diverse functions and dimensions. The most representative spaces are the atrium (3) and the tablinum (7). One can fully appreciate how the decoration, which in the atrium consists of serial and repetitive motifs that can be rapidly perceived, takes on an extreme refinement and becomes a sort of picture gallery in the tablinum, a sitting room that lends itself to analytic observation (Scagliarini, 1998). All the characteristics proper to the late third style are magnificently exemplified here. The walls, whose third-style painting recovered the solidity that had been lost with the perspective breakthroughs of the second style, are divided

Detail of the fresco depicting the discovery of the love affair between Ares and Aphrodite. The scene takes place in the palace of Ares when Helios, the figure in the center with wings on his forehead, comes upon the lovers. It is Helios who will inform Hephaestus, the husband of Aphrodite, with disastrous consequences.

North wall of the tablinum. In the center, the myth of Ares and Aphrodite.

into three vertical segments: a wainscot, a middle area, and an upper section, with the middle section divided into wide panels that house medallions or paintings with mythological subjects. Through the pictorial phase documented in the house, we can recognize today an ever-increasing complexity in the elements that subdivided the panels of the middle zone and a progressive reduction in the dimensions of the paintings in the middle panels.

A thorough study conducted by E.M. Moormann has contributed to the identification of several different hands within the workshop engaged in the decoration of the house. While the simple decorations of the fauces (1), the store-room (2), and another room (8) were most probably entrusted to apprentices, the hands of two painters are clearly discernible in the decorative scheme of the tablinum (7), the bedroom (5), and the atrium (3): one used large and quick brushstrokes, and the other

bedroom (6) and one in the peristyle (9) are worthy of note. In the first room, which is clearly a bedroom for children, a heart-rending scene of filial piety stands out on a splendid yellow-gold ground, *Perona Overcoming Her Modesty and Feeding Her Father Micone at Her Breast, so that He Will Not Die of Hunger in Prison*, as the distich caption informs us. The second, on the other hand, has on its walls a lively scene of *paradeisos* with domestic animals chased by lions, bears and panthers,

Facing page:
Fresco of Narcissus looking at himself in the water of a stream.

Fresco of *Perona Overcoming Her Modesty and Feeding Her Father Micone at Her Breast, so that He Will Not Die of Hunger in Prison*, a touching scene of filial piety.

used finer brushes and was much more attentive to detail. Finally, the four mythological paintings that adorn the walls of the tablinum (7) and the bedroom (5), *Aphrodite and Ares, Dionysus and Ariadne, Theseus and Ariadne,* and *The Toilette of Aphrodite*, must be credited to the hand of an expert *pictor imaginarius*, a painter specializing in representations of mythological subjects and portraits.

Among the paintings belonging to the fourth-style decorative phase, one in the

in homage to the fashion of the time which gave particular attention to the open spaces of dwellings. As in the most noted examples documented in the House of the Little Fountain and the House of the Bear, these narrow green areas were transformed into exotic and luxuriously decorated spaces thanks to landscape paintings of hunting scenes, in some cases embellished by fountain niches ornamented with precious mosaics made of vitreous pastes.
Maria Paola Guidobaldi

House of Meleager (VI, 9, 2): First to Fourth Style

Between the end of the second century B.C. and the middle of the first century A.D., a series of great houses arose along Via di Mercurio, the large street whose exceptional width of over sixteen feet reveals its earlier function as the *cardo maximus* of the north-west quadrant of the city, which is today known as Region VI. All the houses visible today along the two sides of the street in fact show a richness of design and decorative apparatus that has few rivals in other zones of Pompeii, so that the term "noble quarter of the city," coined by the first scholars of Pompeii, is still justified, despite notable changes in our knowledge through successive discoveries in the excavations of the areas surrounding Via dell'Abbondanza. The formation of this residential zone took place gradually, however, as we are reminded by facades in limestone ashlar belonging to dwellings of modest size dating from the third century B.C., which became part of more vast living complexes following the annexation or disintegration of earlier properties. Several houses with prized designs date from the late second century B.C. Among these, the House of the Large Fountain (VI, 8, 20-22) and the House

Corinthian oecus in the House of Meleager.

Facing page:
Decoration of the tablinum: in the center painting is a drunken Silenus held up by two satyrs, with cupids in the painting below. The panels of the side niches house figures in a classicizing style, and the outer ones show figures stepping through half-closed doors (MANN).

276

of the Silver (VI, 7, 20-22) are notable for their double atrium plans and for several architectural schemes used in their interiors. The first has a secondary atrium of the unusual Corinthian type, while in the second the residential quarters were organized around a tetrastyle atrium supported by Ionic tufa columns, accessible from a monumental vestibule punctuated by two Corinthian columns in the same material, truly unique in Pompeii, and culminating in an elegant *cenaculum*, or dining hall, extending above the whole back side.

Other houses preserved only some parts of their oldest floor plans. Among these are: the House of the Centaur, where to the right of the *fauces* it is possible to admire the most notable bedroom with a first-style alcove documented in Pompeii; the House of the Dioscuri, in which the Corinthian-style atrium was surrounded by a veritable forest of columns; and House VI, 7, 25, whose tetrastyle atrium, almost unrecognizable today because of the modifications the house underwent at the time of the expansion of the adjacent House of Apollo, was accessible through an entrance beautified by extremely elegant jambs of the Italo-Corinthian type. Between the end of the Republican era and the early Imperial age, other homes show signs of intense renovation. In fact, the nearly definitive floor plans of the Naviglio, Anchor, Dioscuri and Centaur houses all date from this period and would undergo

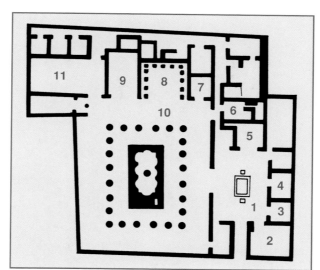

Layout of the house
1. Tuscanic atrium
2. Residential room
3. Bedroom
4. Bedroom
5. Tablinum
6. Bedroom with double alcove
7. Triclinium
8. Corinthian oecus
9. Exedra
10. Peristyle with swimming pool
11. Oecus

few variations in the course of the inevitable rebuilding that took place after the earthquake. In this case too, we note a pursuit of innovation in architecture and—to the extent that we can still perceive it—decoration. Residential spaces organized around a cryptoporticus as in the House of the Anchor, or with double peristyles as in the Dioscuri and Centaur houses, have few rivals in the rest of the city and show in a particularly useful way the wealth, culture and taste of the local ruling class of the time.

The last building fever to seize this small neighborhood took place in the second half of the first century, in the years immediately

Another example of an architectural perspective with stucco figures in relief in the tablinum (MANN).

preceding and following the earthquake of 62 A.D. This often involved partial but significant reconstructions that, besides requiring a complete decorative renewal with fourth-style paintings and floors, introduced the rooms that more than any others are linked to the spirit of the upper classes of the time. These were the gigantic *cenationes,* or dining halls,

that immediately take us back to the world of Trimalchio as described by Petronius, a society whose hedonism stood in the way of any value system independent of the empty, ritualized ovservance of norms and behaviors made obligatory by the model of Rome.

The House of Meleager provides a good example of a dwelling from this period. The

Meleager and Atalanta after the hunt for the monstrous boar that Artemis had unleashed to kill Aeneas, Meleager's father. This fresco is from the tablinum of the House of the Centaur (MANN).

Marble table from the atrium of the house with gryphon-claw feet on which traces of red were found (MANN).

conventional name of this house, in which Wilhelm Jensen set his 1903 novel *Gradiva*, comes from a painting preserved on the north wall of the vestibule that contains a very common fourth-style subject: *Meleager and Atalanta*. Meleager led the heroes who liberated Calydon from the monstrous boar that Artemis had sent to punish Meleager's father Aeneas for the offense of failing to honor her during a sacrifice.

In place of the traditional *impluvium,* the house, of the type with an atrium and peristyle, introduced into the tuscanic atrium a precious fountain pool in marble. Except for the floor of *cocciopesto* with sparse white tiles and colored limestone chips, the furnishings visible today in the room are in fact from the Imperial period. They include small pilasters faced with fragments of marble slabs, originally furnished on the front with a bronze mask used as a water spout, and a table, also of marble, which had trapezoidal legs and gryphon-claw feet, and on which there were traces of red at the time of the discovery. The enormous peristyle, having eight by six columns faced in white and red stucco, and uncovered north of the atrium, was situated

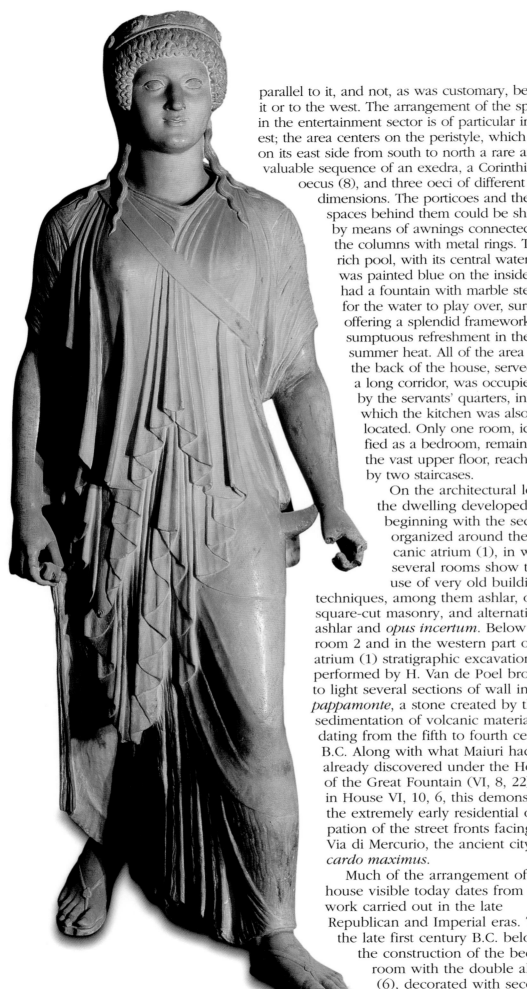

parallel to it, and not, as was customary, behind it or to the west. The arrangement of the spaces in the entertainment sector is of particular interest; the area centers on the peristyle, which has on its east side from south to north a rare and valuable sequence of an exedra, a Corinthian oecus (8), and three oeci of different dimensions. The porticoes and the spaces behind them could be shaded by means of awnings connected to the columns with metal rings. The rich pool, with its central water jet, was painted blue on the inside and had a fountain with marble steps for the water to play over, surely offering a splendid framework for sumptuous refreshment in the summer heat. All of the area to the back of the house, served by a long corridor, was occupied by the servants' quarters, in which the kitchen was also located. Only one room, identified as a bedroom, remains of the vast upper floor, reached by two staircases.

On the architectural level, the dwelling developed beginning with the sector organized around the tuscanic atrium (1), in which several rooms show the use of very old building techniques, among them ashlar, or square-cut masonry, and alternating ashlar and *opus incertum*. Below room 2 and in the western part of the atrium (1) stratigraphic excavations performed by H. Van de Poel brought to light several sections of wall in *pappamonte*, a stone created by the sedimentation of volcanic material, dating from the fifth to fourth century B.C. Along with what Maiuri had already discovered under the House of the Great Fountain (VI, 8, 22) and in House VI, 10, 6, this demonstrates the extremely early residential occupation of the street fronts facing Via di Mercurio, the ancient city's *cardo maximus*.

Much of the arrangement of the house visible today dates from the work carried out in the late Republican and Imperial eras. To the late first century B.C. belongs the construction of the bedroom with the double alcove (6), decorated with second-style tesselation; this work

caused a reduction of the space of the tablinum (5) and modification of the floor above it, which was perhaps occupied until then, when it was transformed into a bedroom, by a cenaculum of the same type as that which was instead preserved to the end of its building history in the nearby House of the Silver (VI, 7, 20-21). The probable expansion of the oldest nucleus of the house toward the north also belongs to this period. The most notable modifications took place during the Imperial era, when a suite of entertainment rooms was built on the east side of the peristyle, and the functions of the alae opening onto the atrium were modified, changing them into bedrooms. Among the spaces in the suite that opened onto the east side of the peristyle, the Corinthian oecus,

282

located between an exedra and a triclinium, is especially noteworthy. This and that of the House of the Labyrinth, dating from 70 B.C., are the only examples of this type of room documented in Pompeii, and it is an indication of a pursuit of original architectural schemes in planning this sector of the house. Much less original, but altogether in line with the spirit of the times, is the open oecus in the north-east corner. Of gigantic proportions, with a floor space of almost 650 square feet, it was decorated with fourth-style painting of rather careless execution in the secondary decorative sections: the lower section decorated with plants and the frame held up by nude male figures. On the other hand, more precisely rendered paintings decorated the center of the walls; the best preserved one,

visible only at the bottom, represented an erotic theme fairly common in the repertory of fourth-style painting, the Judgment of Paris.

Along with the paintings already mentioned belonging to the atrium, many other pictures detached from various rooms of this house are preserved in the National Museum of Archeology in Naples. In particular, besides the painting of Ganymede and Zeus's eagle and that of Hermaphrodite and Panisco, originally from bedrooms 3 and 4, respectively, one notes an architectural perspective in painted stucco with figures in relief: *Dionysus Drunk, Hylas and a Nymph, Actaeon Attacked by His Dogs*, etc. This relief completed the upper zone of the walls decorated with fourth-style painting in the tablinum.

Maria Paola Guidobaldi

Facing page:
Artemis, an important character in the myth of Meleager and Atalanta, in a white marble statue from the Augustan era, which came from the small domestic sanctuary of House VII, 6, 3 (MANN).

Fourth-style frescoes in the oecus (11): the central painting of the facing wall depicts the *Judgment of Paris*.

House of Apollo (VI, 7, 23): Fourth Style

Facing page:
Garden of the House of Apollo, excavated between 1830 and 1840.

Layout of the house

1. Cella penaria
2. Triclinium
3. Kitchen
4. Staircase
5. Courtyard
6. Tablinum
7. Fauces
8. Room
9. Room
10. Summer triclinium
11. Garden
12. Bedroom

Between 1830 and 1840 the excavators uncovered a house at the north end of Via di Mercurio which they named "of Apollo" because of the repeated mention of this divinity on both the wall decoration and the sculptural furniture.

The living plan has a rather irregular form because of the enlargements to gain space for the gardens that were undertaken in the first century A.D., following which the floor area extended to the north end of block VI, 7. Even the sector with the tuscanic atrium was significantly modified: originally lacking side rooms, a characteristic shared with the other houses on this block, the atrium was in fact later furnished with rooms 9 and 8, taken away from the adjacent house VI, 7, 25 and accessible by two steps because they were at a higher level. Passing through the tablinum (6), decorated during the time of Nero with paintings such as *Aphrodite Enthroned* and *Wounded Adonis* and medallions of female busts and cupids, or through the fauces (7), one reached a small courtyard (5) occupied by the precious pyramidal fountain, faced with marble and decorated with statuettes, vases in relief, bas-reliefs, and two-headed herms. The west side of this sector of the house is dominated by the large

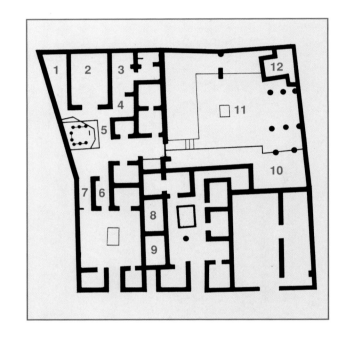

triclinium (2), floored in *opus sectile* of polychrome marbles and flanked by the *cella penaria* (1), and by the kitchen (3), with other service rooms and the stairs to the upper floor (4) adjoining. The most noticeable and

Fourth-style decoration in one of the bedrooms (12) characterized by striking polychrome. The covering of the wainscot with faux marble was never completed, as with the upper zone, which was probably covered with drapery. In the middle zone, on the other hand, the decoration centered on the mythology of Apollo.

Wall mosaic from the garden (11) showing Achilles recognized by Odysseus at Skyros.

characteristic sector of this beautiful *domus* is the garden (11), arranged on two levels and originally belonging to House VI, 7, 25, which had a tetrastyle atrium of the monumental type and was intensely reworked just around the time these spaces were annexed to the House of Apollo. The lower level of the garden is occupied by a large, square flower-bed with a marble fountain containing small angular Corinthian columns and steps to create a water cascade. To the north, on the other hand, opens a summer triclinium (10), paved in

mosaic and covered with a double-sloped roof held up by columns and half-columns and decorated on the back wall by three niches. Near the summer triclinium and in the bedroom located on the opposite side (12), there remain sparse traces of the wall decoration with birds and plants on a red ground, embellished with a coating of false rock and mosaic in vitreous paste.

Of the three mosaic paintings that were discovered on the walls of the garden (11) on April 2, 1839, in the presence of the

Wall mosaic of *Achilles Hurling Himself against Agamemnon*, removed from the walls of the garden (11).

"August Sovereign [Ferdinand II, King of the Two Sicilies], accompanied by his son, Prince Carlo, as well as Prince Leopold and the Princess of Berry," two were detached in June of that very year by the artist Piedimonte and his son. These wall mosaics in polychrome vitreous tiles, framed with shells, are preserved in the National Museum of Archeology in Naples, and they represent, respectively, the *Three Graces*, painted according to a Hellenistic technique that would last throughout the ancient era, and *Achilles Hurling Himself against Agamemnon*, who is seated on a throne in all his royal majesty, with a crown and scepter. The third painting remains on site, on the west wall of the west portico, south of the door to the bedroom (12). It shows Achilles recognized at Skyros by Odysseus: at the center is Achilles with his sword and shield, on which the hero is represented next to the centaur Chiron; on the right is Odysseus and on the left, terrified, one of the daughters of King Lycomedes of Skyros, probably Deiadamia, from whose union with Achilles Neoptolemnus would be born. This subject, replicated in Pompeii in ten or so small pictures inserted into fourth-style paintings, apparently derives from an original by Atheneon of Maronea, a painter of the late-classic age (Pliny, *Natural History*, 35, 134) who was particularly successful during the time of Nero. We owe a re-elaboration of the original, in fact, to the hand of the painter Fabullus, whose work predominated in Nero's *Domus Aurea*. This painting, which can still be admired today in the hall of Nero's royal palace called "of Achilles at Skyros," served as a genuine model for spreading this type of painting to many of those Pompeii dwellings that renewed their decoration after the earthquake of 62 A.D.

Maria Paola Guidobaldi

House of the Tragic Poet (VI, 8, 3.5): Fourth Style

Layout of the house

1. Atrium
2. Tablinum
3. Bedroom
4. Triclinium

An important turning point for the excavations in Pompeii occurred thanks to the direct interest of Queen Carolina, wife of King Joachim Murat, and had long-lasting effects even after the end of French reign in Naples. Between 1824 and 1838, F. Mazois published his prestigious study *Les ruines de Pompèi*. Employing a completely innovative scientific rigor compared to earlier and often useless erudite studies by the Herculaneum Academy, Mazois detailed not only what had been brought to light by the excavations up to that time, but also facts about the lives, customs, and culture of Pompeii. At the same time, following a praxis instituted beginning with the "French" period, the excavations continued to remain open for visits by scholars, antiquarians, learned persons and the ever more numerous educated travellers for whom Pompeii now became an obligatory destination

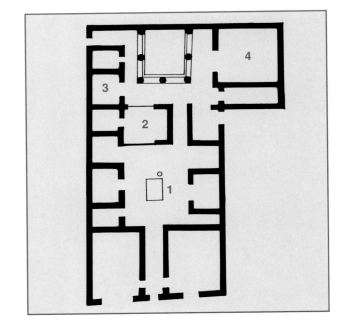

View of the peristyle with the lararium in the background.

on the Grand Tour. Numbered among these were artists, men of letters, and writers, many of whom, with their thoroughly romantic sensibilities, saw in the destroyed city a perfect backdrop for the depiction of human affairs set in the distant past, but inspired by sentiments and vices that were close to the present.

In 1825 Giovanni Pacini composed an opera with a libretto by L. Tottola, *The Last Day of Pompeii*, which premiered at the San Carlo in Naples on November 19 of that same year, with sets by A. Niccolini. In 1834 Edward George Bulwer-Lytton published the most famous modern novel about Pompeii, with an almost identical title, *The Last Days of Pompeii*, but with a completely different plot. His story, centered on the forbidden love between Glaucus and Ione, the perfidy of the Egyptian priest Arbaces, and the self-destructive but belated generosity of Nydia, inspired countless scenarios set in antiquity. It also furnished the ideal locale for many a cinematographer, from the pioneering film by R.W. Paul in 1898 to the strongly innovative "special effects" of E. Rodolfi in 1913, to the rich transposition in a version directed by D. Gallone and A. Palermi in 1926, up to the most recent television abridgments. But at the time of its publication, the novel's real innovation was to place its characters in a city that had been brought back to life for a short time only, setting the plot in motion only days before the city's final destruction and oblivion. To provide a precise setting for the action, Bulwer-Lytton chose as the residence of his refined protagonist a dwelling that had been excavated only a few years earlier, in 1824-25, and discovered almost intact with its rich furnishing of paintings, floors and precious objects. Among them were two splendid gold *armillas*, or bracelets, shaped like serpents, discovered on November 10, 1824 in the excavation of one of the two workshops that opened at the front of the house. In this dwelling—with a regular floor plan and modest dimensions, whose decorative apparatus was extensively

Detail of the polychrome mosaic emblem found in the tablinum, which gave the house its name and which depicts the rehearsal of a chorus for a satyr play (MANN).

Preceding pages:

Detail of the face of Juno in a fresco on the south wall of the atrium; it depicts her wedding to Jupiter, which was celebrated on Mount Ida.

Detail of the face of Briseis in a fresco on the south wall of the atrium.

The entire fresco, which shows Achilles handing over Briseis, who is brought into the presence of Agamemnon's heralds by Patroclus (the figure seen from the back) (MANN).

rebuilt and renovated after the earthquake of 62 A.D.—the writer's minutely detailed descriptions allow us to recognize the House of the Tragic Poet, whose name derives from the polychrome mosaic emblem in the tablinum (2) which shows a chorus rehearsing for the production of a satyr play. That mosaic is now in the National Museum of Archeology in Naples, together with the painting *Admetus and Alcestis* from the same room and many other paintings detached from the walls of the atrium (1).

This atrium was decorated with six large paintings representing episodes from the Trojan War, which were detached in 1836 after having been sketched by Francesco Morelli, one of the official artists in Pompeii from 1791 on, who was alone in also paying attention to the decorative context of each painting.

Beginning with the south wall, arranged in an order independent of the narrative sequence of events, the following scenes unfolded:

1) the *Wedding of Jupiter and Juno* (cfr. *The Iliad*, XIII, 225 *passim*);

2) *Venus [?] with a Dove at her Feet, Gathering a Branch of Myrtle;*

3) a scene variously interpreted as the departure of Cressida, restored to her father by Agamemnon after the pestilence inflicted by Apollo on the Achaean camp (cfr. *the Iliad*, I, 310), or as the abduction of Helen;

4) *Achilles Handing over Briseis to Agamemnon's Heralds* (cfr. *The Iliad*, I, 345);

retained the cocciopesto floor from the end of the first century B.C., the entire upper part of the walls contained a valuable frieze depicting a battle between Greeks and Amazons, clearly based on classical friezes and known today only through Morelli's tempera renderings. In addition to a beautiful black and white mosaic with a central emblem of interlacing circles and semicircles enclosing fish and ducks, the triclinium (4), which was the most representative room in the whole dwelling, displayed a wall decoration with architectural frames supported by caryatids, as well as a black wainscot and a frieze with centaurs and marine monsters, today barely discernible in what remains of the preparatory sketches scratched into the plaster.

Maria Paola Guidobaldi

Fresco from the north wall of the portico in the peristyle, showing Iphigenia, Agamemnon's daughter, being sacrificed so that the Greek fleet can sail for Troy (MANN).

The fauces of the house was guarded by a mosaic dog, with the inscription *cave canem* (MANN).

5) *Poseidon and Amphitrite;*

6) an almost completely vanished battle scene, fortunately reproduced in part in a watercolor.

Bulwer-Lytton writes:

On one side of the atrium, a small staircase admitted to the apartments for the slaves on the second floor; there also were two or three small bedrooms, the walls of which portrayed the rape of Europa, the battle of the Amazons, etc.

You now enter the tablinum, across which at either end, hung rich draperies of Tyrian purple, half withdrawn. On the walls was depicted a poet reading his verses to his friends; and in the pavement was inserted a small and most exquisite mosaic, typical of the instructions given by the director of the stage to his comedians.

You passed through this saloon and entered the peristyle; and here (as I have said before was usually the case with the smaller houses of Pompeii) the mansion ended. From each of the seven columns that adorned this court hung festoons of garlands: the centre, supplying the place of a garden, bloomed with the rarest flowers placed in vases of white marble, that were supported on pedestals. At the left hand of this small garden was a diminutive fane, resembling one of those small chapels placed at the side of roads in Catholic countries, and dedicated to the Penates; before it stood a bronzed tripod: to the left of the colonnade were two small cubicula, or bedrooms; to the right was the triclinium, in which the guests were now assembled.

This sector of the house was richly decorated as well. In bedroom 3, which has

House of the Vettii (VI, 15, 1.27): Fourth Style

A Museum within Pompeii

There are various reasons that the House of the Vettii has become the most famous of all the Pompeii dwellings of the Imperial age: the extraordinary state of preservation in which the building was found at the time of the excavation, completed between 1894 and 1896 under the direction of G. De Petra; the

A cupid riding a crab, from the atrium of the House of the Vettii.

high level of the fourth-style paintings and the considerable number of sculptures and marble furnishings; the possibility of identifying its last owners—the rich freedmen A. Vettius Restitutus and A. Vettius Conviva, the latter a member of the important college of the Augustali—whose names were carved on two seals found near the *arcae*, or chests, located in the atrium; and finally, several "special" aspects of the house, like the discreet little peristyle and the small room in the service area used for prostitution. But all these elements would not necessarily have made this house an obligatory stop on every trip to Pompeii. Other houses excavated during the nineteenth century, such as the House of the Faun, had equally exceptional discoveries, and these did not rescue them from progressive abandonment and from being emptied of their most significant decoration and all their furniture.

The rescue and the fame of the House of the Vettii were due above all to the new direction given to the excavations after the unification of Italy. The decision to preserve the decoration and furnishings of buildings on site and make them useful to the public, by this time a huge number of visitors, provided a tangible symbol for the shift in control over the excavations from the Bourbons to the new Kingdom of Italy. From being the Bourbon king's private property, accessible in the early days only through the sovereign's courtly permission, and open to the public without precise regulation only after 1848, it now became a place of culture for the entire community, where the most modern methodologies of excavation and restoration could converge. No longer an inexhaustible mine for the collections of the King of Naples and his titled guests, it was now an archeological park, in which the topographic and structural contexts could integrate the history, the artistic expressions and the daily life of the ancient Pompeiians. The House of the Vettii was, as noted, the major beneficiary of this new use of archeology as an instrument of royal policy. The excavations, the

A corner of the bedroom (3) used by the house porter, with a frieze depicting various types of fish and marine life in the upper zone.

Wall with fourth-style painting in the triclinium (2). The central picture depicts the fight between Ares and Pan.

restoration, and the publication were effected rapidly and accurately, and a few years after the discovery the house was protected by a roof, at first partial and then extending over all of its considerable area, giving visitors a precise idea of the ancient dimensions for the first time.

With the conclusion of the restoration of the house in 1898, the prediction made fifty years earlier by G. Fiorelli, director of excavations between 1860 and 1875 and then general director of Antiquities and Fine Arts until 1891, came true: "In Pompeii a house will be completely restored; its paintings will have been created by the local artists. Objects found there will be put back in their places, and if bones are found, the skeletons will be reassembled. This house will be shown as the model of a Pompeiian house."

Some Architectural Details

The house plan was probably determined by its position within the block, whose entire short southern side it occupied, situated

Atrium with a view of the peristyle behind it.

Facing page:
Wainscot with painted cupids.

296

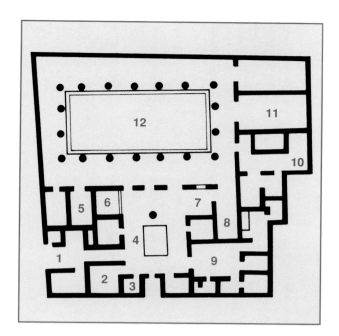

larger (Beck, 1980). If we attribute the unusual structure of the atrium to the last building phase of the house in the Imperial age, the traditional tablinum, present up to that time, would have been suppressed in favor of building a complete peristyle, an indispensable area in any house of rank at the time (Archer).

The decision to suppress the space would have been determined by the ancestry of the last owners, generally believed to have been responsible for the rearrangement of the house, rather than by the architectural norms of the

perpendicular to its main axis. The impossibility of extending beyond the block's perimeter wall and the need to guarantee a hierarchy of space in which, according to the dictates of the time, the greatest possible emphasis must be reserved for the peristyle, probably caused several significant departures from traditional architectural norms. The house was organized around four main nuclei: the tuscanic atrium (4), the peristyle (12), the service atrium (9), and a small private peristyle (10); a service corridor ran between the atrium and a stable, which naturally had a separate street entrance (at Number 27). One immediately perceives two unusual features within a floor plan dominated, in the sectors of the atrium and the peristyle, by a rigid geometric regularity: the absence of a tablinum in the tuscanic atrium, and the existence of a small residential peristyle, whose intimate and private nature is clearly indicted by a door that prevented occasional visitors from using or even seeing it.

The absence of a tablinum, which is not in itself unknown in Pompeii—there are forty-eight other such cases—stands out above all because it was found in a prestigious house where many traditional functions of the rooms were diligently respected, such as, for example, the location of the arcae in the atrium. Various explanations have been formulated to explain the absence of the tablinum, which produced the architectural trick, already used in the Villa of the Mysteries, of making the central point where one passed between the atrium and the peristyle wider than the space between the columns in the colonnade behind it, creating the illusion for the viewer at the level of the fauces that the atrium was much

North ala of the House of the Vettii frescoed with a triumphant cock perched on a gold cup alongside his defeated rivals.

time: the house of freedmen, however prestigious, would not have required an area intended for ceremonies of homage to a patron, since, according to what Vitruvius has indicated, the Vettii brothers would have been the ones to present themselves in the houses of others for the daily rite of the *salutatio* (Tamm, 1973). The displacement of the center of gravity from the atrium to the peristyle in the Imperial era would have involved the replacement of the tablinum by a *cenatium*, or dining hall, which we recognize in the large room (11) (Clarke, 1991, 124). A recent hypothesis, however, has claimed not the Imperial age but the late Republican era for the floor plan visible today, and this renders all previous interpretations meaningless. The suppression of the tablinum would thus not indicate the absence of the practice of the salutatio in the Vettii household, but rather that here the entire atrium would have functioned as a place for receiving *clientes*, the large number of whom would be indicated by the ample proportions reserved for this space (Dickman, 1999).

The nature of the small residential peristyle, reached through a door from the north wing of the main peristyle, was the object of a well-known study by Maiuri, who saw it, both because of its separate and private nature, and because of the erotic and feminine mythological subjects in the pictures (*Drunken Hercules Surprising Augeas*; *Achilles at Skyros Discovered Dressed as a Woman among King Lycomedes' Daughters*), as an area intended for the owner's wife and daughters. It would thus have been configured as a mirror of the feminine peristyles in Greek houses documented by numerous literary sources and in some recent cases recognized in the floor plans of rich Hellenistic homes in Erétria, Pella, and Morgantina. However, it has been shown that neither Vitruvius, who accurately described the women's apartments of Greek houses, nor any other Latin source before the third century A.D., refers to the presence of a *gynaeceum* in a Roman house (Wallace-Hadrill, 1994). But if this small area did not represent an actual gynaeceum, a place, that is, set apart and protected from male indiscretion, its exact function within the house is still somewhat vague. The recognition that the area's "arrangement was planned in a way to give the sensation of increasing privilege as one approached the most intimate areas of the entire house" seems in another way to suggest the sought-after privacy that is intimately connected to the function of the gynaeceum. Perhaps the ancient general definition for *conclave* would most accurately suit

Cupid goldsmiths, painted on one of the altar bases in the sitting room (11).

Facing page:
Fresco in the exedra (5) with *Hercules Strangling the Serpents in the presence of Amphitryon and Alcmene.*

The death of Pentheus, torn apart by maenads; a fourth-style fresco on the middle wall of the exedra (5).

the entire small peristyle: "the most secluded room, located in the most interior part of the house, which can be locked with a key."

Among the building's architectural novelties are two symmetrical rooms (5 and 8) facing the east portico of the peristyle. Both rooms were originally accessible from the peristyle itself and from an anteroom corresponding to the alae of the atrium, receiving their light through a large opening onto the peristyle.

They were decorated with refined fourth-style paintings, in which pictures with mythological subjects inspired by or copied from Greek works of the classical age were reproduced at the center of the walls. Such features argue for recognizing these rooms as two exedras imitating those picture galleries in public buildings and sacred places, as well as in houses owned by rich aristocratic Romans, where original art work was displayed. The function of these rooms appears crucial, therefore, for any possible description of the culture, taste, and ideology of the owners of the House of the Vettii, who commissioned and inspired this cycle of paintings. Still, before lingering in these spaces it would be well to consider the decorative history of the house in its entirety and the pictures found in the other rooms.

A Picture Gallery

Within the fourth-style decoration spread throughout the house, it is possible to recognize not only the activities of different workshops—a more refined one that was active in the residential sector and a more modest one working in the service areas—but also different techniques within the same pictorial style and different periods of execution. In several rooms, such as the alae (6 and 7), there is a well-documented very refined decoration with large, regular, monochrome fields, in this case yellow-ochre, imitating large tapestries hung on the walls, the *aulaea* that according to an ancient tradition were introduced from Pergamum. The backgrounds were interrupted only in the center of the middle section by small paintings with still-lifes and competitions or symbolic subjects. The exedra (8) on the other hand is dominated by a complex and overabundant architectural setting that frames large and refined paintings of mythological subjects. The bedroom (3), almost certainly used by the house porter, shows greater simplicity in the purely decorative sections, where

the viewer's attention is attracted not so much by the small pictures inserted into the centers of the walls as by the large frieze in the upper section representing marine fauna. We are able to establish the absolute chronology of these two rooms through reliable data from the archeological analyses of the ala (6) (Peters, 1977). The ala, in fact, was transformed into a built-in closet during the course of the rebuilding undertaken to repair the damage caused by the earthquake of 62 A.D. It was then that the low wall that supported the wooden closet, easily recognizable near the entrance, was set directly onto the painted wainscot of the east and west walls. The fourth-style painting of the ala, then, dates from before 62 A.D. The date is very important because this is one of the few cases in which we can indicate with certainty a date from the Claudius-Nero era for a painting of this type, whose chronology in Pompeii is usually attributed to the period of great post-seismic rebuilding. This dating has direct consequences for the identical painting in the symmetrical ala (7), evidently going back to the same decorative renovation, while all the other fourth-style paintings documented in the house are certainly later and dateable between the late Nero period and that of Vespasian.

Thus the entrance was watched over by an ithyphallic Pan, a guarantor of prosperity. In the upper zone of the triclinium (2) was a painting of *Jupiter, Leda and Danae,* and there were paintings representing *The Metamorphosis of Cyparissus* and *The Battle between Eros and Pan in the Presence of Dionysus and Ariadne,* all evoking the anxiety, delight, and transfiguration of the amorous experience. The same theme was proposed again, in a more customary manner, in the decoration of another bedroom (3), with paintings of *Leander Swimming towards his Beloved Hero* and *Ariadne Watched over by a Cupid.* Among the figures inserted into the large black panels of the peristyle are Urania, the muse of astronomy, and a generic representation of a poet. These figures alluded to the intellectual activities of the house's owner, trivializing a theme treated in a much more complex form in other painting cycles of the late Republican era like the one found in the House of the Ilion Sanctuary.

In the atrium, figures of children busy making sacrifices to the Penates, or household gods, were reproduced on the wainscot, recalling the cult of the ancestors, always associated with this part of the house. A scene with cupids sacrificing to Fortuna was appropriately inserted to correspond with the large bronze *arca,* while the whole long frieze representing

Corner of the exedras, with frescoes set in the middle of large yellow-ochre panels framed by slender columns. The frescoes depict: *The Infant Hercules Strangling the Serpents Sent by Juno in the Presence of Alcmene, Amphitryon, and his father, Jupiter* and *King Pentheus about to Be Killed by the Maenads.*

Following pages:
Corner of the gallery-exedra (8), decorated in the upper part with sharply-delineated architectural scenery, and with a central field covered by large paintings on a red ground.

cupids at the reins of land and sea creatures constituted a sort of introduction to the more important frieze in the oecus (11). Here ethereal psychai collaborated with the gentle servants of Venus in all the principal productive activities of the time, from producing wine to cleaning clothes, from cultivating flowers to making perfumes, from the labors of goldsmiths to the operation of the forge in a smithy.

illuminates the ancient etymology of *culina*, kitchen, from *colere*, to worship. The famous pornographic paintings in the small bedroom, incorrectly identified as the cook's lodging, reveal its function as the household brothel, a perfect introduction to the profession practiced by the slave Eutychis, whose name appears scratched on a wall of the vestibule with the relevant price, only two *assis*.

Facing page:
Central painting on the east wall of the gallery-exedra (8) depicting the *Torture of Ixion*.

In the triclinium facing the small peristyle the subjects reproduced spoke the language of eroticism in the painting representing Augeas surprised by the drunken Hercules and the language of conflict in the scene of Achilles recognized at Skyros. Even in the service quarters the paintings matched the functions of the rooms: the large masonry lararium with figures representing the Lares, or household gods, and the *genius loci*, or guardian spirit of the place, was situated in the atrium to protect the zone where the hearth was located. This

It is much more complicated, however to interpret the cycle represented by the paintings at the center of the wall in the two exedras (5 and 8), which, because of their structure and their decorative importance, are like two art galleries. The pictures in these rooms probably date from the third quarter of the first century A.D. One of the exedra-galleries in particular (8), has sumptuous architecture and seems to have been influenced by the pictorial innovations of Nero's *Domus Aurea*, built between 64 and 68 A.D. In the

Fresco decoration with rural themes.

other exedra (5) the paintings, centered on great yellow-ochre panels framed with delicate architecture, represent mythic episodes in which, from the point of view of composition, the common theme involves violent movement. On the left is the *Infant Hercules Strangling the Serpents Sent by Juno in the Presence of Alcmene, Amphitryon, and his father, Jupiter*, symbolized here by the eagle perched on the altar. On the right is an episode from Theban myth: two young men, *Amphion and Zethus*, the twin sons of Jupiter and Antiope and future kings of Thebes, are shown tying Dirce, the queen who held their mother in slavery for many years, to a bull. On the main wall, across from the entrance, there was instead a bloody epilogue to the Dionysian narrative: King Pentheus, who had opposed the introduction of the new cult spread by Dionysus, is about to be killed by the maenads, who have already grabbed him by the hair and are throwing stones at him.

The corresponding exedra-gallery (8) was decorated at the edges and in the upper zone with heavy, detailed architectural scenes. Here too there was a center field occupied by large paintings, but dominated by stillness; they are the preludes to later developments in the mythic events they narrated. The painting on the right represents the delivery of the wooden cow built by Daedalus for Pasiphae, the wife of Minos, who asked the mythic craftsman for this particular device so that she could mate with a bull. As the ancient viewer well knew, the monstrous result of this union was the birth of the Minotaur. On the central wall, corresponding with the point in the upper zone where a seated divinity (Concordia?) can be seen with a cornucopia in her hand, was a painting of the torture of Ixion. Here the evil Thessalonian king, who had been saved by Jupiter but then earned eternal divine punishment by making advances to Juno, is already tied to the wheel that will make him turn in the sky. Among the divinities watching this scene, Mercury, Juno, Vulcan, and Iris are clearly recognizable. We can identify the feminine figure in a posture of supplication at the feet of Mercury as Nephele, who was sent by Jupiter as a cloud in the form of Juno in order to trick Ixion into thinking that he had slept with the goddess, and from whose union with Ixion the half-animal line of the Centaurs would originate. The painting on the left wall introduces the peaceful union between a god and a mortal: Dionysus in fact discovers Ariadne asleep on a tiger skin, symbolizing the ends of the earth to which the joyful celebration of the god

extended, while Theseus's ship is leaving the coast of Naxos.

The subjects of the gallery's six paintings have been the focus of various iconographic readings, tending to see the outlines of a deliberate decorative program, which seems justified also by the symmetry of the mythic subjects represented in the paintings displayed in the rooms: punishment in one exedra (5) and monstrous union in the other (8). Based on this, a recent proposal has correctly recognized as the dominant theme "the power of the gods, especially of Zeus and his children, as guarantors of world order: benign toward the innocent and pious, but implacable towards transgressors and those who make themselves hateful in their eyes" (Wirth, 1983).

Facing page:
Central painting on the north wall of the gallery-exedra (8) illustrating the *Delivery of the Wooden Cow*, used by Pasiphae, the wife of Minos, as a means of mating with a bull.

Peristyle of the House of the Vettii photographed at night; in the background is the exedra (5).

Fountain jet in the form of a small boy.

But it is perhaps possible to add some other considerations. In one gallery (5) the common denominator of the mythic episodes illustrated in the paintings seems to be the discovery or revelation of one's predestination to great exploits, represented according to age categories: in childhood by Hercules, in adolescence by the Theban twins, in maturity by Dionysus. A. Vettius Conviva's membership in the Augustali could have inspired this thematic unity, since predestination to power and honors was a favorite subject in the Imperial ideology between the reign of Nero—among whose wonders was his birth at sunrise, interpreted as presaging his future honors (Suetonius, *Life of Nero*, 3)—and that of Vespasian, whose ascent to the throne was predicted by many signs as well as his extraordinary ability to perform miracles (Tacitus, *Histories*, 4, 81; Suetonius, *Life of the Divine Vespasian*, 5). In the selection of mythological episodes painted in the corresponding gallery (8) it is possible to guess the owner's intention to show his own conformity to the new direction the Empire took with the ascension of the Flavian dynasty. A figure of Concordia placed emphatically in front of the entry could in fact allude to a new era of prosperity and peace after the abuse of power that had generated a monster like Nero, comparable on the level of myth only to characters like the Centaurs or the even more terrifying Minotaur. The end of this horror was effectively sealed by the last episode of the Cretan cycle, where the union between Dionysus and Ariadne emphasized, as in the grand hall of the Villa of the Mysteries, the achievement of perfect harmony between gods and humans.

Its notoriety notwithstanding, the sculptural decorative apparatus concentrated in the *viridarium*, or garden, and between the columns of the peristyle is on the whole quite common. What strikes us, if anything, is a sort of *horror vacui* that is almost infantile and that, without taking the qualitative level of the objects into account, goes out of its way to introduce every possible subject for furnishing a typical garden of the period: water jets in the form of little boys, statues of satyrs, Dionysus and Priapus, herms of various types, marble fountain pools, and large tables for exhibiting the rich equipment for use during banquets. We are one step away from the realm of *kitsch*, exemplified by the little park in the "urban villa" of D. Octavius Quartius, which has been compared, with good reason, to modern gardens populated by statues of the Seven Dwarfs and other characters from the fantasy world of Walt Disney (Zanker, 1993).

Fabrizio Pesando

The viridarium inside the peristyle with marble basins and fountains in the form of small boys; thanks to water carried by an aqueduct, the garden was enlivened by a variety of streams and jets.

Facing page:
Two-faced herm representing Dionysus which was located in the garden atop a small marble column decorated with flowers and leaves in relief (MANN).

Praedia *of Julia Felix* (II, 4, 2-12): *Fourth Style*

The Estate of Julia Felix, a grandiose complex that takes up the area of two blocks in Region II, was excavated for the first time between 1755 and 1757 under the direction of R. J. de Alcubierre, assisted by K. Weber. As was customary at the time, all the most valuable objects were removed, and all those pictures that Camillo Paderni, curator of the Museum of Portici, considered best suited to enrich the collections of the Bourbon royal family were cut from the walls. The only act of prudence, on the part of Weber, was to create a relief of the building, numbering the rooms from which the furnishing had been removed, and a separate list of these furnishings. It is really thanks to this scientific scruple of Weber's

that, as will be seen below, it has been possible to attribute a substantial number of fragments belonging to the same pictorial frieze, now housed in the National Archeological Museum in Naples, to specific rooms of the Julia Felix Estate.

The excavation was later covered over, and even though the entire perimeter of the block was revealed between 1933 and 1935, the complex was only brought completely back to light between 1951 and 1952.

The layout is not out of character with the organization of other large villas in the Vesuvius area, such as the Villa of the Papyri in Herculaneum, Villa A at Oplontis, and the Villa San Marco at Stabia. It has a residential

Detail of a capital from the west portico, which was lined with rectangular fluted marble Corinthian pilasters.

West portico of the House of Julia Felix, with luxuriant vegetation and a canal crossed by three small bridges.

Garden in the House of Octavius Quartius with a *euripus*, a small irrigation canal.

View of the garden with the thermal quarters in the background.

nucleus in a quadrangular arrangement organized around an atrium (10), next to a green area of vast proportions centered on a peristyle (15) with a *euripus*, a small irrigation canal, located on a different axis than that of the residential nucleus itself.

The first building phase can be seen in the second-style mosaic floors from around the mid-first century B.C. These have been preserved, both in the tuscanic atrium (10) and the areas around it (8, 9 and 12), and in the other atrium (1), the courtyard (22), and the frigidarium (19), showing that the layout of the villa extended over the entire area from the beginning, including even the thermal quarters themselves. In all probability, in this phase of the villa's life, the main entrance opened onto Via di Nocera through the vestibule (2), which was later closed; consequently, the thermal quarters ended up in a rather marginal position in relation to the actual living area.

After the earthquake of 62 A.D., the complex became involved in a modest but comprehensive decorative renovation, led again by specialists from the workshop on Via

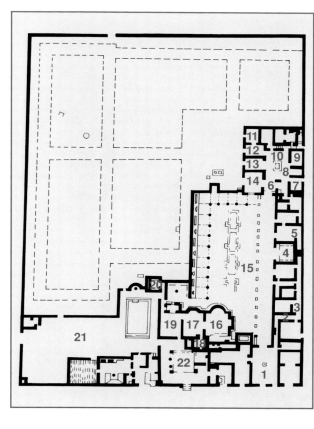

Layout of the house

1. Atrium
2. Vestibule
3. Corridor
4. Summer triclinium
5. Service corridor
6. Room
7. Bedroom
8. Room
9. Room
10. Tuscanic atrium
11. Bedroom
12. Bedroom
13. Tablinum
14. Triclinium
15. Peristyle and Viridarium
16. Caldarium
17. Tepidarium
18. Laconicum
19. Frigidarium
20. Latrine
21. Courtyard
22. Courtyard

313

The canal with three small bridges that crossed the viridarium was furnished with alcoves where fish could deposit their eggs.

Summer triclinium with banquet beds (often covered with fabric and cushions) faced in marble and refreshed by a small water channel that ran alongside it.

di Castricio. Most significantly, the center of gravity was shifted towards Via dell'Abbondanza, where the entrance at number 6 was made larger and more grandiose, including the addition of a distyle portal in brick. The reason for the emphasis on the new entrance, which made the thermal quarters independent, is that the villa's baths were then made available to a select public, as announced in clear letters on a band painted on the facade as a rental notice, later transferred to the museum in Naples: "In the property [*in praediis*] of Julia Felix, daughter of Spurius, elegant baths rented for respectable people, shops

with living quarters above, apartments on the first floor, from the first of next August to August 1 of the sixth year, for five years, with the rental contract expiring at the end of the *quinquennium*." The apartments were above the service corridors (3 and 5). In the difficult years after the earthquake, with the public baths undergoing restoration and a housing crisis caused by the number of dwellings in disrepair, the owners of this grandiose complex decided to take advantage of the enormous available space and structures they were lucky enough to own in a part of the city that was always full of

Still-life (*xenia*) from the upper zone of the walls in the tablinum (MANN).

traffic because it was located in the direction of the Amphitheatre.

In the last phase of its life, then, three different and clearly distinguishable nuclei appeared in the *Praedia* of Julia Felix. The first consisted of a *domus* organized around a tuscanic atrium (10), accessible, once the vestibule (2) was closed, either from the entrance at number 10 or from the bedroom (7). On its east side opened the triclinium (14), the tablinum (13), and bedrooms (12) and (11), all furnished with large windows. On the upper zone of the walls in the tablinum (13) there were imposing still-life paintings, or *xenia*, which are today in the museum in Naples. An especially notable one from this room is a painting with a glass fruit bowl full of apples, among the best examples recovered from the Vesuvian cities; a picture with Dionysian attributes, now also in the museum in Naples, came from another room (possibly 6).

The second nucleus is that oriented around the *viridarium* (15), with the rooms arranged along a longitudinal axis. At the center of the garden was a canal with three small bridges and alcoves where fish could deposit their eggs. Statues of Pan and a fountain in the form of a seashell with crabs suggested the idyllic-sacred atmosphere of this garden, while the image of Pittacus of Mytilene recalled the gardens of the philosophy schools of Greece. The completely restored summer triclinium (4) stands out among the rooms opening onto the west portico, which was punctuated by rectangular fluted marble Corinthian-style pilasters. Atop the walls in this triclinium, which originally had a marble wainscot and frescoes with Nilotic landscapes, was a typical barrel vault that had been refitted as a pseudo-grotto, a particularly suggestive effect obtained by setting cylindrical fragments of porous limestone into a thick layer of stucco and painting them yellow. In contrast to other banquet halls, where couches faced with marble were surrounded by a small canal with water running through it, this room was fed by a niche with a stepped cascade which the water reached

Facing page:
Bronze tripod with ithyphallic satyrs extending the palms of their left hands in an evil-averting gesture (MANN, Secret Cabinet).

Statuette of a philosopher, found in the garden of the house (MANN).

through tubes connected to containers situated above the service corridor (3) behind the room, as in Nero's *Domus Aurea*. The east side of the portico was instead punctuated by alternating semi-circular and rectangular niches with the same pseudo-grotto surface treatment as the vault in the summer triclinium. A small room with a vaulted roof, which may have been a shrine to Isis, opened onto the south edge of the garden area. In fact, the pictures lining the walls showed the goddess carrying an ancient percussion instrument known as a *sistrum*, flanked by Anubis, Serapis, Fortuna, and a guardian spirit offering a sacrifice on the altar of a lararium. From this room comes the famous bronze tripod with ithyphallic satyrs holding out the palms of their left hands in an evil-averting gesture, which is now in the Secret Cabinet in the National Archeological Museum of Naples.

The atrium (1), which must have taken on the function of an entrance at the time when Via dell'Abbondanza assumed a primary role in the city's economic and social life, also belongs to this second nucleus of the Estate. Although the second-style floor from the first building stage has been preserved, the space has lost its original wall decoration because the pictures were renovated during the fourth-style phase. An interesting frieze, with *Scenes of Life in the Forum*, has been attributed to this second and last decorative intervention in the atrium; it is now in the museum in Naples, and its ordered sequence, even including the two solitary fragments of it that remain on site, has been reconstructed relatively recently (Nappo, 1989).

Separating the middle zone, with its panels of red, green, and blue grounds, from the upper zone, which has delicate, fantastic architecture on a white ground, was the frieze, which unfurled along all four walls, with a combined length of almost 102 feet. It provides a precise and suggestive fresco detailing the multiple activities that took place in the Forum: fabric and livestock merchants, metal artisans, bread and vegetable vendors, schoolteachers and scholars, and simple passersby move against a background of monumental porticoes containing equestrian statues. It is claimed by some that the frieze represents specific sections of the Pompeii Forum and further that the frieze in the atrium (1) is oriented in exact correspondence with the public plaza. If this reconstruction is on the mark, this pictorial representation of the Forum, besides satisfying the villa owners' desire to ennoble their own private space using the grandiloquent language of public architecture, could also allude to restoration

Detail of the frieze in the atrium, which depicts several scenes of life in the Forum; three adults and a boy read a public notice written on a long tablet attached to the bases of three equestrian statues (MANN).

activities for which they had been responsible. Several consequences of this interpretation cannot be ignored. In fact, this theory recreates an image of the forum populated with statues and with completely restored buildings, some parts of which we can recognize, such as the porticoes corresponding to the Building of Eumachia and to the *macellum*. These give the forum a look similar to that of nearby Herculaneum, also hit by the effects of the earthquake, and from which numerous marble and bronze statues belonging to the forum area and the main public buildings have come. This, then is a replica that contradicts any notion of desolation or incompleteness in the Pompeii Forum during the years between the earthquake of 62 A.D. and the eruption of 79 A.D., caused by the supposed slow pace of restorations in the public zone after the quake. If we do not consider this to be a purely imaginary pictorial document, it may then appear that there was an almost complete rebuilding of the Forum area after the earthquake, and that its denuded appearance, sealed by the eruption and still visible today, would instead be due to a systematic plundering of the sculptures and the most important architectural elements, probably organized by the Imperial authority itself, a hypothesis that is being argued ever more frequently and plausibly in the most recent studies of the city's last phase (Zevi, 1992).

Another detail of the frieze with a scene of commerce in the Forum (MANN).

Finally, the villa's last distinguishable nucleus consists of the thermal quarters, which, as we have seen above, retained the floors from the ornamental program of the mid-first century B.C., while the wall decoration was actually from the Nero-Flavian age. From a monumental entrance at number 6 Via dell'Abbondanza, one entered a porticoed courtyard (22), furnished with seats along the walls and functioning as a waiting room for clients of the baths. From here there was access to all the standard rooms of a thermal establishment: the frigidarium (19), the tepidarium (17), the laconicum (18), which was circular and had a cupola roof, and the caldarium (16), with an apse on the south and a facade of marble tiles. These tiles were removed by the eighteenth-century excavators, from whose accounts we also learn that the windows of all these rooms were paned with large sheets of glass or talc. Finally, in the courtyard (21), there was a large uncovered swimming pool, which could also be reached from the *taberna* with its entrance at number 7. This taberna was furnished with a bar and an adjacent premises that had a stone triclinium for the clients; at the south-west end of the courtyard there was a large latrine (20), connected to the frigidarium by means of a small channel.

Maria Paola Guidobaldi

Headboard of a bed adorned with putti; this elegant piece of furniture found in Pompeii is similar to those that might have furnished the House of Julia Felix (MANN).

321

House of Menander
(I, 10, 4): Fourth Style

This page and following pages:
The lararium, the atrium, and the
peristyle of the House of Menander,
excavated by Maiuri between 1926 and
1932.

Layout of the house

1. Atrium
2. Ala
3. Tablinum
4. Oecus/Green Salon
5. Peristyle
6. Oecus
7. Triclinium
8. Manager's bedroom

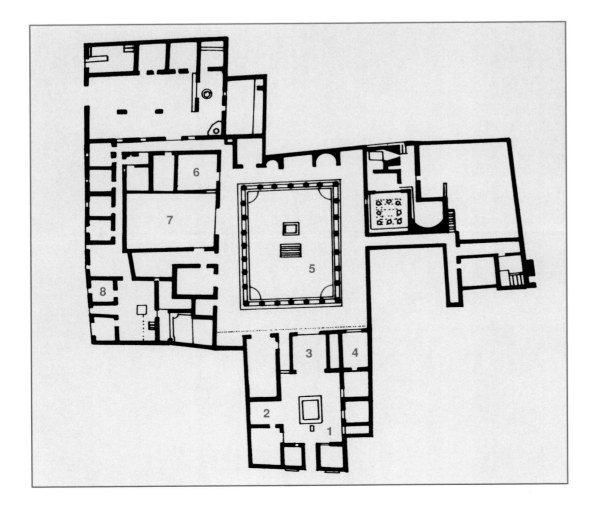

The House of Menander, one of the most
luxurious dwellings located inside Pompeii's
walls, gives us a complete picture of the "urban
villa," with suitable spaces for reception, living,
and service rooms and completely separate
areas for the numerous slave families who
worked on a farm located outside of town.

The house was excavated between 1926
and 1932 by Amedeo Maiuri, who paid
painstaking attention both to archeological
exploration, which included stratigraphic
excavation, and to careful restoration. This
restoration was unfortunately complicated by
some infelicitous and even misleading
reconstructions, which have recently been
remedied through correct displays to the

public, with the furniture and furnishings left
in situ, and the addition of captions that provide a rich didactic and explanatory apparatus.
Maiuri also provided a splendid and timely
description of the house in a monograph
which remained definitive for many years.

This house, one of the few really noble
dwellings in Pompeii, with its imposing
architectural plan, its servants' quarters,
and its rich pictorial and mosaic decoration,
remains one of the most interesting and
valuable examples of a Pompeii dwelling.
The extremely rich treasures found there,
especially the 118 elegantly-embossed silver
pieces, today the pride of the National
Archeological Museum of Naples, make
up one of the most valuable collections
of household objects ever discovered in a

Roman dwelling, not least because of their artistic importance.

The building occupies more than half of one of the square blocks created to the east of Via dell'Abbondanza during one of the oldest urban expansions undertaken in Pompeii. The block is in a fortified position, separated from the other blocks by the city's main axes, Via di Stabia on the west and Via dell'Abbondanza on the north, the so-called *cardo* and

decumanus inferior respectively. Via del Castricio, the main interior axis of Regions I and II begins at about the middle of the block on the east side.

The studies conducted for over ten years by a British team led by Roger Ling have shown that already around 200 B.C., considered to be the earliest date of the house's construction, it occupied a larger lot than the adjacent houses and, more notably, extended farther towards the south. At the time it must have included the space for the rooms located around the atrium, apparently unchanged through the years, and a little garden area to the south behind the tablinum.

During the second half of the second century B.C., the house underwent first a series of

architectural embellishments, carried out in tufa, including the entrance pilasters, two deeply embossed half-columns at the sides of the tablinum, and a series of five columns forming a small portico towards the garden area. Above all, however, its space was later greatly enlarged at the expense of a pre-existing house located on the east side of the block (I 10, 16), and the garden was also furnished with a portico on the east and west sides. At the same time, or at the latest towards the beginning of the colonial period, the building also engulfed the neighboring house to the west, that of the *Fabbro*, or Blacksmith (I 10, 17), thus becoming a double-atrium house, following an architectural model that was extremely widespread in Pompeii at the end of the Samnitic era.

It was in the third quarter of the first century B.C., however, that the house had its most remarkable period of expansion, when it acquired the spaces formerly occupied by buildings to the south. Thanks to terracing, intended to eliminate the natural slope of the terrain, the area of the garden doubled and extended over the demolished parts of one of these buildings. It was then surrounded on all sides by a portico with a series of residential spaces opening around it. Baths were then built on the east side.

Another expansion took place at the end of the first century B.C., when more space was gained at the expense of the house on the north-west corner of the block (I 10, 8), several of whose rooms on the west side were turned into spaces for the kitchen and connected to the peristyle by means of an L-shaped corridor built along the south and west sides of the courtyard of the House of the Blacksmith.

All the connections with the House of the Blacksmith were closed off, however, in the second quarter of the first century A.D., and the area allocated to the house was then reduced around 50 A.D. when a separate workshop (I 10, 6) was created from a room located in the north-west corner, along with other spaces taken from that same adjacent House of the

Blacksmith. Later the ceilings of several rooms located in the area west of the atrium were lowered to create an apartment on the upper floor with an entrance directly from the street (I 10, 5), and another small apartment was created on the upper floor above the atrium rooms at the front of the house, with access from the room to the west of the entrance.

To compensate for this change, sometime around 60 A.D., not only was the entire house (I 10, 16) consolidated into the building, but all the spaces located on the south-east part of the block were completely demolished and rebuilt, in order to make these areas into luxurious sitting and reception rooms and into service quarters with stalls, store-rooms, and carriage houses. This shows that the separation of several rooms from the rest of the house was dictated not by economic necessity but by advantageous income opportunities.

Following the earthquake of 62 A.D., restorations were undertaken to repair the considerable damage and to reorganize several of the rooms. In particular, a second floor was created over the courtyard of the stables, and the room located on the south-east corner of the block was separated from the core of the house and opened towards the street to create a commercial space.

At the time of the eruption renovations were underway in this house, as in many others in Pompeii, possibly made necessary by the earthquake tremors that had preceded the eruption for several days. This might also explain why the household silver had been hidden in the cellars, where assorted debris was also amassed, and why many iron utensils and bronze vessels had been moved into the manager's room, where they would not hamper the work and could also be kept under a watchful eye. It makes no sense to think that such precious silver pieces would have been kept concealed for seventeen years, ever since the earthquake of 62 A.D., without a safer and more suitable location for them being found. The story is completely different, of course, if one attributes the situation to a recent emergency.

At the time of the catastrophe the house extended over an area of about eighteen thousand square feet, equal to a little over half the block. The entrance portal was flanked by Corinthian pilasters, and stone seats on the front of the building along the sidewalk accommodated the clients waiting there from early morning for the *salutatio*. From the vestibule, or fauces, one entered directly into the large, rectangular tuscanic atrium, with its marble impluvium and fourth-style paintings, predominantly in red and black, probably executed after the earthquake of 62 A.D. In the corner to the right of the entrance was

Preceding pages:
Two examples of the precious treasures found in the house: the handle of a silver *patera*, or libation bowl, and a bracelet of gold half-spheres connected with small spherical hooks (MANN).

The *bulla* was probably an amulet in the form of a spherical case of Etruscan origin, worn by newborns to protect them from evil (MANN).

A pair of splendid earrings made from seed pearls and bits of emerald strung on a core of gold threads (MANN).

Ring with a carnelian on which a scene of a charioteer watering his horses is reproduced, also among the treasures from the house (MANN).

the monumental lararium, with its large double front and angular baluster, which was closed by means of wooden partitions. Connected to the impluvium was the ala, on the left as one entered rather than the traditional position. The decorations in the ala have a mainly red background, and in the middle of the vertically-divided walls are images taken from the Cycle of the Sack of Troy. Beginning on the right wall with the earlier episode of Laocoön and his sons strangled by serpents, one moves to the center point on the back wall where the open gates of Troy allow the horse to pass through,

despite Cassandra's vain opposition. Finally we see the epilogue with Priam powerless to oppose the Greeks, while Cassandra is forcibly pulled away from the wooden statue of Athena where she had hidden.

The peristyle extended behind the tablinum along an axis with the entrance. It had wide spaces between the columns corresponding to the main rooms that opened onto it and a low parapet decorated with hunting scenes on the back and herons and plants on the other sides. Inside the vast garden, there was a fountain pool as well as a space for summer banquets.

The olive branch became a widespread decorative theme in the time of the late Republic and lasted for several decades: it referred to a sense of complete *felicitas* that even included nature, reawakened like the rest of creation by the peace of Augustus (MANN).

The green sitting room, in the northwest corner of the peristyle, has a mosaic floor with an emblem in *opus vermiculatum*, a wave pattern, representing scenes of life on the Nile, and in the very subtle fourth-style wall decoration there is a prominent red frieze

The back of a mirror, delicately modelled in a plain style with the image of a female head (MANN).

which ironically recounts the episode of the rape of the Lapith women by the Centaurs during the wedding of the Lapith king Pirithous and Hippodamia.

On the south side of the peristyle, besides an extremely refined chamber with two beds,

which was apparently turned into a library during the final period, there were several exedras of alternating apsidal and rectangular form. In the rectangular one farthest to the west stood an altar for the household cult, under a niche in which were preserved the wax molds of statuettes representing the family's ancestors along with the *lar*, or domestic god. In the other is a seated portrait of the comedy-writer Menander, crowned with laurel and reading a scroll. According to a recently-proposed reading, the now-vanished inscription that could once have been seen on the half-opened scroll emphasized his skill in writing comedies. The opposite wall, on the other hand, would probably have housed a portrait of the tragedian Euripides, now lost, but whose existence is nevertheless suggested by a small table with tragic masks painted on the back wall. Closer to the figure of Menander there must have been a parallel representation of comic masks on another table. In the center between the two tables was the figure of Dionysus, which, because of its position, could be seen from the entrance. In one of the apsidal exedras, there is an image of Venus with landscape scenes in the background, and in the other a depiction of Actaeon being torn to pieces by his dogs for having seen Diana in her bath, with the divinity herself in the foreground.

The most imposing rooms in the house were situated on the east side of the peristyle, the first of these being the grand reception salon, the largest room found in Pompeii, which had an area of 970 square feet and a ceiling over twenty-six feet high. Two other living rooms were on either side of it, one with decorations on a yellow ground, where the skeletons of twelve people trapped inside were found, and the other with decorations on a red ground. Between this room and the grand salon a corridor led to a bedroom set in a more secluded spot.

On the west side of the peristyle were a long L-shaped corridor, which led to the kitchen area with its adjacent garden, and the entrance to the thermal quarters, which centered on an *atriolum*, or antechamber, with eight columns. This atriolum was undergoing restoration at the time of the eruption. The caldarium is a tiny jewel, with its mosaic of sea creatures on the floor and illustrations of various gymnastic exercises on a green ground on the walls. In the vault of the *schola labri*, an apse with a basin, is a stucco seashell ornament. A small mosaic carpet, located just in the entrance to the area, catches the eye with its depiction of a servant bringing lotions for the bath. The thermal plant was completed, finally, by a terrace-solarium. In a subterranean area next to the *praefurnium* a precious treasure trove of silver weighing over fifty pounds was found, along with a coffer containing gold jewels and a cache of gold and silver coins.

From a passageway in the southeast corner of the peristyle, a long corridor led to the imposing servants' quarters, which were in turn connected directly to the street on the east of the block with their own separate entrances. One of these, an actual driveway,

Emblem with a Nilotic landscape: a flotilla of Pygmies rows up the Nile. This type of mosaic, made of tiny tesserae, was composed in the workshop and then transferred to the floor by means of a stone support (MANN).

Fresco with Menelaus grabbing his wife Helen by the hair and Ajax dragging Cassandra away from an effigy of Athena; from the north wall of the ala (MANN).

led directly into the large courtyard around which were arranged the storerooms, stalls, and carriage house, as well as small cells on the upper floor for the slaves, who numbered about thirty.

The entrance at number 16 opened onto the quarters of the procurator, or manager, pivoting around an atrium with a *compluvium* which had meticulously-designed terracotta decorations inserted into a roof with only one peak. Bronze agricultural implements and

Mythological painting showing Cassandra opposing the horse's entry into Troy, predicting that it would cause the city's ruin (MANN).

equipment were stored in one of these rooms, and the man who was found here, along with a baby girl and a purse containing money, wore on his finger a seal with the name Q. Poppaeus Eros.

This discovery led to the supposition that the house might then have belonged to the Poppaea *gens*, one of whose members held the office of *aedile* under Caligula or Claudius. We should not forget, in any case, that this clan had given two consuls to Rome during the Augustan era, and we know that Nero's wife Poppaea Sabina probably came from this very Campania branch of the family and clearly had documented economic interests in the countryside surrounding Pompeii.

If true, this would provide a simple explanation for the graffiti that refer to illustrious members of Nero's entourage. Even though this hypothesis seems the most likely of any proposed, it is still not compelling enough to be accepted unquestionably.

Antonio Varone

Insula *of the Chaste Lovers (IX, 12): Fourth Style*

Faux architecture with doors and columns, sometimes decorated with human figures, is typical of the fresco paintings in the House of the Painters at Work.

Small bowls used by painters for colors, like those found in the House of the Painters at Work next to amphorae full of lime.

Systematic excavation in the south part of *insula*, or block, IX 12 has been conducted since 1987. It was there, in the beginning of the twentieth century, that Vittorio Spinazzola unearthed in its entirety the only architectural facade on the very central Via dell'Abbondanza, elegantly arranged over two floors. Spinazzola then also explored all of the House of the First Colonnaded Cenaculum, situated at numbers 1 and 2, and part of the Second Colonnaded Cenaculum at numbers 3 to 5.

The recent excavation of this block has focused on a bakery, located at number 6 with a secondary entrance at number 8, which has residential spaces connected to it. Among these is a triclinium used as a banquet hall. The bakery itself is now commonly known as the House of the Chaste Lovers. At number 7 is a shop with a store-room, still facing Via dell'Abbondanza. A cenaculum is on an upper floor whose rooms occupy the space

above several rooms of the bakery and are connected by a *maenianum* that protrudes over the street. And finally there is a rich house called the House of the Painters at Work, whose main entrance, not yet excavated, opens onto the lane on the west of the block, and whose secondary entrance is located at number 9, on the lane bordering the block on the east. Of this last house in particular, the only residential spaces unearthed to date are those located around a triporticus that bordered a well-tended garden.

The area of the complex explored so far is over sixteen thousand square feet, but the excavations are currently expanding into the rooms of the rich house located near the main entrance. Because the work is still underway, rather than present a necessarily partial description of the rooms, it is preferable to convey the spirit of the current investigation and at the same time to describe the most

interesting results of the exploration and the new knowledge that has been gleaned from it.

The excavation area is protected by a modular roof and is viewed mainly as a research laboratory where, in line with current trends in archeological investigation, professionals of different cultural backgrounds work in close scientific and technical collaboration. Coordinated by the archeologist, these geologists, vulcanologists, paleobotanists, paleozoologists, chemists, physicists, engineers, architects, etc., are investigating, within their respective areas of competence, those particular cognitive threads that the recovery makes it possible to follow. In this way, data from all sectors can be harmonized in a comprehensive view of this ancient society that takes in daily life, social relationships, the production of goods and services, the people's interaction with the environment and their experience of dramatic natural events like earthquakes and eruptions.

From the beginning, one of the declared objectives of the archeological explorations has in fact been to furnish future users with representative documentation of the impact that the eruption of 79 A.D. had on the inhabited part of Pompeii. There has been a consequent attempt to preserve the evidence as much as possible, no matter how dramatic, just as it appeared to the archeologist, so that it might be perceived in the same way by future visitors. This has required bold technical choices, carried out with the assistance of structural engineers, who made it possible, for example, to preserve *in situ*, in exactly the same position in which it was found, a floor from the upper story in the House of the Chaste Lovers which had settled, after it lost the support of its beams, atop the volcanic materials that filled the room below. Similarly, the upper part of a partition in the workshop at number 7, which one of the seismic shocks that followed the eruption had detached and moved off its base, was preserved where it stood, still erect about ten feet off the floor, engulfed by a mass of volcanic ejecta.

This was achieved by hooking these structures to the tubular frame of the worksite roof and holding them aloft from above or by ensuring permanent static support with tiny rods integrated perceptibly, but utterly discreetly, into the ancient structures. The engineers also made it possible to reconstruct the porticus triplex around the garden in the House of the Painters at Work, revealed to the excavators with the still perfectly delineated arrangement of its roof tiles visible in the impressions in the wood beams and masonry columns. After a historically

accurate restoration and recovery of its various elements, the restructuring could be completed using all the ancient techniques and with the same materials, but following the current norms for areas with elevated seismic risk. Photogrammetric reliefs of the various phases of dismantling the materials and restoring the previously-numbered tiles thus made it possible to completely reassemble the structure with all its original elements preserved in their exact locations.

Another example of a wall decoration with candelabras, garlands of greenery and faux architecture in perspective in the House of the Painters at Work.

Late third style (34-45 A.D.) fresco with a banquet scene set in winter, from the triclinium of the House of the Chaste Lovers. The precious cups arranged on the table in the foreground are of rare beauty.

Truly innovative, however, was the information provided by integrating all the individual data. Paradoxically, the interest in the manufactured goods found there was far inferior to the interest generated by the actual interpretation, systematically sought in the overall context of the interactions within the excavation area, of the various "phenomena" as they expressed both the dynamic flow of life at the time and the impact on it caused by the catastrophe.

Of course, there have been discoveries of immediate and more traditional interest. Examples include the marble fountain-statue representing a golden-haired child crouching beside a dolphin, found in the peristyle of the House of the Painters at Work, and the admirable still-life with fish and crustaceans found in the triclinium. In the bakery there are the millstones for grain, the manual dough-mixer, and the benches for bread-making right next to the baking oven, all in a well-ordered production chain. There is also the cycle of banquet paintings, with

their strong hint of irony, in the bakery's triclinium, quite appropriate for the House of the Chaste Lovers. This cycle is one of the most beautiful examples of a thematic decorative program designed for a specific space, in this case one apparently actually used as a dining room.

The decoration of this triclinium, in splendid late third style, is marked by a simple and refined classicizing color scheme, deliberately playing on a harmonious alternation between red and black panels. In the middle part of the wall, vignettes with small winged figures on the red side panels provide a fitting accompaniment to the splendid scenes depicted on the black central panels. These offer amusing symposium images, preparatory to celebrating the pleasures of drinking, with ironic touches well-suited for lending a properly gay tone to anyone about to host a convivial gathering in the room.

The first of these paintings depicts an indoor scene and clearly refers to the winter season. The second is outdoors in the summer heat under the shady protection of a

canopy with a background of luxuriant vegetation. The third is between seasons in an open space on a portico screened by curtains. All three paintings illustrate the classic theme of a feast with hetairas, showing couples lying on couches busy enjoying the pleasures of the symposium. There are clearly

The still life was highly appreciated in Pompeii, as in all of the Roman Empire. The subjects were not limited to fruit, but could also include various types of food such as game or fish. Here are two examples of still lifes with fish, indirectly intended to celebrate the wealth of the house's owner and the opulence and abundance of his table.

Decoration in the grand salon of the House of the Painters at Work with cupids on chariots drawn by goats.

The fresco of the triclinium that gave the House of the Chaste Lovers its name; two young lovers exchange a modest kiss during a banquet.

explicit appeals to both drunkenness and the passion of love, companions and daughters of the sacred Dionysian liquor. The second scene, in particular, showing the central couple absorbed in a very tender but equally sensual kiss, provided the inspiration for the house's name.

Even the vignettes making up the background of the red side panels, with images of small winged figures holding baskets overflowing with fruit, game, thyrsi and flowers, lances, vases and cornucopias, seem intended to convey opulence and abundance, inviting guests to the delights of the feast and contributing to the creation of a true hymn to the joys of the banquet.

The discoveries that are unexpected, however, have a completely different kind of value, contributing in a less obvious way to the accumulation of information about Pompeii. We note, first of all, the evidence offered by the large oecus in the House of the Painters at Work, where the eruption actually put a halt to the work of a team of painters. An archeological analysis of the parts already frescoed, those already plastered, and those still without plaster, together with a chemical analysis of the pigments discovered in numerous small cups found in the salon along with amphorae full of lime, bronze compasses, mortars and pestles, and other tools, has made it possible to better reconstruct not only the various phases of the decorative process and the different techniques used from one time to another, but also the subdivisions of the labor itself, with their relative timing, among painters of different levels of expertise, who worked at the same time and in the same team in an already predetermined process that also involved the completion of the floor decorations.

The workshop boy was responsible for spreading a uniform background color onto the still-fresh plaster. The *pictor parietarius* painted the side panels with decorations on dry plaster, beginning with a sinopia of just a few lines in a geometric pattern, which was then traced in charcoal with the help of a rule and a compass. The same painter was

which the painters were well aware. A real treasure, finally, was the discovery of a pannier into which a painter had placed the empty color pots, one piled on top of the other, to carry them to the atelier and perhaps fill them anew.

It is clear that such documentation, unique for the detailed analysis it provides about the way a team of painters operated, is most useful in terms of the figurative analysis of the paintings themselves, which are especially valuable in the degree to which they are unfinished and thus able to show interesting connections to those in the salons of the House of the Vettii and the nearby House of Julius Polybius.

Cupids were often painted in Roman houses in various guises: we have seen them on chariots drawn by goats, and here we have a cupid in flight with a wide-brimmed hat (a winged *petasus*), holding in his hands a caduceus, a staff with two intertwined serpents which was the symbol of health.

Statue of a golden-haired child, discovered in the triporticus of the House of the Painters at Work, but which was most likely part of a fountain in the garden (MANN).

perhaps also responsible for making marginal decorations like tapestry borders, garlands, and various grotesques on the monochrome panels, this time, however, using colors made with organic binders. These decorations were painted over the base colors after a preparatory design had been traced, again using a compass, by scratching it into the already-dry background color. Because the final phase of burnishing, the *expolitio*, was never completed, these overpainted colors are perfectly discernible in relief on the walls. Finally, the *pictor imaginarius* undertook the composition of the central paintings on the walls, spreading the colors yet again *a fresco*, after having traced a complex preparatory sinopia in yellow ochre, so that the chiaroscuro effects of the composition were already visible.

The archeological results also permit us to establish the sequence in which the decoration was executed, proceeding in horizontal phases from top to bottom—ceiling, upper zone, central zone, then wainscot—and, within the limits of each area, by vertical panels. The results also indicate that the painters worked simultaneously, at times all facing the same wall to perform their individual tasks. Each color, furthermore, could be mixed starting from different mineral bases, which thus gave different shadings, vibrations, and textures to the same tint, a technique of

Another moment of major scientific effort in the House of the Painters at Work was the excavation of the garden bordered by the triporticus whose reconstruction is mentioned above. This was minutely organized into quadrants of about three feet by three feet and made it possible to discover, thanks to analysis of the pollen and spores and to casts of the holes left in the ground by plant roots, exactly what vegetable species were planted there, namely rose-like plants and evergreens, set into a parterre that was maintained as a lawn. The flower beds were bordered with a trellis, which one often sees in pictures of gardens, but which could now be effectively documented archeologically with fine and detailed evidence. In fact, if one places river reeds of different diameters, such as those which still line the mouth of the Sarno today, into the holes

found in a regular pattern along the edges of the flower beds, it is possible to recreate it visually. Thicker reeds stuck directly into the earth along the beds every three feet created the basic structure, while between them were stuck two fairly fine reeds intersecting at a 45 degree angle to create a perfect rhomboidal grid. The horizontal element that finished the top of the reeds is obviously the only thing missing in the documentation of this system, but we can guess what it was, not only through logic, but in fact from the contemporary garden paintings mentioned above.

One should also note that a pergola made of grapevines covered the wall at the back of the garden, creating a background for the vegetation visible to anyone who was in the oecus with its white background. Garden paths were created between the flower beds,

The portico in the House of the Painters at Work with its garden, whose original appearance has been suggested by the work of scholars from a variety of disciplines.

The plaster cast of a Pompeii victim of the *surges*, the scorching clouds made up of extremely fine ash mixed with thick detritus, which made it impossible for the city's population to breathe.

which were symmetrical but not mirror-images, so that they formed a pathway of functional yet privileged connection between the aforementioned salon and the other reception area of the house, namely the large oecus in which the painters were working, and which was preceded at the front of the garden by a monumental and even pretentious *prothyron,* a sort of porch or vestibule, surely the room that most typifies the house. This further confirmed the importance of the garden to the living space of the classic Roman-era house as the main element connecting its principal open areas; the owner's wealth and luxury were meant to shine there, thanks to suitable and precious furnishings, sculptures, fountains, *tabulae pictae,* and much more.

The shells of edible mollusks found here and there along the garden paths have, on the other hand, documented for us the common habit of consuming such "fruits of the sea" while strolling, and probably conversing, letting the shells fall to the ground.

In the House of the Chaste Lovers, the analysis performed on carbonized vegetal remains found amassed in a storage area on the upper floor has made it possible to establish that these were residues of fodder, mainly made up of oats mixed with *favino,* a mixture still used today for animals subjected to heavy field work. The identification of other vegetal substances marginally present in the fodder has shown us that the scything took place in a field where crops were rotated, according to an ancient technique still in use, the origin of which is lost, but which it has been possible to document

archeologically as definitely used in the Roman era.

Such fodder was undoubtedly used to feed the animals whose carcasses were then physically found in the interior of the plant. Indeed, this space, which was furnished with four mills for grinding grain, had two stalls, in one of which were found the skeletons of five equids, members of the horse family. The other stall was found empty, but the remains of two other equids were discovered

The skeleton of one of the five equids found in a stall at the House of the Chaste Lovers.

Facing page:
Another example of a fresco with
animals: here, a rooster with brightly-
colored feathers is busy pecking at a
pomegranate. In the background is
a still life with pomegranates and pears
(MANN).

Detail of the decoration in one of
the rooms that face the triporticus
in the House of the Painters at Work,
shown on a preceding page in its
context within the house.

in another room of the house, where they probably managed to run in the midst of the eruption. Bone and DNA analyses of these animals has made it possible to exclude their consanguinity. This fact interests archeologists in that it shows that the owner of the bakery had deliberately acquired the beasts, which obviously entailed cost and upkeep, because they were necessary to the functions of the business. It follows then that the production of flour was thus organized around several work shifts with animals alternating at the mills. This indicates a continuous demand for bread that caused such businesses to operate at high speed. It also follows that some of these animals, found as noted in uneven numbers, were used to transport grain or even to distribute bread to the countryside.

In this way, from data ostensibly beyond the normal investigative sphere of the archeologist, we have learned an essential fact relative to the organization of work in that period. We have been able to conclude that because these animals were not born in that stall and were all of an ideal age for this work, the operation of a bakery with four mills required a work force of at least seven animals.

Interesting facts that give a new perspective to the study of the last years of the city's life have appeared regarding the seismic tremors that repeatedly shook the city in the years immediately preceding the eruption of 79 A.D. In fact, it has been possible to identify the damage that occurred following the earthquake of 62 A.D., which had already been repaired for some time, and differentiate it from other damage apparently produced as a result of later shocks, whose time cannot be fixed, up to that produced by an earthquake of equally strong intensity only a short time before the eruption.

The dating of such seismic phenomena can be deduced from the realization that at the time of the eruption four septic gutters in the lane to the east of the complex were all open at the same time, in that they were all found in view and full of lapilli, or lava pebbles. The lane itself was clogged with masses of earth, which, one could reasonably argue, had slid into the channels and was being removed from them in an excavation operation actually underway at the time of the eruption. It is obvious that the most plausible explanation for such underground damage involving several construction projects must be sought indeed in a seismic shock that made the earth located around the channels slide into them and fill them. In

the houses, however, life went on, and in one of them there were even seven equids, which means, as common sense would suggest, that this damage had been discovered only a short time earlier and was therefore being hurriedly repaired.

This causes us to believe that the work underway at the time of the eruption, repeatedly noted in every quarter of the city and generally thought of as restorations following the earthquake of 62 A.D.—even if seventeen years later!—should be connected rather to repairs from a similar earthquake which took place a very short time before the eruption and can undoubtedly be considered its first stage.

This is of paramount importance for the history of Pompeii, given that it causes a complete re-evaluation of the society and economy of the time. This was not then a Pompeii utterly prostrate following the destruction of 62 A.D., such that after many years it could barely manage to recover and begin restorations, but rather a Pompeii not in the least overwhelmed, a city that could conceive of grandiose architectural programs, such as the example of the Main Thermal Baths had already led us to suppose, but which subsequently and repeatedly had to face other earthquakes.

Pliny the Younger himself gives an indication of this phenomenon in his account of the eruption: *praecesserat per multos dies tremor terrae, minus formidolosus quia Campaniae solitus* ("preceding it for many days were earthquakes, less terrible than the ones usual in Campania"), in spite of which the news of the earthquake of 62 A.D. has always kept scholars from seeing why so much work was in process all over Pompeii at the time of the eruption.

In the House of the Chaste Lovers, as a matter of fact, it is possible to see that the damage attributable to the earthquake of 62 A.D. had already been repaired for some time. This is the case, for example, with the large oven, where one can make out a wide angular crack typical of earthquake damage that was repaired with a brick patch and then covered with plaster. After this, the oven remained in use for a long time, blackened with heat and smoke and even crumbled in several places. The rebuilding that was taking place in the room in 79 A.D., therefore, cannot have been made necessary by the same earthquake that caused the crack in the oven, since the crack had already been repaired a long time before.

A thick pile of lime had already been amassed in the triclinium and would have

been used to cover its damaged late third-style pictorial decoration and then recreate it, had not the eruption intervened. A section of the east wall had meanwhile been completely rebuilt and decorated with paintings that, though imitating the earlier ones, are clearly attributable to the fourth style, a period apparently later than the earthquake of 62 A.D. In the section of the wall that had not been redone, there are signs of other patches characteristic of still different

Detail of a fresco painting with a satyr surprising a maenad from behind, on the west wall of the matrimonial chamber in the House of the Painters at Work.

periods. It is therefore not plausible that the work being carried out in A.D. 79 can be ascribed to restorations caused by the earthquake of 62 A.D.

Similarly, in the House of the Painters at Work, we see an equally frenetic situation of work in progress. Piles of lime are spread at intervals along the triporticus, and an enormous pile of stones and other construction materials is amassed in a corner of the garden ready for use. Then, in the *repositorium* near the kitchen, were found heaps of mosaic tiles and river sand, the primary ingredients, along with lime, for preparation of the *rudus*, or rubble-and-lime base, and then the *nucleus* into which the mosaic tiles would be set. Nearby, in an adjacent room, were broken amphorae and a great number of the tools used to prepare these fragments for use in the cocciopesto floor. The consistently high level of disorder in which a wall of the red salon and several other walls of the complex were found should also be noted. It is implausible that a house with such evident signs of life would be left in that precarious condition for seventeen years, and it is also hard to imagine that such damage could have been caused by the violent seismic shocks that accompanied the eruption. The floors of the house are very uneven in several rooms, missing in others and, in contrast, in good condition and quite uniform in the red triclinium, where there is notable damage to the wall structures, almost as if they had just been completely rebuilt. In the salon with the *prostàs*, where pictorial decoration was underway and where there is a mosaic ornament with a central emblem in polychrome *opus sectile*, there are actual depressions in the floor, which, given the context just described, and especially considering the mosaic tiles already amassed in the house and ready for use, seem very difficult to relate to the tremors accompanying the eruption.

The work underway at the same time in the septic channels in the lane, then, not only confirms the breadth of the seismic phenomenon, but also illustrates that it cannot be considered to have been much earlier than the eruption.

The stratigraphic excavation undertaken inside the mass of volcanic materials deposited almost twenty feet deep in the lane west of the block has made it possible, through a comparison between passages from Pliny regarding the eruption and the evidence of the excavation, to finally specify the sequence and the intensity of the eruptions that occurred between August 24 and 25 in

79 A.D. and the effects that each had on people and objects.

Following an initial phase that began about ten a.m. on August 24, at around one p.m. a column of lapilli shaped like a pine tree was violently hurled more than twelve miles into the air. Carried by the wind, the lapilli pelted the city like a very dense hailstorm until around evening, submerging it under about ten feet of debris. Because of their lightness and porosity, lapilli are not generally capable of killing people directly, but in a mass even only twelve to sixteen inches deep their weight can easily collapse a roof, crushing any unfortunates who had expected to find shelter there.

Throughout the night, the eruption had periods of stasis, but during those hours violent earthquake tremors came one after the other. At first light on August 25, many Pompeiians had finally decided to flee, but it was just then that the most dramatic phase of the eruption began. The volcanic cone collapsed and the phreatomagmatic canal emitted surges, the scorching clouds—masses of extremely fine ash mixed with the densest detritus—which, rolling towards the plains like an avalanche, deprived every living being of breath. The first of the surges that reached the inhabited area of Pompeii, the fourth of the series, can be seen in stratigraphy, sedimented, like a petrified layer of ash only an inch or so thick. Its effects were devastating for people and animals. It is actually in this thin layer that were found the skeletons of two fugitives, who after death were dragged and mutilated by the succeeding surge that battered Pompeii with crushing force immediately afterwards, carrying in its wake the connected fragments of roof tiles, beams, and other materials.

This surge, which left sediments more than three feet thick, could only rampage over the cadavers of people who were already dead, but it then violently overran the buildings that had resisted the preceding surge, cutting through and beating down the walls that stood against its advance. A long wall, snapped by the impact in its upper section and toppled a few yards in front of its base, allows us to determine the velocity of the advance of the surge itself.

As it fell, in fact, the wall trapped underneath itself part of the surge that had poured down a contiguous alleyway and, finding no obstructions, was now also spreading onto the slope where the wall was about to fall. Calculating the time of the wall's descent at between four and five tenths of a second and measuring the distance that the unobstructed

flow was able to traverse as the wall reached level ground, it is thus possible to estimate its forward velocity at between forty and fifty miles an hour.

With the people now dead and the buildings collapsed, other surges finished the work of burying the city, in which only the highest points of the walls emerged from a sea of gray ash.

Antonio Varone

Another amorous approach in this delicate fresco with a "flying couple" wrapped in airy drapings on a dark ground.

Villa of the Mysteries

Detail from a third-style fresco in the tablinum decorated with Egyptian motifs; here we see the god Anubis, shown with a jackal's head and sitting on his heels.

The beautiful Villa of the Mysteries, excavated in 1909-1910 and 1929-1930, is for the most part set forward on a square base that made construction possible in spite of the land's slope towards one side.

One of the most beautiful villas in the immediate suburban area of Pompeii, located about a thousand feet from the Herculaneum Gate in the direction of Oplontis, is universally famous as the Villa of the Mysteries because of the scenes of Dionysian rites painted in its salon.

The excavation, which has not yet uncovered the entire area, was carried out in two successive periods, first from 1909 to 1910 under Giulio De Petra, and later by Amedeo Maiuri between 1929 and 1930.

The complex can be dated as far back as the first half of the second century B.C., but it was completely renovated sometime after the arrival of the Roman colony, around 60 B.C. Later it was again enlarged with the addition of a rustic sector, designed to take advantage of the produce from the adjoining farm, which was principally dedicated to grape cultivation. At the time of the eruption it belonged to the Istacidii, a family from an ancient Samnitic line, as the seal of a

freedman found there confirmed. The valuable marble statue found in the peristyle has also been recently attributed to a priestess of this family, after having been incorrectly thought to represent Livia, something which had suggested to many scholars that the villa belonged to Augustus himself, or at least to the Imperial estate.

The villa, a rich dwelling outside the city gates belonging to some magnate of the Samnitic era, shows its peculiar design as a leisure villa in the layout of the main living quarters on the side turned toward the sea, onto which the entertainment rooms faced. Two corner rooms with just one bed each and with windows facing the garden, added to the building during the Augustan era, highlight the privileged status of the occupants. These quarters were served by a terrace on the same level, which also faced the sea. Porticoed and preceded by a hanging garden, it was located over the cryptoporticus that acted as a substructure for the workrooms and as a cool

promenade in summer, and which had an apsidal room at its center.

One approached the villa through a grandiose entrance located on a bend in Via dei Sepolcri, the cemetery road which proceeded towards the suburbs. Under a vaulted passage, which gave the structure an extraordinarily majestic aspect, were benches on which the *clientes* sat while they waited to be received by the patron.

During the last phase of the villa's transformation, additional servants' quarters were created in front of the entrance on either side of the pavement that connected the complex to the street. These were intended for the expansion of agricultural production, which had become dominant by this time.

From the entrance one passed directly into the peristyle, which fits what Vitruvius wrote about the change of position between the atrium and the peristyle in the floor plans of villas. The peristyle acted as the central fulcrum for the rustic sector and the servants' quarters, which also included several bedrooms of a certain quality and rustic apartments with fireplaces, in one of which work implements were found. An apsidal room opened onto the peristyle preceded by an anteroom with marble decorations which suggest that it served as a family lararium. The portico, with Doric tufa columns, was

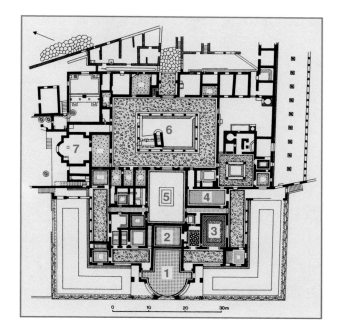

Layout of the house

1. Exedra
2. Tablinum
3. Salon of the Mysteries
4. Oecus
5. Tuscanic atrium
6. Peristyle
7. Room with apse

The frescoed wall in second style that divides the peristyle from the atrium.

This statue, thought for decades to be Livia, actually depicts a priestess of the Istacidii family, *gens* of an ancient Samnitic line, the last owners of the house (MANN).

unusually wide and enclosed a small garden encircled by a tall parapet, at the center of which was an underground passageway leading through a narrow alley to a cellar room, to a large cistern carved out under the residential quarters, and to the center of the three-branched cryptoporticus.

From a corridor located on the north side of the peristyle one passed into the

Preceding pages:
A comprehensive view of the Salon of the Mysteries, the luxurious triclinium space that inspired the name given to the villa by its discoverers.

The matron, spouse, and priestess of the Dionysian cult, depicted next to the passage towards the alcove; seated, she observes the scene that comes to life, already complete, before her eyes.

spaces intended for winemaking, undoubtedly the most widespread activity of the villa's production system. Even though at the current state of excavation it is not possible to ascertain the full extent of the vineyards, the extraordinary dimensions of the large *torcularium*, the room designed for crushing the grapes, and of its two *prela*, or presses, give us a good idea.

The *prelum*, similar in every way to presses still in use in the Vesuvius area until the last century, consisted of a crate filled with weights and connected to a beam, which could be lowered onto the grape clusters underneath it by means of a winch, following a first pressing effected with the feet. This movement was accomplished by the progressive insertion of wedges little by little so that the pressure would reduce the mass of grapes under the weight. The beam and the crate were lifted by means of a rope that passed through a pulley suspended from the ceiling and that was tightened by a winch located in a trap door under the floor. The *mustum*, or must, thus obtained ran off along a small channel into a cistern and was then aged in buried jugs.

The entrance to the spacious kitchen also branched off from the south arm of the peristyle. It boasted an ample oven that ensured the villa's self-sufficiency in the daily production of bread. A smaller oven for baking pastries and the fireplace's long cooking surface give us an idea of how banquets were prepared for large numbers of guests. These were still taking place a short time before the end of Pompeii, as revealed by a graffito found in the Basilica in which a sponger accuses Istacidio, who was perhaps in fact the owner of the villa, of never inviting him to dinner. A lararium niche located in the kitchen itself permitted the servants to offer choice morsels to the household's guardian gods. The cooking apparatus also furnished heat and steam for the baths located on the other side of the wall, although these appear to have been in disuse after the last rebuilding following the earthquake of 62 A.D.

The kitchen was in turn connected to a small, originally tuscanic atrium which must have served as a space for gymnastic exercise in connection with the baths. The construction of several rooms on the floor above and the insertion into one of the thermal halls of a staircase to reach them, caused the transformation and then the disuse of the baths themselves. This small atrium, which had already become a tetrastyle through the insertion of brick columns to support the gallery of the new floor, was then definitively transformed into a cloister with a small, delightful internal garden, which took the place of the original impluvium. Located close to a large sitting room, it thus ended up servicing a matrimonial bedroom, superbly secluded near the hanging garden and constituting, in fact, the center of a truly private sector of the master wing, from which one could also easily reach the large double-colonnaded

portico that ran along the south side of the building. This portico, still not completely excavated, but clearly opening onto the countryside and green vistas, performed the function that in city houses was served by the peristyle. Here, however, the green was no longer imprisoned inside the walls; on the contrary, the portico seems rather to have put the building itself in nature's embrace, and anyone walking there could let his eyes wander freely over cultivated fields.

The nucleus of the apartments that made up the *pars urbana,* or residential sector of the villa, was the large tuscanic atrium, which enjoyed direct access from the west portico of the peristyle and was located in line with the entrance. Its design, without columns on the sides of the impluvium, emphasized its

With an experienced woman nearby to guide her through the ceremony, the initiate listens to the ritual reading of the papyrus by a small nude boy, who is a symbol of purity.

Preceding pages:
A bacchante begins to move in a wild dance to the sound of the lyre of Silenus, symbol of cosmic harmony.

large dimensions and underlined the great expense required for its realization, further indicated by the decoration in extremely prized cinnabar red, which has darkened over time. This decoration created an effect of marble slabs on which Nilotic landscapes were reproduced. There is an interesting graffito on the north wall, a caricature of an honored person with an extraordinary nose and the caption, "This is Rufus."

The master sitting rooms were separated from the rustic quarters, and the large number of bedrooms suggests that this house was also designed to offer lodging to friends. The

original master bedroom, which had a wall closet in the space created by two beds placed at an angle, was subsequently turned into a passageway. In its earliest plan it was functionally and conceptually connected to the salon with the large mystery painting, a sitting room as well as antechamber-prelude to the rites of the alcove. The original second-style decoration is splendid and still perfectly legible; in fact, the most perfect examples of this style are found in the residential rooms of this very villa. In particular, the decoration of bedroom number 16, where two vaulted alcoves were set in an L-shape to leave room

As a possessed bacchante dances naked to the rhythm of clappers she shakes over her head, signaling the climax of the rite, the initiate has a moment of panic and runs to hide in the lap of her initiatrix.

Facing page:
Detail of the initiate hiding in the lap of the woman who accompanies her in the various phases of the rite.

Facing page:
Dancing satyr in a second-style fresco
on the south wall of the double-alcove
bedroom located between the Salon of
the Mysteries and the tablinum.

The initiate prepares to achieve
revelation and acquire the regenerative
power of the phallus, which offers
protection against the adverse forces of
nature, represented here by a winged
demon armed with a whip who must
flee at its sight.

for a closet in the resulting space, can be admired for its perfect architectural perspectives and for the geometric vanishing points that animate the ornate second-style decoration so perfectly that it has been possible to create a computer-generated three-dimensional model of the structures from the painting, almost as if they were real. In the painting a colonnade located in the foreground permits us to see through it to a decoration in vertical panels imitating marble and functioning as vertical stone slabs on which rest horizontal rows, also of multi-colored fake marble, giving the effect of rustic ashlar masonry. The resulting composition, with fanciful architecture that is not overdone, has great balance and dignity.

The third-style decoration in the tablinum, on the other hand, brings us to an extremely rarefied atmosphere of unsurpassed elegance. Located in the traditional position, in line with the entrance behind the atrium, the tablinum has walls with uniform grounds of shiny black and a very delicate decoration with Egyptian-style figures and objects related to Dionysus.

The major fascination of the villa is undoubtedly the second-style decoration in the luxurious triclinium salon with its megalographic frieze and extremely elegant floor in palombino tiles bordered with slate strips. The salon was originally strictly related functionally and architecturally to the master bedroom and even linked to it with visual reminders that, far from appearing accidental, seem in fact to suggest that the ritual acts represented in the pictorial scene actually took place in that room.

This painting, the least damaged and most discussed of those the ancient world has left us, depicts a series of life-sized figures which seem to move ritually as if on stage in a timeless dimension where the real and unreal merge and myth becomes intimately linked to reality. The scene, whose significance still largely escapes us, is the work of a Campania painter of considerable technical and expressive abilities, who was clearly copying and re-elaborating models from the first Alexandrian style. The red ground, obtained with extremely costly cinnabar, and the upper strip in squares that imitate the striations of onyx, call attention to its great value. There have been numerous attempts to interpret the composition, but the results have been extremely controversial, and consequently, explanations not only of the single figures but even of the sequence in which to read them remain uncertain, and interpretations change according to the particular significance that individual scholars have seen in the cycle as a whole.

Some propose a circular and sequential reading of the scenes on the walls. Others prefer a parallel reading of the side walls, which would then converge on the scene of the drunken Dionysus on the wall at the back. Amid the general dissatisfaction with the various interpretations, it still remains uncertain whether the subject is a woman's initiation into an Orphic or Dionysian mystery cult or rather the performance of a drama connected to episodes in the life of Dionysus.

As mentioned above, even the figures have been variously interpreted, according to the approach chosen, but it has not always been possible to arrive at a clear and organic understanding of their various particulars. One persuasive approach sees the scene as a dream in which the seated matron is the protagonist, as well as the bride and priestess of the cult. She is shown in a pensive attitude in the corner next to the passage towards the alcove, meditating on an unfolding scene, the one in fact that is on the walls in front of her and us, and which is already completely and instantly present to her mind. In it the episodes connected to the woman's ritual and sacred initiation into the knowledge of the phallus, seen in a fragmented dimension that precludes any precise temporal sequence, are intertwined in parallel with the manifestation of the divinity at the culmination of the ecstasy, between delirium and the mystic rejoicing of the various personages of her *tiaso*, or religious association.

If we decide to follow a parallel reading of the two side walls, we see first the initiate's

preparations as she adorns herself with the help of a handmaiden, combing her hair and admiring herself in the mirror, in the already-symbolic presence of two cupids, followers of Venus. Then we find the next episode on the opposite wall, where, guided by an already-experienced woman who holds the sacred texts in her left hand, the initiate listens intently as a naked boy, a symbol of purity and innocence, reads the ritual from a papyrus scroll. The ceremony of purification, which follows on the same wall, is the heart of the rite. The woman, sitting with her back to us and crowned with myrtle, receives the purifying water from an officiant who pours it on her right hand, while with her left she uncovers the contents of a basket brought to her by a handmaiden. Another officiant, symbolically pregnant, approaches her to offer the sacred loaf, symbol of the fertility of the earth which provides the harvests.

At this point the scene changes, and the creatures of a Dionysian procession enter the field, superimposing their movements onto those of the initiate in a parallel and imaginary plane. A bacchante begins to move in a vertiginous dance to the sound of the lyre of Silenus, symbol of cosmic harmony. In the background, Pan plays the syrinx and watches as a *panisca*, one of his attendants who is

Detail of the second-style wall decoration in a double-alcove bedroom in the Villa of the Mysteries, depicting an architectural background.

half goat and half woman, suckles a fawn, a reference to universal love. The rite is now about to reach its climax and, on the opposite wall, a possessed bacchante dances nude, accompanying her movements with the obsessive rhythm of the clappers called *crotali*, which she shakes above her head, while one of her companions holds a thyrsus, a staff crowned with a pine cone and garlanded with ivy leaves and vine tendrils that is an attribute of Dionysus. The initiate then has a moment of confusion and fear and would like to escape. She is comforted and encouraged, however, by her initiator, in whose lap she has hidden herself.

The liturgy is brought to completion on the back wall. After having put down the thyrsus and kicked off his sandals, Dionysus, carried away in his own ecstasy, abandons himself to intoxication in the arms of Venus herself, the goddess of love, who presides majestically over the entire scene, a figure which has been only partially preserved and which some have identified, incorrectly, as the mother of Dionysus, Semele, or his wife, Ariadne.

Next, still on a purely mythological plane, to the right of the divine couple Silenus offers a satyr a cup with the *satyrion*, the Bacchic nectar that opens the mind to the comprehension of reality. Behind him another satyr, depicted with a rare portrait-like expressiveness, raises a Silenus mask to his face to indicate the transmission of the knowledge and prophetic wisdom obtained from the magic potion brought to him by Silenus himself. In parallel, to the left of the divine couple on a plane of reality that is by now completely fused with the mythological one, the initiate tries to achieve revelation. She is about to discover the *mystica vannus,* or mystic enigma, and receive knowledge of the phallus, whose regenerative power is capable of counteracting the adverse forces of nature, here in the form of a winged demon armed with a whip ready to strike, but who is forced to retreat instead, powerless at its sight.

The vision is over, the rite has been completed, awareness has been achieved, and the woman, who has become both priestess and matron, can now with dreamy detachment return to the entrance of her nuptial alcove, keeping the memory to herself, mystically enthralled.

The megalographic frieze in the Villa of the Mysteries will probably never reveal its true meaning to us moderns, who can no longer understand its complex symbolism. Any interpretation, in fact, seems reckless. Besides, it had already lost its mystic and religious meaning during antiquity and had only a

decorative importance by the time that the salon, or *procoeton*, the little antechamber-foyer of the alcove, was turned into a triclinium and the alcove itself became a simple passageway. Rather, the meaning is undoubtedly to be found in the enchantment and the evocative power of the images, which seem to be the emblem and synthesis of a civilization and its culture. Such is the suggestive power that animates the movements of the figures, projecting them into a timeless dimension, that it makes the Villa of the Mysteries one of the greatest and most impenetrable documents the Roman world has left us.

Antonio Varone

Another detail of the fresco in the bedroom; to make the effect more realistic, a door was painted on one side of the room.

Villa of Poppea at Oplontis

The covered walkway of the villa, distinguished by a dense line of columns with slender shafts, opening onto a magnificent Mediterranean garden enlivened by olive trees and indigenous plants.

The so-called Villa of Poppea at Oplontis, more precisely defined as Villa A, is without doubt one of the most grandiose examples of a seaside villa, a *villa maritima*, that has come down to us—and it is even in perfect condition. Just a short distance from Pompeii, in what is today Torre Annunziata, the villa appears in a location indicated as Oplontis on a Roman road map of the late Imperial era known as the *Tabula Peutingeriana*. There were no indications of its existence other than what the various discoveries in the area have progressively disclosed.

Largely explored between 1839 and 1840 by the Bourbon excavators who also removed several paintings, the villa was put on view

Detail of one of the frescoes that decorate the rooms of the villa with a theme that is fairly widespread in Pompeii houses, the still life.

Foreshortened view of the peristyle in the servants' quarters; traces of decoration are still visible on the walls and, on the left, amphorae used for stocking oil and wine.

Preceding pages:
What made the excavation of
the Villa of Poppea even more
sensational was the discovery of
still-intact rooms like the one
reproduced here, in which the
barrel ceiling and frescoed walls
are still visible. On the page facing
it is another example of a frescoed
wall with architectural motifs,
a peacock, and a mask.

Fresco with a slender column
decorated by vegetable garlands
and flowers that look like precious
stones.

between 1964 and 1984, although the excavation was far from complete, since more than half of the west wing still lies under today's Via dei Sepolcri and the Bourbon explosives factory. The excavations also had to stop on the south side, where the modern city began, and at the canal of the Sarno, which cut through the Roman structures. This made it impossible to recover the building's southern extension and porticoes, which reached out toward the sea's embrace and the view of Capri and the Sorrento peninsula.

The complex dates from the middle of the first century B.C., but was substantially renovated and enlarged in the first Imperial era, above all in the area around the swimming pool. It underwent further restoration and rebuilding after the earthquake of 62 A.D., but by the time of the eruption it was practically abandoned pending completion of the work made necessary by the more recent seismic shocks. There are several indications that the property may have belonged to the *gens Poppaea* and perhaps even to Emperor Nero's second wife Poppea Sabina herself.

Today the complex is reached by entering from the rear, that is, from the garden at the back that extended the porticoes which bordered it, with their simple fourth-style decorations and white stuccoed columns, in the direction of Vesuvius. Instead of enclosing it within the narrow boundaries of a peristyle, a pleasant covered promenade marked the green space and became a part of it.

The villa's central section was higher than the two lateral ones, which appear to have been symmetrical, even though it has only been possible to excavate a small part of the western wing. At the center of the villa, open toward this garden and in a line with the atrium and the small peristyle, was an

Following pages:
Another example of a still-life fresco in one of the rooms; the rendering of the transparency of the glass vase, through which the pomegranates are visible, is remarkable.

Corner room to the east of the atrium, with the illusion of a wall divided into five sectors, decorated with vitreous vases and a wicker basket containing fruit and stalks of wheat.

enormous distyle sitting room of exceptional height that was a favorite space for enjoying nature. It had, in addition, a large window that opened onto an enclosed garden behind it, thus introducing a recurrent theme in the architecture of this villa, which over and over combined the vision of nature as "free and wild," rambling towards the horizon, with that of nature as "captive and cultivated" within the interior of the house.

From the large window the perspective and the view of green extended as far as the gigantic tuscanic atrium with its solemn second-style decoration of rare refinement. On the west wall, the one best preserved, false architectural recesses with columns frame a faux wooden double door with large bronze knobs at the top of a short staircase. The doors have framed panels in the lower sections and two symmetrical winged Victories holding trophies in the upper. Above them,

in a sacred landscape, figures move between small tetrastyle temples and their *propylaea*, or entrance structures.

Images of women embossed on *clipei*, or round medallions, worked in silver, enhance the upper register. On the two side walls the architectural decoration continues the illusionistic theme, although it is heavily damaged and has some gaps. Here too, we see the motif of closed doors at the top of a staircase, but this time they are framed by a marble colonnade seen in perspective, and more medallions hang in the spaces between the columns.

The noble and austere grandeur of this room, which is already visually enlarged by the fake architectural decoration typical of this period, is further emphasized by the exceptional quality of the pictorial composition, in a style that often reaches its peak in this villa.

In the more properly residential wing of the villa, west of the atrium, is oecus number

Facing page:
Detail of a fresco depicting a garden, luxuriant with vegetation and made even more rich by statues and fountains adorned with anthropomorphic elements.

Proof of the great skill of the decorators is the pictorial representation of construction materials like the marble of the columns.

Facing page:
Fresco was not the only artistic technique used in the villa; here is a refined example of a mosaic decoration with geometric elements and strong chromatic contrasts.

15, which was reached by a folding door, a well-detailed mold of which was recovered from the impression it left in the volcanic ash. Here we see the triumph of second-style painting. The protagonists of the scene are peacocks, represented also in other rooms of the villa and in decorations from different periods. For this reason many have, perhaps

improperly, considered them as symbols. Encountering masks of exceptionally vivid coloring, the creatures wander about, with their characteristic movements, among ethereal and scenic colonnades of two orders topped with columns that act as a theatrical stage in perspective depicting a sanctuary of Apollo. A bronze torch is in the foreground at the

The fresco belonging to the residential ala of the villa reproduces a closed door with gryphons facing each other, above which hangs a gold clipeus.

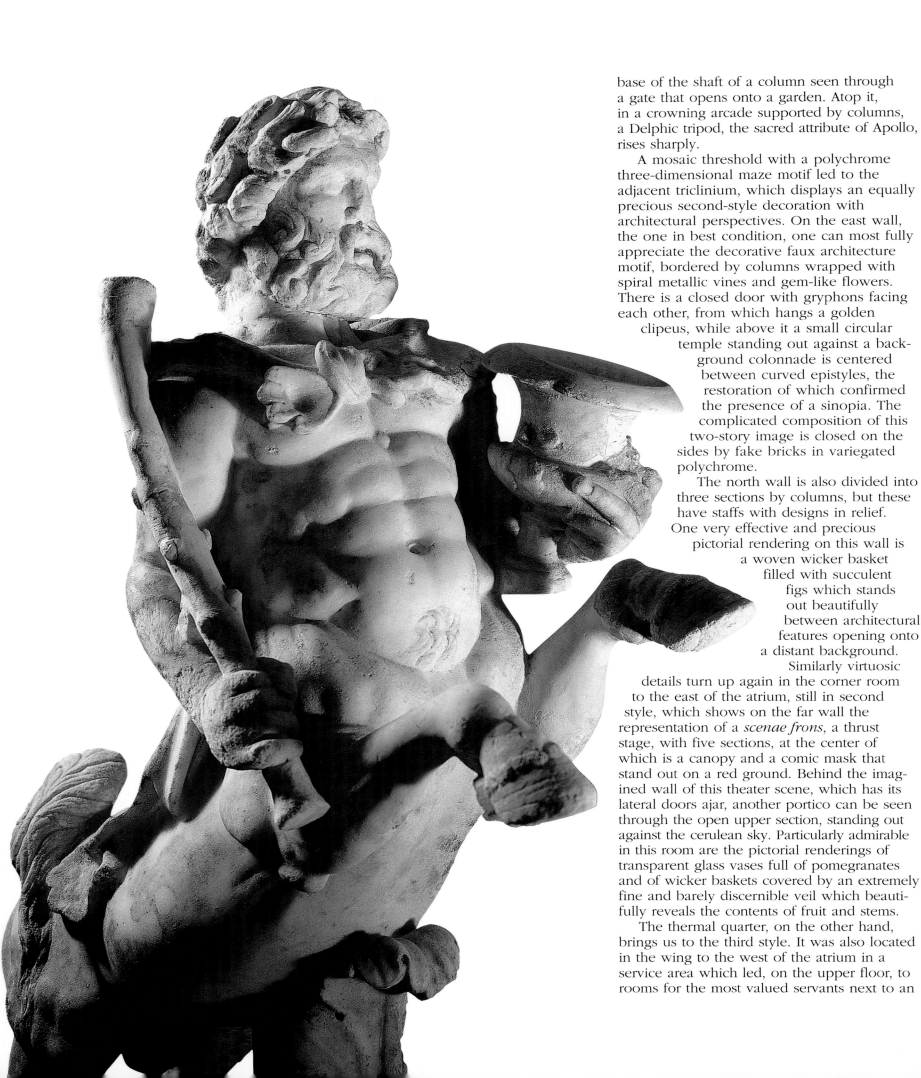

base of the shaft of a column seen through a gate that opens onto a garden. Atop it, in a crowning arcade supported by columns, a Delphic tripod, the sacred attribute of Apollo, rises sharply.

A mosaic threshold with a polychrome three-dimensional maze motif led to the adjacent triclinium, which displays an equally precious second-style decoration with architectural perspectives. On the east wall, the one in best condition, one can most fully appreciate the decorative faux architecture motif, bordered by columns wrapped with spiral metallic vines and gem-like flowers. There is a closed door with gryphons facing each other, from which hangs a golden clipeus, while above it a small circular temple standing out against a background colonnade is centered between curved epistyles, the restoration of which confirmed the presence of a sinopia. The complicated composition of this two-story image is closed on the sides by fake bricks in variegated polychrome.

The north wall is also divided into three sections by columns, but these have staffs with designs in relief. One very effective and precious pictorial rendering on this wall is a woven wicker basket filled with succulent figs which stands out beautifully between architectural features opening onto a distant background. Similarly virtuosic details turn up again in the corner room to the east of the atrium, still in second style, which shows on the far wall the representation of a *scenae frons*, a thrust stage, with five sections, at the center of which is a canopy and a comic mask that stand out on a red ground. Behind the imagined wall of this theater scene, which has its lateral doors ajar, another portico can be seen through the open upper section, standing out against the cerulean sky. Particularly admirable in this room are the pictorial renderings of transparent glass vases full of pomegranates and of wicker baskets covered by an extremely fine and barely discernible veil which beautifully reveals the contents of fruit and stems.

The thermal quarter, on the other hand, brings us to the third style. It was also located in the wing to the west of the atrium in a service area which led, on the upper floor, to rooms for the most valued servants next to an

Elegant bas-relief figure of a nude warrior with a crested helmet, shield, and sword; his features clearly recall Hellenistic art (MANN).

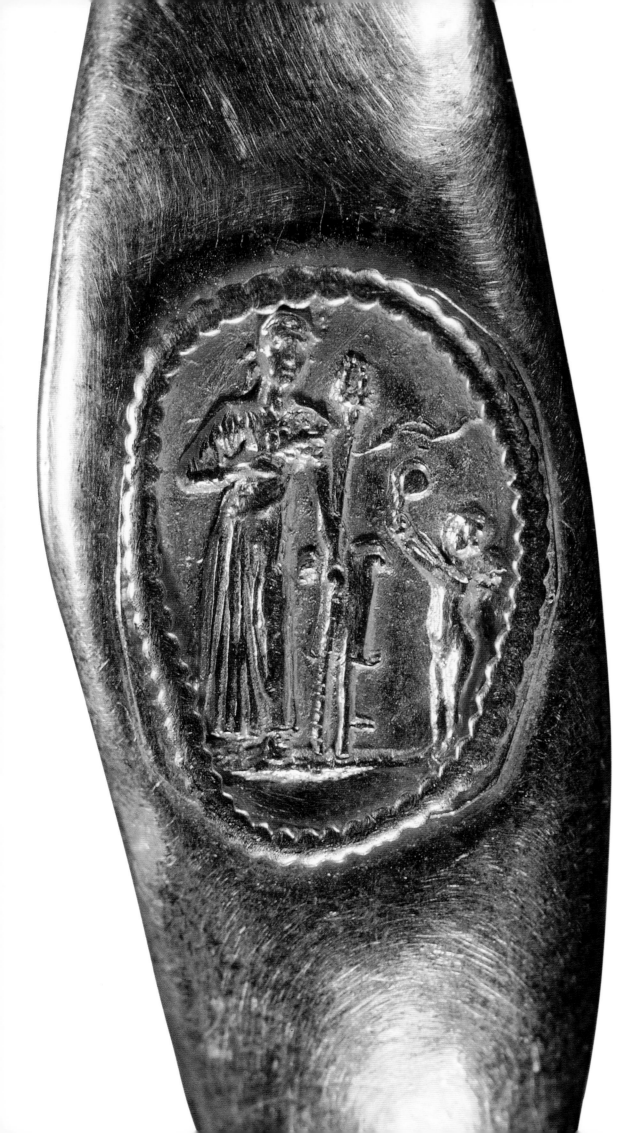

impressive kitchen and close to a showy tetrastyle atrium whose impluvium pool also included spaces for setting out plants. In the upper zone of the wall of the caldarium, within the niche where the bathtub was located, a figure of Orpheus playing a kithara stands out on a yellow ground, while below, in between red partitions, the center painting depicts Hercules in the Garden of the Hesperides.

The heart of the main servants' quarter to the east of the atrium was the porticoed courtyard which framed a small garden enclosed by a tall balustrade. On its west side was a masonry fountain on which stood a statuette from which water cascaded into the basin below. Various bedrooms opened onto this courtyard, as well as rooms for storing tools and stairs leading to other bedrooms located on the upper floor.

The most salient architectural element of this porticoed courtyard was the room that housed the masonry lararium, enclosed in a false apse and opening onto the portico itself through a redundant anteroom. Given that all the tutelary gods of the household were venerated in this space and that the sacred domestic rites were performed here, rites in which all the *familia* of the *dominus* partici-pated, including servants, the amount of space devoted to it speaks eloquently of the number of people, especially those in service, who must have lived in the villa.

Even the latrine, also in the same quarter, appears to have been organized to serve a community. It was built with the usual system of a sewage canal running along three sides of the room, where there were wooden seats with holes. Water dropped from a wash tub that was always full, flushing first the urinals that ran in front of the seats and then pouring into the waste canal, which was thus continu-ously rinsed. A more private space was also reserved behind a little wall.

A long corridor with a very high vault began from the servants' peristyle and functioned as a covered walkway, in the manner of a cryptoporticus. Along its walls, which were decorated in a herringbone pattern of exceptional chiaroscuro effect, a series of red-painted masonry benches encouraged relaxation and conversation. The passage functioned as a connecting hall-way to the sector with the swimming pool, where the villa's luxury reached its most spectacular level.

Along the east side of the pool, which measured a surprising 56 feet by 200 feet, there was a well-endowed gallery of marble statues, copies of Greek originals, placed here and there among the oleanders. From the opposite side a series of rooms for relaxation opened onto a view not only of the pool but also of small windowed greenhouses on several sides, in which real plants were accompanied by paintings of gardens, creating a sophisticated game of tag between the real and the imaginary. From the main salon of this sector, with its splendid marble floors, they could enjoy, in perspectives that were deliberately designed in every detail, priceless foreshortenings in which the wild natural world melded both harmoniously and in a sort of competition with nature as it appeared in the paintings and as it was contained within architectural spaces specifically conceived to house it.

A strong point of the villa, in fact, was also the large garden behind the salon, which opened onto it in a beautiful manner and which complemented the building on the Vesuvius side. Here, amidst small paths and well-tended flower beds, and between flowers and boxwood hedges, were found the impressions of several oleanders and of a row of five plane trees centuries old. Set like immobile guards were the statues of four centaurs, two male and two female.

Nothing, however, could have compared to the large tuscanic portico decorated in fourth style with another herringbone motif, which stretched out its arms towards the sea and its vista. Now the sea is far away, behind a forest of bleak modern buildings, and only our imagination can help us understand what must have been the villa's principal view. The portico, bordering the palace on the south in an almost identical way to that on the opposite side facing the countryside and Vesuvius, was designed to enclose a wide expanse of green in the form of a Mediterranean garden before it met the deep blue of the Tyrrhenian Sea. After the earthquake of 62 A.D., in fact, lemon trees were planted there in huge vases next to every column, and ivy branches rising from smaller vases twisted around fluted shafts covered with white stucco.

In the garden, where several tools for tending the vegetation were found, paleobotanic analyses have shown that in addition to other plants, two great chestnuts grew there and thus provided extensive shade.

Living in such a residence, which is for the most part still to be explored, the owners of the villa at Oplontis, even if they were not already actually associated with the nobility of Rome, certainly had little to envy in the luxury of the Imperial villas at Baia, Capri or Sperlonga.

Antonio Varone

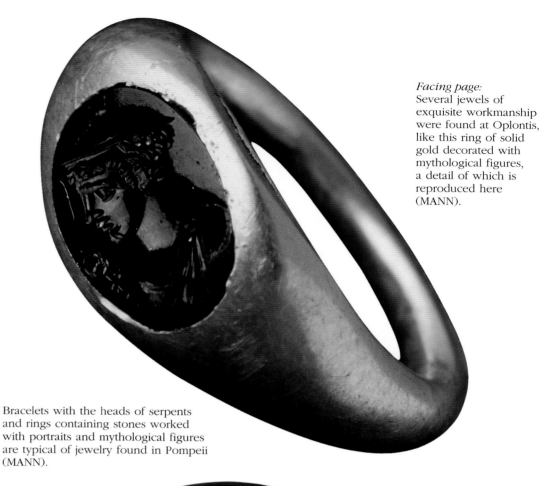

Facing page:
Several jewels of exquisite workmanship were found at Oplontis, like this ring of solid gold decorated with mythological figures, a detail of which is reproduced here (MANN).

Bracelets with the heads of serpents and rings containing stones worked with portraits and mythological figures are typical of jewelry found in Pompeii (MANN).

Following pages:
The Villa of Poppea in all its glory, with graceful columns, porticoes, and gardens.

LEGEND

Unless otherwise indicated, all images are on site
or from Pompeii.

MANN = National Archeological Museum of Naples

SAP = Archeological Superintendence of Pompeii

The Cult of the Dead

Tomb-lined Streets

A stroll through the streets that begin at
the city walls of Pompeii and head toward
various suburban destinations provides the
perfect conclusion to an encounter with this
ancient city and with the endless dialogue
between life and death that it so admirably
illustrates. It is surely significant that the only
Pompeii monument recorded in detail by
Goethe in his *Voyage in Italy* was the tomb of
the priestess Mamia on the road that begins
at the Herculaneum Gate. This tomb is
distinguished mainly by an armchair, from
which the great German intellectual could
admire the sea and the setting sun. The
European neoclassical cultural trend of the
eighteenth century, nourished to a great extent
by the Bourbon excavations of the Vesuvius
cities, was the atmosphere in which Goethe's

View of the Herculaneum Gate, where
the road from Naples reached Pompeii.
In its last stretch, before the entrance
to the city, the road was scattered with
tombs, following a practice common in
the ancient world; one of these, in the
form of an altar, is visible on the left.

On the seat of this evocative tomb
from the Augustan era in the Necropolis
of the Herculaneum Gate, where the
priestess Mamia was buried, Goethe
paused to meditate at the time of his
Voyage to Italy in 1787, observing the
ancient custom of honoring the dead by
resting on their tombs. The background
is dominated by the monumental ruins
of the tomb of the Istacidii, also from
the Augustan era.

Cenotaph of Caius Calventius Quietus from the Nero-Flavian era, in the Necropolis of the Herculaneum Gate. It resembles an altar with pulvini, ornamental stone cushions, and it belongs to a personage who received the honor of the *bisellium*, the right to sit in special seats during theatrical spectacles.

View of the Necropolis of the Nucera Gate with its typical row of tombs in various styles, in the immediate vicinity of the south-east section of the city walls of Pompeii.

visit to Pompeii took place. A short time later, that same scenario and atmosphere, although he never experienced them directly, inspired the poet Foscolo to write the lofty verses of his *Sepulchres*, many of which managed to directly express the basis for the connection that the ancients felt to the dead:

Testimonies to the great were the tombs,
and altars to their sons; and from them come
the answers of the domestic Lares, and feared
was the oath on the ashes of their farewells.

The displays of wealth and social prestige, the sacredness and actual domestic intimacy of the ancestor cult, and the need to ensure some balance between one's own living experience and the world located beyond the last threshold of existence, mysterious and unfathomable in so many ways, are actually perceptible along the sepulchral roads of Pompeii. This is true in every other place in the ancient world where similar documentation survives, such as the stretch of the Appian Way beyond Porta San Sebastiano. Despite some irrational and superstitious

elements, their intimacy with death, suggested by the very location of the tombs on the city's access roads, seems to signal precisely a vision of the world that combines their essential sense of life's transience with an existential wisdom perhaps more farsighted than and preferable to the modern world's shallow and neurotic tendency to banish the very thought of death from our daily lives. Furthermore, in order to avoid a purely estheticized notion of the connection between the ancients and their necropolises, undoubtedly real but quite misleading if left unqualified, we should not forget that the narrow spaces between the tombs themselves could accommodate furtive encounters of mercenary love, involving prostitutes of the lowest class, winking at passersby and offering themselves for a very small fee. In Pompeii this is attested even by an erotic epigraph scratched on a tomb in the Necropolis of the Nucera Gate, giving a particular price and explicitly describing the service, a worthy vulgar rival to some savory lines by the Imperial era poets Juvenal and Martial that allude to similar mingling of sex and tombs.

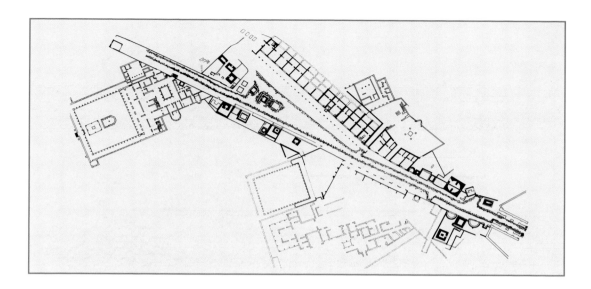

Diagram of the Necropolis of the Herculaneum Gate.

very few tombs from the oldest periods. This picture is full of very marked contrasts in terms of wealth and personal fortune. Such social demarcations were very evident even during the funerals themselves. These were usually sumptuous for members of the ruling classes, who were buried with great pomp

A nineteenth-century drawing by G. Genovese from the famous work *Le case e i monumenti di Pompei* edited by Fausto, Felice, and Antonio Niccolini, and published between 1854 and 1896; it illustrates the tomb said to be that of Aulus Umbrecius Scaurus, with its famous gladiator friezes, which unfortunately have not survived.

Beyond the general impressions that a visit to the Pompeii funerary complexes can offer, in the sense we have just tried to describe, a pause amid these ancient tombs makes it possible to visualize Pompeii's complicated social picture, recognizable even from this particular perspective, especially as it concerns the last two centuries of the city's life, since there are

after their remains had been exhibited for public homage for no less than a week; on the other hand, they were quick and perfunctory for the destitute, who were buried at night, almost furtively, a short time after death. Funeral rites were not uniform either, alternating between burial and cremation, but with an obvious predilection for the latter, especially

The Tomb of the Blue Glass Vase in the Necropolis of the Herculaneum Gate owes its name to this splendid vase in glass cameo from the Julio-Claudian era. It was created by an unusual technique that involved superimposing one vitreous layer on top of another, the first an extremely intense color and the second a layer of white which was then removed in places according to the desired ornamental design. This is one of the most famous examples of artistic craftsmanship in Pompeii. The piece is Dionysian in spirit, as we can see from its shape as an amphora for wine and from the subjects illustrated, which include cupids harvesting grapes and playing music (as seen here) in a refined setting made of an elaborate vegetal motif of vines and of garlands enlivened by birds (detail, facing page) (MANN).

during the period of most thorough Romanization. Naturally, another essential topic of interest is the notable stylistic variety of the tombs, which provide an extraordinary anthology of architectural forms, often with valuable esthetic refinements, as a final testimony to the cultural vitality not just of Pompeii, but of the entire Roman world between the Hellenistic period and the early Imperial era.

A precious epigraphic document, known up to now through four identical inscriptions found outside the Marina, Vesuvius, Nucera, and Herculaneum Gates, is singularly related to the interconnection between life and death, and thus specifically to Pompeii itself. The inscription, going back to the time of the Emperor Vespasian, records how the tribune Titus Suedius Clemens, by explicit order of the emperor, had provided for the restitution to the Pompeii community of several public lots unlawfully seized by private citizens, among them undoubtedly lands used for building tombs. But this epigraph, and in particular the copy found outside the Herculaneum Gate in 1763, fifteen years after the beginning of the

excavations, had great importance in the return to life of the city that had been buried by Vesuvius. The text of the inscription definitively demonstrated that what was coming to light actually belonged to Pompeii and not to Stabia, as the Spanish military engineer Roque de Alcubierre, the first investigator of the Pompeii archeological area, had until then erroneously maintained.

We now turn more closely to the Pompeii necropolises and their most significant funeral monuments, the subject of these lines from Shelley's famous *Ode to Naples*:

Around me gleamed many a bright sepulchre
Of whose pure beauty, Time, as if his pleasure
Were to spare Death, had never made erasure.

The tombs evoked by the romantic poet are unfortunately not as well preserved as they were at the time of their archeological discovery, now some two and a half centuries ago.

Necropolis of the Herculaneum Gate

Outside the Herculaneum Gate, at a place with one of the most evocative landscapes in all Pompeii, where the eye can take in the imposing mass of Vesuvius as well as gentle views of the nearby coast, there are about thirty monumental tombs excavated thus far, belonging for the most part to the last century and a half of the city's life, from the founding of the Sulla colony in 80 B.C. to the phase immediately preceding the eruption. Even today these tombs, located along both sides of the street that ran to Herculaneum and to Naples, as well as on several short side streets, give the impression of being naturally enmeshed in what must have been normal daily activities in an area of intense movement of men, carts and goods, their plots almost merging with those of the sumptuous patrician villas nearby. The stylistic diversity of the funeral monuments reflects not only the demands of esthetic and architectural taste, but real differences of sensibility regarding burial rites and the modes of honoring and immortalizing the memory of the dead, both in the strictly private sense of familial piety and nobility, and in the completely interrelated sense of a public celebration of the wealth and power attained in life by one's own relatives. Regarding this last point, it is useful to emphasize, before moving on to the specific examination of several tombs in the necropolis, that one of the focal points of Roman funerary ideology

Altar tomb with pulvins—actually a monumental cenotaph—built in the time of Nero in honor of the freedwoman Naevoleia Tyche; the bas-relief shown here illustrates a ship sailing toward port, an explicit metaphor for the soul's descent into Hades at life's inevitable end.

between the late Republican period and the early Imperial era was, generally speaking, the spread of individual sepulchral monuments designed to heroicize the deceased, a custom clearly derived from Greece, in connection with the absolutism of the eastern Mediterranean and several aspects of Stoicism, also well represented in this Pompeii necropolis, in addition to tombs inspired by continuity with earlier ideological models.

This significant overlapping is recognizable in the first famous group of tombs located just outside the gate on the south side of the street. These are five monumental tombs, built at different times between the Sulla era and the Flavian age, each with its own particular characteristics. Four of these, adjacent to one another, are typical individual tombs with inscriptions that specifically record, besides the names of the deceased, the municipal council's public grant of the burial site. The oldest tomb belonged in all probability to a moneyed personage of colonial Pompeii, the very same Marcus Porcius who, as duovir quinquennalis, had financed the construction of both the Amphitheater and the covered theater. His tomb had the appearance of a quadrangular altar crowned with *pulvini*, or cushion-like structures, conceived as a monument whose mass would cover the bare earth where his ashes had been deposited. The tomb of this important magistrate is preceded and followed by two other tombs, similar to

each other in conception and style, but not from the same era. They can be dated respectively to the end of the Republican era and the late Augustan age. These are two tufa monuments shaped like semicircular chairs,

An evocative image of the Necropolis of the Herculaneum Gate with its row of tombs; the ancient "cities of the dead" were usually located along the first section of the roads that exited the city gates, almost as if to indicate the need for daily and affectionate intimacy with the dead and the common destiny of all mortals.

with the funeral inscription on the back, and elegant winged lion paws. The first and older tomb must have been created from a statue of the deceased, later lost, the magistrate Aulus Veius, while the second was the last dwelling of Mamia, a priestess of Venus. Their ashes would undoubtedly have been deposited, as in the tomb of Marcus Porcius, in the earth underneath. The particular shape of these two tombs, called *a schola*, directly reveals the need for a burial site capable of accommodating different but complementary requirements: not only the gathering of familiars on the occasion of commemorations or funeral banquets and the explicit desire to perpetuate the buried person's memory, but also, and of no less importance, a very human dialogue intended for the passerby, who is almost invited to sit on the chair and meditate on the precariousness of our destiny in a scenario that is moreover rendered less grim by the site's natural enchantment. The fourth individual monument of this group is the tomb of an augustal (a priest of the Imperial cult) from the Nero or Flavian era, Marcus Cerrinius Restitutus, a tomb essentially set atop an altar around which are arranged stonework chairs.

Behind the tomb of Mamia, however, turned towards a bend in the main sepulchral road, we find a fifth funeral monument, completely different from those examined up to now, and one which documents the persistence during the high Augustan age of ancient customs that reflect the old aristocracy's way of thinking. This is the famous tomb of the Istacidii, an imposing structure with two floors. Below was a quadrangular podium with half-columns against the walls, enclosing a burial chamber surrounded by a dozen niches intended for cinerary urns (of the founders of the family, their descendants, and even of one of their slaves), obviously always accessible on the occasion of funeral rites. Above, unfortunately lost, was a small circular temple, a *thólos,* with an open colonnade that contained the statues of several persons buried in the tomb. This group tomb, linked to a *gens* that was prominent in Pompeii during the Augustan era, is important also because it has yielded various aniconic gravestones, actual tombstones in the form of a bust topped by a disc suggesting a featureless head, bearing an inscription with the name of the deceased on its breast.

Several other fairly significant tombs survive in the Necropolis of the Herculaneum Gate. First we should note the Tomb with the Blue Glass Vase, which takes its name

from a splendid cinerary urn of the Julio-Claudian era, with white cupids in relief on a blue ground, busy with the grape harvest, clearly an allusion to the redemptive symbology connected to Bacchus; second, the tomb said to be that of Aulus Umbricius Scaurus, whose gladiatorial frieze, unfortunately lost, is mentioned in the chapter on theatrical spectacles; and finally, the two monumental cenotaphs, honorary tombs for personages buried elsewhere, both from

the Nero era and in the form of altars with pulvini, related respectively to the augustal Caius Calventius Quietus and to the freedwoman—that is, a liberated former slave—Naevoleia Tyche. Noteworthy in the reliefs of the former is a *bisellium*, the wide theater seat assigned to citizens who distinguished themselves through particular public munificence; in those of the second is a ship with its sail lowered heading toward port, an explicit metaphor for life and its inevitable conclusion.

Necropolis of the Nucera Gate

Excavated at different times, in 1886-1887 and especially in the 1950s under Maiuri, the Necropolis of the Nucera Gate presents another extraordinary group of tombs, often of notable architectural inventiveness, which we will illustrate primarily, but not exclusively, through inscriptions on the most interesting of them. There are almost fifty monuments, falling within the last century and a half of the city's life, as is the case with the Necropolis of the

The Necropolis of the Herculaneum Gate in a drawing proposed by the scholar William Gell, an intellectual of the early nineteenth-century who lived the last twenty years of his life in Naples, from his great masterpiece *Pompeiana: The Topography, Edifices and Ornaments of Pompeii. The Result of Excavations since 1819,* published in London in 1832.

The tomb of the Flavii (50-30 B.C.) is distinguished by a broad facade with many open niches, originally filled with tufa busts, of which only a few traces remain; through the central arched passage one entered a double burial chamber covered with barrel vaults.

Detail of the tomb of the freedman Publius Vesonius Phileros, from the Augustan era, with the inscription containing his invective against a friend who had betrayed his trust.

Herculaneum Gate. For more than 650 feet, the tombs line both sides of the street that runs parallel to the walls outside the Nucera Gate, proceeding south-west toward the Stabia Gate—near which it apparently intersected the suburban road to Stabia—and north-east towards the Nucera plain. In fact, along this sector of the road, there is a tomb from the Flavian era, consisting of a base with elegant Corinthian pilasters and a central niche, into which were scratched two elegant lines of erotic verse dedicated to a beautiful Nucera woman, Novellia Primigenia. She is known also from other Pompeii epigraphs in which she was celebrated for her beauty and for her availability as a prostitute, in all probability a high-priced one. The brief poetic piece, comparable to many verses of Virgil and Ovid, made use of an image that was as efficient as it was sensual:

> *Would that I could be for but an hour that gem*
> *[in the ring I give you]*
> *so that I could kiss you as your mouth affixed*
> *the seal.*

These lines, a clear reference to gems set in rings which could be used as personal seals, reveal, thanks to their lofty literary tone, the elevated social origins not only of their author but also of his lover herself.

It is in the other sector of the necropolis, however, the one going towards the Stabia Gate, where the most significant monuments are clustered. The first of these is a large tomb, in *opus incertum* with traces of the original stucco coating, of a freedman of the important late-Republican Ceii family, owners of a beautiful *domus* not far from the House of Menander. This freedman, Lucius Ceius Serapius, whose family name seems to suggest Egyptian origin, held the office of *argentarius*, as the inscription reminds us, and is therefore probably the earliest banker documented in Pompeii. Next to this grave is an unusual funeral monument, also from the late-Republican era. It opens in front through the center of an arch, lined by three niches on each side intended for an equal number of aniconic gravestones, only a few of which have been preserved. Above, set back slightly, is a second row of eight niches, two of which still hold coarsely-made tufa busts; through the central arch mentioned above, one entered two sepulchral chambers covered by barrel vaults, where burial niches were situated for the urns. This collective tomb, which we know by epigraphic evidence to belong to the freed-men of a certain Publius Flavius, was most probably managed by a funerary board, a sort of corporation in charge of this specific task.

The most monumental tomb in the entire necropolis is without doubt the tomb of Eumachia, the priestess of Venus who died in the time of Tiberius and who is linked to the construction of the important building in the Forum that was named after her in modern times. It is a true mausoleum, with a large enclosure in front and the main part of the structure in the form of a large concrete exedra faced with elegant slabs of Nucera tufa. This semicircle, above the sepulchral chamber, was once dominated by a larger-than-life statue of the priestess, only a few fragments of which, unfortunately, remain. Thirty or so feet away, on a high podium, stands an Augustan aedicula-style tomb containing three tufa statues, two male ones on the sides and a female one in the center. The major point of interest in this tomb may be the epigraph carved into the center of the podium:

Passerby, stop a moment if it does not disturb you, and learn that against which you must beware. A friend, one I had hoped was really such to me, accused me falsely; in court, by the grace of the gods and in virtue of my innocence, I was absolved of every charge; may those who defame us be welcomed neither by the Penates nor by the underworld divinities.

These are the bitter reflections, addressed to anyone who found himself along the road,

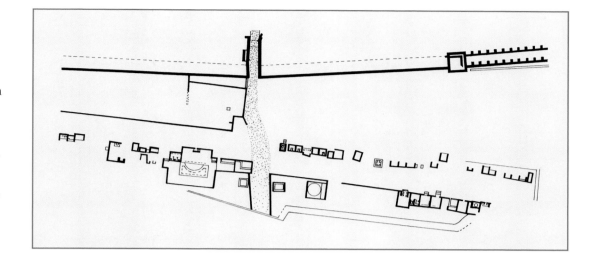

Diagram of the Necropolis of the Nucera Gate.

offered with a generous moral purpose but an equal measure of rancor towards his false friend, by the freedman Publius Vesonius Phileros, whose effigy is in the statue on the left, next to his patroness, Vesonia. His trust had been betrayed by Marcus Orfellius Faustus, also a freedman, who is depicted, one might say for future ignominy, in the statue on the right.

The corpses of many Pompeiians who perished in the vain flight from the fury of the volcano were found in the excavation of the tombs in this necropolis completed by Maiuri. The great archeologist, who recorded with emotional words the final human act of every one of those desperate persons, wanted to leave the casts of thirteen victims next to the graves of the Nucera Gate, almost as if to contrast the death of those who had the good fortune to die in bed with the fate of those who were torn from life by a blind and terrible violence.

Other Funerary Structures

Another three necropolises, unfortunately much less well known than the two described above, are located close to two other city gates. The Samnitic-Roman necropolis discovered a few hundred yards outside the Stabia Gate in the 1910s has particular historic significance—even more than the three tombs *a schola* excavated up to then, the most interesting of which is possibly that of Marcus Tullius, almost certainly the founder of the Temple of the Fortuna Augusta. This funerary area was used for more than four centuries, beginning at the end of the fourth century B.C., and the more than forty burial tombs here, going back to the Samnitic period, are worthy of note

Full view of the tomb of Publius Vesonius Phileros, characterized by its niche constructed of brick, in which stand three tufa statues, effigies, respectively, of the deceased, his patron, and his false friend.

Facing page
Mosaic from the Augustan era that decorated the open triclinium of *domus* I, 5, 2; it is an allegory of the fleeting nature of earthly pleasures and of the levelling power of death. Below the skull, a butterfly and a wheel evoke the soul and its fate, while on the right and left, in a perfectly mirrored balance assured by the scale held up by the skull, are the figurative symbols of wealth (the sceptre and purple toga) and of poverty (the beggar's crook and knapsack) (MANN).

above all for their absolute simplicity and relative poverty. These graves, which resemble those in a Pompeii necropolis found outside the Herculaneum Gate, attest to a notable dissimilarity between their intentional modesty and the opulence of the houses contemporary with them, a possible indication of funeral customs from ancient Sabellian traditions, predating the influence of ideological models from the Hellenistic East. From this same necropolis come several *tabellae defixionum*, lead tablets from the first century B.C. on which were carved

Priscus, who died at the young age of twenty-two, shortly before the eruption. His inscription records, among other things, that the decurions voted a substantial contribution for his funeral. An equal honor was also reserved for the duovir quinquennalis of the Imperial era, Marcus Obellius Firmus, buried in a monumental tomb with an enclosure outside the Nola Gate. Another Pompeii notable, a duovir with jurisdictional power, Numerius Herennius Celsus, a wealthy personage of the Augustan era, was buried nearby in an elegant tomb *a schola*. But this

This fresco, still *in situ* in the tomb of the Flavian-era aedile Caius Vestorius Priscus in the Necropolis of the Vesuvius Gate, gives a very accurate picture of a table laid with sumptuous silverware and was intended to record for posterity the wealth of the deceased.

maledictions against enemies and rivals, whose untimely misadventures and death were hoped for. These tablets were deposited in the center of the graves, evidently in the certainty, also linked to primitive rituals of magic and superstition, that the evil eye would thus be more effective.

Among the only four known tombs in the Necropolis of the Vesuvius Gate, the one which stands out above all is a tomb decorated with interesting pictures of various subjects and formed by an enclosure around an altar with pulvini on a tall base. This was the final abode of an aedile, Caius Vestorius

same necropolis has also revealed thirty-six very pitiable cinerary urns, buried with the sparsest of provisions along the *pomerium,* the consecrated land left free of construction on both sides of the city walls. These are the graves of humble Pompeiians, barely remembered by aniconic tombstones or by inscriptions scratched on the walls, an incisive testimony to class distinctions that not even the common destiny of death could erase.

Emidio de Albentiis

Glossary

compiled by Emidio De Albentiis

Aedicula (Latin, "little temple," from *aedes,* "temple"): small structure often annexed to a larger building, usually consisting of two columns or half-columns with a pediment on top, to serve as an ornament and protection for sacred images, celebratory representations, epigraphs, etc.

Aedile (Latin, from *aedes,* "temple"): an official in charge of public works and games, police, and the grain supply.

Agger (from Latin *agger -eris,* "rampart, embankment"): an embankment that reinforces the defensive line of a fortification, obtained by excavating a deep trench and tossing the dirt inward along the edge; the threshold of the embankment was usually later reinforced with a wall.

Ala (Latin, "wing"): a side wing or corridor opening right or left at the far end of an atrium.

Ambulacrum (Latin, from *ambulare,* "to walk"): a term established in modern archaeology to indicate a covered, porticoed walkway; also indicates the corridor placed between a perimeter colonnade and the *cella* (q.v.) of a classical temple. The Romans used the term *ambulatio* to indicate an uncovered walkway or tree-lined avenue.

Aniconic (from Greek *an,* "without" + *icona,* "image"): non-figurative.

Antefix (from Latin *antefixa -orum,* "placed in front of"): decorative element which closed off the ends of roof tiles that served as ducts or rainspouts on Greek temples; generally and especially originally of painted terra-cotta, later of stone or marble, and often decorated with figurative motifs in high relief.

Apse (from late Latin *absida -ae,* crossed with classical Latin *absis -idis,* Greek *hapsis -idos,* "joint, arch, vault"): architectural structure in the form of a semicircular, polygonal or square niche, surmounted by a bowl-shaped vault in a quarter-sphere; found in classical architecture, especially Roman, with important Greek precedents; widely used in Christian architecture from its beginnings up to the present.

Arca, -ae (Latin): box, chest, money box, safe, prison cell.

Architectural terra-cotta: typical ornamental elements on sacred buildings in the Etrusco-Italic tradition; made of terra-cotta mostly cast from molds, and used as facings for the various wooden elements that formed the framework of a building's roof; in addition to their protective function, they had great decorative value because of the various figurative, geometric and stylized motifs that distinguished them.

Ashlar masonry: square-cut or rusticated stone.

Atellana (from Latin *fabula atellana,* "a fable from Atella," an Oscan locality in the Campania region): a comic genre in Latin literature, possibly originating around 300 B.C.; acquired some literary respectability at the time of Sulla in the early part of the first century B.C. thanks to the works of Novius and Pomponius. It was a kind of lively and realistic farce, rich in salacious jokes and allusions, with plots concerning comic mix-ups and themes taken from country life having to do with simple folk and common laborers.

Atrium (from Latin): a central connecting room in the Roman house, with an opening in the roof for collecting rainwater (see *impluvium*).

Bucchero ware (from Spanish *bucaro* and Portuguese *pucaro*): pots made from a reddish earth used extensively in the seventeenth and eighteenth centuries in Portugal, and very fashionable in Italy during the Baroque era. At the end of the seventeenth century, when excavations in the Etruscan necropolises first began, the many vases recovered there that were created from a polished black clay were called "buccheri" by analogy with the recently introduced Iberian vases. Vases in bucchero are among the most typical artisanal products of ancient Etruria, especially in the archaic period from the seventh to sixth centuries B.C.

Caldarium (Latin, from *calor,* "heat"): the hot room in the baths; also *calidarium.*

Cardo (from Latin *cardo-,* "hinge, pivot") and **Decuman** (from Latin *decumanus,* variant of *decimanus,* from *decimus,* "tenth"): the principal axes on which the urban grid was oriented, generally consisting of streets intersecting at right angles, the cardo north-south and the decuman east-west; also used for military encampments and the subdivision of agricultural land into regular lots. Derived from the ancient rites of the augurs, the priests charged with the interpretation of signs, they were the imaginary lines which bordered the so-called augural temple, the holy area in which to observe the divine *signa.*

Catachthonic (from Greek *kata,* "down" + *chthon,* "earth"): having to do with the subterranean deities of the underworld; sometimes confused with "chthonic" (q.v.).

Cella (Latin, "small room, storeroom, cellar"): in ancient temple architecture the most sacred part of the temple, designed to house the cult statue; usually a closed space bordered by perimeter walls and accessible only by the persons responsible for the cult.

Cella Penaria (Latin): a *cella* (q.v.) dedicated to the Penates, gods of the storeroom, who were, with the Lares, protectors of the household.

Cenaculum (Latin): upstairs dining room; also upper floor.

Cenatium (Latin): dining hall.

Choreutic space (from the Greek *choreutikos,* "having to do with choral dance"): in ancient classical theatrical productions an area generally connected to the orchestra and reserved for choral movements.

Chthonic (from Greek *chthon,* "earth"): refers to pagan deities directly connected to the earth; sometimes used to indicate underworld deities more properly referred to as catachthonic (q.v.).

Client (from Latin *cliens -entis*): a free citizen dependent on the aid and protection of a powerful citizen called a patron.

Clipeus (Latin): a circular metal or marble medallion, also one painted in murals, depicting divinities and heroes, usually only the head or bust; from a circular shield used by Roman soldiers during the Republican era and the Empire.

Cocciopesto (from Italian *coccio*, "terracotta," + *pesto*, "crushed"): a compact combination of clay fragments and broken pottery mixed with lime mortar and crushed; used as a lining for cisterns, bathtubs, terraces and *impluvia* because of its impermeability, and also for flooring, sometimes decorated with marble tiles.

Comitia (Latin, plural of *comitium*, "a meeting place," from *com*, "together" + *ire*, "to go"): public assemblies for the exercise of legislative, judicial, and electoral functions.

Compluvium (Latin, from *compluere*, "to flow together," *pluere*, "to rain"): a square opening in the roof of the atrium toward which the roof sloped and through which the rain fell into the *impluvium* (q.v.).

Crepidine (from Latin *crepido -inis*, Greek *krepis -idos*, "base, foundation"): in classical architecture, a stone base for a temple building, consisting of three steps.

Crotali (Latin, from Greek *krotalon*, from *krotos*, "noise"): a pair of clappers made of wood, ivory or even metal that the musician, holding the lower one, caused to clack against each other like castanets; a percussion instrument found in ancient classical and oriental civilizations; sing. *crotalum*, each of the two clappers.

Cryptoporticus (Latin, from Greek *kryptos*, "hidden" + Latin *porticus*, "gallery"): a hidden or enclosed portico or gallery.

Deambulatorium (late Latin, from *deambulare*, "to walk"): the part of a building that, within the overall architectural context, has a complementary function with respect to another part, e.g. a passageway alongside a main corridor, as in the apse of a Gothic cathedral where the deambulatorium follows the curving and polygonal route of the chancel; in Roman architecture it can indicate a separate corridor intended as a private passage.

Decuman see Cardo.

Distich (from late Latin *distichum*, Greek *distichon*, "poem of two lines"): strophe composed of two lines; in classical meter used mainly to indicate the unit formed by one line of hexameter and one line of pentameter, known as the elegiac distich.

Distyle (from Latin *di-*, Greek *dis*, "twice" + Latin *stilo*, Greek *stylos*, "column"): indicates a temple with two columns on the facade, placed in front of the doorway to the *cella* (q.v.) or between the doorways; also indicates a large space with two columns on the entrance side.

Domus (Latin, from Greek *domos*, "house, room" and *demo*, "build"): house or dwelling.

Donarium (Latin, from *donum*, "gift"): indicates both the place where offerings to the gods were housed, and the individual votive gift itself; donariums could often be massive in both construction and appearance.

Double cortina wall (from late Latin *cortina* and Latin *cors, cortis*, "court, courtyard" derived from Greek *aulaia*, "curtain, court" and *aule*, "hall, court"): in ancient military architecture a cortina wall designated the entire arrangement of elements in a fortification, including the towers; in double-cortina walls, a construction technique originating with the Greeks, two stone walls ran parallel to each other with the space in-between filled with stone chips and packed earth.

Duovir iure dicundo (Latin): a two-man team of magistrates; every five years the duovir iure dicundo assumed the title of *quinquennales* and as Roman censors had to conduct the census and revise the list of decurions.

Emblem (from Latin *emblema*, Greek *emblema*, literally "a thing inserted," from *en* + *ballo*, "throw"): a mosaic image created by fixing tiny polychrome tiles onto a thin sheet of marble or onto a large tile which is then imbedded in a tessellated floor.

Emporium sanctuary (from Latin *emporium*, Greek *emporion*, derived from *emporos*, "traveler or trader," in turn from *poros*, "passage"): an important ancient sacred complex located in a market; a wholesale commercial center, usually situated on the coast, functioning as a place for the receipt and distribution of merchandise for one or more regions.

Epistyle (from Greek *epistylion*, from *epi*, "above" + *stylos*, "column"): in classical architecture an architrave consisting of marble blocks positioned horizontally atop columns with their junctures on the axis of the columns.

Exedra (from Greek, *ex*, "out, from" + *hedra*, "place for sitting"): a portico where discussions are held; in private homes a vestibule used for conversation.

Fauces (Latin): passage from the entrance to the interior of a house.

Frigidarium (Latin, from *frigus*, "frost, cold"): room with a cold bath.

Graffito (from Italian *graffiare*, "to scratch"): a design or inscription carved into the surface of an object, or more often onto a rock or the walls of a building, according to a practice already documented in prehistoric times.

Gymnasium (from Greek *gymnasion*, derived from *gymnazo*, "exercise naked," and *gymnos*, "nude"): in ancient Greece the place where men and boys exercised naked and took part in athletic games; later, a center for spiritual education and a meeting place for banquets, parties, theatrical productions, lessons, conferences, etc.

Heraion (from Greek *Hera*): a temple or sanctuary consecrated to the Greek female divinity Hera, the wife of Zeus, called Juno by the Romans.

Hortus (Latin): garden.

Impluvium (Latin, from *pluere*, "to rain"): a cistern or pool in the atrium or peristyle that collects rainwater through the *compluvium* (q.v.).

In situ (Latin, "in position"): an archeological term indicating that an object was discovered in its original position and has not been moved elsewhere.

Insula (Latin, "island"): a block of houses or an apartment block.

Laconicum (Latin, from Greek *lakonikos*,

a Spartan): steam bath, possibly based on a model originating in Sparta and found in Greek gymnasia.

Lapis niger (Latin, "black stone"): the black stone floor of the Comitia.

Lararium (Latin): a small shrine dedicated to the Lares, tutelary gods or spirits worshipped as guardians of the household.

Latericius (Latin, from *later* "brick, tile"): brick; fictile material composed of clay, calcium carbonate, iron oxide and cinders; widely used in Roman architecture.

Maenianum (Latin): in Roman architecture a protrusion beyond the vertical line of a wall or portico on the upper portion of a building, in the manner of a loggia or balcony; named after Caius Maenius, Roman consul in 318 B.C., who was the first to introduce this architectural element in the buildings around the Roman Forum.

Megalographic (from Greek, *megalo-*, "large," and *graphia*, "writing, drawing"): indicates pictures of larger-than-life size or of morally elevated subjects; used in archeology to indicate a picture cycle containing large figures.

Monopteros (Greek): term mentioned by Vitruvius, indicating a temple with a single row of exterior columns around the cella (q.v.), also a round temple with a circular colonnade supporting the roof and without a cella.

Mystica vannus (Latin, "mystic vessel"): in Dionysian rituals a basket that contained the instruments necessary for the celebration of the mystery cult.

Nucleus (from Latin): the upper layer of the composite preparation required for the completion of a pavement; placed over the *rudus* (q.v.), the *nucleus* was a cementitious layer about five inches thick made of crushed earthenware and lime which could function either as a pavement itself, mixed with large ceramic or marble fragments, or as a bed on top of which to lay a tessellated pavement.

Oecus (Latin, from Greek *oikos*, "house"): an apartment, room, or hall in an ancient Roman house.

Opus incertum (Latin): term mentioned by Vitruvius indicating a cement surface that is in irregular layers; a concrete wall faced with stones of irregular shape.

Opus sectile (Latin, from *sectilis, sectus, secare* "to saw or cut"): an inlay or mosaic in colored marble where the pieces are cut to follow the outline of a geometric or figurative design and to which other polychrome materials such as enamel and vitreous paste can be added; of Greek origin and widespread throughout the Roman world in both the late-antique and early-Christian eras.

Opus vermiculatum (Latin, from *vermis*, "worm"): a mosaic using small pieces of marble arranged in patterns of curving or wavy lines.

Orthostates (from Greek *orthos*, "erect" + *histemi*, "make stand"): vertical stone slabs with which the lower line of the foundation walls was constructed, double or triple the height of the upper rows.

Oscan (from Latin *Osci* or *Opsci*): member of an ancient Italic population of the Campania region; the language of the Oscans.

Penates (Latin): Roman gods of the storeroom and protectors of the household.

Peripter (from Greek *peripteros*, derived from *peri-*, "around" + *pteron*, "wing"): a classical temple with a row of columns on all sides, whether the *cella* (q.v.) was round or rectangular.

Peristyle (from Greek *peri*, "around" + *stylos*, "pillar"): a colonnade or row of columns surrounding a temple or court.

Pertica (Latin, of Italic origin): unit of measure equal to a length of ten feet, used by the ancient Romans, who also called it a *decempeda*.

Pinax (Greek): a table or board; in particular a wooden tablet used for calculations or, when coated with wax, for writing and painting.

Poliade (from Greek *polias -ados*, feminine adjective derived from *polis*, "city," the "protectress of the city"): describes a divinity more closely linked to one specific city than to any other, with the special role of protectress for which she was venerated with a particularly solemn cult.

Pomerium (Latin, from *post*, "behind" + *moerus, murus*, "wall"): in ancient Rome and in the colonies, a strip of consecrated land that ran along the city walls both inside and outside and that was kept free of construction.

Portico (from Latin *porticus* and *porta*, "gate"): an open, colonnaded, covered space serving as a porch at the entrance to a building or as an ambulatory.

Porticus triplex (Latin): portico which extended along three sides.

Posterula (late Latin, feminine diminutive of *posterus*, "one who stands behind"): in ancient fortifications a small hidden doorway far from the main door that ensured a link between the interior and the exterior of the enclosure, to be used in unusual circumstances.

Praefurnium (Latin): stove or boiler for heating water and air in the ancient public and private baths.

Propylaeum (Latin, from Greek *propylaion*, from *pro-*, "in front of" + *pyle*, "gate"): in classical architecture a stately, monumental complex of buildings at the entrance to a city or plaza; also an imposing vestibule or entryway at the front of an enclosure, building, or temple.

Prostas (Greek, from *pro-*, "in front of" + *histemi*, "make stand"): the space at the front of a Greek or Hellenic building in between the thick piers on the sides of the portico; a sort of monumental vestibule.

Prostylos (Latin, from Greek *pro-*, "in front of" + *stylos*, "column"): a type of classical temple with a row of at least four columns in a front portico only.

Prothyron (Greek, *pro*, "before" + *thyra*, "door"): a front door; the space before a door; a porch or veranda.

Proto-history: an intermediate period between pre-history, for which there are no written records, and history, for which there are written texts; specifically, the ancient period to which classical authors refer when they write about remote epochs of which they themselves had only a vague notion which was passed down orally without the support of any written documents.

Pseudoperipteros (Latin, from Greek *pseudes*, "false" + *peri-*, "around" + *pteron*, "wing"): a type of temple, especially in Roman times, adapted from the peripteral type (q.v.), where the *cella* (q.v.) opened up to incorporate the colonnade, which was reduced to a row of half-columns or pilasters jutting out from the walls.

Quadriporticus (Latin): a portico running along the four sides of a quadrilateral courtyard.

Repositorium (Latin): a space used as a warehouse or store room.

Rudus (Latin): the intermediate layer of the composite preparation required for the completion of a pavement; placed over the *statumen*, a layer of large pepples, the *rudus* was about ten inches thick and composed of gravel, sand, stones and lime, forming a sort of concrete on which the *nucleus* (q.v.) was laid.

Rustic (Latin *rusticus*, from *rus*, "open land"): rural, relating to the country; describes a rough-hewn building or wall with conspicuous joints.

Sacellum (Latin, diminutive of *sacrum*, "sacred enclosure"): a small round or quadrangular enclosure open to the sky with an altar consecrated to a divinity; also the name for other special kinds of cult sites such as niches, aedicules, rocky hollows, etc.

Salutatio (Latin): a visit paid to someone at home in order to show respect, especially by a client (q.v.) to a patron as an act of particular deference.

Scenae frons (Latin): a wall structure, articulated in various ways, that delimited the theatrical stage, separating the front, where the action took place, from the backstage area.

Sinopia (from Latin, Greek *sinopis*, from Sinop, an ancient port on the Black Sea): a red to reddish-brown earth pigment used for preliminary drawings of frescoes on top of a rough sketch done in charcoal; a drawing using this pigment.

Social War (from Latin *socii*, "allies"): a war against former allies; the war between Rome and eight Sabellian cities, including Samnitic Pompeii, from 90 to 88 B.C.,

which ended with Rome's offer of citizenship and most of their other demands to its defeated enemies.

Stratigraphy (from Latin *stratus*, past participle of *sternere*, "to spread out"): a method of analysis that distinguishes the successive layers in which archeological material is found in order to document various periods and fix relative dates.

Strigil (from Latin *strigilis*): an iron or bronze scraper used to clean sweat, dirt and oil from the body after gymnastic exercise and the bath; made of a straight handle and a curved, concave blade that was passed over the body.

Synoecismus (late Latin, from Greek *syn*, "together" + *oikeo*, "inhabit"): the concentration in a single city of a population previously spread among villages and farmlands, with the grant of political rights equal to those of the existing citizens; also the formation of a new city from several pre-existing ones.

Tablinum (Latin, from *tabula*, "record, writing tablet, tablet, board"): a room, alcove, or patio opening off the atrium opposite the main entrance and used as a gallery to store family archives, pictures, statues, etc.

Tabula picta (Latin): a painted plank, synonymous with a painting.

Telamon (from Latin, Greek *telamon*, "bearer, supporter"): a sculpted male figure used as a column or pilaster to support an architectural framework.

Tepidarium (Latin, from *tepidus*, "moderately warm"): room with a warm bath.

Terminus ante quem (Latin, "the end before which"): a time or date established as the moment before which the thing being discussed must have occurred; used to date events, the construction of buildings, etc.

Tetrastyle (from Greek *tetra*, "four" + *stylos*, "column"): describes a temple having four columns along the front; also describes an atrium whose roof is supported by four columns in a square configuration.

Thermae (Latin, from Greek *therme*, "heat"): a public bathing establishment

usually of great size with rooms (*caldarium, tepidarium, frigidarium*, q.v.) of varied heat intensity and facilities for exercise and relaxation; also similar rooms of smaller size in private homes.

Thólos (Latin and Greek): a circular building, especially a beehive-shaped tomb approached through a horizontal passage in the side of a hill.

Triclinium (Latin, from Greek *triklinion*, from *tri*, "three" + *klineo*, "lean, recline"): a couch that extends around three sides of a table; a room or open area furnished with a triclinium and used for dining.

Tripod (from Latin, Greek, *tri-*, "three" + *pod-, pous*, "foot"): a three-footed stand, usually of bronze but sometimes of gold, copper, marble or terra-cotta, used to support braziers, candelabra, receptacles, etc.; the famous tripod of Delhi was a three-legged stool, the seat of the priestess of Apollo when delivering oracles.

Trivium (Latin, *tri-*, "three" + *via*, "road"): the place where three roads intersect.

Tuscanic (from Latin *tuscanus*, "from Tuscia, Etruscan"): an order of architecture that is Etruscan in origin, distinguished by a plain style with slightly tapered columns that have smooth shafts resting on large bases of varying shapes and capitals similar to the Doric.

Vestibule (from Latin, *vestibulum*, origin unknown): an open space at the entrance to a room; a hall or passage between the outer door and the interior of a building; the portico at the front of a temple whose atrium was created by the forward extension of the walls of the *cella* (q.v.); the space in front of a tomb.

Viridarium (Latin, from *viridis*, "green"): a garden or wooded park.

Xenia (Latin, from Greek *xenos*, "guest" and *xenion*, "hospitality"): a present given to a guest or stranger, especially to a foreign ambassador; also the still-life paintings used for such gifts.

Xystus (Latin, from Greek *xystos*, "scraped, polished"): a long, open portico with a smooth floor used for athletic exercises during winter or stormy weather; also a walk lined with trees.

Bibliography

Urban Development

Bonghi Jovino, M (cur.). *L'insula 5 della* Regio *VI dalle origini al 79 d. C.*, Roma 1990.

De Caro, S. "La città sannitica. Urbanistica e architettura," *Pompei*, Ed. F. Zevi, Napoli 1991, 23-48.

____. "Lo sviluppo urbanistico di Pompei, *Atti e Memorie della Società Magna Grecia*, 3a ser. I, Roma 1992, 67-90.

Eschebach, H. *Die Städtebauliche Entwicklung des antiken Pompeji, Römische Mitteilungen*, Suppl. 17, Heidelberg 1970.

Fiorelli, G. *Descrizione di Pompei*, 1875 Napoli 2001.

Geertman, H. "Lo studio della città antica. Vecchi e nuovi approcci," *Pompei. Scienza e società*, Milano 2001, 131-135.

Gerkan, A. von. *Der Stadtplan von Pompeji*, Berlin 1940.

Maiuri, A. *Alla ricerca di Pompei preromana*, Napoli 1973.

Sgobbo, I. "Un complesso di edifici sannitici e i quartieri di Pompei per la prima volta riconosciuti," *Rendiconti dell'Accademia di Archeologia, Lettere e Belle Arti di Napoli* 6, 1942, 15-41.

Sogliano, A. *Pompei nel suo sviluppo storico: Pompei preromana*, Roma 1937.

Walls and War

Chiaramonte Treré, C. *Nuovi contributi sulle fortificazioni pompeiane*, Milano 1986.

De Caro, S. "Nuove indagini sulle fortificazioni di Pompei," *Annali dell'Istituto Universitario Orientale. Sezione di Archeologia e Storia Antica*, 7, 1985, 75-114.

Maiuri, A. "Studi e ricerche sulle fortificazioni di Pompei," *Monumenti Antichi dei Lincei* 33, 1929, cc. 120-296.

Government and the Forum

Castrén, P. "Ordo Populusque Pompeianus. Polity and Society in Roman Pompeii," *Acta Instituti Romani Finlandiae* 8, Roma 1975.

Dobbins, J. J. "Problems of Chronology, Decoration, and Urban Design in the Forum at Pompeii," *American Journal of Archaeology* 98, 1994, 629-694.

Franklin, J. *Pompeii: the Electoral Programmata, Campaigns and Politics, A. D. 71-79, Papers and Monographs of the American Academy in Rome* 28, 1980.

Jongman, W. *The Economy and Society of Pompeii*, 2nd Ed., Amsterdam 1991.

Lauter, H. "Zur Chronologie der Forumsbauten von Pompeji, *Jahrbuch der Institut* 1979, 416-436.

Lo Cascio, E. "La società pompeiana dalla città sannitica alla colonia romana," *Pompei* I, a cura di F. Zevi, Napoli 1991, 113-128.

____. "Pompei, dalla città sannitica alla colonia sillana: le vicende istituzionali, Les élites municipales de l'Italie péninsulaire des Gracques à Néron." *Actes de la Table Ronde internationale de Clermont-Ferrand* (1991), Napoli-Roma 1996, 111-123.

Onorato, G. *Iscrizioni pompeiane. La vita pubblica*, Napoli 1950.

Savino, E. "Note su Pompei colonia sillana: popolazione, strutture agraria, ordinamento istituzionale," *Athenaeum* 80, 1998, 439-461.

Sogliano, A. *Il Foro di Pompei, Memorie dell'Accademia dei Lincei* 6, 1, 1925, 221-272.

The Sacred

Carrol, M., Godden, D. "The Sanctuary of Apollo at Pompeii: Reconsidering Chronologies and Excavation History," *American Journal of Archaeology* 104, 2000, 743-745.

Coarelli, F. "Il culto di Mefitis in Campania e a Roma," *I culti della Campania antica. Atti del convegno internazionale di studi in ricordo di Nazarena Valenza Mele* (Napoli 1995), Roma 1998, 185-190.

De Caro, S. *Saggi nell'area del tempio di Apollo a Pompei: Annali dell'Istituto Orientale di Napoli. Sezione di archeologia e storia antica* 3, 1986.

Della Corte, M. "Venus Pompeiana," *Ausonia* 10, 1921, 68-87.

De Waele J. (cur.). *Il tempio dorico del Foro Triangolare di Pompei*, Roma 2001.

Elia, O., Pugliese Carratelli, G. "Il santuario dionisiaco di Pompei," *La Parola del Passato* 34, 1979, 442-480.

Jacobelli L., Pensabene, P. "La decorazione architettonica del tempio di Venere a Pompei: contributo allo studio e alla ricostruzione del santuario," *Rivista di Studi Pompeiani* 7, 1995-1996, 45-75.

Russo, D. *Il tempio di Giove Meilichio a Pompei*, Napoli 1991.

Torelli, M. "Il culto imperiale a Pompei," *I culti della Campania antica. Atti del convegno internazionale di studi in ricordo di Nazarena Valenza Mele* (Napoli 1995), Roma 1998, 245-270.

Tran Tam Tinh, V. *Le culte d'Isis à Pompéi*, Paris 1964.

Zevi, F. "I Greci, gli Etruschi, il Sele (*note sui culti arcaici di Pompei*)," *I culti della Campania antica. Atti del convegno internazionale di studi in ricordo di Nazarena Valenza Mele* (Napoli 1995), Roma 1998, 1-25.

Alla ricerca di Iside. Analisi, studi e restauri dell'Iseo pompeiano del Museo di Napoli, Napoli 1992.

"Alla ricerca di Iside," *La Parola del Passato* 49, 1994, fasc. I, 2.

Economics and Industry

Andreau, J. "Histoire de séismes et histoire économique. Le tremblement de terre de Pompéi (62 ap. J.-C.)," *Annales E.S.C.*, 28, 1973, 369-395.

____. *Les affaires de Monsieur Jucundus*, Roma 1974.

____. "Le tavolette cerate," *Pompei 79*, Napoli, 1979, 272-277

____. "Remarques sur la société pompéienne (à propos des tablettes de L. Caecilius Iucundus)," *Dialoghi di Archeologia* 7, 1973, 213-254.

____. "Sull'economia di Pompei," *Pompei. Scienza e società*, Milano 2001, 109-110.

Breglia, L. "Circolazione monetale ed aspetti della vita economica a Pompei," *Pompeiana*, Napoli 1950, 41-59.

Carrington, R. C. "Studies in the Campanian *Villae Rusticae*," *Journal of Roman Studies*, 21, 1931, 110-130.

Casella, D. "La frutta nelle pitture pompeiane," *Pompeiana*, Napoli 1950, 355-386.

Castrén, P. *Ordo populusque pompeianus. Polity and Society in Roman Pompeii*, Roma 1975.

Ciarallo, A. "La regione vesuviana al 79 d.C.," "Il territorio vesuviano nel 79 d.C.," *Pompei 1992*, 9-13.

Curtis, R. I. *Garum and Salsamenta. Production and Commerce in Materia Medica*, Leiden-New York 1991.

____. *The Production and Commerce of Fish Sauce in the Western Roman Empire: a Social and Economic Study*, Ann Arbor (Mich.) 1992.

Dapoto, P. "Circolazione monetale a Pompei. Cenni su problemi di economia," *Rivista di Studi Pompeiani* 1, 1987, 107-110.

D'Arms, J. "Ville rustiche e ville di 'otium'," *Pompei 79*, Napoli 1979, 65-86.

Day, J. "Agriculture in the Life of Pompeii," *Yale Classical Studies* 3, 1932, 165-208.

Eschebach, L. "Hafenstadt Pompeji," *Antike Welt* 20, 1989, 40-54.

Étienne, R. *La vita quotidiana a Pompei*, Milano 1973, 146-235.

Frank, T. "Economic Life of an Ancient City," *Classical Philology* 13, 1918, 225-240.

Geist, H. *Pompejanische Wandinschriften*, München 1960.

Heurgon, J. "Les Lassii pompéiens et l'importation des vins italiens en Gaule," *La Parola del Passato* 7, 1952, 113-118.

Jongman, W. M. *The Economy and Society of Pompeii*, Amsterdam 1988.

Kolendo, J. "Le attività agricole degli abitanti di Pompei e gli attrezzi agricoli ritrovati all'interno della città," *Opus. Rivista internazionale per la storia economica e sociale dell'antichità* 4, 1987, 111-124.

La Torre, G. F. "Gli impianti commerciali e artigianali nel tessuto urbano di Pompei," *Pompei. L'informatica al servizio di una città antica*, Roma 1988, 73-102.

Lepore, E. "Orientamenti per la storia sociale di Pompei," *Pompeiana*, Napoli 1950, 144-166.

Mau, A. *Pompeji in Leben und Kunst*, Leipzig 1908, 403-424.

Moeller, W. O. *The Wool Trade of Ancient Pompeii*, Leiden 1976.

Moritz, L. A. *Grain Mills and Flour in Classical Antiquity*, Oxford 1958, 74-90.

Onorato, G. O. *Iscrizioni pompeiane. La vita pubblica*, Firenze 1957.

Rostovtzeff, M. I. *The Social and Economic History of the Roman Empire*, Oxford 1926.

Savio, A. "Sui prezzi del frumento e del pane a Pompei," *Numismatica e antichità classica*, vol. 3, Lugano 1974, 121-126.

Sgobbo, I. "Un complesso di edifici sannitici e i quartieri di Pompei per la prima volta riconosciuti," *Memorie della Reale Accademia di Archeologia Lettere e Belle Arti di Napoli*, 6, 1942, 15-41.

Staccioli, R. A. *Pompei. Vita pubblica di un'antica città*, Roma 1979.

Stazio, A. "Moneta e vita economica a Pompei. Un restauro di conoscenza e di immagine della città antica," *Restaurare Pompei*, Milano 1990, 83-94.

Tchernia, A. "Amphores et marques d'amphores de Bétique à Pompéi et à Stabies," *Mélanges de l'École Française de Rome*, 76, 1964, 419-449.

____. "Il vino: produzione e commercio," *Pompei 79*, Napoli 1979, 87-96.

Varone, A. "La struttura insediativa di Pompei: l'avvio di una indagine computerizzata per la conoscenza della realtà economica e sociale di una città campana della prima età imperiale," *Pompei. L'informatica al servizio di una città antica*, Roma 1988, 25-48.

____. *Paesaggio e colture agrarie di Pompei nei documenti storici, archeologici ed epigrafici*, Pompei 1992, 14-21.

____. *Pompei. I misteri di una città sepolta*, Roma 2000, 129-144.

The *Macellum*

De Ruyt, C. *Macellum. Marché alimentaire des Romains*, Louvain 1983.

Fedele, L. *Mercati e piazze antiche. Storia ed architettura*, Napoli 1954.

Nabers, N. "The Architectural Variations of the Macellum," *Opuscula Romana*, 1973, 173-176.

Pagano, M. "Note sui 'Macella' del mondo romano," *Rendiconti della Reale Accademia di Archeologia Lettere e Belle Arti di Napoli* n.s. 59, 1984, 111-121.

Small, A. "The Shrine of the Imperial Family in the Macellum at Pompeii," *Journal of Roman Archaeology*, suppl. 17, 1996, 115-136.

The *Mensa Ponderaria*

Bidder, G. P. "The Mensa Ponderaria of Pompeii," *The Academy* 47, 1895, 319-320.

Romanelli, D. "Modulo di antiche misure trovato nel 1816 negli scavi di Pompei," *Giornale enciclopedico di Napoli* 11, vol. 3, 1817, 257-270.

The Building of Eumachia

Fentress, E. "A Slave Market at Pompeii," in *Selling People: Slave Markets in the Roman World*, Conference held at the British School at Rome, June 28, 2001.

Mau, A. "Osservazioni sull'edificio di Eumachia in Pompei," *Römische Mitteilungen* 7, 1892, 113-143.

Moeller, W. O. "The Building of Eumachia. A Reconsideration," *American Journal of Archaeology*, 76, 1972, 323-327.

____. "The Date of Dedication of the Building of Eumachi," *Cronache Pompeiane* 1, 1975, 232-236.

Richardson, L., Jr. "Concordia and Concordia Augusta: Roma and Pompeii," *La Parola del Passato* 33, 1978, 260-272.

Spano, G. "L'Edificio di Eumachia in Pompei," *Rendiconti della Reale Accademia di Archeologia Lettere e Belle Arti di Napoli* 36, 1961, 3-35.

Wallat, K. "Der Marmorfries am Eingangsportal des Gebäudes der Eumachia (VII 9, 1)" *Pompeji und sein ursprünglicher Anbringungsort*, *Archäologischer Anzeiger*, 1995, n. 2, 345-373.

Shops, Taverns and Cafes

Gassner, V. *Die Kaufläden in Pompeji*, Wien, 1986.

Kleberg, T. *Hôtels, restaurants et cabarets dans l'antiquité romaine. Études historiques et philologiques*, Uppsala, 1957.

Magaldi, E. "Il commercio ambulante a Pompei," *Atti dell'Accademia Pontaniana* 60, 1930, 61-88.

Packer, J. E. "Inns at Pompeii: a Short Survey," *Cronache Pompeiane* 4, 1978, 5-53.

The Fullery of Stephanus

Spinazzola, V. "Pompei. Continuazione dello scavo della via dell'Abbondanza e scoperte quivi avvenute nel mese di agosto 1912," *Notizie degli Scavi di Antichità*, 1912, 281-283.

____. *Pompei alla luce degli scavi nuovi di Via dell'Abbondanza (Anni 1910-1923)*, vol. III, Roma 1953, 763-785.

Workshop of Marcus Vecilius Verecundus

Angelone, R. *L'officina «coactilaria» di M. Vecilio Verecondo a Pompei*, Napoli 1986.

Matz, F. L. J. "Der Gott auf dem Elefantenwagen," *Abhandlungen der Akademie der Wissenschaften und der Literatur von Mainz* 10, 1952, 717-764.

Moeller, W. O. "The Felt Shops of Pompeii," *American Journal of Archaeology* 75, 1971, 188-189.

Pais, E. "Venere vincitrice ed il trionfo di Pompeo Magno. Osservazioni a proposito di un dipinto pompeiano," *Studi storici per l'antichità classica* 6, 1915, 241-257.

Spano, G. "Abitanti di Pompei chiedenti protezione ai pianeti," *Annali dell'Istituto Superiore di Scienze e Lettere S. Chiara di Napoli* 2, 1950, 207-221.

Spinazzola, V. *Pompei alla luce degli scavi nuovi di Via dell'Abbondanza (Anni 1910-1923)*, vol. I, Roma 1953, 189-210.

Bakery of Numerius Popidius Priscus

Mau, A. "Su certi apparecchi nei pistrini di Pompei," *Römische Mitteilungen*, 1, 1886, 45-48.

Mayeske, B. J. B. *Bakeries, Bakers, and Bread at Pompeii: a Study in Social and Economic History*, Ann Arbor (Mich.) 1974.

A Rustic Villa: the Villa of Pisanella at Boscoreale

Antiquarium di Boscoreale. Uomo e ambiente nel territorio vesuviano, Pompei, 1990.

Baratte, F. J. *Le trésor d'orfèvrerie romaine de Boscoreale*, Paris, 1985.

Canessa, C. "Le trésor monétaire de Boscoreale," *Le Musée* 6, 1909, 259-265.

Casale, A. *Salvatore di Giacomo e le ville romane di Boscoreale*, Boscoreale, 1985; *Il tesoro di Boscoreale. Una collezione di argenti da mensa tra cultura ellenistica e mondo romano. Pitture, suppellettili, oggetti vari della «Pisanella»*, Milano, 1988.

Lipinsky, A. "Il trafugamento del tesoro di Boscoreale, oggi al Louvre," *Napoli Nobilissima* 18, 1979, 234-238.

Oettel, A. *Bronzen aus Boscoreale in Berlin*, Berlin, 1991.

_____. *Fundkontexte römischer Vesuvvillen im Gebiet um Pompeji. Die Grabungen von 1894 bis 1908*, Mainz, 1996.

Oliver, A. *Silver for the Gods: 800 Years of Greek and Roman Silver*, Toledo 1977.

Pasqui, A. "La villa pompeiana della Pisanella, presso Boscoreale," *Monumenti Antichi dell'Accademia dei Lincei* 7, 1897, 397-554.

Pernice, E. A. *Hellenistische Silbergefässe*, Berlin, 1898.

Sambon, A., Toudouze, G., De Foville, J. "La banlieu de Pompeï: Boscoreale, Boscotrecase et la marine de Sarno," *Le Musée* 3, 1906, 159-212.

Schoenberger-Muench, K. *Die Silberbecher von Boscoreale: Ein interpretatorischer Versuch*, Berlin, 1989.

Social Life: Spectacles, Athletic Games, Baths

André, J.-M. *Recherches sur l'otium romain*, Paris 1962.

Bieber, M. *The History of the Greek and Roman Theater*, Princeton 1961.

Delorme, J. "Étude architectural sur Vitruve, V, 11, 2," *Bulletin de Correspondence Hellenique* 73, 1949, 398-420.

_____. *Gymnasion. Étude sur les monuments consacrés à l'education en Grèce (des origines à l'Empire romain)*, Paris 1960.

Étienne, R. *La vita quotidiana a Pompei*, Milano 1973, 379-443.

Franklin, J. L., Jr. "Pantomimists at Pompeii: Actius Anicetus and His Troupe," *American Journal of Philology* 108, 1987, 95-107.

Galsterer, H. "Politik in römischen Städten. Die «seditio» des Jahres 59 n. Chr. In Pompeji," *Studien zur antiken Sozialgeschichte. Festschrift Friedrich Vittinghoff*, Köln-Wien 1980, 323-338.

Gigante, M. "La cultura letteraria a Pompei," *Pompeiana*, Napoli 1950, 111-143.

_____. "La vita teatrale nell'antica Pompei," *Studi salernitani in memoria di Raffaele Cantarella*, Salerno 1981, 9-51.

Jorio, A. "Sistema di riscaldamento nelle antiche terme pompeiane," *Bullettino della Commissione Archeologica Comunale di Roma* 86, 1978-1979, 167-189.

Krell, O. *Römische Heizungen*, München-Berlin,1901.

Lugli, G. "Le terme dei Romani," *Le meraviglie del passato*, Milano 1929, 1331-1340.

Maiuri, A. "Pompei e Nocera," *Rendiconti della Reale Accademia di Archeologia Lettere e Belle Arti di Napoli* 33, 1958, 35-40.

_____. *Sport e impianti sportivi nella Campania antica. Mostra storica allestita dal Museo Nazionale di Napoli, Giochi della XVII Olimpiade*, Roma 1960.

Maiuri, B. "Ludi ginnico-atletici a Pompei," *Pompeiana*, Napoli 1950, 167-205.

Moeller, W. O. "The Riot of A.D. 59 at Pompeii," *Historia* 19, 1970, 84-95.

Neilsen, I. *Thermae et Balnea. The Architecture and Cultural History of Roman Public Baths*, Aarhus 1990-1991.

Pesando, F. "Gladiatori a Pompei," *Sangue e arena*, Roma 2001, 175-197.

Sabbatini Tumolesi, P. *Gladiatorum paria. Annunci di spettacoli gladiatorii a Pompei*, Roma 1980.

Szulczyk, J. "The Gladiatorian Games at Pompeii," *Acta Pompeiana*, Warsaw 1984, 89-94.

Varone, A. *Pompei. I misteri di una città sepolta*, Roma 2000, 145-178.

Ville, G. *Le gladiature en Occident des origines à la mort de Domitien*, Roma 1981.

Weber, M. *Antike Badekultur*, München, 1996.

The Triangular Forum

Coarelli, F. "Il Foro Triangolare: decorazione e funzione," *Pompei. Scienza e società*, Milano 2001, 97-107.

De Waele, J. A. K. E. et al. *Il tempio dorico del Foro Triangolare di Pompei*, Pompei 2001.

Koldewey, R., Puchstein, O. *Die griechische Tempel in Unteritalien und Sicilien*, Berlin 1899, 45-49.

Mau, A. "Die Säulenstümpfe des dorischen Tempels in Pompeji," *Römische Mitteilungen*, 23, 1908, 103-106.

Onorato, G. O. "La sistemazione stradale del quartiere del Foro Triangolare di Pompei," *Atti dell'Accademia dei Lincei. Rendiconti della classe di scienze morali, storiche e filologiche*, ser. 8, 6, 1951, 250-264.

Pesando, F. "Il fregio fittile con scene di battaglia da Pompei. Ipotesi di localizzazione," *Ostraka* 6, 1, 1997, 51-62.

Richardson, L., Jr. "The Archaic Doric Temple of Pompeii," *La Parola del Passato* 29, 1974, 281-290.

Sogliano, A. "Il Tempio nel Foro Triangolare di Pompei," *Monumenti Antichi dell'Accademia dei Lincei* 1, 1890, coll. 189-200.

Spano, G. "L'Hekatonstylon di Pompei e l'Hekatonstylon di Pompeo," *Atti dell'Accademia Pontaniana* 49, 1919, 157-210.

Von Duhn, F., Jacobi, L. *Der griechische Tempel in Pompeji*, Heidelberg 1890.

The Samnitic Gymnasium

La Regina, A. "Appunti su entità etniche e strutture istituzionali nel Sannio antico," *Annali dell'Istituto Orientale di Napoli. Sezione di Archeologia e Storia antica* 4, 1982, 134-137.

Poccetti, P. "Il testamento di Vibio Adirano," *Rendiconti della Reale Accademia di Archeologia Lettere e Belle Arti di Napoli* n. s. 57, 1982, 237-245.

Seki, T. "Doryphoros in Naples. A Critical Study on the Roman Copy," *Akten des XIII Internationalen Kongresses für klassische Archäologie*, Mainz 1990, 514-516.

Tagliamonte, G. "Alcune considerazioni sull'istituzione italica della Vereia," *La Parola del Passato* 44, 1989, 361-376.

Weber, M. "Der Speer des Doryphoros und die Binde des Diadumenos von Polyklet," *Archäologischer Anzeiger*, 1992, 1-6.

Weinstock, H. "Zur Statuenbasis in der Samnitischen Palästra von Pompeji," *Römische Mitteilungen* 104, 1997, 519-526.

The Theaters and Gladiator Barracks

Broneer, O. T. *The Odeum*, Cambridge (Mass.) 1932.

Byvanck, A. W. "Das grosse Theater in Pompeji," *Römische Mitteilungen* 40, 1925, 107-124.

Comparetti, D. "L'*Eneide* negli altorilievi di un elmo gladiatorio pompeiano," *Atene e Roma* 22, 1919, 113-127.

De Albentiis, E. "Attività edilizia ed evergetismo in Italia: il caso di C. Quinctius Valgus," *Italia e Hispania en la crisis de la República romana*, Madrid 1998, 277-293.

Graefe, R. *Vela erunt*, Mainz 1979.

Harvey, P. B. "Socer Valgus, Valgii, and C. Quinctius Valgus," *Classical and Classical Tradition. Essay Presented to R. E. Dengler*, Philadelphia 1973, 79-94.

Lauter, H. "Theater der Samniten und Latiner," *Hellenismus im Mittelitalien*, Göttingen 1976, 415-418.

Mau, A. "Das grosse Theater in Pompeji," *Römische Mitteilungen* 21, 1906, 1-56.

Maiuri, A. "Saggi nella cavea del 'Teatro grande,'" *Notizie degli Scavi di Antichità*, 1951, 126-134.

Meinel, R. *Das Odeion*, Frankfurt am Main 1980.

Murolo, M. "Il cosiddetto 'Odeo' di Pompei ed il problema della sua copertura," *Rendiconti della Reale Accademia di Archeologia Lettere e Belle Arti di Napoli* 34, 1959, 89-101.

Neppi Modona, A. *Gli edifici teatrali greci e romani. Teatri-Odei-Anfiteatri-Circhi*, Firenze 1961.

Petersen, E.A.H. "Über die sogennante Gladiatorenkaserne in Pompeji," *Römische Mitteilungen* 14, 1899, 103-104.

Polacco, L. "Rapporti tra i teatri greco-italici e i teatri sicelioti," *Ercolano 1738-1988. 250 anni di ricerca archeologica*, Roma 1993, 147-153.

Puchstein, O. "Das grosse Theater in Pompeji," *Jahrbuch des Deutschen Archäologischen Instituts zu Berlin* 21, 1906, coll. 301-314.

Spano, G. "Il teatro delle Fontane in Pompei," *Memorie della Reale Accademia di Archeologia Lettere e Belle Arti di Napoli* 2, 1911, 109-148.

____. "Osservazioni intorno al *theatrum tectum* di Pompei," *Annali dell'Istituto Superiore di Scienze e Lettere S. Chiara di Napoli* 1, 1949, 111-139.

Zangemeister, K.F.W. "Sopra l'iscrizione del teatro piccolo di Pompei," *Bullettino dell'Instituto di Corrispondenza Archeologica*, 1866, 30-31.

The Large Gymnasium

Della Corte, M. "'Campus' di Pompei," *Atti dell'Accademia dei Lincei. Rendiconti della classe di scienze morali, storiche e filologiche*, ser. 8, 2, 1947, 555-568.

____. "Pompei. Le iscrizioni della «Grande Palestra» ad occidente dell'Anfiteatro," *Notizie degli Scavi di Antichità*, 1939, 239-327.

Devijver, H., Von Wonterghem, F. "Il 'Campus' nell'impianto urbanistico delle città romane: testimonianze epigrafiche e resti archeologici," *Acta Archaeologica Lovaniensa* 20, 1981, 33-68.

Le Roux, P. "L'armée romaine au quotidien: deux graffiti légionnaires de Pompéi et Rome," *Epigraphica* 45, 1983, 65-77.

Maiuri, A. "Pompei. Scavo della 'Grande Palestra' nel quartiere dell'Anfiteatro (1935-1939)," *Notizie degli Scavi di Antichità*, 1939, 165-238.

Pierre, A. "La grande palestra de Pompéi," *Revue Archéologique*, ser. 6, 15, 1940, 106-107.

The Amphitheater

Étienne, R. "La naissance de l'amphithéâtre: le mot et la chose," *Revue des Études Latines* 43, 1965, 213-220.

Girosi, G. M. "L'anfiteatro di Pompei," *Memorie della Reale Accademia di Archeologia Lettere e Belle Arti di Napoli* 5, 1936, 27-57.

Golvin, J.-C. *L'amphithéâtre romaine. Essai sur la théorisation de sa forme et de ses fonctions*, Paris 1988.

Jones, M. W. "Designing Amphitheatres," *Römische Mitteilungen* 100, 1993, 391-442.

Spano, G. "Alcune osservazioni nascenti da una descrizione dell'anfiteatro di Pompei," *Annali dell'Istituto Universitario di Magistero di Salerno* 1, 1949-1950, 355-419.

Welch, K. "The Roman Arena in Late-Republican Italy: a New Interpretation," *Journal of Roman Archaeology* 7, 1994, 59-80.

The Thermal Baths

Bargellini, P. "Le Terme Centrali di Pompei," *Les thermes romains*, Roma 1991, 115-128.

Cantarella, E. *Pompei. I volti dell'amore*, Milano 1998, 33-40.

De Simone, A., Nappo, S. C. (a cura di). *. . . mitis Sarni opes. Nuova indagine archeologica in località Murecine*, Napoli, 2000.

De Simone, A., Rinauro, A. *Pompei, Terme Suburbane*, in *Restaurare Pompei*, Milano 1990, 77-93.

Eschebach, H. "La documentazione delle Terme del Foro a Pompei," *La regione sotterrata dal Vesuvio. Studi e prospettive*, Napoli 1982, 313-319.

____. "*Schola labri*. Die Entwicklung der «Schola labri» in den Vesuvstädten, dargestellt am «labrum» des Männercaldariums der Stabianer Thermen," *Cronache Pompeiane* 3, 1977, 156-176.

____. "Zur Beheizung der Forumsthermen in Pompeji," *Jahresberichte aus Augst und Kaiseraugst* 3, 1983, 87-100.

Eschebach, H. et al. *Die Stabianer Thermen in Pompeji*, Berlin, 1979.

Eschebach, L. "Die Forumsthermen in Pompeji, *Regio* VII, *Insula* 5," *Antike Welt* 22, 1991, 257-287.

Hartmann, R. "Das Laconicum der römischen Thermen," *Römische Mitteilungen* 35, 1920, 152-169.

Jacobelli, L. *Le pitture erotiche delle Terme Suburbane di Pompei*, Roma, 1995.

____. "Vicende edilizie ed interventi pittorici nelle Terme Suburbane a Pompei," *Mededelingen van het Nederlands Historisch Instituut te Rome* 54, 1995, 154-166.

Mau, A. "Le terme centrali di Pompei," *Bullettino dell'Instituto di Corrispondenza Archeologica*, 1877, 214-223, 1878, 251-254.

Maiuri, A. "Pompei. Nuovi saggi di esplorazione nelle Terme Stabiane," *Notizie degli Scavi di Antichità*, 1932, 507-516.

Schween, G. *Die Beheizungsanlage der Stabianer Thermen*, Hamburg 1938.

Varone, A. *Conservazione di pitture e stucchi: Pompei, Regio II, insula 9 e Terme Suburbane, Restaurare Pompei*, Milano 1990, 97-110.

The *Lupanare*

Giornale degli Scavi di Pompei, 1862, 44-59.

Guzzo, P., Scarano Ussani, V. *Veneris figurae. Immagini di prostituzione e sfruttamento a Pompei*, Napoli 2000, 9-12.

Inscriptions:

CIL IV 2173-2296.

Varone, A. *Erotica Pompeiana. Iscrizioni d'amore sui muri di Pompei*, Roma 1994, *passim*.

Paintings:

Clarke, J. R. *Looking at Lovemaking*, Berkeley-Los Angeles, London 1998, 196-206.

Dierichs, A. *Erotik in der Römischen Kunst*, Mainz 1997, 73-75.

Prostitution:

Cantarella, E. *Pompei. I volti dell'amore*, Milano 1998, 68-115.

Varone, A. *Erotica Pompeiana. Iscrizioni d'amore sui muri di Pompei*, Roma 1994, 133-144.

The House

For the numerous studies on Pompeii houses, refer to the bibliographies contained in the monographs published after 1990, cited below:

Clarke, J.R. *The Houses of Roman Italy. 100 B.C.-A.D. 250. Ritual, Space and Decoration*, Berkeley 1991.

De Albentiis, E. *La Casa dei Romani*, Milano 1990.

Dickmann, J.-A. *Domus frequentata. Anspruchsvolles Wohnen im pompejanischer Stadthaus*, München 1999.

Laurence, R., Wallace-Hadrill, A. eds., *Domestic Space in the Roman World: Pompeii and beyond* (*Journal of Roman Archaeology*, suppl. 22), Portsmouth 1997.

Pesando, F. *"Domus". Edilizia privata e società pompeiana fra III e I secolo a.C.* (Monografie della Soprintendenza Archeologica di Pompei 12), Roma 1997.

Pirson, F. *Mietwohnungen in Pompeji und Herkulaneum. Untersuchungen zur Architektur, zum Wohnen und zur Sozial- und Wirtschaftsgeschichte der Vesuvstädte*, München 1999.

Wallace-Hadrill, A. *Houses and Society in Pompeii and Herculaneum*, Princeton 1994.

Zaccaria Ruggiu, A.P. *Spazio privato e spazio pubblico nella città romana*, Roma 1995.

Zanker, P. *Pompei. Società, immagini urbane e forme dell'abitare*, Torino 1993.

Zevi, F. "La città sannitica. L'edilizia privata e la Casa del Fauno," *Pompei*. F. Zevi (*a cura di*), Napoli 1991, 47-74.

____. "Il terremoto del 62 e l'edilizia privata pompeiana," *Pompei*, F. Zevi (a cura di), Napoli 1992, 39-58.

On Roman houses according to Vitruvius:

Romano, E. *La capanna e il tempio. Vitruvio o dell'Architettura*, Palermo 1987.

Vitruvius, *De Architectura*, (a cura di P. Gros, traduzione e commento di E. Romano e A. Corso), Torino, 1997.

On Pompeii houses with atriums:

Evans, M. *The Atrium Complex in the Houses of Pompeii*, I-II, Diss. U. of Birmingham, 1980.

For a picture of Pompeii dwellings not limited to the canonical type of house:

Hoffmann, A. "Ein Beitrag zum Wohnen in vorrömischen Pompeji," *Architectura* 10, 1980, 162-164.

Miele, F. "La casa a schiera I, 11, 16, un esempio di edilizia privata a Pompei," *Rivista di Studi Pompeiani* 3, 1989, 165-184.

Nappo, S.C. "Alcuni esempi di tipologie di case popolari della fine del III, inizio II secolo a.C. a Pompei," *Rivista di Studi Pompeiani* 6, 1993-1994, 77-104.

For a synopsis of Roman dwellings of the Republican era, excluding the houses of Pompeii and Herculaneum:

Pesando, F. "Forme abitative e controllo sociale: la documentazione archeologica delle colonie latine in età repubblicana," *Habitat et société*, *Actes des recontres*, October 1998, Antibes 1999, 237-254.

Texts Specifically Cited in the Introduction (among more than 250 publications by Maiuri, only the excavations of the House of Menander and the Villa of the Mysteries were published in monograph form):

Breton, E. *Pompeia décrite et dessinée*, Paris 1855.

Bulwer-Lytton, E.G. *The Last Days of Pompeii*, London 1834.

Eschebach, L., Müller-Trollius, J. *Gebäudeverzeichnis und Stadtplan der antiken Stadt Pompeji*, Köln-Weimar-Wien 1993.

Fiorelli, G. *Pompeianarum Antiquitatum Historia*, I-III, Napoli 1860-1864.

____. *Descrizione di Pompei*, Napoli 1875.

Gell, W., Gandy, J.P. *Pompeiana: The Topography, Edifices, and Ornaments of Pompeii*, London 1817-1819.

Maiuri, A. *La Casa del Menandro e il suo tesoro di argenteria*, Roma 1932.

____. *La Villa dei Misteri*, Roma 1931.

Mau, A. *Geschichte der decorativen Wandmalerei in Pompeji*, Leipzig 1882.

____. *Pompeji in Leben und Kunst* (Bearb. von F. Drexel), Leipzig 1913.

Mazois, F., Gau, F.Chr. *Les ruines de Pompéi, dessinées et mesureés*, Paris 1824-1838.

Nissen, H. *Pompeianische Studien zur Städtekunde des Alterthums*, Leipzig 1877.

Overbeck, J. *Pompeji in seinen Gebäuden, Alterthümern und Kunstwerken*, Leipzig 1884.

Pompei. L'informatica al servizio di una città antica. Analisi delle funzioni urbane, Roma 1988.

Pompéi. Travaux et envois des architects français de Rome au XIXe siècle, Naples 1981.

Spinazzola, V., Aurigemma, S. (a cura di). *Pompei alla luce degli Scavi Nuovi di Via dell'Abbondanza*, Roma 1953.

Staël, Mme. de. *Corinne ou l'Italie*, Paris 1807.

For a contextualization of the history of the excavations of Pompeii before and after Italian unification:

De Caro, S. "Giuseppe Fiorelli e gli scavi di Pompei," *A Giuseppe Fiorelli nel primo centenario della morte, Atti del convegno (Napoli 19-20 Marzo 1997)* (a cura di) S. De Caro, P.G. Guzzo, Napoli 1999, 5-23.

Zevi, F. *La storia degli scavi e della documentazione: Pompei 1748-1980. I tempi della documentazione*, Roma 1981.

For a detailed description of the pictorial and mosaic decorations of all the houses in Pompeii, see:

Baldassarre, I. (coordinamento di). *Pompei. Pitture e Mosaici*, Roma, Ist. dell'Enciclopedia Italiana, Roma 1990-1999 (a collection of contributions by the major experts on Pompeii painting and by authors of monographs on individual housing complexes).

Schefold, K. *Die Wände Pompejis. Topographisches Verzeichnis der Bildmotive*, Berlin 1957.

The most recent and exhaustive synthesis on Roman pictorial styles documented in Pompeii is:

Strocka, W.M. *Enciclopedia dell'Arte Antica*, Suppl. 1970-1994, Roma 1996, s.v. *Pompeiani Stili*.

Principal monographs dedicated to individual dwellings:

Franklin, J. M., Jr. *Pompeii: The "Casa del Marinaio" and Its History* (Monografie della Soprintendenza Archeologica di Pompei 3), Roma 1990.

Peters, W. J. H. Th. *La Casa di Marcus Lucretius Fronto e le sue pitture*, Rome 1993.

Richardson, L., Jr. *Pompeii: The Casa dei Dioscuri and Its Painters* (Memoirs of the American Academy in Rome 23), Rome 1955.

Zevi, F. *La Casa Reg. IX, 5 18-21 a Pompei e le sue pitture* (*Studi Miscellanei* 5), Roma 1964.

Very important for its level of research and notable editorial commitment is the *Häuser in Pompeji* series, 9 titles of which have appeared to date:

Ehrhardt, W. *Casa dell'Orso* (VII, 2, 44-46), (2), München 1988.

____. *Casa di Paquius Proculus* (I, 7, 1.20), (9), München 1998.

Frölich, Th. *Casa della Fontana Piccola* (VI, 8, 23.24), (8), München 1996.

Michel, D. *Casa dei Cei* (I, 6, 15), (3), München 1990.

Seiler, F. *Casa degli Amorini Dorati* (VI, 16, 7), (5), München 1992

Staub, M. *Casa del Granduca* (VII, 4, 56) *und Casa dei Capitelli Figurati* (VII, 4, 57), (7), München 1994.

Stemmer, K. *Casa dell'Ara Massima* (VI, 16,15), (6), München 1992.

Strocka, W.M. *Casa del Labirinto* (VI, 11, 8-10), (4), München 1991.

____. *Casa del Principe di Napoli* (VI 15, 7.8), (1), Tübingen 1984.

There are very few systematic studies of *insulae* or of the Pompeii neighborhoods. For the extent of their efforts and the results achieved we note especially the publication of the quarter facing the southwest edge of the city plateau, corresponding to part of Regions VII and VIII:

Noack, F., Lehmann-Hartleben, K. *Baugeschichte Untersuchungen am Stadtrand von Pompeji*, Berlin 1936.

In the last few years studies have begun on entire *insulae*; among these we note:

Carocci, F., De Albentiis, E., Gargiulo, M., Pesando, F. *Le insulae 3 e 4 della Regio VI di Pompei*, Roma 1990.

De Albentiis, E. "Indagini sull'*Insula Arriana Polliana* di Pompei," *Dialoghi di Archeologia* 3a serie, 7,1, 1989, 43-84.

Ling, R. "The Insula of the Menander at Pompeii: Interim Report," *Antiquaries Journal* 63, 1983, 34-57.

House of the Surgeon

Building history of the house:

Chiaramonte Treré, C. "Sull'origine e lo sviluppo dell'architettura residenziale di Pompei sannitica," *ACME* 43, 3, 1990, 3 *passim*.

Maiuri, A. in "Notizie degli Scavi" 1930, 380 *passim*. = *Alla ricerca di Pompei preromana (Saggi stratigrafici)*, Napoli 1973, 2 *passim*.

Decorations:

Sampaolo, S. in *Pompei. Pitture e Mosaici* IV, Roma 1993, 53-84.

For discoveries of archaic dwellings built with the use of local tufa ("pappamonte"), which was also used in the construction of the oldest city walls of the sixth century B.C., see:

De Caro, S. "Lo sviluppo urbanistico di Pompei," *Atti e Memorie della Società Magna Grecia* 3, 1, 1992, 67-90 (especially p. 71-72), which is a collection of all the references to excavations carried out by A. Maiuri.

Other archaic structures of the same type have been noted under the atrium of the House of Meleager in an unpublished excavation carried out by H. B. Van der Poel in 1962:

Curatolo, E. "La Casa di Meleagro (*regio* VI,9,2): scavi Van der Poel," *Pompei. Scienza e società. 250° Anniversario degli Scavi di Pompei, Convegno Internazionale Napoli 25-27 Novembre 1998* (a cura di) P.G. Guzzo. Milano 2001, 240.

Guidobaldi, M.P., Pesando, F. "Variazioni di proprietà nell'insula VI, 9: indagine nella Casa del Centauro (VI, 9, 3-5 e 10-12)," *Rivista di Studi Pompeani* 9, 1998 [2000], 224.

The remains of an archaic building also emerged in Region I:

Fulford, M., Wallace-Hadrill, A. "Towards a History of Pre-Roman Pompeii. Excavations beneath the House of Amarantus (I, 9, 11-12), 1995-8," *Papers of the British School at Rome* 67, 1999, 37-127 (especially 103-112).

Also very important are the structures created with earth walls (*opus formaceum*) found in the excavation of the atrium of the House of the Vestals, dating from the fourth century B.C., which find solid comparisons in the Italic and Roman world, above all in the houses of the Latin colony of Fregellae; for the results of these excavations see:

Bon, S.E., Jones, R., Kurchin, B., Robinson, D.J. "Research in Insula VI, 1 by the Anglo-American Project, 1994-6," *Rivista di Studi Pompeiani*, 7, 1995-96 [1998], 153-157.

The importance of these last discoveries, which could describe a period of private building in Pompeii ("the earth wall era") comparable to the best-known periodizations used in the manuals ("limestone era," "tufa era"), is highlighted by:

Guzzo, P.G. "Alla ricerca della Pompei sannitica," *Studi sull'Italia dei Sanniti*, Milano 2000, 109.

Pesando, F. "Forme abitative e controllo sociale: la documentazione archeologica delle colonie latine in età repubblicana," *Habitat et société*, *Actes des recontres 22-23-24 octobre 1998*, 1998, Antibes 1999, 247.

An unjustifiably primitive vision emerges from the pre-Roman reconstruction of Pompeii proposed by:

Carandini, A. "Nuovi progetti, nuove domande, nuovi metodi," *Pompei. Scienza e società. 250° Anniversario degli Scavi di Pompei, Convegno Internazionale Napoli 25-27 Novembre 1998* (a cura di) P.G. Guzzo. Milano 2001, 127-129, which regards the city as populated until the second century B.C. by modest houses of two or three rooms surrounded by a small garden. The results of the sample analyzed, however, are so exiguous (parts of two buildings of under a hundred square feet on an urban area of 63 hectares) and in contrast with the other evidence cited that they cannot be extended to all of Pompeii of the fourth to third centuries B.C. without risking a hermeneutic error.

House of the Faun

In the interest of brevity, this essential bibliography cites only the most recent contributions or those to which explicit reference has been made in the text and in which the reader will find a more extensive bibliography.

Architecture and decorative apparatus:

Hoffmann, A. "Die Casa del Fauno," *Basileia. Die Paläste der hellenistischen Könige*, (hrsg) W. Hoepfner-G. Brands, Berlin 1996, 258 *passim*.

Hoffmann, A., De Vos, M. in *Pompei. Pitture e mosaici*, vol. V, Roma 1994, 80-141.

Pesando, F. "Autocelebrazione aristocratica e propaganda politica in ambiente privato: la casa del Fauno a Pompei," *Cahiers du Centre Gustave Glotz* VII, 1996, 189-228.

____. *"Domus". Edilizia privata e società pompeiana tra III e I secolo a.C.* (Monografie della Soprintendenza Archeologica di Pompei 12), Roma 1997, 80-130.

Zevi, F. "Die Casa del Fauno in Pompeji," *Römische Mitteilungen* 105, 1998, 21 *passim*.

____. "La Casa del Fauno," *Abitare sotto il Vesuvio*, (edd.) M. Borriello, A. d'Ambrosio, S. De Caro, P.G. Guzzo (Catalogo Mostra Ferrara), Ferrara 1996, 65-71.

____. "L'edilizia privata e la Casa del Fauno," *Pompei**, (a cura di) F. Zevi, Napoli 1991, 66-71.

____. "Pompei: Casa del Fauno," *Studi sull'Italia dei Sanniti*, Milano 2000, 118-137.

Mosaic of Alexander and aspects of the decoration of the house:

Andreae, B. *Das Alexandermosaik aus Pompeji*, Reckinghausen 1977.

Coarelli, F. "La pompé di Tolomeo Filadelfo e il mosaico nilotico di Palestrina," *Ktema* 15, 1990, 225-251 = *Revixit Ars*, Roma, 1996, 102-137 (recognizes the pavilion reproduced in the mosaic of *Praeneste* as the *skené* of Ptolemy II).

Cohen, A. *The Alexander Mosaic*, Cambridge 1997.

Fuhrmann, H. *Philoxenos von Eretria. Archäologische Untersuchungen über zwei Alexandermosaike*, Göttingen 1931.

Goldman, B. "Darius III, the Alexander Mosaic and the 'Tiara Ortho'," *Mesopotamia* 18, 1993, 51-69 (on the unusual form of the turban worn by the Persian king, a loose representation of the *tiara orthè* described by Xenophon, based not on a specific model, but on a re-elaboration of different iconographs of Oriental head coverings).

Meyboom, F. *The Nile Mosaic of Palestrina. Early Evidence of Egyptian Religion in Italy*, Leiden-New York-Köln 1995, 167-172 (connects the name of the Samnitic *gens* of the *Sadirii* and the statue-totem of the house, according to a reading similar to that proposed here).

Moreno, P. *Apelle. La Battaglia di Alessandro*, Roma 2000 (attributes the original to Apelles and identifies the battle reproduced with Gaugamela in 331 as the final decisive encounter between Alexander and Darius).

____. *EAA suppl.* 1971-1994, vol. IV, Roma 1996, s.v. *Nikomachos*.

____. *EAA suppl.* 1971-1994, vol. V, Roma 1997. s.v. *Skìrtos* (for the identification of the faun with the "leaping satyr").

____. *La pittura greca*, Roma 1987, 103-107 (attributes the Tomb of Persephone at *Aigai* to Nicomachus and proposes the interpretation of the *pictura compendiaria* invented by Philoxenus as the application of interchangeable silhouettes on similar iconographic schemes).

____. *Sabato in museo. Letture di arte ellenistica e romana*, Milano 1999, 36-38.

____. *Scultura ellenistica* I, Roma 1994, 292-296.

Nylander, C. "Il milite ignoto: un problema nel mosaico di Alessandro," *La regione sotterrata dal Vesuvio*, Napoli 1982, 689-695 (proposes a Persian nobleman as the creator of the mosaic of Alexander).

Perrin, Y. "A propos de la 'bataille d'Issos'. Théâtre, science et peinture: la conquête de l'espace ou d'Uccello à Philoxène," *Cahiers du Centre Gustave Glotz* IX, 1998 [2000], 83-116.

Stewart, A. *Faces of Power. Alexander's Image and Hellenistic Policy*, Berkeley 1993, 130 *passim* (proposes recognizing Issus as the theater of the war between Alexander and Darius reproduced in the mosaic).

Zevi, F. "Il mosaico di Alessandro e i Romani: qualche appunto," *Ultra Terminum Vagari: Scritti in onore di C. Nylander*, Roma 1997, 385-397 (outline of the possible connections between the family of the creator of the mosaic and the feats of Alexander the Great and Alexander of Molossus).

____. *I mosaici della Casa del Fauno*, Napoli 1998.

House of the Diadumeni or of Epidius Rufus

Architecture:

Lauter, H. "Zur Siedlungsstruktur Pompejis in samnitischer Zeit," *Neue Forschungen in Pompeji*. B. Andreae and H. Kyrieleis (heraus von), Recklinghausen 1975, 152.

Pesando, F. "Atriis quia Graeci non utuntur." *Ambienti di tradizione ellenistica nel settore dell'atrio nelle case pompeiane di età sannitica*, Acts of the Third Annual Meeting (European Association of Archaeologists), Ravenna, September 24-28 1997, 1998.

____. *"Domus". Edilizia privata e società pompeiana fra III e I secolo a.C.*, Roma 1997, 259-261.

Richardson, L., Jr. *Pompeii. An Architectural History*, Baltimore 1988, 112-114.

Decoration:

Sampaolo, V. in *Pompei. Pitture e mosaici* VIII, Roma 1998, 916-955.

Recent excavations in the servants' quarter and in the andron connected to the garden:

Gallo, A. "Saggi di scavo nella casa di Epidio Rufo IX, 1, 20," *Rivista di Studi Pompeiani* 8, 1997 [1999], 153-157.

For the sculptural group from the Temple of Neptune in the Circus of Rome:

Coarelli, F. *Il Campo Marzio*, Roma 1997, 431-446.

House of the Labyrinth

Building and decorative history:

Strocka, W.M. *Casa del Labirinto* (VI, 11, 8-10), (Häuser in Pompeji 4), München 1991.

For the question of the spaces used in the city by the Sulla colonists:

Zevi, F. "Pompei dalla città sannitica alla colonia sillana: per un'interpretazione dei dati archeologici," *Les élites municipales de l'Italie péninsulaire des Gracques à Néron*. M. Cebellaic-Gervasoni (dir.), Naples-Roma 1996, 125-138.

On the oldest "farms" of the Pompeii area:

Cicirelli, A. in *Casali di Ieri, Casali di Oggi. Architetture rurali e tecniche agricole nel territorio di Pompei e Stabiae*, Napoli 2000, 71-83 (Ville di Terzigno).

De Caro, S. *La villa rustica in località Villa Regina a Boscoreale*, Roma 1994.

Oettel, A. *Fundkontexte römischer Vesuvvillen im Gebiet um Pompeji. Die Grabungen von 1894 bis 1908*, Mayence 1996.

Stefani, G. "La Villa del fondo Prisco in località Civita," *Casali di Ieri, Casali di Oggi. Architetture rurali e tecniche agricole nel territorio di Pompei e Stabiae*, Napoli 2000, 45-47.

On the "urban villas" of Pompeii:

Noack, F., K. Lehmann-Hartleben, *Baugeschichte Untersuchungen am Stadtrand von Pompeji*, Berlin 1936 (Insula VIII, 2).

Strocka, W.M. "Ein Haus mit Privatbibliothek," *RM* 100, 1993, 341-351 (on the "urban villa" VI, 17, 42).

On the identifications of the owners of the houses of Pompeii:

Della Corte, M. *Case e abitanti di Pompei*, Napoli 1965.

Critiques on the method used:

Castrén, P. "Ordo Populusque Pompeianus. Polity and Society in Roman Pompeii," *Acta Instituti Romani Finlandiae* 8, Roma 1975, 31.

On the labyrinth mosaic:

Strocka, W.M. *Casa del Labirinto* (VI, 11, 8-10), (Series: Häuser in Pompeji 4), München 1991, 107. A critical position on the self-celebratory reading of the mosaic proposed by the scholar is expressed by B. Germini, in a review of W.M. Strocka, *Casa del Labirinto* (VI, 11, 8-10), in *Ostraka* I, 2, 1992, 303-305. He agrees with the German scholar, recognizing the labyrinth as a metaphoric illustration of the good government of the city after the colonial decommissioning.

Grassigli, G. L. *La scena domestica e il suo immaginario. I temi figurati nei mosaici della Cisalpina*, Napoli-Perugia 1999, 101-104.

The "Pompeiian" mosaic from Cirta:

Picard, G. "Une mosaïque pompéienne à Cirta," *Revue Archéologique* 1980, 185-187.

House of the Silver Wedding

Building History:

Pesando, F. *"Domus". Edilizia privata e società pompeiana fra III e I secolo a.C.*, (Soprintendenza Archeologica di Pompei, Monografie 12), Roma 1997, 62-68.

In anticipation of a complete edition concerning the house in the series *Häuser in Pompeji*, edited by W. Ehrhardt, several early reports have been issued on the decorative and building history of the house in:

Meyer-Graft, R., Ehrhardt, W. "Untersuchung der putzträer und der Malereien in der Casa delle Nozze d'Argento in Pompeji und Präsentation der Ergebnisse aus der Sicht des Restaurators und des Archälogen," *Roman Wall Painting: Materials, Techniques, Analysis and Conservation*. Proceedings of the International Workshop, Fribourg 7-9 March 1995, Fribourg 1997, 317-327.

Decoration:

Archer, W.C. "The maturing of the Fourth Style: the *Casa delle Nozze d'Argento* at Pompeii," *Journal of Roman Archaeology* 7, 1994, 129-150.

Ehrhardt, W. "Die Malerwerkstatt Casa delle Nozze d'Argento/Casa dell'Orso," *Mededelingen Rom* 54, 1995, 140-155.

Parise Badoni, F. *Pompei. Pitture e mosaici* III, Roma 1991, 676-772.

House of the Cryptoporticus and of the Ilion *Sanctuary*

Descriptions of the houses and the building phases:

Pesando, F. *"Domus". Edilizia privata e società pompeiana fra III e I secolo a.C.*, (Soprintendenza Archeologica di Pompei, Monografie 12), Roma 1997, 35-45.

Spinazzola, V., S. Aurigemma (a cura di). *Pompei alla luce degli Scavi Nuovi di Via dell'Abbondanza*, Roma 1953, 437-593.

Decoration:

Aurigemma, S. in *Pompei alla luce degli Scavi Nuovi di Via dell'Abbondanza* (a cura di) V. Spinazzola, S. Aurigemma, Roma 1953, 869-970.

Beyen, H.G. *Die Pompejanische Wanddekoration vom 2. bis zum 4. Stil*, II, Den Haag 1960, 87-119.

Blanc, N. "L'enigmatique "Sacello iliaco" (I,6,4E); contribution à l'étude des cultes domestiques," *I temi figurativi nella pittura parietale antica (IV sec.a.C. IV sec. d.C.)*, Bologna 1997.

Bragantini, I. *Pompei. Pitture e mosaici*, I, Roma 1990, 193-329.

Schefold, K. *Die Wände Pompejis. Topographisches Verzeichnis der Bildmotive*, Berlin 1957, pp.17-24.

House of Julius Polybius

Descriptions of the house and its decoration:

De Franciscis, A. "La casa di Giulio Polibio a Pompei," *Rivista di Studi Pompeiani* 2, 1988, 15-36.

Laidlaw, A. *The First Style in Pompeii: Painting and Architecture*, Roma 1985, 285-301.

Pesando, F. *"Domus". Edilizia privata e società pompeiana fra III e I secolo a.C.*, (Soprintendenza Archeologica di Pompei, Monografie 12), Roma 1997, 137-141.

Zevi, F. "La Casa di Giulio Polibio," *Abitare sotto il Vesuvio* (Catalogo Mostra Ferrara), M. Borriello, A. d'Ambrosio, S. De Caro, P.G. Guzzo (edd.), Ferrara 1996, 73-79.

For the antiquarian pieces found in triclinium EE:

Zevi, F., M.L. Lazzarini, "Hydria bronzea da Pompei," *Atti e Memorie della Società Magna Grecia* 3, 1, 1992, 91-97.

House of Marcus Lucretius Fronto

Peters, W. J. Th. *La casa di Marcus Lucretius Fronto a Pompei e le sue pitture* (with contributions by E.M. Moormann, T.L. Heres, H. Brunsting and S.L. Wynia), Amsterdam 1993.

Scagliarini Corlàita, D. "La pittura parietale nelle domus e nelle villae del territorio vesuviano," *Romana pictura. La pittura romana dalle origini all'età bizantina*, (a cura di) A. Donati, Milano 1998, 57-64.

House of Meleager

Bragantini, I. in *Pompei. Pitture e mosaici*, IV (Regio VI, parte prima), Roma 1993, 660-818.

Curatolo, E. "La Casa di Meleagro (regio VI,9,2): scavi Van der Poel," *Pompei. Scienza e società. 250° Anniversario degli Scavi di Pompei*, (a cura di) P.G. Guzzo, Convegno Internazionale Napoli 25-27 Novembre, Milano 2001, 240.

Dickmann, J.-A. *Domus frequentata. Anspruchsvolles Wohnen im pompejanischer Stadthaus*, München 1999, 186-189.

House of Apollo

Caso, L. "Gli affreschi interni del cubicolo "amphithalamus" della casa di Apollo," *Rivista di Studi Pompeiani* 3 (1989), 111-130.

Sampaolo, V. in *Pompei. Pitture e mosaici* IV, Roma 1993, 470-524.

Zanker, P. *Pompei. Società, immagini urbane e forme dell'abitare*, Torino 1993, 172-176.

House of the Tragic Poet

Borriello, M. "La casa del Poeta Tragico in Pompei," *Abitare sotto il Vesuvio* (Catalogo Mostra Ferrara), (edd.) M. Borriello, A. d'Ambrosio, S. De Caro, P.G. Guzzo, Ferrara 1996, 98-101.

Parise Badoni, F., Narciso, F. in *Pompei. Pitture e mosaici* IV, Roma 1993, 527-603.

Wood, N. *The House of the Tragic Poet–Full Size Reconstruction Project in London*, London 1996.

House of the Vettii

General Works:

Clarke, J.R. *The Houses of Roman Italy. 100 B.C.-A.D. 250. Ritual, Space and Decoration*, Berkeley 1991, 208-235.

Sampaolo, V. in *Pompei. Pitture e Mosaici* V, Roma 1994, 468-572.

On several architectural details:

Archer, W.C. *The Casa dei Vettii in Pompeii* (Diss.), 1983.

Bek, L. *Towards Paradise on Earth: Modern Space Conception in Architecture: A Creation of Renaissance Humanism* (Analecta Romana Studi Danici, suppl. 9), Rome 1980, 185.

Dickmann, J.-A. *Domus frequentata. Anspruchsvolles Wohnen im pompejanischer Stadthaus*, München 1999, 104-108; 139-141.

Maiuri, A. "Ginecèo e "Hospitium" nelle case pompeiane," *MemAccLinc*, ser. 8, 5, 1954, 449-467.

Tamm, B. "Some Notes on Roman Houses," *Opuscola Romana* 9, 1973, 53-60.

Wallace-Hadrill, A. *Houses and Society in Pompeii and Herculaneum*, Princeton 1994, 58.

A hall of paintings:

Guzzo, P.G. and V. Scarano Ussani, *Veneris figurae, immagini di prostituzione e sfruttamento a Pompei*, Milano 2000, 28 (on the pornographic paintings of the so-called cook's room).

Peters, W. J. Th. "La composizione delle pareti dipinte nella Casa dei Vettii a Pompei," *MededRome* 39 (n.s. 4), 1977, 95-128.

Wirth, Th. "Zum Bildprogramm der Räume N und P in der Casa dei Vettii," *Römosche Mitteilungen* 90, 1983, 449-455.

Praedia of Julia Felix

Nappo, S.C. "Fregio dipinto dal "praedium" di Giulia Felice con rappresentazione del foro di Pompei," *Rivista di Studi Pompeiani* 3, 1989, 79-96.

Parslow, C.C. "Documents illustrating the Excavations of the Praedia of Iulia Felix in Pompeii," *Rivista di Studi Pompeiani* 2, 1988, 37-48.

____. *The Praedia Iuliae Felicis in Pompeii* (Diss. Duke University), Durham 1989.

____. "Preliminary Report of the 1997 Fieldwork Project in the *Praedia Iuliae Felicis* (Regio II,4) Pompeii," *Rivista di Studi Pompeiani* 9, 1998 [2000], 199-207.

____. *Rediscovering Antiquity. Karl Weber and the Excavations of Herculaneum, Pompeii and Stabiae*, Cambridge 1995, 107-122.

Sampaolo V. in *Pompei. Pitture e mosaici* III, Roma 1991, 184-310.

House of Menander

De Vos, A. and M. *Pompei, Ercolano, Stabia*, Bari 1982, 90-96.

Ling, R. *The Insula of the Menander at Pompeii*, in "Antiquaries Journal" LXIII 1983, 34-57.

____. "La casa del Menandro," *Pompei. Abitare sotto il Vesuvio*, Ferrara 1996, 65-71.

____. *The Insula of the Menander at Pompeii. Volume I: The Structures*, Oxford 1997.

Maiuri. A. *La casa del Menandro e il suo tesoro di argenterie*, Roma 1933.

The Thermal Quarters:

Ling, R. "The baths of the Casa del Menandro," *Pompeii Herculaneum Stabia* I 1983, 49-60.

The Silver Treasure:

Painter, K. *The Insula of the Menander at Pompeii. Volume IV: The Silver Treasure*, Oxford University Press, forthcoming.

Paintings:
Pompei: pitture e mosaici II. Regio I, parte seconda, Roma 1990, 240-397.

Wall Inscriptions:
Varone. A. *The Insula of the Menander at Pompeii. Volume III: The Wall Inscriptions*, Oxford University Press, forthcoming.
____. "Gli abitanti della casa," *La casa del Menandro*, G. Stefani (cur.), forthcoming.

Insula of the Chaste Lovers
Preliminary Notices on Excavations in Process:
Varone, A. "Pompei. Attività dell'Ufficio Scavi: 1987-1988," *RStPomp* II, 1998, 146-148.
____. "Scavo lungo via dell' Abbondanza," *RStPomp* III 1989, 231-238.
____. "Pompei, Via dell' Abbondanza: scavi 1987," *BdArch*, 1-2, 1990, 233-238.
____. "Pompei. Attività dell' Ufficio Scavi: 1990," *RStPomp* IV 1990, 201-211.
____. "Pompei. Attività dell' Ufficio Scavi: 1991," *RStPomp* V 1991, 195-200.
____. "New finds in Pompeii. The excavation of two buildings in Via dell'Abbondanza," *Apollo* (London), July 1993, 8-12.
____. "Nuovi rinvenimenti a Pompei lungo via dell' Abbondanza," *Boll.Ass.Arch. Ticinese* VII 1995, 4-8.
____. "Gli scavi in corso nell'*insula* dei Casti Amanti," *Pompei. I misteri di una città sepolta,* Roma 1990, 314-329.

Intervention Methodologies:
Varone, A. "L'apporto delle scienze alla conoscenza del mondo antico: l'esempio del recente scavo pompeiano lungo via dell' Abbondanza," *Proceedings of the XVth International Congress of Classical Archaeology,* Eds. R. F. Docter, E. M. Moormann, Amsterdam 1999, 432-435.

Decorative Programs:
Varone, A. "Scavi recenti a Pompei lungo via dell'Abbondanza (Reg. IX, ins. 12, 6-7)," *Ercolano 1738-1988 250 anni di ricerca archeologica,* L. Franchi dell'Orto (cur.), Roma 1993, 617-640.
____. "Un nuovo pavimento musivo pompeiano in corso di restauro al momento dell'eruzione vesuviana del 79 d.C.," *Atti del V Convegno AISCOM* (Bordighera 6-10 dicembre 1995), Bordighera 1996, 681-694.
____. "Pompei: il quadro Helbig 1445, "Kasperl im Kindertheater", una nuova replica e il problema delle copie e delle varianti," *Atti del Convegno A.I.P.M.A.* (Bologna, 1995), Bologna 1998,149-152.
____. "Un nuovo programma decorativo a soggetto erotico," P.G. Guzzo, V. Scarano Ussani, *Veneris figurae. Immagini di prostituzione e sfruttamento a Pompei,* Napoli 2000, 61-65.

Pictorial Works in Process:
Varone, A. "L'organizzazione del lavoro di una bottega di decoratori: le evidenze dal recente scavo pompeiano lungo via dell' Abbondanza," in *MedRom* 54, 1995, 124-136.
____. "Un pittore al lavoro a Pompei," *Romana Pictura,* A. Donati (cur.), Milano 1998, 302-304.
Varone, A., Bearat, H. "Pittori romani al lavoro: materiali, strumenti, tecniche. Evidenze archeologiche e dati analitici di un recente scavo pompeiano lungo via dell'Abbondanza (Reg. IX, ins.12)," *Roman Wall Painting: Materials, Techniques, Analysis and Conservation* (Acts of Fribourg International Conference, 1996), Fribourg 1997, 199-214.

Wall Inscriptions:
Varone, A. "Iscrizioni parietarie inedite da Pompei (Reg. IX, ins. 12),"

Miscellanea Epigrafica in onore di Lidio Gasperini, G. Paci (cur.), Tivoli 2000, 1071-1093.

The Restoration and Conservation of the Complex:
Varone, A. "Fouilles, documentation et conservation de la maison pompeienne des 'Casti Amanti'," *Vestiges archéologiques. La conservation in situ* (Acts of the III international ICAHM (ICOMOS) conference: Montreal, October 1994), Montreal 1996, 224-236.
____. "Ricostituzione del tetto del triportico nella casa dei Pittori al Lavoro a Pompei (Reg. IX, ins. 12)," *Arkos, I grandi Restauri,* 1, 2000, 12 *passim*.

The Excavation of the Garden:
Varone, A., Ciarallo, A., Mariotti Lippi, M. *Parchi e giardini storici,* Roma 1991,171-177.

The Earthquake of 79 AD:
Varone, A. "Piú terremoti a Pompei? I nuovi dati degli scavi di via dell'Abbondanza," *Archäologie und Seismologie,* München 1995, 29-35.

The Dynamics of the Eruption of 79:
Dal Maso, C. Maturano, A., Varone, A. "Pompei. Il racconto dell'eruzione," *Le Scienze,* luglio 1999, 58-65.
Varone, A., Marturano, A. "L'eruzione vesuviana del 24 agosto del 79 d.C. attraverso le lettere di Plinio il Giovane e le nuove evidenze archeologiche," *RStPomp* VIII 1997, 57-72.

Villa of the Mysteries
Bonacasa, N. "Villa dei Misteri," *E.A.A. Suppl. 1970,* Roma 1973, 916-922.
De Petra, G. "Villa Romana presso Pompei," *NotSc* 1910, 139-145.
Della Corte, M. "Scavi eseguiti da privati nel territorio di Pompei," *NotSc* 1922, 480-485.
____. "'La Giuliana' o vera denominazione spettante alla così detta 'Villa dei Misteri'," *Atti del V Congresso Naz. Di Studi Romani,* vol.2, Spoleto 1940, 350-356.
Maiuri, A. *La Villa dei Misteri,* Roma, 1931.

Inscriptions:
Della Corte, M. *Le iscrizioni della Villa Giuliana, o "dei Misteri",* Napoli, 1940.

Megalographic Frieze:
Aoyagi, M. "Uno studio sul fregio megalografico della Villa dei Misteri, *Annuario Ist. Giapponese di Cultura* 7, 1969-1970, 97-116.
Bastet, F. L. "De Fries uit de zg. Villa dei Misteri," *Pompeii,* den Haag 1973-1974, 29-36.
____. "Fabularum dispositas explicationes," *BABesch* 49, 1974, 206-240.
Bendinelli, G. "Il fregio dionisiaco della Villa dei Misteri a Pompei," *Misc. Fac. Lettere Univ. Torino,* ser. 1, Torino 1936, 17-56.
____. "Ultime considerazioni intorno alla villa pompeiana detta dei Misteri," *Latomus* 27, 1968, 823-831.
Bieber, M. "Der Mysteriensaal der Villa Item," *JdI* 43, 1928, 298-330.
Boyancé, P. "Dionysos et Sémélé," *RendPontAccRomArch* 38. 1965-6, 79-104.
____. "Ménè-Hekate à la Villa des Mystères," *RACrist* 42, 1966, 5771.
Brendel, O.J. "Der grosse Fries in der Villa dei Misteri," *JdI* 81, 1966, 206-260.
Byvanck, A.W. "De groote schildering in de Villa dei Misteri bij Pompeji," *MededRome,* ser. 2, 9, 1939, 19-39.
Comparetti, D. *Le nozze di Bacco e Arianna. Rappresentazione pittorica spettacolosa nel triclinio di una villa suburbana di Pompei,* Firenze, 1921.

Frova, A. *La Villa dei Misteri a Pompei,* Milano 1965.

Grieco, G. "La grande frise de la Villa des Mystères et l'initiation dionysiaque," *Studi su Ercolano e Pompei (ParPass* 34, fasc. 188-189), Napoli 1979, 417-441.

Herbig, R. "Zwei Strömungen späthellenistischer Malerei," *Die Antike* 7, 1931, 135-160 (esp.135-141).

____. *Neue Beobachtungen am Fries der Mysterien-Villa in Pompeji,* Baden Baden, 1958.

Little, A. *A Roman Bridal Drama at the Villa of the Mysteries,* Kennebunk (Maine) 1972.

____. "The Damaged Central Figures at the Villa of the Mysteries," *CrPomp* 5, 1979, 150-155.

Macchioro, V. *La Villa dei Misteri in Pompei,* Napoli 1925.

Maiuri. A. "Note e commenti al dipinto della Villa dei Misteri," *ParPass* 3, 1948, fasc.8, 185-211.

Pappalardo, U. "Nuove osservazioni sul fregio della "Villa dei Misteri" a Pompei," *La regione sotterrata dal Vesuvio. Studi e Prospettive,* Napoli 1982, 599-622.

Rizzo, G. E. "Dionysos Mystes. Contributi esegetici alle rappresentazioni di misteri orfici," *MemAccNap* 3, 1914, 37-102.

Sauron, G. *La grande fresque de la villa des Mystères à Pompéi: mémoires d'une dévote de Dionysos,* Paris 1998.

Simon, E. "Zum Fries der Mysterienvilla bei Pompeji," *JdI* 76, 1961, 111-172.

Toynbee, J. "The Villa Item and a Bride's Ordeal," *JRS* 19, 1929, 67-87.

Turcan, R. "Le Dieu-Prêtre de la Villa item," *MEFRA* 72, 1960, 169-179.

____. "La démone ailée de la Villa Item," *Hommages . . . Renard,* Bruxelles 1969, 586-609.

____. "Pour en finir avec la femme fouettée," *RA* 1982, 291-302.

Wesenberg. B. "Zur Bildvorstellung im grossen Fries der Mysterienvilla," *KölnJahrbVorFrühgesch* 24, 1991, 67-72.

Zuntz, G. "On the Dionysiac Fresco in the Villa dei Misteri at Pompeii," *Proceedings of the British Academy* 49, 1963, 177-201.

Villa of Poppea at Oplontis

De Caro, Lagi, A. "Oplontis: Villa A o villa di Poppea," *Pompeii-Herculaneum-Stabiae* 1, 1983, 364-375.

Fergola, L. *Oplontis,* Napoli 2000.

Franciscis, A. de. "La villa romana di Oplontis," *PP* 28, 1973, fasc. CLIII, 453-466.

____. "La villa romana di Oplontis," *Neue Forschungen in Pompeji,* Recklinghausen 1975, 9-38.

____. "Oplontis," *La regione sotterrata dal Vesuvio. Studi e prospettive,* Napoli 1982, 907-925.

Painting:

Andreae, B. "I pavoni della villa di Oplontis," *La Regione sotterrata dal Vesuvio. Studi e prospettive,* Napoli 1982, 531-533.

Clarke, J. R. "Early Third Style at the Villa of Oplontis," *RM* 94, 1987, 267-294.

____. "Landscape paintings in the Villa of Oplontis," *JRA* 9, 1996, 81-107.

Franciscis, A. de. *Gli affreschi pompeiani nella villa di Oplontis,* Recklinghaus, 1975.

Tybout, R. A. "Oplontis," *Hermeneus* 51, 1979, 263-283.

Sculpture:

De Caro, S. "Sculture della villa di Poppea in Oplontis," *CronPomp* II 1976, 184-225.

____. "The Sculptures of the Villa of Poppaea at Oplontis: a Preliminary Report," *Ancient Roman Villa Gardens,* Washington, D.C. 1987, 77-133.

Franciscis, A. de. "La dama di Oplontis," *Eikones,* Bern 1980, 115-117.

Gardens:

Andreae, B. *Am Birnbaum. Garten und Parks im antiken Rom, in den Vesuvstädten und in Ostia,* Mainz am Rhein 1996, 25-30.

Jashemski, W. "Recently Excavated Gardens and Cultivated Land of the Villas at Boscoreale and Oplontis," *Ancient Roman Villa Gardens,* Washington, D. C. 1987, 31-75.

Inscriptions:

De Caro, S. "Un graffito e altre testimonianze del culto della Magna Mater nella villa romana di Oplontis," *Studia Pompeiana et Classica in Honor of W.F. Jashemski* 1, New Rochelle, N.Y. 1988, 89-96.

Franciscis, A. de. "Beryllos e la villa "di Poppea" ad Oplontis," *Studies in Classical Art and Archaeology .. to P. H. Blanckenhagen,* Locust Valley, N.Y. 1979, 231-233.

The Cult of the Dead: Tomb-lined Streets

Borrelli, L. *Le tombe di Pompei a schola semicircolare,* Napoli 1937.

Compostela, C. "Banchetti pubblici e banchetti privati nell'iconografia funeraria romana del I secolo d.C.," *Mélanges de l'École Française de Rome* 104, 1992, 659-689.

De Franciscis, A., Pane, R. *Mausolei romani in Campania,* Napoli 1957.

Étienne, R. *La vita quotidiana a Pompei,* Milano 1973, 365-378.

Gabelmann, H. *Römische Grabbauten der frühen Kaiserzeit,* Stuttgart 1979.

____. "Römische Grabbauten in Italien unsd den Nordprovinzen," *Festschrift F. Brommer,* Mainz 1977, 101-117.

Ghedini, F. "Raffigurazioni conviviali nei monumenti funerari romani," *Rivista di archeologia* 14, 1990, 35-62.

Kockel, V. "Im Tode gleich? Die sullanische Kolonisten und ihr kulturelles Gewicht in Pompeji am Beispiel der Nekropolen," *Römische Gräberstrassen,* München 1987, 183-198.

Pellegrino, A. "Considerazioni sulle tombe a «labrum» di Pompei," *Pompei* 79 (= suppl. al n. 15 di *Antiqua* 4, 1979), 110-115.

Varone, A. *L'area vesuviana. (Le strade. Le necropoli pompeiane. Monumenti), Viae Publicae Romanae,* Roma 1991, 95-104.

____. "Note di archeologia sarnese: i cippi funerari a stilizzazione antropomorfa," *Apollo* 6, 1985-1988, 195-260.

____. *Pompei. I misteri di una città sepolta,* Roma 2000, 27-30.

Zanker, P. "Grabreliefs römischer Freigelassener," *Jahrbuch des Deutschen Archäologischen Instituts zu Berlin* 90, 1975, 267-315.

Necropolis of the Herculaneum Gate

Kockel, V. *Die Grabbauten vor dem Herkulaner Tor in Pompei. Mit einem Plan von B. Weber,* Mainz 1983.

Sogliano, A. "La necropoli preromana di Pompei," *Memorie della Reale Accademia di Archeologia Lettere e Belle Arti di Napoli* 2, 1913, 207-229.

Necropolis of the Nucera Gate

D'Ambrosio, A., De Caro, S. "Fotopiano e documentazione della necropoli di porta Nocera," *Un impegno per Pompei,* Milano 1983, 23-42.

____. "La necropoli di porta Nocera. Campagna di scavo 1983," *Römische Gräberstrassen,* München 1987, 199-228.

Elefante, M. "Un caso di *defixio* nella necropoli pompeiana di Porta Nocera?," *La Parola del Passato* 40, 1985, 431-443.

Giordano, C. *L'epigramma a Novellia Primigenia. Un discendente del Catilinario Cetego a Pompei,* Pompei, 1957.

Other Funerary Structures

De Caro, S. "Scavi nell'area fuori Porta Nola a Pompei," *Cronache Pompeiane* 5, 1979, 61-101.

Della Corte, M. "Pompei. Di un sepolcreto della necropoli sannitica di Pompei, scoperto presso la Porta Stabiana," *Notizie degli Scavi di Antichità*, 1911, 106-111.

____. "Sui monumenti scoperti fuori la Porta del Vesuvio. Brevi note di epigrafia pompeiana," *Memorie della Reale Accademia di Archeologia Lettere e Belle Arti di Napoli* 2, 1911, 177-200.

De Franciscis, A. "Sepolcro di M. Obellius Firmus," *Cronache Pompeiane* 2, 1976, 246-248.

Dentzer, J.-M. "La tombe de C. Vestorius dans la tradition de la peinture italique," *Mélanges de l'École Française de Rome* 74, 1962, 533-594.

Jongman, W. M. "M. Obellius M. f. Firmus, Pompeian duovir," *Talanta* 10-11, 1978-1979, 62-65.

Mols, S. T. A. M., Moorman, E. M. "*Ex parvo crevit*. Proposta per una lettura iconografica della Tomba di Vestorius Priscus fuori Porta Vesuvio," *Rivista di Studi Pompeiani* 6, 1993-1994, 15-52.

Pozzi Paolini, E. "Exedra funeraria pompeiana fuori Porta di Nola," *Rendiconti della Reale Accademia di Archeologia Lettere e Belle Arti di Napoli* 35, 1960, 175-186.

Sogliano, A. "Scoperte fuori la Porta Stabiana," *Notizie degli Scavi di Antichità*, 1891, 273-275.

Spano, G. "La tomba dell'edile C. Vestorio Prisco in Pompei," *Atti dell'Accademia dei Lincei. Rendiconti della classe di scienze morali, storiche e filologiche*, ser. 7, 3, 1942-1943, 237-315.

____. "Pompei. Relazione degli scavi eseguiti negli anni 1908-1909. Scavi fuori Porta di Nola. Scavi fuori Porta del Vesuvio," *Notizie degli Scavi di Antichità*, 1910, 385-416.

Photography

Alfredo and Pio Foglia, Naples
except:

Magnus Edizioni: p. 32 (below), p. 39 (above), p. 52 (below), p. 57 (below), p. 60 (below), p. 69, p. 79, p. 91, p. 94 (below), p.150, p.173 (above), pp. 176-177, p. 381, p. 385.

SIME, Treviso: pp. 42-43, p. 206.

Alinari, Florence: p. 45, p. 59, p. 77 (below), p. 229.

Vatican Museums, Rome: pp. 204-205